W9-CTA-258

Contra Costa Edition
2008/2009

A Reference Guide for Mothers and Families in
Contra Costa County

BAY AREA
Mama™
HANDBOOK

PRINTED IN CHINA

Copyright © 2008 Bay Area Mama's Handbook
Cover Illustration by Alison Jay

Table of Contents

Advertiser Index

Places to Go and Things to Do

Bored? There's no reason to be! There's so much to do in the East Bay! In this chapter you'll find general activities to entertain you and your children. Remember that the Bay Area Mama's Handbook is full of great ideas, so be sure to check out The Great Outdoors, and Theatre and the Arts chapters for more ideas. When you see this icon 🎂 in this chapter, the listing offers group party packages!

Amusement Places & Arcades

Children's Fairyland

699 Bellevue Avenue
Oakland, CA 94610
www.fairyland.org
510-238-6876

Just imagine: a ten-acre park on the shores of Oakland's Lake Merritt where children's literature comes to life and kids can be kids. Since 1950, Children's Fairyland has been delighting children and their parents with whimsical storybook sets, gentle rides, friendly animals, wonder-filled puppet shows, and inspired live entertainment. Special performances and arts and crafts each weekend. Perfect for the younger child!

Chabot Space & Science Center

10000 Skyline Blvd.
Oakland, CA 94619
www.chabotspace.org
510-336-7373

Places to Go and Things to Do

Hours: Wed.–Thurs. 10 am–5 pm, Fri.–Sat. 10 am–10 pm, Sun. 11 am–5 pm

Give your family the Moon, the Stars and the Universe. Parents and kids alike are in for an out-of–this-world experience when they visit our 86,000-square foot Space Center set amidst 13-acres of park land. Immerse yourself in our state-of-the-art digital dome planetarium, giant screen MegaDome theatre and hands-on interactive exhibits and demonstrations. Marvel at the wonders of the Universe through the largest public telescopes in the Western United States.

CrusingCo.com

DianeC@cruisingco.com

925-932-4646

For 20 years, we have planned over 70,000 magical vacations for clients. As Authorized Disney Vacation Planners, we specialize in Disney vacations; Disneyland, Walt Disney World, Disney Cruiseline, and the new Adventures by Disney for worldwide escorted tours with a Disney touch. We look forward to custom-tailoring your next Disney vacation and making it truly memorable.

Golf N Games Family Fun Center

501 Auto Center Drive
Antioch, CA 94509
www.golfngames.com

925-754-5053

Hours: See website for complete details.
Price: Rock wall $3.50/2 climbs, Billiards $7/half-hour, $10/hour, Miniature golf Children (5–11) $5.50, Adults $7, Seniors (55+) $6, Under 4 Free with paid adult; Batting cages Tokens $1.75 each or 8 for $12, Go-karts Slick Track $5.75 (must be 56" or taller), Kid karts $5 (must be 44" to 56" to ride)

Miniature golf, arcade, billiards, redemption games, go karts, batting cages, and rock climbing wall. Group and Birthday Party packages available.

Jungle Fun and Adventure

1975 Diamond Blvd.
Concord, CA 94520
www.thejunglefun.com

925-687-4386

Hours: Sunday–Thursday 10 am–9 pm, Friday & Saturday 10 am–10 pm
Price: Monday–Friday unlimited play $7.95, toddlers (12–36 months) $5.95, Saturday, Sunday and Holidays unlimited play $8.95, toddlers $6.95, Sunday–Thursday after 5 pm all children $5.95, Toddler Tuesday toddlers $3.48 all day. Parents always play FREE!

An indoor family entertainment center, with play structures, skill games, and gourmet family dining all in a fun-filled, jungle-themed environment. Group and Birthday Party packages available.

Children's Fairyland

is an enchanting,
10-acre outdoor park that brings children's
literature to life, through fairytale exhibits,
animals, rides, puppet shows, children's theatre
and "talking storybooks."

Special performances and arts and crafts each
weekend. Perfect for the younger child!

(510)238-6876
699 Bellevue Ave, Oakland, CA
www.fairyland.org

Pixieland Amusement Park

2740 East Olivera Road
Concord, CA 94519
www.pixieland.com

925-689-8841

Hours: Vary by season

Pixieland Amusement Park is a hidden gem right here in our own backyard! Pixieland, located in Concord, has been one of the Bay Area's best kept secrets for more than 50 years! The Park features 7 rides that the tots will love including the famous G-16 Train, the "Dragon" Roller Coaster, Antique Cars, Frog Hopper, Red Baron Airplanes, Tea Cups and a Carousel. Visit for an hour, or stay the whole day with free admission and parking. Enjoy their famous hand dipped corn dogs, freshly spun cotton candy (two of many items) or bring your own snacks! Pixieland is the perfect setting for your special Birthday Party celebration! Open February through November. Please visit their website or call for more information.

Prewett Family Park-Antioch Water Park

4701 Lone Tree Way
Antioch, CA 94531
www.ci.antioch.ca.us/CitySvcs/Prewett

925-776-3070

Hours: See website for details.

Price: Children 2 and under free with paying adult. Monday–Friday $6, Saturday, Sunday & Holidays $8, Everyday after 4 pm $4.

A great place for little kids. Even those 30" and above can enjoy the Otter Slide! No outside food is allowed into the park. Group and Birthday Party packages available.

Q-Zar at the Entertainment Zone

2295 Willow Pass Road
Concord, CA 94520
www.q-zar.com

925-521-9663

Hours: Monday–Thursday Noon–10 pm, Friday Noon–12 am, Saturday 10 am–12 am, Sunday Noon–10 pm

Price: 1 Game $8/person, 2 Games and 20 Tokens $18/person, 3 Hours of Laser Tag and 20 Tokens $25/person, 5 Hours of Laser Tag and 20 Tokens $30/person. One 30 Minute laser tag experience includes briefing, vesting, 15 minute live action laser tag game, de-vesting and scores.

An action-packed game which combines the ever-popular games of hide and seek, tag, and capture the flag with state-of-the-art interactive computer and laser technology. Group and Birthday Party packages available.

Places to Go and Things to Do

Small World Park

2551 Harbor Street
Pittsburg, CA 94565
www.ci.pittsburg.ca.us
/Pittsburg/Government/Departments/Recreation/rec-worldpark.htm.htm

925-439-4879

Hours: See website for details. Park is closed on Mother's and Father's Day.

Price: Adults (15+) $3.50, Senior $2, Child (1–14) $1.75. Under 1 free.

Picnic, play or enjoy the rides. Drop-in, or for those special occasions, reserve a large picnic site or the party castle. Group and Birthday Party packages available.

Waterworld USA

1950 Waterworld Pkwy.
Concord, CA 94530
www.waterworldcalifornia.com

925-609-1364

Hours: Waterworld USA will open for its season in May, 2008. See website for details.

Price: $29.99 for General Admission ticket which includes unlimited use of over 25 attractions from family rides to thrill rides, $23.99 General Admission Ticket (walk up anytime for one low price), $23.99 Under 48" $23.99, Senior Admission Ticket (must present valid ID age 62 and over) $23.99, Military Admission Ticket (must present valid ID) $23.99. Parking $10 (cash only) per non-commercial vehicle.

In addition to a slew of cool, fast water rides, little ones can enjoy Tot Town and walk into shallow waters of Wild Water Kingdom. Climb on turtles, walk into waterbrellas and climb a mini slide built just for them. Group and Birthday Party packages available.

Animals

Deer Hill Ranch

3232 Deer Hill Road
Lafayette, CA 94549
www.deerhillranch.org

925-283-1197

Hours: Please call

Deer Hill Ranch is a nonprofit experiential education center serving youth ages 4–18, as well as adults. They also have a special outreach effort to at-risk youth. Utilizing experiential learning techniques and adventure education in the intimate setting of a family ranch. Deer Hill Ranch programs empower participants by building self-esteem, increasing their communication skills, and improving interaction with other people, other living creatures, and the environment. Group and Birthday Party packages available.

Lindsay Wildlife Museum

1931 First Avenue
Walnut Creek, CA 94597
www.wildlife-museum.org

925-935-1978

Hours: See website for details. Closed Holidays.
Price: Adults (18+) $5, Children (3–17) $4, under 3 free.

Connect with wildlife and learn about the animals found in your backyard and open spaces. Kids will love close encounters with many live, non-releasable wild animals such as an eagle, hawk, fox, snake or mountain lion. The museum also features changing art and natural history exhibits, classes for children and adults, and a discovery room with hands-on activities for children.

Old Borges Ranch

1035 Castle Rock Road, Shell Ridge Open Space
Walnut Creek, CA 94596
www.walnut-creek.org

925-934-6990

Hours: Ranch is open daily. Visitor center open on Saturdays 1 pm–4 pm and on the 1st Sunday of the month Noon–4 pm.
Price: Free, although donations are appreciated.

This historic site boasts a working cattle ranch complete with cattle, chickens, goats, geese, horses, pigs, and sheep.

Bowling

Clayton Valley Bowl

5300 Clayton Road
Concord, CA 94521
www.claytonvalleybowl.com

925-689-4631

Hours: Sun.–Thurs. 10 am–Midnight, Fri.–Sat. 10 am–1 am.

This is where families and friends come to play! If you haven't been to Clayton Valley Bowl in awhile, stop by to see all the improvements that have been made. They have video games, a café, a cocktail lounge and a party room available to host your next party or meeting. Clayton Valley Bowl also has many specials throughout the week such as Freaky Funday on Sunday nights with $5 cover & $1 games, shoes, hotdogs, sodas, and small beers. Digital Thunder for kids on Friday nights 4 pm–6 pm. Visit their website or call for more information.

Places to Go and Things to Do

Danville Bowl

200 Boone Court
Danville, CA 94526
www.davnvillebowl.com

925-837-7272

*Hours: Sunday and Monday 9 am–11 pm, Tuesday 9 am–1 am, Wednesday and Thursday
11 am–1 am, Friday 11 am–1:30 am, Saturday 9 am–1:30 am*

Price: Many specials to choose from including After School specials. See website for details.

Group and Birthday Party packages available.

Delta Bowl

3300 Delta Fair Blvd.
Antioch, CA 94509
www.deltabowl.net

925-757-5424

Hours: Sunday–Thursday 9 am–11:30 pm, Friday and Saturday 9 am–1:30 am

Price: Many specials to choose from including Daytime Cosmic bowling. See website for details.

Group and Birthday Party packages available.

Diablo Lanes

1500 Monument Blvd., Suite G
Concord, CA 94520
www.diablolanes.com

925-671-0913

Hours: Monday–Thursday 9 am–1 am, Friday and Saturday 9 am–2 am, Sunday 9 am–Midnight
Price: Many specials to choose from. See website for details.

Group and Birthday Party packages available.

Harvest Park Bowl

5000 Balfour Road
Brentwood, CA 94513
www.harvestparkbowl.com

925-516-1221

Hours: Sunday–Thursday 9 am–11 pm, Friday and Saturday 9 am–1:30 am
Price: See website for details

Group and Birthday Party packages available.

Paddock Bowl

5915 Pacheco Blvd
Pacheco, CA 94553
www.paddockbowl.homestead.com

925-685-7812

Hours: Daily 9 am–11 pm. Fridays open until 1 am, Saturdays open until 1:30 am.
Price: 6 pm–Midnight $4.50, Before 6 pm Adults $4, Seniors $2.75, Juniors $2.75, Bumpers $3.
Shoes (with socks) $3.50. Free shoes for juniors before 6 pm on weekdays.

Group and Birthday Party packages available.

Historical Sites

Black Diamond Mines

(Also known as Black Diamond Mines Regional Preserve)
5175 Somersville Road
Antioch, CA 94509
www.ebparks.org/parks/black_diamond

925-757-2620

Places to Go and Things to Do

Hours: 8 am to dusk, unless otherwise posted or permitted. (Closing time varies seasonally.)
Price: Parking is $5/vehicle (when kiosk is attended); $4 per trailered vehicle. There is also a
dog fee of $2/per dog. Guide/service dogs are free.

The Preserve includes the remains of several coal mines and the sites of five long gone coal mining towns. The area is an ideal location for hiking, picnicking and nature study.

East Brother Island Lighthouse

At the tip of Point San Pablo

117 Park Place
Richmond, CA 94801
www.ebls.org

510-233-2385

Hours: Dusk to dawn
Price: Day visitors may come to the island for free to visit and enjoy the vistas, but must provide
their own transportation.

The lighthouse was opened in 1874 and automated in 1969. The former keeper's house began
operating as a bed and breakfast in 1980 and offers guests an expensive and elegant getaway. The
lighthouse was opened in 1874 and automated in 1969. Visiting East Brother Island is an adven-
turesome outdoor experience. Accessing the island requires the physical stamina and strength to
climb from a bobbing boat up a vertical ladder 4 to 12 feet in height, depending on tides. Children
are welcome for day-use activities only and must be under the supervision of parents at all times.
Parents with small children are encouraged to bring or plan activities for the 4–1/2 hour stay.
Minimum age of overnight guests is 18 years unless special arrangements are made.

Eugene O'Neill National Historic Site

Danville, CA 94526
eugeneoneill.areaparks.com

925-838-0249

Hours: Public visitation (by advance reservation only), Wednesdays through Sundays, with guid-
ed tours at 10 am and 12:30 pm. Allow 2 1/2 hours. Closed Mondays, Tuesdays, Thanksgiving,
Christmas and New Year's Day.
Price: Free including a free shuttle. (All visitors are shuttled to the site on National Park Service
vehicles from the Town of Danville. Directions to the pick-up location are provided when reserva-
tions are made. 1–2 week advance reservation is recommended.)

America's only Nobel Prize winning playwright, Eugene O'Neill, chose to live in Northern California
at the climax of his writing career. The 13-acre grounds of the site are accessible from hiking and
mountain biking trails in the Las Trampas Regional Wilderness. Bordered by regional park land,
this site remains an open greenbelt area, much like when the O'Neills themselves lived there.
Don't be surprised to see black tailed mule deer, coyotes, bobcats, red-tailed hawks, or wild
turkeys during your visit!

Forest Home Farms

19953 San Ramon Valley Blvd.

San Ramon, CA 94583

www.ci.san-raMondaycа.us/parks/historic/boone.htm

925-973-3281

Hours: Tours are available by appointment on Thursdays and Saturdays

Price: $3 per person

This historic site is on the National Register of Historic Places. It is home to 21 structures including the Boone House (built in 1900), the David Glass House (built in 1877) and the Tractor Museum. The Boone House will eventually serve as a retreat and meeting center after it is renovated and the David Glass House will become a historic house museum.

The Tractor Museum can be rented for your next unique celebration!

John Muir National Historic Site

4202 Alhambra Avenue

Martinez, CA 94553

925-228-8860

Hours: The Muir Home is available for self guided tours from 10 am–5 pm, Wednesday–Sunday. Public tours are available at 2 pm Wednesday–Friday, and 2 pm and 3 pm on weekends. Closed Mondays and Tuesdays, as well as on Thanksgiving, Christmas and New Year's Day.

Price: Individuals 16 and older are $3 each, good for 7 days. Children 15 and under are free when accompanied by an adult.

The Martinez Adobe, built in 1849, is also on site and open to the public. The two downstairs rooms of the adobe have exhibits about John Muir, the Martinez family and early California history. Mount Wanda is available for sauntering seven days a week, sunrise to sunset. It is one mile uphill to get to the top. Always bring water and wear comfortable shoes when setting out for the 640 foot summit. Wildflower walks, Bird walks and Full Moon walks are available on Mt. Wanda. For the kiddos, be sure to ask for the free Jr. Ranger Book at the Visitor Center. Have the kids complete it and return it to the ranger at the front desk for a Jr. Ranger badge! (Books are geared toward 8–12 year olds.)

Patrick Rodgers Farm

(Also known as Rodgers Ranch)

315 Cortsen Road

Pleasant Hill, CA 94523

www.rodgersranch.org/eventsandfundraisers.html

925-387-0158

925-939-8436

Hours: The house is open to the public on the second Sunday of each month from 2 pm–4 pm.

Price: Free

Enjoy hands-on experiences of family farm life over the years, displays of historic farm tools and equipment and workshops and activities related to the heritage of the region.

Places to Go and Things to Do

Red Oak Victory Ship

1337 Canal Blvd., Berth 6A
Richmond, CA 94804
www.ssredoakvictory.org

510-237-2933

Hours: Tours are available from 10 am–3 pm on Tuesdays, Thursdays, Saturdays and Sundays
Price: A donation of $5 for adults, $4 for seniors and $2 for children under 5 is requested.

Of the 747 ships launched at Richmond during the War, only this vessel remains to tell the story of that incredible time.

Rosie the Riveter/World War II Home Front National Historical Park

1401 Marina Way South
Richmond, CA 94804
www.rosietheriveter.org

510-232-5050

Hours: The Visitor Center is open Monday–Friday 8:30 am–5 pm except major holidays. The Rosie the Riveter Memorial in Marina Bay Park is open year round, dawn to dusk, as are the other city parks within the National Park's boundaries.
Price: Free

The park encompasses an array of historic properties in the city which were constructed during the 1940s to support America's entry into World War II. The memorial began as a public art project for the City of Richmond in the 1990's. During the creation of the memorial, the National Park Service was invited to participate, and this partnership led to the founding of this National Park.

Shadelands Ranch House
(Also known as Shadelands Ranch Historical Museum)
2660 Ygnacio Valley Road
Walnut Creek, CA 94598
www.ci.walnut-creek.ca.us/header.asp?genericId=1&catId=3&subCatId=159
925-935-7871
Hours: Wednesday and Sunday (tours offered) 1 pm–4 pm. The Museum is closed each year from the beginning of November until the first Sunday in February. The annual hiatus allows them to hold the Holiday Faire and Victorian Teas and to work on the interior of the house. Office hours are Monday-Thursday 9 am–4 pm.
Price: Adults $3, students ages 6–17 $1, children under 6 and Walnut Creek Historical Society members, free.

Built by Walnut Creek pioneer Hiram Penniman, this 1903 redwood-framed house is a showcase for numerous historical artifacts, many of which belonged to the Pennimans. It also houses a rich archive of Contra Costa and Walnut Creek history in its collections of old newspapers, photographs and government records. The Sherwood Burgess Room is open Wednesdays from 1 pm–4 pm for individuals who wish to do research on local history.

Libraries

Contra Costa County Library System
Each branch may vary in what they offer. Please go to www.contra-costa.lib.ca.us and check with your local branch to find out the times and dates of the programs you're interested in. You may also find detailed information on www.bayareamama.com.

Programs include:
Patty Cakes: For babies to 3 years—Child attends with caregiver
Picture Book Time: For 3 to 5 year olds—Child may attend without caregiver
Spanish/English Storytime: Bilingual storytime in Spanish and English for preschoolers.
Family Storytime: For children ages 3 and up and their families
Kids' Book Club: For kids in grades 4–6
Teen Programs: For Ages 12–18

Places to Go and Things to Do

Library Administration
Contra Costa County Library

75 Santa Barbara Road
Pleasant Hill, CA 94523
925-646-6423
Hours: Monday–Friday 8 am–5 pm. Closed Saturday and Sunday.

Adult Literacy: Project Second Chance

75 Santa Barbara Road
Pleasant Hill, CA 94523
925-927-3250
Hours: Monday, Tuesday, Wednesday and Friday 8:30 am–5 pm, Thursday 8:30 am–8 pm. Closed Saturday and Sunday.

Offers free, confidential, one-on-one basic literacy instruction to people who are over 16 years of age and out of school. Tutoring is done by trained volunteers who meet with their students twice a week, providing customized, personal lessons.

Branch Locations

Antioch

501 West 18th Street
Antioch, CA 94509
www.contra-costa.lib.ca.us/locations/antioch.html

925-757-9224
Hours: Monday, Tuesday and Wednesday 10 am–8 pm, Thursday Noon–8 pm, Friday Noon–6 pm, Saturday 10 am–6 pm. Closed Sunday.

Bay Point

205 Pacifica Avenue (in the Riverview Middle School)
Pittsburg, CA 94565
www.contra-costa.lib.ca.us/locations/baypoint.html

925-458-9597
Hours: Monday, Tuesday and Thursday 10:30 am–8 pm, Friday 2:30 pm–6 pm, Saturday Noon–5 pm. Closed Wednesday and Sunday.

Brentwood

751 Third Street
Brentwood, CA 94513
www.contra-costa.lib.ca.us/locations/brentwood.html

925-634-4101
Hours: Monday, Tuesday, Wednesday and Thursday 10 am–8 pm, Friday and Saturday 10 am–6 pm. Closed Sunday.

Clayton

6125 Clayton Road
Clayton, CA 94517
www.contra-costa.lib.ca.us/programs/cla.html

925-673-0659

Hours: Monday and Wednesday, 1 pm–9 pm, Tuesday, Thursday and Saturday 10 am–6 pm, Sunday 1 pm–5 pm. Closed Friday.

Concord

2900 Salvio Street
Concord, CA 94519
www.contra-costa.lib.ca.us/programs/conc.html

925-646-5455

Hours: Monday and Thursday Noon–9 pm, Tuesday and Wednesday 10 am–6 pm, Friday and Saturday 10 am–5 pm, Sunday 1 pm–5 pm

Crockett

991 Loring Avenue
Crockett, CA 94525
www.contra-costa.lib.ca.us/programs/cro.html

510-787-2345

Hours: Monday, Wednesday and Friday 11 am–5 pm, Saturday 11 am–4 pm. Closed Tuesday, Thursday and Sunday.

Danville

400 Front Street
Danville, CA 94526
www.contra-costa.lib.ca.us/programs/dan.html

925-837-4889

Hours: Monday, Tuesday, Wednesday and Thursday 10 am–8 pm, Friday and Saturday 10 am–6 pm, Sunday 1 pm–5 pm

Dougherty Station

17017 Bollinger Canyon Road
San Ramon, CA 94582
www.contra-costa.lib.ca.us/programs/srl_dsl.html

925-973-3380

Hours: Monday and Thursday 10 am–8 pm, Tuesday and Wednesday Noon–8 pm, Friday and Saturday 10 am–5 pm. Closed Sunday.

Places to Go and Things to Do

El Cerrito

6510 Stockton Avenue
El Cerrito, CA 94530
www.contra-costa.lib.ca.us/programs/ecl.html

510-526-7512

Hours: Monday and Tuesday Noon–8 pm, Thursday 10 am - 6 pm, Friday 1 pm–5 pm, Saturday 10 am–5 pm. Closed Wednesday and Sunday.

El Sobrante

4191 Appian Way
El Sobrante, CA 94803
www.contra-costa.lib.ca.us/programs/esl.html

510-374-3991

Hours: Monday and Thursday Noon–8 pm, Tuesday Noon–6 pm, Friday 1 pm–5 pm, Saturday 10 am–5 pm. Closed Wednesday and Sunday.

Hercules

109 Civic Drive
Hercules, CA 94547
www.contra-costa.lib.ca.us/programs/her.html

510-245-2420

Hours: Monday and Tuesday 1 pm–9 pm, Wednesday, Thursday and Saturday 10 am–6 pm, Sunday Noon–5 pm. Closed Friday.
Homework Room Hours: Monday and Tuesday 3 pm–8 pm, Wednesday and Thursday 3 pm–6 pm. Closed Friday, Saturday and Sunday.

Kensington

61 Arlington Avenue
Kensington, CA 94707
www.contra-costa.lib.ca.us/programs/ken.html

510-524-3043

Hours: Monday and Tuesday Noon–8 pm, Thursday 10 am–6 pm, Friday 1 pm–5 pm, Saturday Noon–5 pm. Closed Wednesday and Sunday.

Lafayette

952 Moraga Road
Lafayette, CA 94549
www.contra-costa.lib.ca.us/programs/laf.html

925-283-3872

Hours: Monday and Thursday 10 am–6 pm, Tuesday and Wednesday Noon–8 pm, Friday and Saturday 1 pm–5 pm. Closed Sunday.

Martinez

740 Court Street
Martinez, CA 94553
www.contra-costa.lib.ca.us/programs/mtz.html
925-646-2898
Hours: Monday Noon–8 pm, Tuesday 10 am–8 pm, Wednesday and Friday Noon–5 pm, Saturday 10 am–5 pm. Closed Thursday and Sunday.

Monument Futures

2699 Monument Blvd., Suite G
Concord, CA 94520
www.contra-costa.lib.ca.us/locations/monument.html
925-680-2844
Hours: Weekdays 6 am–Noon

Library service is available to the Monument area of Concord. Residents are able to pick up reserved materials at Monument Futures, located at 2699 Monument Blvd., Suite #G, Concord, and are able to access the collection of the County Library system via computer terminals. Library card holders are able to access the Library databases, search the Internet and request books and books-on-tape, videos, DVDs and other library material to be sent to Monument Futures for pick-up. A library book drop is available outside Monument Futures for 24-hour use by residents to return County Library materials.

Moraga

1500 Street Mary's Road
Moraga, CA 94556
www.contra-costa.lib.ca.us/programs/mor.html
925-376-6852
Hours: Tuesday and Thursday Noon–8 pm, Wednesday 10 am–6 pm, Friday 1 pm–5 pm, Saturday 10 am–5 pm. Closed Monday and Sunday.

Oakley

1050 Neroly Road (Located in Freedom High School)
Oakley, CA 94563
www.contra-costa.lib.ca.us/programs/oak.html
925-625-2400
Hours: Tuesday and Wednesday 10 am–9 pm, Thursday 2 pm–9 pm, Friday 2 pm–6 pm, Saturday 10 am–6 pm. Closed Monday and Sunday.

Places to Go and Things to Do

Orinda

26 Orinda Way
Orinda, CA 94563
www.contra-costa.lib.ca.us/programs/ori.html

925-254-2184

Hours: Monday, Tuesday, Wednesday and Thursday 10 am–8 pm, Friday and Saturday 10 am–6 pm, Sunday 1 pm–5 pm.

Pinole

2935 Pinole Valley Road
Pinole, CA 94564
www.contra-costa.lib.ca.us/programs/pnl.html

510-758-2741

Hours: Monday and Wednesday 1 pm–9 pm, Tuesday and Saturday 10 am–6 pm, Thursday and Friday 1 pm–6 pm. Closed Sunday.

Pittsburg

80 Power Avenue
Pittsburg, CA 94565
www.contra-costa.lib.ca.us/programs/pit.html

925-427-8390

Hours: Monday Noon–8 pm, Tuesday, Wednesday and Thursday 10 am–8 pm, Friday Noon–6 pm, Saturday 10 am–6 pm. Closed Sunday.

Pleasant Hill (Central)

1750 Oak Park Blvd.
Pleasant Hill, CA 94523
www.contra-costa.lib.ca.us/programs/phl.html

925-646-6434

Hours: Monday, Tuesday and Thursday Noon–8 pm, Wednesday, Friday and Saturday 10 am–6 pm. Closed Sunday.
Computer Lab Hours: Monday, Tuesday and Thursday 5 pm–7:30 pm, Saturday 10 am–5:30 pm. Closed Wednesday, Friday and Sunday.

Richmond Public Library

325 Civic Center Plaza
Richmond, CA 94804
www.ci.richmond.ca.us/index.asp?NID=105

510-620-6555

Hours: Monday and Tuesday Noon–8 pm, Wednesday 10 am–8 pm, Thursday and Saturday 10 am–5 pm, Friday Noon–5 pm. Closed Sunday.

Rodeo

220 Pacific Avenue
Rodeo, CA 94572
www.contra-costa.lib.ca.us/programs/rod.html

510-799-2606

Hours: Monday and Saturday 11 am–5 pm, Tuesday and Thursday, 1 pm–7 pm. Closed Wednesday, Friday and Sunday.

San Pablo

2300 El Portal Drive (Located in the Community Resource Center)
San Pablo, CA 94806
www.contra-costa.lib.ca.us/programs/spl.html

510-374-3998

Hours: Monday and Tuesday Noon–8 pm, Wednesday 10 am–6 pm, Friday 1 pm–5 pm, Saturday 10 am–5 pm. Closed Thursday and Sunday.

San Ramon

100 Montgomery Street
San Ramon, CA 94583
www.contra-costa.lib.ca.us/programs/srl_dsl.html

925-973-2850

Hours: Monday, Tuesday, Wednesday and Thursday 10 am–8 pm, Friday and Saturday 10 am–5 pm, Sunday: 1 pm–5 pm.

Walnut Creek Downtown

1644 North Broadway
Walnut Creek, CA 94596
www.contra-costa.lib.ca.us/programs/wcl.html

925-646-6773

Hours: Monday, Tuesday, Wednesday and Thursday 10 am–8 pm, Friday and Saturday: 10 am–6 pm. Closed Sunday.

Ygnacio Valley

2661 Oak Grove Road
Walnut Creek, CA 94598
www.contra-costa.lib.ca.us/programs/yvl.html

925-938-1481

Hours: Monday, Tuesday, Wednesday and Thursday 10 am–8 pm, Friday and Saturday 10 am–6 pm. Closed Sunday.

Book Clubs for Children & Teens

Al's Book Club

www.msnbc.msn.com/id/18179145

The loveable Today show weatherman has his own book club for kids.

American Girl Book Club Kit

Cost: $10.95

www.store.americangirl.com

This kit includes everything your girl needs to start her own club:

- Invitations, bookmarks, and calendars to help her get a club off the ground
- Theme cards offering suggestions for books to read and discuss
- 40 question cards that will keep girls talking about any book they read
- A handbook full of start-up suggestions and advice to help your girl take her book club from fun to fabulous!

The Kid Lit Book Club

bookclubs.barnesandnoble.com/bn/board?board.id=kl

From baby books to teen novels, come here to join fellow readers—and the B&N Jr. department editor Matt West—as you share ideas, recommendations, and opinions about books for children and teens of all ages.

Scholastic's Flashlight Readers: A Book Club for Kids Who Love Books

www.scholastic.com/flashlightreaders

Kids can play cool games and activities that take them into their favorite books. Get exclusive author information, including photos, audio, and notes from the authors themselves. Connect about books, authors, and reading on the Flashlight Reader message boards.

www.kidsreads.com and www.teenreads.com

Kidsreads and Teenreads have all the answers to Book Club questions, and some guides to help lead a good discussion with friends.

Literacy Programs

Reading is Fundamental

www.rif.org

Parents can find articles, tips on motivating kids to read, guidelines for choosing good books, suggestions on school involvement and reading aloud with your child. You can also search books by age group and content, get ideas for family activities, and explore other reading and literacy links.

Starfall

www.starfall.com

Offered free as a public service, Starfall presents a leveled reading program that begins with basic phonics. Primarily designed for first grade, Starfall is also useful for pre-kindergarten, kindergarten and second grade.

Story Time

Barnes & Noble
Slatten Ranch Shopping Center
5709 Lone Tree Way
Antioch, CA 94531
www.bn.com
925-978-1031
Mondays 10 am, Preschool Storytime (ages 3–6), Mondays 11 am, Storybook Character Storytime, Pre-school (ages 3–6) and Beginning Readers (ages 5–8), Saturdays 11 am, Preschool (ages 3–6) and Begging Readers (ages 5–8)

Walnut Creek
1149 South Main Street
Walnut Creek, CA 94596
925-947-0373
Toddler Tuesdays 10 am & Saturday Storytime 11 am

Pleasant Hill
552 Contra Costa Blvd Ste 90
Pleasant Hill, CA 94523
925-609-7060
Tuesdays 10:30 am, Children's Storytime & Saturdays 2:30 pm, Children's Storytime

Borders
www.borders.com

Pleasant Hill
120 Crescent Drive
Pleasant Hill, CA 94523
925-686-4835
Wednesdays 10 am, Children's Storytime
Saturdays 11 am, Children's Storytime

Places to Go and Things to Do

San Ramon

120 Sunset Drive
San Ramon, CA 94583
925-830-1190
Wednesdays 10:30 am, Children's Storytime

Clayton Books

5433 Clayton Road, Suite D
Clayton, CA 94517
www.claytonbookshop.com
925-673-3325
Children's storytime every Thursday at 10 am. A special guest will share some of their favorite stories.

Pottery Barn Kids

1139 South Main Street
Walnut Creek, CA 94596
www.potterybarnkids.com
925-932-5022
Kids of all ages are invited to story time on Tuesdays 10 am–10:30 am. Members receive an official Book Club Card at their first story time, and a special gift after attending five story times.

Storyline Online

www.storylineonline.net

An online streaming video program featuring Screen Actors Guild members reading children's books. Requires Flash Player plug-in.

Museums

Bay Area Discovery Museum
Fort Baker

557 McReynolds Road
Sausalito, CA 94965
www.BayKidsMuseum.org
415-339-3900

The nationally recognized Bay Area Discovery Museum is a one-of-a-kind indoor/outdoor children's museum that offers a full range of programs for children ages 6 months to 8 years. Located on seven and a half acres in the Golden Gate National Recreation Area, the Museum's unique programs feature hands-on art, science and environmental exhibitions, performances, special events, and cultural festivals... all with a focus on fun!

Benicia Fire Museum

900 East 2nd Street
Benicia, CA 94510
www.beniciafiremuseum.org

707-745-1688

*Hours: The museum is open the first three Sundays of the month and Thursdays, from
1 pm–4 pm.*
Price: Admission is free. Donations are gratefully accepted.

The Museum houses many treasures of fire service equipment, including the Phoenix Engine
which is believed to be the first fire engine to arrive in California. Fire equipment from the former
Benicia Arsenal Military Reservation in also on display.

Benicia Historical Museum at the Camel Barns

2060 Camel Road
Benicia, CA 94510
www.beniciahistoricalmuseum.org

707-745-5435

Hours: Wednesday–Sunday 1 pm–4 pm
*Price: Adults $5, Seniors/students $3, Children (6–12) $2, Children 5 and under are free as are
Wednesdays.*

Build a nest, create art, test the wind and waves, learn
about other cultures and more with hands-on interactive
exhibits and programs for young children and families.

**Bay Area
Discovery
Museum**
557 McReynolds Road
Sausalito, CA 94965
www.BayKidsMuseum.org
(415) 339-3900
Open Tuesday – Friday 9 a.m. – 4 p.m.
Saturday – Sunday 10 a.m. – 5 p.m.

Places to Go and Things to Do

The name, Benicia Historical Museum at the Camel Barns, comes from Benicia's contribution to US Military history. In the 1850's and 1860's the US Army experimented using camels imported from the Mideast as pack animals. After the advent of the Civil War the experiment was abandoned. The remaining camels were shipped to the Benicia Arsenal where they were auctioned to the public.

Blackhawk Museum

3700 Blackhawk Plaza Circle
Danville, CA 94506
www.blackhawkmuseum.org
925-736-2277

Hours: Wednesday–Sunday 10 am–5 pm

Price: $8 for Adults, $5 for Students (with valid ID) and Seniors (65 & older); Free for Children under 6 (Must be accompanied by a paid adult); Free for Active Military Personnel

Kids will love looking at the significant automotive treasures blending art, technology, culture and history. In addition to the Museum's rolling sculptures, educational lectures are scheduled each month and rotating exhibitions are presented in each of two 2,100 square foot galleries. An Automotive Research Library and the Museum's Shop & Bookstore are located just off the Main Lobby. Blackhawk displays about 90 cars, many of which are on loan from Museum friends in many different parts of the world. Car collectors enjoy sharing their automobiles and Blackhawk has the most dramatic presentation of coachbuilt cars in the world.

Children's Discovery Museum of San Jose

180 Woz Way
San Jose, CA 95110
www.cdm.org
408-298-5437

One of the Ten Best Children's Museums in the nation (Child Magazine) as well as one of the largest, CDM invites children and families to test, tinker, explore, create, and wonder in a warm and inviting setting. You'll find over 150 hands-on exhibits, performing and visual arts, an early childhood gallery, and surprises (check our Website for details on current exhibits) in the provocatively-purple building in Discovery Meadow.

Clayton Historical Society Museum

6101 Main Street
Clayton, CA 94517
www.claytonhistory.org/default.aspx
925-672-0240

Hours: Summer Hours (June–Sept.), Wednesdays 2 pm–4 pm and 6 pm–8 pm, Sundays 2 pm–4 pm

Price: Free

The Clayton Historical Society was founded in 1974 to research, collect, record, preserve, display, borrow, share, and interpret local history information and memorabilia, and to promote understanding of Clayton origins and development. In addition to maintaining regular museum hours, the Society hosts student classes and special tours and opens the Museum upon request.

Concord Historical Museum

1987 Bonafacio Street
Concord, CA 94520
www.conhistsoc.org
925-689-2677
Hours: Tuesday–Sunday 1 pm–4 pm
Price: Free

In addition to a broad coverage of Concord-specific history, heritage, and preservation materials, the Concord Historical Society maintains detailed data and photo coverage of several subjects unique to Concord including airfields and railroads.

Crockett Historical Museum

900 Loring Avenue
Crockett, CA 94525
510-787-2178
Hours: Wednesdays and Saturday 9 am–3 pm
Price: Free

East Contra Costa Historical Society & Museum

3890 Sellers Avenue
Brentwood, CA 94513
www.theschoolbell.com/history
925-634-8651
Hours: Thursdays, Saturdays and every third Sunday of the month 2 pm–4 pm
Price: Free

The museum is filled with memorabilia, documents, and photos from the rich history in East Contra Costa County. Visitors will enjoy parading through the building's unique period rooms, including the parlor, kitchen and office, as well as several bedrooms. Plus, the museum houses several pieces of farm equipment.

Golden State Model Railroad Museum

900-A Dornan Drive
Point Richmond, CA 94801
www.gsmrm.org
510-234-4884

Places to Go and Things to Do

Hours: During the months of April through December, the museum is open and trains are running every Sunday from Noon–5 pm. They are also open Saturdays from Noon–5 pm and Wednesdays from 11 am–3 pm with free admission, but there aren't any trains running. The museum will be closed for the winter break from January through March.

Price: $4 for Adults, $2 for Senior Citizens and Children under 12, $9 for Families

Inside the museum, you'll find three large, operating model railroads constructed and operated by the East Bay Model Engineers Society (EBMES).

Habitot Children's Museum

2065 Kittredge Street
Berkeley, CA 94704
www.habitot.org

510-647-1111

Hours: Tuesday–Thursday 9:30 am–1 pm, Friday–Saturday 9:30 am–4:30 pm. Closed most Mondays. Open Sundays for private rentals only. Hours subject to change—please check website.

Habitot is the East Bay's award-winning place for arts and hands-on play for young children, 7 months to 7 years. A full Art Studio and ten, interactive theme-based exhibits like Little Town Grocery and Cafe, Waterworks and Recycling Center help young children learn through play. Check website for upcoming special events, children's classes, birthday party rentals and free parent education programs. Daily drop-in fees and annual memberships available.

Lawrence Hall of Science
U.C. Berkeley
Located on Centennial Drive below Grizzly Peak in the Berkeley Hills
Berkeley, CA 94720
www.lawrencehallofscience.org
510-642-5132
Hours: Open daily 10 am–5 pm

Spend quality family time indoors and out. Traveling exhibits in 2008 include SPEED! And Engineer It. Outdoors, take in a spectacular 180-degree view of San Francisco Bay in the science park Forces That Shape the Bay. Play Mother Nature with hands-on demonstrations that show how earthquakes, erosion, wind and weather helped shape the Bay. Climb a whale and crawl through a DNA jungle gym on our Plaza.

Martinez Museum
1005 Escobar Street
Martinez, CA 94553
www.martinezhistory.org/index.html
925-228-8160
Hours: Tuesday and Thursday 1:30 am–3 pm, First four Sundays 1 pm–4 pm
Price: Free

Find maps, the city's property assessment books from 1884 to the late 1940's, a massive collection of historic photographs, artifacts from the city and county, the county census from 1860–1920 including some other parts of California, and other interesting things to see. Plus, be sure to visit the rooms of the historic building where work has been done to restore the structure to an approximation of its original appearance.

Mount Diablo Summit Museum
Located in the historic stone building atop Mt. Diablo's highest peak
Clayton, CA 94517
www.mdia.org/museum.htm
925-837-6119
Open daily from 10 am–4 pm
Price: Free

Impressive exhibits chronicle the history of the mountain and capture its majesty. A rock wall with instructional video examines the geological forces which created the mountain. Panels describe the Native American history of the region. A diorama, complete with native sounds, offers an overview of the park's ecosystems. A model of the mountain acquaints visitors with important park locations. Splendid photographs enhance the visitor's experience. Plus, telescopes are mounted on the deck to help you enjoy one of the finest views in the world.

Places to Go and Things to Do

MOCHA the Museum of Children's Art

538 Ninth Street
Historic Oakland, CA 94607
www.mocha.org

510-465-8770

510-465-8770 x308 Reservations

Hour: Tuesday–Friday 10 am–5 pm; Saturday & Sunday Noon–5 pm

Admission: $7/child for hand-on studio admission, Members & Adults FREE!

MOCHA, is a joyful, lively place to celebrate children's art. Join in art-making activities or view exhibitions of children's art. For under-fives and their caregivers, visit the Little Studio designed especially for hands-on fun for little ones. Weekends participate in family extravaganza workshops for all ages. Plan a birthday, holiday, art party or field trip. MOCHA artists provide age appropriate projects and materials while guiding and encouraging your artistic endeavors. Paint, build, sculpt...create!

Museum of the San Ramon Valley

205 Railroad Avenue
Danville, CA 94526
www.museumsrv.org

925-837-3750

Hours: Tuesday–Friday 1 pm–4 pm, Saturday 10 am–1 pm

Price: Free. Donations welcome

The Valley's past is featured in a permanent exhibit that includes artifacts, an historical narrative frieze and pictures of historic buildings. The Museum collects, stores and protects artifacts from the San Ramon Valley. A Museum Store offers exciting gifts and remembrances for visitors. In addition to a permanent exhibit on Valley history, the Museum sponsors revolving exhibits and several guided tours including the Alamo Cemetery and Old Town Danville.

Pittsburg Historical Society & Museum

515 Railroad Avenue
Pittsburg, CA 94565
www.pittsburgca.net/sites/pittsburghistoricalsociety/index.aspx

925-439-7501

Hours: Wednesdays 1 pm–4 pm, Saturdays 10 am–2 pm

Price: Free. Donations welcome.

Richmond Museum of History

400 Nevin Avenue
Richmond, CA 94802
www.richmondmuseumofhistory.org/mapdirections.htm

510-235-7387

Hours: Wednesday–Sunday 1 pm–4 pm. Closed Holidays.

Price: Free

Valley Children's Museum

www.valleychildrensmuseum.org

925-461-6574

Valley Children's Museum is currently a traveling exhibit program that has appeared in venues throughout the community. Valley Children's Museum has provided thousands of local children with hands-on, play-based activities, make-and-take projects and learning experiences. It has offered its exhibits and programs at festivals, fairs and public libraries in the Tri-Valley and surrounding community, including San Ramon and Danville elementary schools. Valley Children's Museum expects to open the doors of a permanent museum in Dublin, California within a few years.

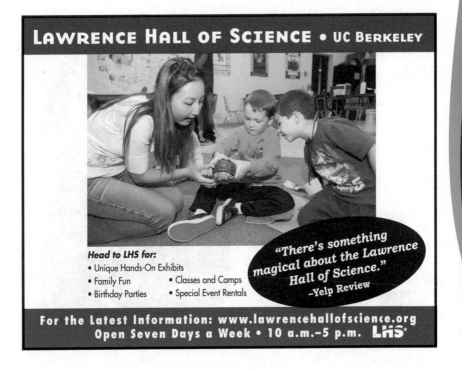

Places to Go and Things to Do

Skating

The Golden Skate

2701 Hooper Drive
San Ramon, CA 94583
www.thegoldenskate.com

925-820-2525

Hours: See website for open session and lesson hours.
Price: Saturday 10 am–Noon, $9; Regular Daytime $9; Evenings $9; Extra Session $4. Rentals: Roller Skates $4, Inline Skates $5

A full-service inline and quad skating rink for kids of all ages. Open skate sessions, lessons, and a hockey program are offered. Group and Birthday Party packages available.

The Rink at the Lafayette Community Center

500 Street Mary's Road
Lafayette, CA 94549
www.ci.lafayette.ca.us

925-284-2232

Hours: Varies by sport. Please call for details.
Price: Varies by sport. Please call for details.

This brand new multi.-sport outdoor facility is located at the Lafayette Community Center. Several sports to choose from including roller hockey, basketball and electric remote-control car drops! Don't miss Family Skate Nights for lights, music, fun and games. Food and drink available for purchase. Group and Birthday Party packages available.

RollerHaven

West 10th Street and Fairgrounds Park
Antioch, CA 94509
www.rollerhaven.com

925-779-0200

*Hours: Public Skating Weekdays 1 pm–3:30 pm and 3 pm–5 pm, Friday 4 pm–6:30 pm,
6 pm–8:30 pm and 8:30 pm–11 pm, Saturday Noon–2:30 pm, 2:30–5 pm and 7:30 pm–10 pm,
Sunday 1 pm–3:30 pm, 2:30 pm–5 pm*
Price: General Admission $8, Quad skate rental free with paid admission. Inline skate rentals available for an additional $3.

Tuesday is Roll'n and Stroll'n day at Roller Haven during the public skating session from 3 pm to 5:30 pm. Bring your strollers in and skate with your little ones. It's a fun way to get exercise, spend time with your toddlers, meet and network with other new parents in the East County area. And, every stroller gets a FREE colorful helium-filled balloon attached! Moms/Dads skate & stroll for just $7. Skating pre-schoolers accompanied by you skate for only $3. Babies or toddlers get a FREE ride for being your exercise partner. Bring your own skates or use theirs, skate rental is FREE!

Unique Parks

Antioch Paintball Park

1201 West 10th Street
Antioch, CA 94509
www.antiochpaintballpark.com

925-757-2468

Hours: Saturday and Sunday 8 am–4 pm. Friday nights are available on demand for groups.
Price: $15 allows for play in one 3 hour session. $20 allows for play in two 3 hour sessions. Players must be at least 10 years of age. Spectators are free. Half Day is $49 and provides you with one session (in either AM or PM), marker, face mask, barrel cover, 500 paint balls, and one air fill to power your equipment. All Day is $59 and provides you with two sessions, marker, face mask, barrel cover, 500 paint balls, and unlimited air to power your equipment.

Places to Go and Things to Do

Castro Park and Clubhouse

1420 Norvell
El Cerrito, CA 94530
www.el-cerrito.org/recreation/parks.html

510-215-4300

Castro Park features a large playground and grassy area. It's adjacent to Castro School's blacktop (basketball courts and kickball diamond) and features tennis courts, a barbecue and picnic table.

Central Park

12501 Alcosta Blvd.
San Ramon, CA 94583
www.ci.san-ramon.ca.us

925-973-3200

A fantastic playground, picnic areas and water play makes this park a favorite for East Bay families. It is also home to the San Ramon Community Center and Pool.

Concord Community Park

North side of Cowell Road (between Hale Drive and Sheridan Road) next to El Monte School
Concord, CA 94518
www.ci.concord.ca.us/recreation/parks/parks.htm

925-671-3444

This park features the Concord Community Pool, an Olympic size swimming pool, with diving facilities, wading pool and heated changing rooms with showers and lockers. Park facilities include seven unlighted tennis courts, handball/tennis practice wall, ball field and backstop, large open turf area, and a children's play area with a castle theme. There are two group picnic/barbecue areas that can be reserved and many individual picnic tables with barbecues scattered throughout the park.

Crockett Park

Empire Avenue
Oakley, CA 94561
www.ci.oakley.ca.us/subPage.cfm?page=176673

925-625-7011

Amenities include a lawn area, BBQ's, tot lot with play structure, picnic benches, a large grass field, tennis court, basketball court, and walking trails.

Diablo Vista Park

1000 Tassajara Ranch Drive (at Crow Canyon Road)
Danville, CA 94506
925-314-3400

This 20-acre park is known for the mosaic water-snake that winds down a hillside. The park also has a children's play area, sand volleyball court, covered picnic area, lighted sports fields and two tennis courts. The sports fields, tennis courts, picnic area, and a snack shack are available for rent.

Dougherty Valley Aquatic Park

10550 Albion Way (on the new Dougherty Valley High School Campus)
San Ramon, CA 94582
www.ci.san-ramon.ca.us/parks/aquatics/dvac.htm

925-973-3335

Hours: Recreation Swim will begin in April. Please call for schedule.
Price: Children (1–6) $2.25, Youth (7–17) $2.75, Adults (18+) $3.50. Swim passes available for residents only.

Completed in September, 2007, this aquatic park boasts an Olympic size pool (starts at 4 1/2 feet) and a small kids water play structure. Everyone who enters the facility is required to pay the recreation fee, whether or not they are swimming.

Foxboro Park & Tennis Courts

1025 Canterbury Avenue
Hercules, CA 94547
www.ci.hercules.ca.us/New/Rec/parks.htm

510-799-8291

Highlights of this park include a recreation building, children's tot lot, two tennis courts, a basketball court, four picnic tables, four BBQ pits, a multi-use field, a jogging trail, restrooms, drinking fountain and street parking.

Heather Farm Park

North San Carlos Drive at Ygnacio Valley Road
Walnut Creek, CA 94598
www.walnut-creek.org/header.asp?genericId=1&catId=5&subCatId=686

925-943-5858

This 102 acre park features the Clarke Swim Center, tennis courts, picnic areas, community center, equestrian center, bike paths, tot lots, a sand volleyball court, fishing pond, nature pond (with ducks and geese galore), six athletic fields, restrooms, and connection to the Iron Horse Trail. The tot lots feature swings, slides, a rock-climbing wall, and plenty of sand to make little masterpieces.

Lafayette Reservoir

Mt. Diablo Blvd. (between First Street & Moraga Road)
Lafayette, CA 94549
www.ci.lafayette.ca.us

925-284-2232

Places to Go and Things to Do

Price: The daily entry fee to the park is $6, and hours of operation range from 6 am to 9 pm, depending on the season. Discounts for seniors and disabled persons are available also.

This all-year, day-use area is ideal for hiking, jogging, fishing, boating and picnicking. Rowboats and pedal boats can be rented. Private rowboats, canoes, kayaks and small sailboats are allowed if carried atop your auto (no gasoline engines). Launching docks and a small bait shop are added conveniences. A daily fishing access fee ($3) is required. Families, groups and companies can reserve picnic areas holding 50 or 200 people. Many individual tables and barbecues accommodate smaller groups. Two play areas offer lively fun for children. The park has restrooms and a disabled-access fishing dock with adjacent parking.

Larkey Park

Buena Vista Avenue and First Avenue
Walnut Creek, CA 94597
www.walnut-creek.org/header.asp?genericId=1&catId=5&subCatId=658

925-943-5858

Amenities include children's play areas, connection to walking trails, open turf area, picnic areas, restrooms, sand volleyball court, swimming (May–September) and tennis. Larkey Park is also home to the Lindsay Wildlife Museum and the Walnut Creek Model Railroad Society.

Moraga Commons

1799 Street Mary's Road (corner of Moraga Road and Street Mary's Road)
Moraga, CA 94556
www.ci.moraga.ca.us/moraga_park_rentals.php

925-376-2521

The park offers picnic areas, tot lots, swings, a few water elements, sand volleyball, horseshoes, bocce ball, and half court basketball, along with lots of room to relax under shade trees. The group picnic area, located near the bandshell is available for rent and accommodates up to 85 persons. An addition to the Commons Park in 2004 was the Lamorinda Skatepark. The skatepark is open from 9 am to dusk daily.

Oak Hill Park

3005 Stone Valley Road
Danville, CA 94526
www.ci.danville.ca.us/default.asp?serviceID1=178&Frame=L1

925-314-3400

Oak Hill Park offers a quiet country setting with a spectacular Mt. Diablo backdrop, an idyllic location for family picnics, weddings, and other special occasions. This 43-acre park features a small lake that supports a variety of wild birds, including migratory ducks and geese. Adventurous visitors to Oak Hill Park will enjoy a scenic hike or horseback ride along the trail that meanders through the hills overlooking the park. An exercise course is incorporated into the trail. Here too is the future site of the All Wars Memorial.

A sand volleyball court and group picnic area are available for rent. The picnic area includes seven tables and three barbecue pits. Nearby, four lighted tennis courts can also be reserved.

Orinda Community Center Park

26 Orinda Way
Orinda, CA 94563
www.ci.orinda.ca.us/parksandrec
925-254-2445

The Community Park is located next to the Orinda Community Center. The Park is available for use on a first come, first served basis. This large park includes a big open grass area (perfect for throwing a Frisbee), two playground areas (one featuring a water play area), picnic and barbecue areas along with three tennis courts with lights.

Osage Station Park

816 Brookside Drive
Danville, CA 94526
www.ci.danville.ca.us/default.asp?serviceID1=563&Frame=L1
925-314-3400

Osage Station Park is known for its beautiful memorial rose garden and children's play area with train station and water attraction. This 35-acre park features four tennis courts, four baseball diamonds, several soccer fields, plus a path around the park that has a distance of 7/10 (.7) mile. The tennis courts and sports fields can be rented.

Pinole Valley Park

3790 Pinole Valley Road
Pinole, CA 94564
www.ci.pinole.ca.us/recreation/parks_locations.html
510-724-9002

This very large (231 acres!) and popular park has many convenient facilities including a fenced ball field, full-sized soccer field, bleachers, playground, restrooms, drinking fountain and play areas. Adjacent to the park is a dog park, consisting of two play areas—one for large dogs and one for small dogs and the Hazel Downer-Thornton Picnic Grove with picnic tables and restrooms.

Pleasant Hill Park

147 Gregory Lane
Pleasant Hill, CA 94523
www.pleasanthillrec.com/Rentals.htm#Parks
925-676-5200

This popular park has a new five and under play area, two baseball diamonds, three reserved picnic areas, two open picnic areas, two sand volleyball courts, a children's playground and basketball court. Next to the park is the Pleasant Hill Aquatic Park with a Diving Pool that is 25 yards long with a depth of 3 1/2 to 10 feet; two one-meter Diving Boards, and two or more lifeguards on duty. The new Sprayground features interactive, active, and passive play for all age groups and people with disabilities. There will even be a "No Splash Zone" for young toddlers and infants.

San Ramon Olympic Pool and Aquatic Park
9900 Broadmoor Drive
San Ramon, CA 94583
www.ci.san-raMondayca.us/parks/aquatics/srop.htm
925-973-3240
Hours: Hours fluctuate by season. Please see website for details.
Price: Daily Fee—Children (1–6) $2.25, Youth (7–17) $2.75, Adult (18+) $3.50. Everyone who enters the facility is required to pay the recreation fee, whether or not they are swimming.

A public facility offering outdoor lap swimming, swim lessons, recreation swimming, including a very cool water play park for the kids, lifeguard certification courses, and a variety of other programs. Get fitness for the whole family with the Family Lap Swim. Fee is $3.50 per person, ages 7–17. Group and Birthday Party packages available.

Shadow Cliffs Regional Recreation Area
2500 Stanley Blvd.
Pleasanton, CA 94566
www.shadowcliffs.com
925-829-6230
Hours: Summer Hours: Open Daily 10:30 am–5:30 pm, June 9 through Labor Day and on weekends through September.
Price: Half-hour $5, 1 hour $7, Half Day $10 (9:30 am–2 pm or 2 pm–5:30 pm), All Day $15.

Located at Shadow Cliffs East Bay Regional Park, the Rapids Waterslides are a hit with families. And, a brand new waterpark, California Splash! is currently in construction, scheduled to open in May 2008. Picnic areas, softball, swimming, barbecues, fishing, paddleboats and windsurfing are also available. Riders must be at least 42" tall.

Sycamore Valley Park
2101 Holbrook Drive (at Camino Tassajara)
Danville, CA 94506
925-314-3400
Sycamore Valley Park has a children's play area with popular recreational fountain, a reflection pond with waterfall and a jogging path that meanders through the park. The picnic area includes eight picnic tables and barbecue pits. The picnic area and five baseball diamonds and soccer fields can be reserved.

Veterans Park

3841 Balfour Road
Brentwood, CA 94513
925-516-5444

Located adjacent to the Brentwood Family Aquatics Complex, this park features covered group picnic areas which can be reserved, a sand volleyball court, four bocce courts with oyster shell surfacing and a horseshoe court. This facility also has a restroom, children's play area with unique play equipment and a 10-foot wide walking path around the perimeter of the park.

Vincent Park

End of the Peninsula
Richmond, CA 94804
www.ci.richmond.ca.us/index.asp?NID=242
510-620-6793

Panoramas, playground, offshore fishing, and shipyard stories, make this park a favorite for all ages. The S.S. Red Oak Victory, launched in 1944, is being restored at the former Kaiser Shipyard #3 visible across the harbor to the West.

Waterfront Park

North Court Street via Ferry Street.
Martinez, CA 94553
www.cityofmartinez.org/depts/recreation/parks/waterfront.asp
925-372-3510

Four ball fields are included in this complex with concessions and restrooms, soccer field, picnic areas, playground areas, horseshoe pits and bocce ball courts, restroom, the Marina and fishing pier. In addition, there's a twelve-hundred seat amphitheater and skateboard park.

Other Cool Finds

Cribs, Kids & Teens

7260 San Ramon Road
Dublin, CA 94568
www.cribskidsandteens.com
info@cribskidsandteens.com
925-833-2020

Cribs, Kids & Teens provides one-stop shopping, which means you can select your children's furniture, bedding and accessories in just one trip! Along with kids and teenager selections, we offer cribs, nursery furniture, and strollers. They're only young once...Give them a room to remember!

Downtown Pleasanton Association

830 Main Street
Pleasanton, CA 94566
www.pleasantondowntown.net

925-484-2199

Charming, historic downtown Pleasanton, California is an enjoyable place to shop, dine and meet friends in the heart of the city. Downtown will greet you with unexpected finds and uncommon treasures. The pedestrian-friendly, tree-lined streets offer a vibrant blend of parks and historic buildings, specialty shops and service businesses, fine dining and coffee shops

East Bay Dads

dads@eastbaydads.org

East Bay Dads is group of fathers with babies, toddlers and pre-schoolers in the East San Francisco Bay Area. They meet almost every Monday morning at a local park, museum, or other fun place. And most Thursday mornings there is a hike for dads with kids still young enough to go in a front- or backpack or jog stroller. East Bay Dads is open to any and everyone: no fee, no commitment, etc.

Grateful Dads, East Bay Chapter
Contact: Allen, 510-532-8322

www.gratefuldads.com

On any given weekend, six to 20 dads show up with babes in tow. They tote them in slings or back-packs, slather on the sunscreen and tramp the trails with water bottles and tied-on baby toys flapping against the pack frames. The East Bay group mixes the pace, opting for the paved path around the Lafayette Reservoir one month and the steeper trails of Joaquin Miller Regional Park the next. There are no fees, no RSVP's, and no one takes roll. You just show up.

Stoneridge Shopping Center

One Stoneridge Mall Road
Pleasanton, CA 94588
www.shopstoneridge.com

925-463-2778

Stoneridge is the East Bay's premier shopping center, featuring Nordstrom, Macy's, JCPenney and Sears. Stoneridge is also home to over 165 specialty stores and restaurants that include Apple, Ann Taylor, Banana Republic, The Cheesecake Factory, Children's Place, Gap Kids & Baby Gap, Gymboree, Janie & Jack, Limited Too, P.F. Chang's, Pottery Barn & Pottery Barn Kids, Motherhood Maternity, Williams-Sonoma and much more. Be sure to visit Guest Services to find out about the Stoneridge Kidgits club, a kids club for kids ages 3–8 that hosts monthly events at the shopping center. You can also visit www.simonkidgitsclub.com for more information.

Chapter 2

Day Trips and Northern California Vacations

W e live in one of the most beautiful areas of the country! We've researched some great places to visit with your family, right here in our own back yard. Take advantage of all these offerings . . . without having to get on a plane!

Central Coast

Charles Paddock Zoo

9305 Pismo Avenue
Atascadero, CA 93422
www.charlespaddockzoo.org
805-461-5080
Hours: Summer Hours (April 1–October 31) 10 am–5 pm; Winter Hours (November–March 31) 10 am–4 pm.
Price: Adults 12 & over $5 , Children 3–11 $4 , Seniors 65+ $4.25, Members Free.

Located within beautiful Atascadero Lake Park is the Charles Paddock Zoo. Although the zoo is quite small, it has over 100 animals including jaguars, Bengal tigers, Flamingos, a Black Bear, porcupines, Mere Cats and Mangabey monkeys. Make sure to spend some time at the petting zoo where the kids can touch the animals.

Cayucos State Beach

Five miles north of Morro Bay, at the foot of Cayucos Drive
Cayucos, CA 93430
www.parks.ca.gov
805-781-5930
Hours: Open Sunrise to Sunset
Price: Free

41

Cayucos State Beach is a haven for boogie boarding, surfing, swimming, and tide pooling. Next to the beach, kayaks and boogie boards are available for rent; Rent a kayak and paddle out into Estero Bay or take a lesson in surfing. With its gentle waves and flat sandy shore, the beach is perfect for splashing in the water and for building sand castles. Lifeguards are on duty from Memorial Day to Labor Day. There are also picnic tables, restrooms, and outside showers. The fishing pier is a great place for whale watching or spotting sea otters. After the sun sets, the pier is lit for night fishing. North of the pier is Hardie Park which has a play structure, a grassy area, picnic tables, barbecue grills, and a public swimming pool. Cayucos is a charming beachside town with a relaxed atmosphere, wonderful unspoiled beaches, historic buildings, a popular beachside boardwalk and a pier for fishing and enjoying the beautiful sunsets. There are several small family-owned budget-friendly motels and quaint restaurants that offer traditional seaside fare like chowder, fish n' chips and gourmet seafood. This little town is perfect for a relaxing family get-away and makes a great place to stop en-route to Southern California.

Montaña de Oro State Park

Pecho Road
Los Osos, CA 93402
www.parks.ca.gov
805-772-7434

Hours: Open Sunrise to Sunset
Price: Free for day use. Call for campground fees.

Montaña de Oro State Park is one of California's largest state parks, consisting of 8,000 acres with seven miles of spectacular coastline and over fifty miles of trails for hiking, jogging, bicycling, horseback riding, and mountain biking. Favorite activities here include surfing, tide pool exploring, whale watching, picnicking and camping. This park features rugged cliffs, secluded sandy beaches, coastal plains, streams, canyons, and hills, including 1,347-foot Valencia Peak. The park's name, "Mountain of Gold," comes from the golden wildflowers that bloom in spring. Day use facilities at Spooners Cove and Coon Creek include picnic tables and woodstoves. Pit toilets are located nearby. There are fifty primitive campsites located on a bluff above the beach, alongside a creek which flows into the ocean. The campsites are available from Memorial Day to Labor Day. Picnic tables and woodstoves are provided and primitive non-flushing toilets are nearby. There are no showers at this campground. Guided tours depart from the visitors' center located in the Spooners Ranch House, which is open daily during the summer and on weekends during the rest of the year.

Morro Bay State Park Museum of Natural History

20 State Park Road
Morro Bay, CA 93442
www.morrobaymuseum.org
805-772-2694

Hours: The Museum is open daily from 10 am–5 pm; Closed Thanksgiving, Christmas and New Year's Day.

Price: Adults $2, Children 16 and under Free.

The Morro Bay State Park Museum of Natural History sits on a hill above the Morro Bay Estuary and offers a panoramic view of the coastline and of world-famous Morro Rock.

There are 26 interactive hands-on exhibits which teach visitors about tidal forces, geology, erosion and how humans affect the Earth. Visitors can build a sand dune, operate the hydrologic cycle and dig into the food pit to create their own food chains. At the tide pool exhibit, friendly tour guides offer binoculars so visitors can spy on the spotted seals.

Pismo Beach Oceano Campground

555 Pier Avenue
Pismo Beach, CA 93449
www.parks.ca.gov

805-473-7223

Hours: Call Reserve America at 800-444-7275

Price: Sites without hook-ups are $20/night, sites with hook-ups $29/night

Pismo Beach Oceano Campground has 42 campsites which will accommodate tents or RVs. Campground amenities include restrooms with quarter-operated showers, direct beach access, a small lake, hiking trails, and the Pismo Beach Nature Center which offers guided tours, gardens to stroll through, and special programs to campers. A restaurant is located nearby. Bring your own firewood as it can be expensive to purchase it near the campground.

The Monarch Butterfly Grove

Highway 1, South Pismo Beach
Pismo Beach, CA 93449
www.monarchbutterfly.org

805-773-4382

Hours: Butterfly viewing anytime; guided tours from 11 am and 2 pm daily from November until February.

Price: Free

Beginning in November, hundreds of thousands of Monarch butterflies return every year to the Monarch Butterfly Grove and remain throughout the winter until February. This Pismo Beach habitat is believed to be the largest in the Western United States. Though docents provide telescopes, bring your own binoculars so you can take your time beholding the thousands of butterflies flitting about the Eucalyptus grove. During the monarch season, the grove is staffed every day from 10 am to 4 pm with docent talks at 11 am and 2 pm. Free parking is available inside the North Beach Campground, just north of the trees. Drive into campground and park in campsite #78. There are signs to the grove over the creek.

Bay Area Day Trips and Family Vacations

Pismo Beach Nature Center

555 Pier Avenue
Pismo Beach, CA 93449
www.morrobaymuseum.org/pismo_nature_center.html
805-473-7223

Hours: Open Saturday–Sunday only during the winter from 11 am–2 pm and 7 days a week during the summer from 11 am–2 pm.

Price: Free

Located in the Pismo State Beach Oceano Campground, this Nature Center provides visitors information about the plants, animals and cultural history of the State Park.

Interactive, hands on exhibits on birds, animals, Monarch butterflies, the fresh water Lagoon, native plants and Chumash culture make learning fun for all ages. Docents are available to lead guided walks and to answer questions. A "walk through" garden area has easy paths that wind their way through native plants, which are identified with markers. There are benches with a view of the lagoon, where visitors can enjoy the flowers, butterflies, and birds. Adjacent to the Walk through Garden is the Dune Interpretive Garden, which has been planted with plants native to the Sate Park dunes. The freshwater lagoon adjacent to the Oceano campground is encircled by the one mile Guiton Trail which is a pleasant walk through a grove of willows where birdwatchers can see migrating warblers during the months of September and October.

Monterey Coast

Big Sur

Julia Pfeiffer Burns State Park

Highway 1
Big Sur, CA 93920
www.parks.ca.gov
831-667-2315

Hours: Open 1/2 hour before sunrise to 1/2 hour after sunset.

Price: $8 per vehicle. Two campsites are available for $20 each per night; Reservations are required.

Julia Pfeiffer Burns State Park is located 37 miles south of Carmel on Highway 1, and 12 miles south of Pfeiffer Big Sur State Park. It's most stunning feature is an 80-foot waterfall that drops from granite cliffs into the ocean. The trail to the waterfall is an easy hike and stroller accessible. In December and January the bench at the end of Overlook trail is an excellent place to watch for gray whales. Many whales swim close to shore during this time and one will occasionally come into the mouth of the cove. In March and April, the whales can be seen returning north to their summer feeding grounds in the North Pacific. Sea otters can sometimes be seen in the cove, as well as harbor seals and California sea lions. Many sea and shore birds also make an appearance.

There are only two campsites within this park and they are located above the waterfall. While the setting is spectacular, the sites are remote and can only be reached on foot with picnic tables being the only amenity. Restrooms are located near the parking area away from the campsites.

Pfeiffer Big Sur State Park

Big Sur Station #1
Big Sur, CA 93920
www.parks.ca.gov
831-667-2315
Hours: Open 1/2 hour before sunrise to 1/2 hour after sunset.
Price: $8 per vehicle. Campsites $20 per night.

Located 26 miles south of Carmel on Highway 1, this beautiful park features redwoods, conifers, oaks, sycamores, cottonwoods, maples, alders and willows as well as open meadows. Hikers can enjoy the many scenic trails, including a self-guided nature trail. The campground also has a trail to a waterfall as well as a river perfect for swimming, wading and tubing. There are several very spacious tent sites with picnic tables, barbecue grills, fire rings and water spigots. Restrooms with warm-water showers are nearby (bring quarters for the showers). Other amenities include a fairly well-stocked store and laundry facilities. Though the store stocks firewood, it's best to bring your own as it's rather expensive to buy it at the campground. For those who would rather not camp, Big Sur Lodge is located within the park. The lodge has 61 guest rooms, a café, and a grocery store. This option is more expensive and the cabins are rustic, but the lodge is nicely located inside the redwood forest near hiking trails and most cabins have been newly refurbished. Some cabins have fireplaces and useful amenities such as kitchens or mini-refrigerators. Cabins are situated near the swimming pool and looped around a lawn where children can play close by.

Carmel

Carmel Beach

Ocean Avenue
Carmel-by-the-Sea, CA 93923
www.carmelcalifornia.org
831-755-4500
Hours: Open Sunrise to Sunset
Price: Free

Pack the sand toys and a picnic blanket and stroll down to the end of Ocean Avenue to kid-friendly Carmel Beach. This beach is clean and wide and great for building sandcastles, taking long walks along the shore and enjoying the incredible view. There is a busy parking lot adjacent to the beach so consider parking up the hill where you can pick up a picnic lunch or dine at one of the many restaurants before heading towards the beach. Restrooms are available next to the beach.

Bay Area Day Trips and Family Vacations

Mission San Carlos Borromeo de Carmelo

3080 Rio Road
Carmel, CA 93923
www.carmelmission.org
831-624-1271

Hours: Monday–Saturday from 9:30 am–5 pm; Sunday 10:30 am–5 pm. Call the Mission at ext. 210 for the holiday schedule.

Price: Adults $5, Seniors $4, Children under 17 $1. Includes access to the mission, garden and museums.

Founded by Father Junipero Serra on June 3, 1770, the Carmel mission is the second founded in California and one of the most beautiful with its lovely gardens, unique architecture, and view of the sea. Explore the gardens, the mission, the museum and the small cemetary. Complimentary docent tours may be available at 10 am and 2 pm during the week if docents are on the grounds. You can call ext. 213 to check on their availability. Most people explore the mission on their own with the aid of a brochure offered by the mission. Be aware that the mission is an active parish and holds mass as well as weddings, funerals and baptisms which may limit access to certain parts of the mission.

Point Lobos State Reserve

Route 1
Carmel, CA 93923
www.pt-lobos.parks.state.ca.us
408-624-4909

Hours: Open daily at 9 am to half hour after sunset (posted daily at the entrance). A schedule of guided walks for the month is posted at the entrance station. The museums are open as staffing permits, generally from 11 am until 3 pm.

Price: $8 per car and $1 for map. Includes entrance to museums and tours.

Point Lobos is known as "the crown jewel of the State Park System" and for good reason. Not only is it in a spectacular ocean setting, it offers many activities including hiking, nature study, picknicking, whale watching and scuba diving. Kids will love spying on the otters and seals and exploring the many tidepools. Hiking trails are wide and level and accessible for young hikers. Visit Whalers Cabin where there are displays of harpoons, whaling tools, whale-oil barrels, a model of a whaling boat and photographs of the old Monterey Peninsula whalers. China Cove and Gibson Beach are white sand beaches accessible via long stairways. Swimming and wading are allowed but the water is icy cold. Hike to Bird Island which is home to hundreds of birds. Come early, especially during the summer months when the number of visitors allowed inside the park is limited, and plan to spend a good part of the day—there is a lot to see and do. Bring a picnic, comfortable shoes, layered clothing, lots of water and binoculars if you have them. Food is not allowed on the beach in order to protect the wildlife, but picnic areas are available. Restrooms are available as well.

Monterey

Dennis the Menace Park

777 Pearl Street
Monterey, CA 93940
831-646-3866

Dennis the Menace Park has a fun combination of old and new play structures. There is a big rock climbing wall, tall slides, a bridge, a maze, a staionary locomotive donated by Southern Pacific Company that kids love to climb and a variety of climbing and play structures. The park is near the Monterey Bay Aquarium, the wharf, museums and Cannery Row and a must-do if you are visiting the area with children. There are restrooms, picnic tables, grassy areas and a concession stand that sells burgers, fries, drinks and ice-cream treats. There is a free parking lot adjacent to the park which can fill up quickly on busy days so be prepared to cruise around for street parking if you come on a weekend, especially during the summer.

Skateboard Park

Located just behind Dennis the Menace Park, bordering Lake El Estero, is a newly constructed skate park. Bring a helmet and skateboard or in-line skates and practice jumps and turns on the challenging ramps and corners.

El Estero Boating

Del Monte & Camino Aguajito
Monterey, CA 93940
831-375-1484

Hours: Open seven days a week from 10 am weather permitting. Closed on Mondays during the winter.

Price: $20/hour, $15/half-hour.

Rent a paddle boat, kayak, or canoe and join the ducks for a cruise around the fresh waters of El Estero Lake surrounding Dennis the Menace Park.

Monterey Bay Aquarium

886 Cannery Row
Monterey, CA 93940
www.mbayaq.org
831-648-4800

Hours: 10 am–6 pm Daily; Holidays 9:30 am–6 pm; Closed Christmas Day
Price: Adults $24.95, Child (3–12) $15.95, Under 3 Free, Student $22.95, Senior (65+) $22.95, Memberships available.

The Monterey Bay Aquarium is the biggest and the best aquarium in the country and the main attraction in Monterey. There are many exhibits that will enchant children and adults of all ages—shimmering pink and purple jelly-fish, silvery swirling circles of anchovies and swaying underwater kelp forests. See the Great White Shark cutting through the water, watch the penguins enjoy a meal at feeding time, touch a bat ray as it swims past or pick up a starfish in the tide-pool exhibit. Let the kids play in the children's learning area where they can learn about marine life through the hands-on exhibits. These are just a few of the many wonders at this fascinating underwater showcase. To avoid the dense crowds, it is best to visit during the fall and winter months and mid-week during the busy summer months. Food and drinks may not be consumed inside the aquarium but the aquarium does provide picnic areas for guests. Also, within the aquarium, the Portola Restaurant is a full-service restaurant, serving seafood entrees in a panoramic ocean view setting. There is also a self-service café where pizza, burgers, sandwiches and salads are served. Avoid the long line and purchase tickets on-line in advance as the museum draws big crowds.

Montery Bay Whale Watch

84 Fisherman's Wharf
Monterey, CA 93940
www.montereybaywhalewatch.com

831-375-4658

Hours: Ships depart daily at 9 am and 2 pm. Reservations are required. Closed Thanksgiving and Christmas.

Price: 9 am tour (4 1/2 hours) Adult $43, Children (12 and under) $33, 2 pm tour (3 1/2 hours) Adult $34, Children $23 .

Monterey Bay is one of the best places to observe the many types of wildlife that inhabit the bay. Depending on the season, a variety of mammals, birds and other sea creatures can be seen from one of the several boat tours available from Fisherman's Wharf. Monterey Bay Whale Watch is unique in that tours are led by experienced marine biologists. Wear warm clothing and bring a snack or lunch.

MY Museum

601 Wave Street, Suite 100
Monterey, CA 93940
www.mymuseum.org

831-649-6444

Hours: Monday–Saturday 10 am–5 pm; Sunday Noon–5 pm; Closed Wednesday.
Price: Children and Adults $5.50, Children under 2 Free, 10-visit Card/$30; Every Tuesday $2 for all visitors.

Located on Cannery Row in Monterey, MY Museum is a great place to take children ages 6 and under. The museum is packed with hands-on fun including the Creation Station, stocked with art supplies and several bins of assorted recycled materials that kids can use to create a myriad of art projects to take home. There is a theater with puppets, costumes, and a working TV camera, a build-your-own house exhibit, a restaurant with a kid-size kitchen stocked with dishes, utensils and play food, and several other hands-on exhibits. Food is not permitted inside but there are several dining options just outside the museum's doors. Register on-line and get the scoop on free days and events. For an ideal way to spend the day with younger tots, plan a daytrip to MY Museum then bring a picnic lunch to Dennis the Menace Park. After lunch, let the kids run around the playground. This is a great way to wear them out for the long ride home!

Old Fisherman's Wharf

Old Fisherman's Wharf #1
Monterey, CA 93940
www.montereywharf.com

The historic wharf is where families can dine at any of several restaurants, shop for gifts, candy or souveniers, cruise around the Monterey Bay on one of the many boat tours, catch a glimpse of gray whales or see a play at the The Bruce Ariss Wharf Theater. Stroll to the end of the pier and say hello to the barking sea lions. Take a few minutes to visit the website before you visit the wharf to explore the possibilities.

Steinbeck's Spirit of Monterey Wax Museum

700 Cannery Row, Suite II
Monterey, CA 93940
www.wax-museum.com

831-375-3770

Hours: Open all week from 10 am–8 pm except on Saturdays 10 am–9 pm and Tuesdays 11 am–7 pm.
Price: $8.95 Adults, Seniors (60+) $6.95, Teens (13–17) $5.95, Youth (6–12) $4.95, Children (5 and under) $2.95

Take a glimpse into Monterey's fascinating history at Steinbeck's Spirit of Monterey Wax Museum. The wax museum takes up an entire floor of the 700 Cannery Row building, just one block from the Monterey Bay Aquarium and features over 100 life-size wax figures set in animated scenes. See Cannery workers, fishermen, and bandits of the past come to life. The tour is narrated by the taped voice of John Steinbeck.

Vision Quest Safari Ranch

400 River Road
Salinas, CA 93908
www.wildthingsinc.com

831-455-1901

Hours: Public tour is available every day at 1 pm except Thanksgiving and Christmas. There is an additional tour at 3 pm during the months of June, July, and August. Reservations are not required.
Price: Basic Tour—Adults $10, Children (14 and under) $8. Other tour options are available at additional cost. Check website for other options.

Vision Quest Safari Ranch is home to professionally trained animals working in film, education, television and other productions. Vision Quest also takes in retired animals which might otherwise not fare as well elsewhere. After a short video presentation, guests may take a one hour tour of the animal compound and visit with lions, leopards, tigers, exotic birds, bears, elephants, reptiles, bugs, baboons and more! Other tour packages are available for those who are interested in a more in-depth and hands-on experience with the animals.

Santa Cruz

Big Basin State Park
Big Basin Redwoods State Park

21600 Big Basin Way
Boulder Creek, CA 95006
www.parks.ca.gov

831-338-8860

Hours: The park is open every day year round from 6 am to 10 pm. Office hours are currently 9 am to 5 pm Sunday-Thursday, and 8 am to 8 pm Friday and Saturday. The museum is open 9 am to 5 pm.

Price: Day use fee is $6 per vehicle. Family Camps $25, Senior Camps $23, $6 per additional vehicle. Family campsites may be reserved through Reserve America up to 7 months in advance —800-444-07275. Campsites will accommodate one vehicle, one towed vehicle and up to 8 people.

Big Basin is California's oldest State Park and home to the largest continuous stand of Ancient Coast Redwoods south of San Francisco. The park has over 80 miles of trails. Be sure and pick up a map at park headquarters before your hike. The park has a surprising number of waterfalls, a wide variety of environments from lush canyon bottoms to sparse chaparral-covered slopes, many animals including deer, raccoons, and an occasional bobcat, and lots of bird life. Food, beverages, essential camping supplies, single speed bike rentals and more are available at the Big Basin Redwoods Store located across the street from Park Headquarters (open daily 10 am–4 pm and closed during the months of December and January). Next to the General Store is a gift shop where postcards and gifts can be purchased. Visit the museum where visitors can see photographs of the area from years past, learn about redwood forests, and see the many birds, reptiles, insects and mammals that live in Big Basin. Campsites can be reserved. Big Basin Redwoods State Park also features charming one-room tent cabins to rent through a private concession. To make Tent Cabin reservations, call 800-874-8368.

Costanoa Coastal Lodge and Camp

2001 Rossi Road at Hwy 1
Pescadero, CA 94060
www.costanoa.com

650-879-1100

Price: Prices will vary anywhere from $40 to $365 per night depending on the type of lodging and number of nights at Costanoa. Please call or check the website for available options.

Costanoa may be the answer for those parents who may not necessarily enjoy "roughing it" with the kids, yet want them to experience the joy of camping and the great outdoors. Located between Santa Cruz and Half-Moon Bay, Costanoa is a good home base for many state parks in the area and offers many amenities and activities for both parents and children. Visitors may bring their own tents or opt to stay in the Lodge, a tent bungalow or in one of the Douglas Fir Cabins. Each of the rooms in the Lodge has many amenities including bathrobes, a mini refrigerator, stereo, telephone, coffee maker, thermostat controlled heat, and double French doors which open onto a patio or deck. Tent sites, which accommodate up to four people, have a wooden platform where campers can set up a tent, electricity, water and a parking space. Tent bungalows have electricity, sliding windows, a locking door and heated mattress pads. Visitors who opt for one of the cabins can choose a cabin with either a king or two double beds which all include a fireplace, skylights, bathrobes, bath amenities, a mini refrigerator, stereo, telephone, coffee maker, thermostat controlled heat and double French doors which open onto a shared deck. Campers and visitors who are not staying in the lodge have access to comfort stations which feature restrooms, indoor hot showers, heated concrete floors, a 24 hour dry sauna and an outdoor fireplace. Costanoa also offers spa treatments, yoga classes, kids' camp, horseback riding, nature hikes, biking and other activities. A restaurant, general store, barbecuing and picnicking facilities are all available on-site. Just short drives away are the towns of Pescadero and Davenport, berry-picking farms, and several state parks including Big Basin and Ano Nuevo State Reserve.

Henry Cowell Redwoods State Park

101 North Big Trees Park Road
Felton, CA 95018
www.parks.ca.gov

831-438-2396

Hours: Sunrise to Sunset

Price: Day use fee $5

This park features about 20 miles of trails of varying difficulty and terrain, a picnic area and the San Lorenzo River. Located in the Santa Cruz Mountains, the park is home to majestic redwoods, ponderosa pines, Douglas fir and oak trees. The Redwood Grove Trail is perfect for families with small children with its flat, stroller-friendly loop around the giant redwoods and restrooms at the half-way point. There is a visitor's center and a gift shop located within the park. Camping is also available. Call for fees and to make reservations.

Manresa State Beach

400 San Andreas Road
La Selva Beach, CA 95076
www.santacruzstateparks.org/parks/manresa

831- 724-3750

Hours: Sunday–Saturday 8 am–1/2 hour after sunset.

Price: $6 day use parking fee

Just off Highway 1 in Aptos, Manresa State Beach offers a wide stretch of beach, perfect for building sandcastles, swimming, and surfing. Restrooms, picnic tables and outdoor showers are available. Food is available nearby.

The Mystery Spot

465 Mystery Spot Road
Santa Cruz, CA 95065
www.mysteryspot.com

831-423-8897

Hours: Summer Hours 9 am–7 pm (first tour at 9:30 am, last tour at 7 pm, from Memorial Day to Labor Day); Winter Hours 9 am–5 pm (first tour at 9:30 am, last tour at 5 pm, from Labor Day until Memorial Day).

Price: General Admission $5, Children 3 and under Free. Parking $5 per car. Cash and ATM only (there is a $2 service charge for ATM). Credit Cards may be used in the gift shop only.

Prepare to be baffled. It's not very big (only about 150 feet in diameter) but strange things seem to happen in this part of the woods. Balls roll uphill; two people standing on opposite sides of a level surface appear to change height, people can walk up walls or balance at precarious angles. This is an interesting stop while visiting other attractions in the area.

Natural Bridges

2531 West Cliff Drive
Santa Cruz, CA 95060
www.santacruzstateparks.org/parks/natbridges

831-423-4609

Hours: Open daily 8 am to sunset.
Price: $6 day use parking fee.

Known for its famous natural bridge, Natural Bridges is an excellent place to view shore and ocean birds, migrating whales, and seals and otters playing offshore. Further along the beach, tide pools offer a glimpse of life beneath the sea. Low tides reveal sea stars, crabs, sea anemones, and other colorful sea creatures. The park also includes areas of coastal scrub meadows with bright native wildflowers in the spring. Natural Bridges State Beach is world-renowned for its yearly migration of monarch butterflies. In mid-October to late January, thousands of Monarch Butterflies can be seen migrating to the Eucalyptus grove. Inside the Visitor's Center there are displays on the monarch butterflies and an aquarium which features animals found in the tide pools. A video is also available for viewing. There are restrooms and picnic tables available and food can be purchased nearby.

Roaring Camp

Off of Graham Hill Road
Felton, CA 95018
www.roaringcamp.com

831-335-4484

Hours: Departure times vary. Call or check on-line for current schedule.
Price: Beach Train Roundtrip Fare: Adult (13 & up) $20.95, Children (3–12) $15.95, Under 3 Free.
Steam Train Roundtrip Fare: Adult (13 & up) $18.95, Children (3–12) $12.95, Under 3 Free.
Parking: $6.

Get your tickets and hop on board the Steam Train to Bear Mountain (1 1/2 hours round trip) or the Beach Train to the Santa Cruz Beach Boardwalk (3 hours round trip). Roaring Camp's steam engines are among the oldest and most authentically preserved narrow-gauge steam engines which still provide regularly scheduled passenger service in America. Beach Trains travel through Henry Cowell Redwoods State Park, down the scenic San Lorenzo River Gorge, across a 1909 steel truss bridge, and through an 1875 tunnel before arriving at the Santa Cruz Beach Boardwalk. You can get off at the Boardwalk and enjoy the beach and attractions before boarding one of the afternoon trains returning to Roaring Camp. Bring a hat, water and a camera for the steam train ride. Cars are uncovered and it can get hot under the sun. Trips may be long for very young children.

Santa Cruz Beach Boardwalk

400 Beach Street
Santa Cruz, CA 95060
www.beachboardwalk.com

831-423-5590

Hours: Memorial Day to Labor Day, the park is open daily from 11 am–10 pm. Operating hours vary depending on the weather so call or check the website for current calendar and operating hours. Open weekends and holidays from 11 am–5 pm or 6 pm; closed Christmas.
Price: Boardwalk access is free; All-Day Unlimited Rides Wristband $28.95 allows you to ride as often as you like all day; 60-Ticket Strip $37.95 is good for 10-20 rides depending on ride choices; Individual Rides $2.25–$4.50—tickets are 75 cents each and each ride requires 3–6 tickets. Season passes and on-line discounts available. Check the website for current offers. Parking fees: Varies by lot. Meter parking is also available.

The Santa Cruz Beach Boardwalk is an historic amusement park adjacent to Santa Cruz's mile-long beach. The Boardwalk includes more than 34 rides and attractions including the Giant Dipper, an historic wooden roller coaster built in 1924, and the 1911 Looff Carousel with its beautifully carved wooden horses. The Boardwalk also features more than 300 arcade games at the Casino Arcade, miniature golf in Neptune's Kingdom, a 3,400 square foot laser tag arena, a 26-lane bowling alley, and several restaurants and shops. Free Friday Night Concert Series in the summer.

Bay Area Day Trips and Family Vacations

Seymour Marine Discovery Center

100 Shaffer Road
Santa Cruz, CA 95060
www.seymourcenter.ucsc.edu

831-459-3800

Hours: Tuesday–Saturday 10 am–5 pm; Sunday Noon–5 pm; Closed Monday. Closed Labor Day, Veteran's Day and Thanksgiving.
Price: Adult $6, Student or Senior (64+) $4, Children (4–16) $4. Admission is free the first Tuesday of each month.

Located at the edge of West Cliff Drive and near Natural Bridges State Park, the Seymour Marine Discovery Center is a working marine laboratory where children can learn how scientists do their work in a real lab. Unlike habitat tanks, many of the tanks are laboratory-like with exposed seawater pipes and valves. Visit the seawater table and hold an assortment of sea creatures such as sea stars, sea urchins, hermit crabs, sea anemones, and different types of kelp. Just outside is an 87-foot long skeleton of a blue whale. A limited number of tours are offered each afternoon, and space is limited. Tours are filled on a first come, first serve basis. Sign-up begins one hour before tour time. Tours are scheduled as follows: Lab-wide tours depart at 1 pm, 2 pm, and 3 pm.

East Bay

Berkeley

Berkeley Marina

160 University Avenue
Berkeley, CA 94710
www.ci.berkeley.ca.us/marina

510-981-6740

The Berkeley Marina offers more than just a place for boats to dock. Take a walk on the pier, let the kids build a clubhouse at the Adventure Playground, learn about nature and marine life at Shorebird Park Nature Center and the Straw Bale Nature Center, or fly kites at Cesar Chavez Park where there are great views of the Bay and Golden Gate Bridge.

Adventure Playground

162 University Avenue, Berkeley Marina
Berkeley, CA 94710
www.ci.berkeley.ca.us/marina/marinaexp/adventplgd.html

510-981-6740

Hours: Saturdays & Sundays year-round 11 am–5 pm, Monday–Friday 9 am–5 pm during the summer; Closed weekdays during the school year.

Price: Free for four children or less if accompanied by adults. Reservations are required for groups of five or more children.

Adventure Playground is an innovative playground and is one of the Top 5 play spaces in the country. Kids can create, build and paint their own playground, climb on the hanging tires, glide through the air on a zip line and play on the kid-designed play structures. Don't be surprised to find hammers, nails and saws for the kids to build with. Make sure kids wear sturdy shoes (no sandals or flip-flops) and clothes that they can get dirty in. The playground is recommended for children ages 7 and older, but younger ones are welcome as long as parents are within arms reach. Restrooms and picnic areas are on site.

Chabot Space & Science Center

10000 Skyline Blvd.
Oakland, CA 94619
www.chabotspace.org

510-336-7373

Hours: Wed.–Thurs. 10 am–5 pm, Fri.–Sat. 10 am–10 pm, Sun. 11 am–5 pm.

Give your family the Moon, the Stars and the Universe. Parents and kids alike are in for an out-of–this-world experience when they visit our 86,000-square foot Space Center set amidst 13-acres of park land. Immerse yourself in our state-of-the-art digital dome planetarium, giant screen MegaDome theatre and hands-on interactive exhibits and demonstrations. Marvel at the wonders of the Universe through the largest public telescopes in the Western United States.

Shorebird Park Nature Center and Straw Bale Building
Berkeley Marina

Berkeley, CA 94710
510-981-6720

Hours: Shorebird Park Nature Center is open 9 am–5 pm Tuesday–Saturday; Straw Bale Visitor Center is open to the public 1 pm–5 pm Tuesday–Friday and Saturdays 9 am–5 pm.
Price: Free

Shorebird Park Nature Center is the first municipal straw bale building in the United States. It has a solar hot water system to provide heating year-round in the cool marina climate, and a solar electrical system to power the aquariums, computers, lighting and other equipment. The new Straw Bale building houses the Nature and Visitors Center and contains a 50 gallon salt-water tank, marine mammals and birds.

Habitot Children's Museum

2065 Kittredge Street
Berkeley, CA 94704
www.habitot.org

510-647-1111

Bay Area Day Trips and Family Vacations

Hours: Fall/Winter Hours (Beginning Oct. 1): Open Tuesday, Wednesday, and Thursday from 9:30 am–1 pm; Friday and Saturday from 9:30 am–4:30 pm. Sunday: Private parties only; Closed on Mondays. Closed Thanksgiving, Christmas, and New Year's Day. Summer Hours (through September 30): Wednesday, Friday and Saturday 9:30 am–1 pm.

Price: Adult $6 (Senior/Disabled 10% discount), Children/$7, Under 1/Free.

Habitot is the East Bay's discovery museum for young children. This museum is small and won't take all day, but it's a nice add-on to your itinerary if you have very young children and are visiting other attractions in the area. Children can shop in the miniature grocery store, take orders at the café, or play dress up. There are hands-on exhibits, drop in art studios and events for children up to 6 years. There are several parking garages nearby so bring extra cash for the parking fee.

Hall of Health

2230 Shattuck Avenue (Lower Level)
Berkeley, CA 94704
www.hallofhealth.org

510-549-1564

Hours: Open 10 am–4 pm, Tuesday–Saturday

Price: Admission is $5 per person, age 4 and older.

The Hall of Health, sponsored by Children's Hospital & Research Center at Oakland, is a community health-education museum and science center dedicated to promoting wellness and individual responsibility for health. Visitors of all ages have used the Hall's interactive, hands-on exhibits to learn about the workings of the body, the value of sound diet and exercise, and the destructive effects of smoking and drug abuse. Interactive exhibits include: Displays and models, Games and puzzles, Electronic quizzes, Medical equipment, and Computers. The Hall of Health sponsors special programs and events for families, including health and safety festivals, and puppet shows on physical, mental, medical, and cultural differences.

Lawrence Hall of Science

Centennial Drive
Located on the UC Berkeley Campus above the Botanical Gardens
Berkeley, CA 94720
www.lhs.berkeley.edu/lhshome.html

510-642-5132

Hours: Daily from 10 am–5 pm

Price: Adults (ages 19–61) $10, Students, Senior, Disabled (ages 5–18 & 62+) $8, Child (ages 3–4) $5.50, LHS Members and Children under 3 Free.

Lawrence Hall of Science is an educational center for kids of all ages focusing on science and math. There are on-going and featured exhibits, games, hands-on activities, workshops, classes, as well as a biology discovery lab where kids can learn about a variety of living things. For an additional fee (Adults $3; 3 and under $2.50), visit the William Knox Holt Planetarium where children can explore the skies (check for show times and age restrictions). Also within LHS are a museum shop, a café, vending machines and birthday party accommodations.

Tilden Regional Park

The park can be reached via Canon Drive, Shasta Road, or South Park Drive, all off of Grizzly Peak Boulevard or off of Wildcat Canyon Road
Berkeley, CA 94708
www.ebparks.org/parks/tilden.htm

510-843-2137

Hours: Daily 5 am–10 pm unless otherwise posted.

Tilden Regional Park is a 2,079 acre wildlife preserve and park and offers many activities for the whole family including hiking, picnicking, swimming in Lake Anza, strolling through the botanical gardens, learning about nature at the educational center, riding the merry-go-round and the steam train, and visiting with animals.

Lake Anza

Canon Drive and Wildcat Canyon Road
Berkeley, CA 94708

510-843-2137

Beach Access Fee: Adult $3.50 (ages 16–61), Youth $2.50 (ages 1–15), $2.50 Senior (62+) and disabled, under 1 Free.

A sandy beach, changing rooms, lifeguards, a refreshment stand (currently closed for renovation), and picnic grounds makes Lake Anza a great place for the family to spend the day. The lake is also open for fishing throughout the year. A state fishing license is required for ages 16 and over.

The Little Farm & Environmental Education Center (EEC)

North End of Central Park Drive
www.ebparks.org/parks

510-525-2233

Hours: Little Farm is open daily 8:30 am–4 pm. EEC is open Tuesdays–Sundays 10 am–5 pm, closed Thanksgiving, Christmas Eve at 1 pm, Christmas Day and New Year's Day.

Meet with farm animals at Little Farm or learn about nature through the programs at EEC. Weekday programs require a reservation, but weekend programs are open to everyone.

The Herschell Spillman Merry-Go-Round

Wildcat Canyon Road
www.ci.berkeley.ca.us/coolthings/parks/Tilden/Carousel.html

510-524-6773

Hours: Open 11 am–5 pm on weekends and holidays and weekdays during school breaks and summer vacation
Price: $1 per ride, $10 for a 13-ride ticket book

Take a ride on this antique merry-go-round with its whimsical hand-carved wooden carousel animals.

Bay Area Day Trips and Family Vacations

Redwood Valley Railway

The Steam train is located at the south end of Tilden Park, at the intersection of Grizzly Peak and Lomas Cantatas.

www.redwoodvalleyrailway.com

510-548-6100

Hours: Open weekends 11 am–dusk year-round; weekdays 11 am–5 pm from Jun 18–Aug 3, no trains after Labor Day weekend.

Price: Single Ticket Ride $2, 5 Ride or Family Ticket $8 can be used for a single person or a group of riders.

Redwood Valley Railway will take you on a scenic 1.25 mile ride through Tilden Regional Park on a scaled down steam train. Tickets and souvenirs may be purchased at the ticket booth.

The Botanic Garden

Canon Drive (Take Canon Drive off Grizzly Peak Boulevard)
Berkeley, CA 94708

www.ebparks.org/parks/vc/botanic garden

510-525-2233

Hours: 8:30 am–5 pm October 1–May 31; 8:30 am–5:30 pm June 1–September 30; closed New Year's Day, Thanksgiving and Christmas.

Price: Free

The Botanic Garden in Tilden Regional Park contains the most extensive collection of plants native to California. The visitor center offers free docent-guided tours and lectures throughout the year. The garden is stroller and wheelchair accessible and restroom facilities are available.

The UC Berkeley Botanical Gardens

200 Centennial Drive
Berekeley, CA 94720

www.botanicalgarden.berkeley.edu

510-643-2755

Hours: Daily 9 am–5 pm; The Garden Shop and The Plant Deck 10:30 am–4:30 pm; Mather Redwood Grove and Greenhouses close at 4 pm. Closed first Tuesday of each month, Thanksgiving, December 24–25, December 31 and January 1, Martin Luther King, Jr. Day

Price: Adults $7, Seniors (65+) $5, Juniors (13–17) $5, Children (5–12) $2, Children under 5 Free; First Thursday of every month FREE for all. Parking fees for the lot across from the garden: $0.75 for first half hour, $1.50 for one hour, $0.50 for each half hour thereafter.

An extensive collection of plants from all over the world composes this garden in the Berkeley Hills. Tours and programs geared toward the younger set are available. Check the website to download a current schedule. Plants, books and gifts are available for sale at the Garden Shop and the Plant Deck. Food is not available at the Botanical Gardens but you may bring your own picnic.

Fairfield

The Jelly Belly Factory

One Jelly Belly Lane
Fairfield, CA 94533
www.jellybelly.com

707-428-2838

1-800-953-5592 For tour information

Hours: Visitor Center is open daily from 9 am–5 pm. Tours are daily from 9 am–4 pm and depart approximately every 15 minutes and last approximately 40 minutes. Closed Thanksgiving, Christmas, New Year's Day and Easter.

Weekend Tours: Tours are available but candy making machines do not run on weekends.

Price: Free

See how Jelly Bellys, taffy, chocolates and gummy candy are made in this candy factory. Take a 40-minute tour and learn how over 150 different types of sweets are made. After the tour head to the Visitor Center and taste the finished products at the Sampling Bar. Order a jelly-bean shaped pizza, hamburgers, or an ice-cream cone at the Visitor Center Café. The Visitor Center and candy factory are stroller and wheelchair accessible. Wait times for tours during Easter, Spring, Summer, and holiday breaks can be as long as 90 minutes. Typical wait is 15 minutes. Reservations for tours are not required. Fairfield is about an hour's drive northeast of San Francisco.

Fremont

Ardenwood Historic Farm

34600 Ardenwood Blvd.
Fremont, California 94555
www.ebparks.org/parks/ardenwood

510-796-0663

Hours: Open Tuesdays–Sundays, year round, including Labor Day and Memorial Day. Closed Thanksgiving and Christmas Day. Open Space Days are Tues. & Wed.; Historic Days (Naturalist Programs, Tours, Horse drawn train and Blacksmith shop are open. Farmyard Café is open on Sunday only) Thurs., Fri. & Sun.; Family Saturdays (Naturalist Programs, House Tour for additional fee, Blacksmith shop and café are open.). Park is closed Mondays.

Price: November 21–April 1, Tuesday–Sunday Adults (18+) $2, Children (4–17) $1. After April 1, Tuesday, Wednesday and Saturday Adults $2, Senior (62+) $2, children $1; Thursday, Friday and Sunday Adults $5, Seniors $4, Children $4. Additional cost for special events.

Ardenwood Historic Farm is a 205-acre, fully functioning farm in the heart of the Silicon Valley where kids can learn about life in the 1800's. They can feed the farm animals, sample cookies cooked on a wood burning stove, ride on a horse drawn railroad, help docents dressed in period costumes with chores, and visit a blacksmith shop and an old- fashioned Victorian house. Visit during the holidays when Ardenwood is decorated for an old-fashioned Christmas and offers a variety of holiday programs.

Bay Area Day Trips and Family Vacations

Oakland

Chabot Planetarium

10000 Skyline Blvd.
Oakland, CA 94619
www.chabotspace.org

510-336-7300

Hours: Wednesday–Thursday 10 am–5 pm , Friday–Saturday 10 am–10 pm, Sunday 11 am–5 pm; Closed Monday–Tuesday; Closed July 4th, Thanksgiving and Christmas Day.

Price: General Admission includes daily planetarium show. Adult $13, Senior (65+) $10, Youth (3–12) $9, 2 and under Free, Members Free. Additional fee for Megadome Theater: Adults $8, Youth, Senior and Students $7. Evening Planetarium Shows: Adults $8, Youth, Senior and Students $7.

Nestled in the hills of Oakland, Chabot Space & Science Center is an 86,000 square foot facility where visitors can explore space, science and technology through classes, lectures, workshops and interactive exhibits. There are free telescope viewings Friday and Saturday evenings from dusk until 10 pm.

Children's Fairyland

On the shore of Lake Merritt at Grand Avenue and Bellevue
Oakland, CA 94610
www.fairyland.org

510-452-2259

Hours: 10 am–4 pm from Sep. 5–Oct. 28 on Wednesday–Sunday and national holidays; 10 am–4 pm from Nov. 2–Dec. 9 on Friday–Sunday and national holidays; Noon–7 pm from Dec. 14–23 (Fairy Winterland); Closed Dec. 24–Jan. 4. Check website for details about special and seasonal events.

Price: General Admission includes rides and shows $6 ages 1–100, ages 1 and under free. Discount passes available. There may be additional costs for special and seasonal events. Magic keys to activate Storybooks are $2 at the gate.

Favorite storybooks come to life at Children's Fairyland. This theme park is especially designed for younger children. There are puppet shows, story-time, a petting zoo, gardens and kid-friendly rides including a Ferris wheel, boat ride, train and carousel.

Jack London Square

Broadway at Embarcadero
Oakland, CA 94607
www.jacklondonsquare.com

510-514-6000

Jack London Square is a charming and historic site nestled on the water's edge offering an array of options for dining, shopping, and entertainment. This is a fun place to take the kids for a bite to eat and people-watching if you are in the area or as part of your itinerary to tour the USS Potomac which is located on the square. Several seasonal events are held at the square throughout the year. Check the website for the current calendar and maximize your visit by timing it to coincide with one of the special events.

Museum of Children's Art (MOCHA)

538 9th Street
Oakland, CA 94607
www.mocha.org

510-465-8770

Hours: 10 am–5 pm Tuesday–Friday; Noon–5 pm Saturday–Sunday
Price: Gallery tours are free; additional fee for classes or workshops; for drop-in workshops for kids and families, cost is typically $7 per child (includes adult).

MOCHA is an art studio for kids from ages 18 months to 18 years. Downstairs, in the Little Studio, kids can make their own works of art from recycled materials. Tour the gallery and view exhibits of original artworks created by children. Upstairs, The Big Studio offers classes, workshops and camps for kids of all ages.

Oakland Museum of California

1000 Oak Street
Oakland, CA 94607
www.museumca.org

510-238-2200

Hours: Wednesday–Saturday, 10 am–5 pm; Sunday Noon–5 pm; First Friday of each month open until 9 pm; Closed Mondays and Tuesdays; Closed New Years Day, July 4th, Thanksgiving Day, Christmas Day.
Price: Adult $8, Senior (65+) $5, Students $5, Children 6 and under free;
Admission is free the second Sunday of each month.

The Oakland Museum of California is a graceful, three-tiered blend of spacious galleries, terraces, patios, sculpture gardens and ponds. The museum houses permanent exhibits on California history, California natural sciences, and California art. The art gallery contains an interesting collection of sculptures, photographs, paintings, ceramics, jewelry and prints. The natural sciences gallery takes visitors through California, from the coast to the mountains. Kids will enjoy the dioramas of animals in their natural habitats. In the California history gallery, visitors can walk through the state's history from the Spanish explorers on to the "Summer of Love." Within the museum are the Museum Café and Museum Store.

Bay Area Day Trips and Family Vacations

Oakland Zoo

9777 Golf Links Road
Oakland, CA 94605
www.oaklandzoo.org

510-632-9525

Hours: Daily from 10 am–4 pm; rides open 11 am; Closed Thanksgiving and Christmas. In the event of inclement weather, the Zoo may be closed.

Price: Adults $9.50, Seniors (55+) $6, Children (2–12) $6, Under 2 Free. Group discount rates and memberships are available. Parking: $6 per car. No bills over $20 are accepted. Additional fee for rides.

Nestled in the hills of 525-acre Knowland Park, the Oakland Zoo is home to more than 440 native and exotic animals. Some of the highlights for the kids are the petting zoo, the playground and the small amusement park next to the zoo. The Skyfari Ride will take you up into the hills for a beautiful view of the Bay and an aerial view of the animals below. There are concession stands and picnic and barbecue areas.

USS Potomac

540 Water Street
Oakland, CA 94604
www.usspotomac.org

510-627-1667

Hours: Tours are scheduled Tuesdays and Thursdays, rain or shine, from May-November and depart from Jack London Square at 11 am.

Price: Adult (13–59) $40, Senior (60+) $35, Youth (6–12) $20, 6 and under Free; Group discounts are available. Purchase tickets in advance on the web.

Called the "Floating White House," the USS Potomac served as Franklin Delano Roosevelt's presidential yacht until his death in 1945. This 165 foot National Historic Landmark is one of the few floating museums in the country. Guests watch a 15-minute video in the Visitor Center prior to the cruise. The Potomac then sets off for a narrated two-hour cruise around the San Francisco Bay. Emphasis is placed on the impact Franklin Delano Roosevelt's administration had upon the Bay Area and surrounding landmarks. While on board, guests may elect to take a docent led tour or self guided tour. Coffee, tea and water are available. Park in the Washington Street Garage between 2nd and Embarcadero Streets, one block from the Potomac.

Vallejo

Six Flags Discovery Kingdom

1001 Fairgrounds Drive
Vallejo, CA 94589
www.sixflags.com/discoveryKingdom

707-643-6722

Hours: Hours Vary. Check website for current calendar and operating hours.
Price: General Admission $49.99 (or buy on-line for $34.99), Child (under 48") $29.99, 2 &
under Free. Season passes and on-line discounts available. Check the website for current offers.
Parking Fee: $15 per vehicle

Six Flags Discovery Kingdom is a 135-acre park featuring rides for all ages, animal exhibits and shows, and interactive animal experiences. Thrill-seekers will find some of the fastest and wildest roller coasters in the state at Discovery Kingdom. Younger kids will enjoy the rides at Tava's Jungleland, Looney Tune's Seaport and the new Thomas Town which features Thomas the Train. The park also includes several restaurants and gift shops. Plan to visit when attendance is lightest. Best bets: weekdays during the summer and any regular operating day during the months of April, May, September and October. Pick up a show schedule at The Explorer's Outpost and take note of the show times of shows your family would like to see. To avoid crowds, plan to start your day at attractions farthest from the main entrance. Also, ride your favorite rides when the park first opens or after 5 pm.

San Francisco

Asian Art Museum

200 Larkin Street
San Francisco, CA 94102
www.asianart.org

415-581-3500

Hours: Tuesday–Wednesday 10 am–5 pm, Thursday 10 am–9 pm, Friday–Sunday 10 am–5 pm,
Closed Monday.
Price: Adults $12, Seniors (65+) $8, Students with ID and Youths (13–17)$7, Children (12 and
under) Free, Thursday evening after 5 pm $5, First Tuesday of each month Free to all visitors.

The Asian Art Museum of San Francisco houses one of the largest collections of Asian Art with over 17,000 artworks spanning 6,000 years of history. The Asian Art Museum's interactive Family Programs allow parents and children to explore the many aspects of Asian art and culture together. All Family Programs are free with museum admission. Programs include AsiaAlive, an interactive, drop-in program for all ages, featuring live artist demonstrations, hands-on activities, and videos and books on rotating themes. See the website to view the upcoming AsiaAlive schedule. At The Family Art Encounter program, children can sculpt, paint doodle or create a masterpiece. Join the museum storytellers every Sunday at 1 pm and the first Saturday of the month at 11:45 am as they bring to life the myths and folktales of Asia. The museum also holds a variety of performances, festivals, and events. Check the website's Calendar of Events to learn about current happenings at the museum. Within the museum, there is a café serving a variety of food and beverages and a museum store selling a variety of Asian-themed merchandise from around the world.

Bay Area Day Trips and Family Vacations

California Academy of Science

875 Howard Street
San Francisco, CA 94103
www.calacademy.org

415-321-8000

Hours: Open every day year-round, including holidays 10 am–5 pm except on the third Thursday of every month when the museum is open 5 pm–9 pm.

Price: Members Free, Adults$10, Youth (12–17), students with ID, and seniors (65+) $6.50, Children (4–11) $2, Children 3 and under Free; Free admission on the first Wednesday of each month; $5 from 5 pm–9 pm on the third Thursday of each month.

Founded in 1853 to survey and study the vast resources of California and beyond, the California Academy of Sciences is the oldest scientific institution in the West and the fourth largest natural history museum in the country. The museum is home to Steinhart Aquarium, Morrison Planetarium (closed until the museum re-opens in Golden Gate Park in 2008), and the Kimball Natural History Museum (also closed until 2008). The Academy has temporarily relocated to its current downtown location while the original building in Golden Gate Park is completely rebuilt. The museum includes the Nature Nest for children five and under which provides nature themed books, costumes, puppets, puzzles and blocks to encourage exploration through creative play. Come Saturday morning during Story time for 3–5 year olds.

Chinatown

Grant Avenue and Jackson Street
San Francisco, CA 94133

Hours: Open day and night year round. The best time to visit with kids is during the day.

Price: Free

San Francisco's Chinatown is one of the largest and oldest in North America. Enter Chinatown through the pagoda at Bush Street and Grant Avenue and step into a world of exotic smells, sights and sounds. Stroll through Stockton Street and see authentic Chinese markets selling medicinal herbs, produce, chickens, frogs, fish and other Chinese delicacies. Visit the tiny Fortune Cookie Company tucked away in Ross Alley and see how the crispy cookies are made. There are bakeries, restaurants and dim sum shops where an inexpensive meal or snack can be had. Inexpensive souvenirs can be purchased from one of the many shops selling interesting knick knacks. At Portsmouth Square, located at Walter Lum Place, is a playground where kids can play and watch elderly men play chess. There are several parking garages in the area but they can be rather expensive. Drive around and find a lot that charges a reasonable flat rate. If you visit Chinatown during the Chinese New Year you are likely to see a dragon dancing down the street to the sound of firecrackers and drums. Chinatown draws many tourists and it can be difficult to maneuver with a stroller, but it's definitely a fun and interesting way to expose children to a very authentic cultural experience without having to leave the Bay Area.

The Exploratorium

Exploratorium at the Palace of Fine Arts

3601 Lyon Street

San Francisco, CA 94123

www.exploratorium.edu

415-561-0360

Hours: Open Tuesday–Sunday 10 am–5 pm. Closed Mondays (Except Martin Luther King Day, President's Day, Memorial Day and Labor Day). Closed Thanksgiving, Christmas Eve at 3 pm., Closed Christmas Day.

Price: Adults (18–64) $14, Students (18+ with ID) and Seniors (65+) $11, Disabled $11, Youth (13–17) $11, Children (4–12) $9, 3 and under Free. Tactile Dome $17 ages 7 and over only, general admission included. Admission is free the first Wednesday of each month.

Housed within the walls of San Francisco's Palace of Fine Arts, the Exploratorium is a collage of hundreds of science, art, and human perception exhibits. It provides access to, and information about, science, nature, art, and technology. Through the many hands-on exhibits, children can learn about the human body, machines, food, motion, society, culture, living things, space, and so much more. This museum will provide hours of educational fun for kids of all ages. Inside the Tactile Dome, children ages 7 and older can take an interactive journey through total darkness, where the sense of touch becomes their only guide.

Fisherman's Wharf and Pier 39

Fisherman's Wharf and Pier 39 are tourist magnets that attract millions of visitors each year. Come in the morning before the crowds get too heavy. Beware the overpriced restaurants and attractions—some can be disappointing. Finding street parking at this tourist mecca is nearly impossible but there are many parking lots and garages in the area. Some restaurants will validate. Also, check on-line for discount coupons and city passes that give discounts for multiple attractions in San Franciso. Below are some attractions that are worth a visit.

Alcatraz Island

Pier 41 at Fisherman's Wharf

San Francisco, CA 94123

www.nps.gov/alcatraz

Hours: Hours vary depending on the season. Boats depart daily about every half hour throughout the day from 9 am. Evening tours are also available. Alcatraz is open year-round except Christmas and New Year's Day.

Price: There is no entrance fee to Alcatraz. However there is a ferry charge to get to the island. Prices will vary depending on the ferry/tour company. Visit the website for schedules and prices and to compare and select tickets and tour packages. Alcatraz tours sell out quickly so make sure to purchase tickets a few weeks in advance.

Bay Area Day Trips and Family Vacations

Just a 10-minute boat ride from Fisherman's Wharf is the infamous Alcatraz Island, once a maximum security prison housing notorious criminals such as Al Capone, "Machine Gun" Kelly, and the "Birdman of Alcatraz" Robert Stroud. Take a short ride on the ferry and explore the prison and the marine and wildlife on the island. Self-guided audiocassette tours or guided ranger-led tours are available. Alcatraz Kidz Tours provides a weekly guided tour and special programs geared towards families with kids. Check their website www.alcatrazcruises.com for programs and age restrictions. Make sure to wear comfortable walking shoes and layers of clothing. Food is not available on the island but you can enjoy a snack on the boat before you arrive. Restrooms and water are available.

Angel Island

Located in the middle of San Francisco Bay, Angel Island is accessible by private boat or public ferry from San Francisco, Tiburon and seasonal service from Oakland and Alameda.
www.angelisland.org

415-435-5390

Hours: 8 am–Sunset, every day, year-round. Ferry service is limited in the winter.

Price: Prices will vary depending on ferry service. State park admission is included with the purchase of a ferry ticket.

From San Francisco see www.blueandgoldfleet.com for fares and schedules. From Tiburon see www.angelislandferry.com. Fares are usually less than $15 per person for a round trip ticket. Credit cards may not be accepted so bring cash or checks to purchase tickets for the ferry.

Angel Island State Park offers an array of outdoor activities along with a spectacular view of the entire Bay. From its vantage point in the middle of the San Francisco Bay, you can see the Golden Gate Bridge, the San Francisco Skyline, the Marin Headlands, and Mt. Tamalpais. Visitors can enjoy hiking, biking, volleyball, baseball, kayaking, and fishing. You can bring your own bikes or rent bikes on the island. Also available are tram tours and Segway tours (a Segway is an electrictronic, self-balancing, personal-transportation device designed to travel miles on a single electrical charge). You can bring your own picnic or purchase food at the Cove Café.

Aquarium of the Bay
Pier 39

Embarcadero at Beach Street
San Francisco, CA 94133
www.aquariumofthebay.com

415-623-5300

Hours: From Memorial Day to Labor Day, hours are 9 am–8 pm daily. The rest of the year, the Aquarium is open from 10 am–7 pm Monday–Thursday, and 10 am–8 pm Friday–Sunday. The aquarium is open 364 days a year, and closed on Christmas. Hours sometimes vary. Call 415-623-5300 for specific hours on the day you plan to visit.

Price: Adult $13.95, Senior (age 65+) $7, Child (3–11) $7, Under 3 Free; Family Pack (two adults and two children) $33.95. Behind the Scenes Tours are an additional $6.

The Aquarium of the Bay is the only aquarium that focuses specifically on the aquatic life and distinctive ecosystems of the San Francisco Bay. There are three different exhibits that feature the underwater life beneath the Bay. The Aquarium's expert naturalists are on hand to answer questions throughout your visit. Walk through clear underwater tunnels and see underwater creatures up close and touch live bat rays and leopard sharks at the touch pool.

Aquatic Park

2998 Hyde Street
San Francisco, CA 94109
www.nps.gov
415-447-5000
Hours: Always open
Price: Free

The Aquatic Park has a sandy beach and relatively calm waters. It's a great place for kids to dig in the sand, build sand castles and mingle with the kite-fliers. There are park benches where parents can sit back and relax while the kids play in the sand. This is the perfect place to relax and take a break while exploring the sites on Fisherman's Wharf.

Bay Cruises

Explore San Francisco Bay by boat. Take a one-hour cruise past the San Francisco waterfront, Sausalito and Angel Island, around Alcatraz and under the Golden Gate Bridge. It gets windy on the water so dress in layers for the boat ride. Don't forget to bring a camera—the views are fantastic.

The Blue and Gold Fleet
Pier 39 Marine Terminal
The Embarcadero at Beach Street
San Francisco, CA 94133
www.blueandgoldfleet.com
415-705-8200
Hours: Frequent daily departures. Check website for current schedule.
Price: Varies depending on tour or destination. Check website for current fares.

The Blue and Gold Fleet provides a variety of sightseeing tours of the Bay and Alcatraz as well as ferry service to Tiburon, Sausalito, Oakland/Alameda, Angel Island and Vallejo. The Blue and Gold Fleet offers a snack bar on the boat where you can get a hot dog, drinks and other snacks.

The Red and White Fleet
Pier 43 1/2
San Francisco, CA 94133
www.redandwhite.com
415-673-2900

Bay Area Day Trips and Family Vacations

Hours: Frequent daily departures. Check website for current schedule.

Price: Varies depending on tour. Check website for current fares.

The Red and White Fleet offers sightseeing tours of the San Francisco Bay. There is a snack bar on board offering lunch, snacks and drinks. The Red and White Fleet does not offer ferry service to or tours of Alcatraz.

Hyde Street Pier Ships

2905 Hyde Street
San Francisco, CA
www.nps.gov/safr

415-447-5000

Hours: 9:30 am–5:30 pm (Memorial Day to September 30), 9:30 am–5:30 pm (October 1 to May 27), Closed Thanksgiving, Christmas and New Year's Day.

Price: A ticket is needed for entrance to the historic vessels on Hyde Street Pier. The cost is $5 per person and the ticket is good for seven days. Entrance to the ships is free for supervised children under 16. The ticket booth is located on the pier.

Explore the exhibits in the Visitor Center, stroll down Hyde Street Pier and visit the historic ships. Guided tours are available on the Balcultha, Eureka and Hercules. There are also a variety of activities including crafts, demonstrations, concerts, workshops and lectures. Kids ages 6–12 can pick up a free Junior Ranger activity book at the ticket booth or in the Visitor Center and learn about the park and earn a badge. There is no designated parking area for the park. There is metered street parking (bring lots of quarters), and garages and parking lots that charge anywhere from $10 to $20 per day.

Musee Mecanique
Fisherman's Wharf

Pier 45 Shed A at the end of Taylor Street
San Francisco, CA 94133

415-346-2000

Hours: Monday–Friday 10 am–7 pm; Saturday–Sunday and Holidays 10 am–8 pm.

Price: Free.

The Musee Mecanique houses one of the world's largest privately owned collections of mechanically operated musical instruments and antique arcade machines. There are 200 coin operated machines, all in working order. The collection includes a miniature carnival, hand cranked music boxes, player pianos, pinball machines, fortune teller machines, vintage video and arcade games and other mechanical toys from the past.

Pier 39

Beach Street & The Embarcadero
San Francisco, CA 94133
www.pier39.com

Hours: Vary by season and by attraction. Check web site for current schedule and hours of operation.
Price: Free. Fee for attractions.

Two blocks east of Fisherman's Wharf, this 45-acre complex is home to two levels of entertainment and houses shops, ocean view restaurants and numerous attractions. At Pier 39 you can ride the San Francisco Carousel, test your skills at Riptide Arcade, visit Pier 39's internationally renowned sea lions, take cruise on the Bay, and experience "The Great San Francisco Adventure" on a big screen. There are street performers, comedians, jugglers, acrobats, dancers and clowns on the Center Stage. The shows are free. Daily Show Times: 12:15 pm, 1:30 pm, 3 pm, 4:30 pm, 5:45 pm, 7 pm, 8 pm and 9 pm.

USS Pampanito Submarine

At Pier 45 in the center of Fisherman's Wharf

415-775-1943

Hours: From October 14–May 23: 9 am–6 pm Sunday–Thursday; 9 am–8 pm Friday–Saturday; From May 23–October 13: 9 am–8 pm every day except Wednesday; 9 am–6 pm Wednesday.
Price: Self-guided tour is included in the ticket price. Adults $9, Children (6–12) $3, Children 6 and under are free with an adult, Seniors (62+) $5, Active Duty Military with current ID $4, Family ticket $20 (admits two adults and up to four children under 18).

Take a tour of the USS Pampanito, a World War II Fleet submarine museum and memorial at San Francisco's Fisherman's Wharf. Inside the submarine, kids can discover what life was like aboard this submarine. The tour will take you through the functional, but tiny galley kitchen, the crew's quarters, the torpedo room, and the engine and radio rooms.

The Wax Museum at Fisherman's Wharf

145 Jefferson Street
San Francisco, CA 94133
www.waxmuseum.com

800-439-4305

Hours: Daily 10 am–9 pm Open every day of the year—rain or shine. Call 415-202-0402 for special Holiday Hours.
Price: Adult (18–54) $12.95, Junior (12–17) $9.95, Child (6–11) $6.95, Senior (55+) $9.95.

If your children want to see life-size wax clones of famous celebrities including Beyonce, Will Smith, Halle Berry, Angelina Jolie and Brad Pitt, it may be worthwhile to visit the Wax Museum at Fisherman's Wharf at least once. One of the world's largest wax museums, the fully restored San Francisco attraction has recreated the tomb of King Tut, features a Chamber of Horrors (may not be appropriate for younger children), and contains wax creations of royalty, political figures, and all types of performers and celebrities.

Bay Area Day Trips and Family Vacations

Golden Gate Park

Off of Fulton and Stanyan Streets, Lincoln Avenue and Highway 1
San Francisco, CA 94117
www.nps.gov/goga.com

415-831-2700

Hours: Open All Year Daily Sunrise–Sunset
Price: Entrance to park is free but a fee is required for attractions in the park.

Spanning from Stanyan Street to the Pacific Ocean, San Francisco's Golden Gate Park is larger than Central Park in New York and offers something for everyone. There are walking and jogging trails, biking, horseback riding, boating, playgrounds, baseball and soccer fields, golf courses, tennis courts, lawn bowling and gardens and museums—just to name a few.

Some of the highlights in the park include:

The Conservatory of Flowers

JFK Drive, at the eastern end of Golden Gate Park
San Francisco, CA 94117
www.conservatoryofflowers.org

415-666-7001

Hours: Tuesday–Sunday, 9 am–4:30 pm; The Conservatory is closed Mondays. Open on major holidays.
Price: Adults $5, Youth (12–17), Senior (65+) and Students with ID $3, Children (5–11) $1.50, Children 4 and under Free. The Conservatory is free to all visitors on the 1st Tuesday of every month.

The oldest glass-and-wood Victorian greenhouse in the Western Hemisphere, the Conservatory of Flowers is a spectacular living museum of more than 10,000 rare and beautiful plants from around the world. A must-see for kids is the current "Chomp" exhibit featuring hundreds of carnivorous plants. Kids can peek through magnifying lenses and get a close-up look at these meat-eating plants. Don't miss the giant lily pads that are so big they can hold the weight of a small child.

The Japanese Tea Garden
Music Concourse, Golden Gate Park
San Francisco, CA 94118
415-752-4227
Hours: Open daily from 9 am–4:45 pm.
Price: Adults $4 , Children and seniors $2. Free on the first Wednesday of the month. Cash only.

Originally created as part of the World's Fair of 1894, the Japanese Tea Garden in Golden Gate Park is one of the oldest public Japanese Gardens in the United States. Within this five-acre park are winding pathways, koi-ponds, a waterfall, native Chinese and Japanese trees, plants, and flowers, a pagoda, bridges, and the largest bronze sculpture of Buddha outside of Asia. Children love to climb the curved moon bridge in the Tea Garden. Enjoy a pot of tea and sesame-almond cookies in the open air teahouse after exploring the gardens. Tip: Admission into the garden is free after 4 pm.

The Koret Children's Quarter

Once known as the Children's Playground, the Koret Children's Quarters is a newly renovated playground located in the southeast part of the park. Featuring a climbing wave wall, a watery play canal, sea caves and tide pools and a tree house play structure, the playground is geared more toward the 2–5 year old set, however, the thrilling concrete slides remain much to the delight of older children.

The Herschell-Spillman Carousel

320 Bowling Green adjacent to the Koret Children's Quarter
San Francisco, CA 94117
Hours: During September and October (depending on the weather) the Carrousel is open Wednesday–Sunday, including Labor Day, from 10 am–4:30 pm.
Price: Adults $1.50; Children (6–12) $.50 per ride, Children 5 and under are free if accompanied by a paying adult.

The Herschell-Spillman Carousel, with its beautifully carved and painted animals, has been a fixture at the Children's Playground since the playground opened in 1888.

M.H. de Young Museum
Golden Gate Park

50 Hagiwara Tea Garden Drive
San Francisco, CA 94118
www.thinker.org

415-750-3600

Hours: Tuesday–Sunday 9:30 am–5:15 pm, Fridays until 8:45 pm. The tower closes at 4:30 pm Tuesday–Sunday and 8 pm Fridays. Closed January 1st, July 4th, Thanksgiving Day, and December 25th. The museum closes at 4 pm on December 24th and 31st.
Price: Adults $10, Seniors (65+) $7, Youths (13–17) $6, Students with ID $6, Children 12 and under FREE. Admission tickets to the de Young may be used on the same day for free entrance to the Legion of Honor. First Tuesday of each month FREE. There maybe additional fees for special exhibits.

In addition to the newly installed permanent collection of American, African, Oceanic, American Indian, New Guinea, Maori and Filipino art on the first and second floors, visitors can see treasures from Egypt's Golden Age in special exhibition galleries. Outside, children and adults alike will enjoy the sculpture garden. Get a taste of the Bay Area in the de Young Café where, as part of the "Farm to Fork" program, ingredients are grown or produced within 150 miles of the kitchen where they are prepared. For kids the Saturday art program for 3 1/2 to 12 year olds features tours of current exhibitions which are followed by studio workshops taught by professional artist-teachers. The program runs every Saturday 10:30 am to noon, excluding holiday weekends. The program is free with museum admission. Reservations are not necessary, but register 15 minutes before class as space is limited. Call 415-750-3658 for a schedule and more information.

Bay Area Day Trips and Family Vacations

San Francisco Botanical Garden at Strybing Arboretum

Ninth Avenue at Lincoln Way, Golden Gate Park

San Francisco, CA 94122

www.sfbotanicalgarden.org

415-661-1316

Hours: The San Francisco Botanical Garden is open daily, 365 days a year. Weekdays 8 am–4:30 pm. Weekends & Holidays 10 am–5 pm. Free guided walks are given daily at 1:30 pm.

Price: Free

This 70-acre garden has more than 6,000 plant species including plants and flowers from around the world. The Garden of Fragrance is a treat for the senses. Make sure to take the kids to watch the butterflies in the Children's Garden. Visit the Helen Crocker Russell Library of Horticulture during story time held every 1st and 3rd Sunday of each month at 10:30 am. The Library also has an excellent collection of books for children on plants, natural history, general science, and nature-related myths and stories.

Stow Lake

Stow Lake Drive, Golden Gate Park

San Francisco, CA 94118

415-752-0347

Hours: Monday–Sunday 10 am–4 pm

Price: $13/hour row boats; $17/hour paddle boats (Cash only)

Within Golden Gate Park is Stow Lake where visitors can have a picnic, feed the ducks, or rent a boat. The Boathouse rents electric boats, pedal boats, and rowboats. For those who prefer to cruise through the park on land, the Boathouse also rents roller blades, bicycles and quad-cycles.

Randall Museum

199 Museum Way

San Francisco, CA 94114

www.randallmuseum.org

415-554-9600

Hours: The Randall Museum is open to the public 10 am–5 pm, Tuesday–Saturday. All exhibits are closed on Sundays and Mondays. The Randall Museum is closed on the following legal holidays: New Year's Day, July 4th, Veteran's Day (Nov 11th), the fourth Thursday in November and the following Friday, Thanksgiving, and Christmas Day.

Price: Free

Though the Randall Museum is tucked away within the off-the-beaten-path neighborhood of Corona Heights, it's definitely worth a visit. The Museum houses changing science, art, and interactive exhibits. Permanent areas of the Museum include a live animal exhibit, a woodshop, art and ceramics studios, a lapidary workshop, a 188-seat theater, a greenhouse, and gardens. Kids can test their puzzle solving skills at the current A-MAZE-ing Puzzles exhibit, a giant labyrinth located in the museum lobby. Inside the Animal Exhibit, there are over 100 animals that make their home in the Museum. For toddlers, the Tree House has a safe and fun carpeted climbing structure, plus age-appropriate books and toys. The Randall Museum also hosts a number of family-friendly special events each year including Bug Day, Family Halloween Fest, and Holiday Craft Day. Check the website for the current calendar to find out when these events take place. Behind the museum, kids can hike along the trails on Corona Heights Hill. Walking distance from the museum is a playground. Bring a picnic lunch to enjoy at the park before or after touring the museum as there are no restaurants in the immediate area. Free parking is available in the parking lot on nearby States Street and Roosevelt Way, but be aware that the parking lot tends to get busy on Saturdays and during special events.

San Francisco Zoo

Entrances located on the Great Highway and Sloat Boulevard & 47th Avenue.
San Francisco CA 94132
415-753-7080

Hours: 10 am–5 pm daily, 365 days a year, including Thanksgiving and Christmas Day. The Children's Zoo is open daily from 10 am–4:30 pm. Within the Children's Zoo, the Animal Resource Center and Family Farm are open daily from 10:30 am–4:30 pm.
Price: Adults (18–64) $11, Youths (12–17) and Seniors (65+) $8, Children $5, 2 and under Free. All-day parking $6. Exit tickets may be purchased at the Ticket counter at the main entrance prior to leaving the parking lot.

The San Francisco Zoo is Northern California's largest zoological park and conservation center. The Zoo features 250 different animal species in naturalistic surroundings, and many Zoo activities and events. Activities for children include grooming livestock or collecting eggs at the Family Farm, peering through microscopes in the Insect Zoo, crawling through a child-sized burrow at the Meerkats and Prairie Dogs exhibit, carousel and steam train rides, animal feedings, special educational programs, and a playground with swings, slides, and a climbing structure. Visitors can dine at Leaping Lemur Café, an indoor restaurant with a wide variety of food choices including made-to-order pasta and pizza. Free street parking is available along Sloat Blvd and a pedestrian drop-off area is located on Sloat Blvd. and 47th Avenue with a grand walkway leading directly to the main entrance.

Yerba Buena Gardens

Yerba Buena Gardens is bounded by Mission, Folsom, Third and Fourth Streets.
San Francisco, CA 94103
www.yerbabuenagardens.com
415-820-3550

Hours: Open daily to the public from 6 am–10 pm.
Price: Free. Fee for some attractions.

Bay Area Day Trips and Family Vacations

The rooftop garden offers a playground, a hand-carved Carousel, an interactive museum, and an Ice Skating and Bowling Center. The play circle includes a sand circle, play stream, a xylophone and 25 foot tube slide. Made of hedges, the Labyrinth is a child size version of those found in ancient castles. At the Stream & Fountain, children can interact with the flow of water, creating dams or irrigating the gardens. Next to the Shaking Man Statue, there are eight granite game boards that can be used for checkers or chess. Bring your own playing pieces. You can bring a picnic to enjoy in the gardens or dine at one of the several restaurants within and surrounding the park.

Zeum

221 Fourth Street at Howard Street
San Francisco, CA 94103
www.zeum.org

415-820-3320

Hours: Wednesday–Friday 1 pm–5 pm; Saturday–Sunday 11 am–5 pm.
Price: Youth (4–18) $6, Students & Seniors $7, Adults $8, 3 and under Free.

The only Bay Area museum where kids and families can combine hands-on use of animation, digital technology, electronic media, traditional and non-traditional materials, and the power of their imaginations to create high quality stories, movies, performances, music, art and more. Street parking is difficult to find in this busy area. Park at the Fifth and Mission Parking Garage, located on Mission Street, one block from Zeum.

Sausalito

Bay Area Discovery Museum
East Fort Baker

557 McReynolds Road
Sausalito, CA 94965-2614
www.badm.org

415-339-3900

Hours: Tuesday–Friday 9 am–4 pm; Saturday–Sunday 10 am–5 pm; Closed Mondays except when noted. The Museum is closed on Easter, Memorial Day, 4th of July, Labor Day, Thanksgiving Day, Christmas Day, New Years Day and the last two weeks of September.
Price: Adults $10, Children (1–17) $8, Seniors (62+ years) $8, Under 1 Free.

Just across the Golden Gate Bridge and set in a former military base, the Bay Area Discovery Museum has a lovely view of the Bay and features many fun hands-on indoor and outdoor exhibits that will thrill the youngest visitors. Outside is the Lookout Cove where kids can hike along the Lookout Trail and take in the incredible views of the Bridge and the Bay. Along the way, they can stop and build a giant birds' nest out of sticks and twigs. Kids will love exploring the Fishing Boat, a Shipwreck, the sea cove and the rocky shore. Indoors, there are two art studios, one for younger artists and another for artists 6 years and older, where kids can explore different art mediums. The Tot Spot is where crawlers, toddlers and preschoolers can explore exhibits themed around animal homes and habitats. Bay Hall features an expansive train set and a child-size interactive display of the Bay Area with an "Underwater" Tunnel, Fishing Boat and a small scale Fisherman's Wharf where kids can go fishing and crabbing. While the museum does have a café, it's best to bring snacks or a picnic to enjoy on the pier. Check the calendar on-line to check for current exhibits, workshops, and events.

South Bay

Gilroy

Gilroy Gardens Family Theme Park
3050 Hecker Pass Highway (Highway 152)
Gilroy, CA 95020
www.gilroygardens.org

408-840-7100

Hours: Operating hours vary. Check website for current calendar and operating hours.
Admission: 2 and under FREE, General (7–64) $39.99, Children (3–6) $29.99, Senior (65+) $29.99. Check online for special offers. VIP and Season Passes are also available. Parking Fee: $8.

Gilroy Gardens includes rides, a water park, beautiful gardens, educational exhibits, food concessions, carnival games, shows and attractions. Bring a bathing suit, towel, sunscreen and waterproof shoes (required) if your little ones plan to play in the water.

Make sure to visit the park during the Gilroy Gardens Holiday Lights event. Admission is FREE when you purchase a Season Pass for the following year. During the winter season, the park is a-glow with millions of twinkling lights and offers many holiday activities for the whole family to enjoy. Ice-skate under the stars, roast chestnuts, shop for gifts, visit with Santa in his workshop, or enjoy a holiday feast at Snowflake Palace, complete with ham and turkey and all the fixings (check website for holiday feast pricing). Plan to visit the park on the weekdays during the summer months and any weekend in the fall when crowds are lightest.

Palo Alto

The Children's Library
1276 Harriet Street
Palo Alto, CA 94301
www.cityofpaloalto.org/depts/lib

650-329-2436

Hours: Sunday 1 pm–5 pm; Monday–Wednesday 10 am–9 pm; Thursday Noon–9 pm; Friday–Saturday 10 am–6 pm.
Price: Free

Bay Area Day Trips and Family Vacations

The Children's Library is the oldest free standing children's library in the United States. Built in the Spanish Colonial Revival style, it features a hand-molded Mission tile roof, a lovely fireplace tiled with scenes from fairy tales, child-sized furniture, and a new Tree Top Room which opens into the brick-wall-enclosed Secret Garden. Newly re-opened in September 2007, the library has added two new wings with comfortable seating, art work and an expanded collection of books. If you are visiting the museum and the park next door, make sure to stop and read a few stories to your little ones in this delightful library. You can use the parking lot in front of the Junior Museum and Rinconada Park on Middlefield Road.

Museum of American Heritage

351 Homer Avenue
Palo Alto, CA 94301
www.moah.org
650-321-1004

Hours: Open from 11 am–4 pm on Friday–Sunday, except during exhibit changeover weeks. Call the museum to check the schedule.
Price: Free

The museum exhibits the evolution of American invention through its collection of preserved artifacts. Children and adults will marvel at the gadgets from the past displayed in realistic settings. Permanent exhibits include a Kitchen of the 1920–30's, an early 20th Century General Store, a Radio Repair Shop of the 1940's and a Print Shop of the 1920–30's. There is also a garden that is undergoing restoration. There are other interesting exhibits that rotate every four months so check the website to see what is current. The museum also offers classes and workshops for kids and families.

Palo Alto Junior Museum and Zoo

1451 Middlefield Road
Palo Alto, CA 94301
www.city.palo-alto.ca.us
/depts/csd/activities_and_recreation/attractions/junior_museum.asp
650-329-2111

Hours: Tuesday–Saturday 10 am–5 pm; Sunday 1 pm–4 pm; Closed Monday. Please note that bedtime for the animals is 4:30 pm.
Price: Free but donations are welcome.

The Palo Alto Junior Museum and Zoo is a small museum adjacent to Rinconada Park. There's not much to this little museum but little kids love it. You can make a day of it if you combine a visit along with the Children's Library next door and the park just outside. The museum has hands-on exhibits that will teach them the concepts of velocity, momentum, and energy including things that spin, roll, stack, stick and tumble. The small zoo includes a bobcat, raccoons, bats, an owl, geese, peacocks and snakes. The Zoo also recently added a 500-gallon salt water tank containing sharks.

Rinconada Park

777 Embarcadero Road
Palo Alto, CA 94301
www.city.palo-alto.ca.us

650-493-4900

Price: Free; Additional fee for swimming pool.

Rinconada Park is a neighborhood park shaded by California Live Oak trees. Next to this park you will find the Palo Alto Junior Museum, the Community Theater/Children's Theatre, and the Children's Library. The park includes a toddler playground with sand, swings and a climbing structure and a play area with an adventure ship. There is also a more challenging climbing structure for older kids. Near the swimming pool, the park also includes a water play area, so don't forget to pack bathing suits and towels if you visit during the warmer months. The park also has tennis courts (reservations required) and shuffle board courts. Bring a blanket and picnic lunch and dine al fresco at the park before or after a visit to the museum and the Children's Library next door.

Santa Clara

Great America

4701 Great America Parkway
Santa Clara, CA 95054
www.pgathrills.com

408-988-1776 x8858

Hours: Operating hours vary. Check website for current calendar and operating hours.
Price: Adult (ages 3–61 and 4 ft. and taller) $51.95, Junior/Senior (ages 3–61 or under 4 ft. and ages 62+), Check online for special e-ticket offers and other discounts. Season Passes are available. Parking Fee is $10. Premium Parking is $15 (Premium Parking allows guests to park closer to the main entrance and is available on a first come first serve basis). Season passes and online discounts available. Check the website for current offers.

Great America offers rides for all ages, live shows, attractions, water parks, restaurants and food stands, gift shops, arcades and carnival games. Make sure to visit Kidzville which features smaller rides and play structures for younger children. Plan to visit the park when attendance is lightest. Best bets are weekdays during the summer and any day during the months of June and October. Great America offers daily stroller rentals for a single passenger at $8 per day, and a double passenger stroller at $13 per day. Check out strollers in the morning, as supplies are limited.

Bay Area Day Trips and Family Vacations

San Jose

San Jose Discovery Museum
Children's Discovery Museum of San Jose

180 Woz Way
San Jose, CA 95110
408-298-5437

Hours: Tuesday–Saturday 10 am–5 pm; Sunday Noon–5 pm;
Members–Only Hour: Sunday 11 am–Noon. Closed Mondays.
Price: Adult (18–59) $8, Child (1–17) $8, Senior (60+) $7, Under 1 Free

This 52,000 square foot purple building is where children can learn and discover through many hands-on exhibits. There is a post office, a fire engine, a pizza restaurant, water play area, a bank, a bubble exhibit, an art loft, a garden where kids can water the plants, and more! Inside the Wonder Cabinet, the youngest explorers can make big discoveries. This is the Discovery Museum's newest exhibit, where younger kids can explore the Woodland Puppet Forest, Giant Dragon, Sand Science Laboratory, Crawl-Through Tunnel and Child-Sized Kaleidoscope. Also within the museum is the Kid's Café where lunch and snacks can be purchased. Outside the museum is Guadalupe River Park where there is lots of space to picnic and play. There is also a giant 930 square foot Monopoly Board where players throw giant dice to determine where they will land on the board. Use the parking lot on Woz Way where parking is $5. Make sure to bring exact bills ($1 bills or $5 bill) for the machine—it does not make change.

The Tech Museum of Innovation

201 South Market Street
San Jose, CA 95113
408-294-8324

Hours: Open 7 days a week 9 am–9 pm. Closed Christmas Day.
Price: Museum entry + 1 IMAX feature $8, Additional IMAX feature $4, IMAX Feature Film
(includes museum entry) $10. There may be an additional fee for special exhibits.

The Tech Museum of Innovation is a hands-on technology and science museum located in the heart of the Silicon Valley. Visit the Exploration Gallery and see the sun's atmosphere in 3D. In Green by Design, experience the design of renewable resources. In Genetics: Technology with a Twist, explore new advances in the field of genetics. The Hackworth IMAX Dome Theater at The Tech is the ultimate movie experience. With crystal clear images up to eight stories high and 13,000 watts of wrap-around digital surround sound, the IMAX Dome experience is a powerful and immersive movie experience. Call or check the website for special 3D viewings of current movies.

The Winchester Mystery House

525 South Winchester Blvd.

San Jose, CA 95128

408-247-2101

Hours: Check website for tour schedules and restrictions.

Price: Adults (13–64) tours range from $20.95–$28.95, Seniors from $19.95–$25.95, Children (6–12) from $17.95–$25.95, Children under 5 are Free.

Wealthy widow, Sarah Winchester began construction on this 160-room Victorian mansion in 1884. Construction did not stop until her death 38 years later. No expense was spared in the construction of this architectural wonder with its exquisite details and extraordinary craftsmanship. The mysteries are the doors that open into walls, stairs that lead to ceilings and a host of mysterious symbols which Sarah Winchester hoped would protect her from the spirits. Make sure to take a stroll through the lovely Victorian gardens planted with trees, shrubs and flowers from all over the world. There is a café, a museum and a shop on the grounds. House tours are not stroller accessible and would best be enjoyed by children ages six and older.

Bay Area Day Trips and Family Vacations

Gold Country

Angels Camp

Highway 49
Angels Camp, CA 95222
www.angelscamp.gov

209-736-2181

Now a quiet mountain town located in the Gold Country, Angels Camp was once a city booming with the roar of the stamp mills and the music of the many saloons and dance halls. A stroll down Main Street, with its old-fashioned store fronts will take your family back to the days of the gold rush. Visit the Chicken Ladder on Hardscrabble Street, once constructed by residents living on the narrow, "nearly vertical" street. Angel Camp is also known as the "Home of the Jumping Frog." In 1865, Mark Twain wrote his famous tale "The Celebrated Jumping Frog of Calaveras County." Every May, Angels Camp holds a jumping frog contest and people from all over the world come to see how far their frogs can jump. Visit the Angels Camp Museum and see carts and wagons, minerals and mining equipment, and a variety of antique household wares. After a stroll through town and a visit to the museum, take a moment to play and rest at tree-shaded Utica Park which has grassy areas, a playground, and picnic tables.

Apple Hill

See website for individual locations
www.applehill.com

530-644-7692

Hours: See website for individual days and hours of operation.
Cost: Free but additional cost to purchase products or for special events and attractions.

Apple Hill is a cooperative of orchards, farms, ranches and vineyards, which began 40 years ago and now has 50 farms to visit. Each farm has a variety of attractions, including bakeries offering pies, cider and doughnuts and the famous "Apple Hill Cake." There are country stores, fruit picking, tractor, pony, train and hay rides, animals to visit and picnic tables for picnicking. In October the Apple Hill Shuttle runs from 10 am to 5 pm every weekend. The shuttle is free and allows families to visit as many farms as they wish.

Columbia State Historic Park

11255 Jackson Street
Columbia, CA 95310
www.parks.ca.gov

209-588-9128

Hours: Columbia is a real town and never actually closes. Most businesses are open from 10 am to 5 pm.
Price: Free

The town of Columbia has been carefully preserved with shops, restaurants, hotels and a variety of businesses including a dentist's office, a blacksmith shop, and an old Chinese apothecary. Take a trip back in time to the 1850's when you visit the old jailhouse, drug store and schoolhouse. Experience a bygone era watching proprietors in period clothing conduct business in the style of yesterday. Ride a 100 year-old stagecoach, take a horseback ride, pan for gold, or tour an active gold mine. Come to the Museum for a free docent-led town tour each Saturday and Sunday at 11 am, year-round, and every day at 11 am from July 5th-Labor Day. The Museum is open daily from 10–4, and closed on Thanksgiving and Christmas. Gold Rush days are on the 2nd Saturday of each month. Many special exhibits are open and hands-on activities are conducted throughout the day.

Discovery Museum Gold Rush History Center

101 I Street
Old Sacramento CA 95814
www.thediscovery.org

916-264-7057

Hours: Tuesday–Sunday 10 am–5 pm with last ticket sold at 4:30 pm. Hours subjet to change — call before visiting to confirm hours. Closed Mondays with the exception of some Holidays and School Tours. Please call for holiday hours. Closed Thanksgiving Day, Christmas Eve, Christmas Day, New Year's Eve and New Year's Day.
Price: Adults (18+) $5, Seniors (60+) $4, Youth (13–17) $4, Children (4–12) $3, Children 3 and under Free.

The Gold Rush History Center is a great place to learn about the gold rush era. In the Central Gallery, at the Glass Floor Exhibit, visitors can view historical artifacts and objects displayed beneath a beautiful glass floor. At the Agricultural Gallery, see how farmers once lived. At the Lure of Gold Exhibit, check out the how the miners lived during the gold rush. In the Reading Corner, children can find a comfortable spot and peruse the materials on science and history.

Marshall Gold Discovery State History Park

310 Back Street
Coloma, CA 95613
www.parks.ca.gov

530-622-3470

Hours: 8 am to Sunset
Price: Parking fee $5. Museum and Park entry $2.

Marshall Gold Discovery State Historic Park is the place where James W. Marshall found shining flecks of gold in the tailrace of the sawmill he was building for himself and John Sutter. This discovery in 1848 changed the course of California and the nation's history. See a replica of the original sawmill and over 20 historic buildings including mining, house, school and store exhibits. Try panning for gold in the American River, take a hike, or enjoy a picnic under oak trees. Overlooking the beautiful river canyon, see the statue of James Marshall. Throughout the year the park provides daily interpretive programs at the sawmill replica. Participate in special events, exhibits and "Live History Days" planned regularly throughout the year. Contact the Gold Discovery Museum and Visitor Center for details.

Bay Area Day Trips and Family Vacations

South Yuba River State Park

17660 Pleasant Valley Road
Penn Valley, CA 95946
www.parks.ca.gov

530-432-2546

Hours: Call for park operating hours and trail conditions.
Price: Free

South Yuba River State Park offers visitors a chance to see many scenic vistas—from the rapid water rushing over massive granite ledges to the historic toll crossings and bridges that tell a story of day-to-day life during the Gold Rush era. Visitors can enjoy swimming, hiking, panning for gold, beautiful wildflowers, or exploring the trails leading to historic mining sites like the Miner's Tunnel and Jones Bar. Docent-led history, nature, and gold-panning tours are offered at selected times throughout the year.

Napa Valley & Sonoma

While Napa Valley is usually associated with adult activities such as wine tasting, golf, and gourmet adventures, it also has much to offer as a family getaway. Nestled in a picturesque valley close to several state parks and surrounded by lakes, rivers, and historic small towns, there are many activities in the area that will entertain both adults and children alike.

Copia: The American Center for Wine, Food and the Arts

500 First Street
Napa, CA 94559
www.copia.org

707-259-1600

Hours: Open daily except Tuesday 10 am–5 pm. Closed Tuesdays and the following holidays: Thanksgiving, Christmas Eve, Christmas Day, New Year's Day.
Price: Admission and Day Pass: Adults (18–61) $5, Seniors (62+) $4, Students with valid ID $4, Children (12 and under) Free. Day Pass includes entrance to the Edible Gardens, Forks in the Road exhibit, changing exhibits, Sensory Stations offering mini-tastings, and daily wine tastings.

Budding chefs and food-lovers will enjoy a visit to Copia. In the Kids Garden, children can wander through an organic garden which includes a Fruit Tree Orchard a Chicken Coop, a Rabbit Hutch, a Habitat Walk, Compost Bins, and "Dig In," an area where children can dig and design their own mini-garden. Children are encouraged to see, smell and touch to learn how plants are grown for food. At the interactive 'Forks in the Road' exhibit, kids can test their sense of smell, view silent film clips and cartoons, guess at the use of mystery kitchen gadgets, and explore the special language of short-order cooks.

Cornerstone Festival of Gardens

23570 Hwy 121
Sonoma, CA 95476
www.cornerstonegardens.com
707-933-3010
Hours: Gardens are open daily 10 am–5 pm. Café is open daily 9 am–5 pm.
Price: Free for self-guided tours; $6 for private group tours (10 or more). Reservations required for group tours. Tour & Lunch Package are available for groups of 10 or more.

Located along the main gateway to Sonoma and Napa Valley, Cornerstone Festival of Gardens is a gallery of 20 different gardens, each designed by a world-famous landscape architect. There are many strange and wonderful things to see at Cornerstone and children will marvel at some of the installations. The garden also has a Café, several shops, galleries and spacious event gardens.

The Downtown Napa Trolley

Downtown Napa
www.nctpa.net
707-252-2600
Hours: Runs every 30–45 minutes. Call or check on-line for a current schedule.
Price: Free

Take a free ride around Downtown Napa on the Trolley. Stops are located wherever you see a green sign that says "Trolley Stop." The trolley stops at various shops, restaurants and near Copia and the Wine Train.

Napa Fire Fighters Museum

1201 Main Street
Napa, CA 94559
707-259-0609
Hours: Wednesday–Saturday and some Sundays 11 am–4 pm
Price: Free

This museum has an interesting collection of vintage fire trucks, hand and horse-drawn carts and steamers, fire hydrants, extinguishers, clothes patches, firefighting toys, photo collections, newspaper clippings and fire house pictures from around the world.

Napa Valley Model Railroad
In the Napa Valley Expo

575 Third Street
Napa, CA 94559
www.napavalleyexpo.com/f-railroad.html
707-253-4900

Hours: Friday evenings 7 pm to Midnight
Price: Free

For those who have kids who love trains, visit the Napa Valley Expo, conveniently located in the center of Downtown Napa. The Napa Valley Expo houses a permanent exhibit for The Napa Valley Model Railroad Historical Society, including a vast HO Scale Layout. The layout has over 1500 feet of track with a railroad line that runs from Napa through Lake County.

Napa Valley Wine Train Family Fun Nights

1275 McKinstry Street
Napa, CA 94559
www.winetrain.com

707-253-2111

Hours: Family Fun Nights Boarding Schedule: 5:30 pm Check In, 6 pm Boarding, 6:30 pm Depart Napa, 9:30 pm Return to Napa.
Price: Adult prices vary depending on dinner package selected. Children ages 3–12 free with paid adult—one child per adult. Reservations are required.

Twice a month the Napa Valley Wine Train treats parents to a quiet, intimate and uninterrupted gourmet dinner. While parents are enjoying dinner, children (ages 3–12) are entertained by a professional care-giver in a separate railcar with games, movies, and their own child-friendly meal. The gourmet dinner may not quite live up to expectation, but it's a fun way for kids to spend the evening while parents enjoy a quiet dinner and some "alone time." This popular dinner excursion package is available twice monthly on Fridays during the school year and on Sundays in the summer. Call or check on-line for the next event date.

The Petrified Forest

4100 Petrified Forest Road
Calistoga, CA 94515
www.petrifiedforest.org

707-942-6667

Hours: Open daily 9 am–7 pm; Winter hours 9 am–5 pm.
Price: Adults $6, Seniors (over 60) $5, Juniors (12 to 17) $5, Children (6 to 11) $3.

Over 3 million years ago, Mt. St. Helena erupted and blanketed the valley with lava, turning the trees to stone. The California Petrified Forest has been a tourist attraction since 1870 when a petrified stump was discovered. Children will marvel at the trees turned to rock. The Queen of the Forest is the largest tree on the property at 8 feet in diameter and 65 feet long. There are picnic tables and a gift shop where visitors can browse the polished rocks and petrified stones.

Sterling Vineyards

1111 Dunaweal Lane
Calistoga, CA 94515
www.sterlingvineyards.com

800-726-6136

Hours: Open Daily 10:30 am–4:30 pm. Closed New Years Day, Easter Sunday, Thanksgiving Day, Christmas Day.

Price: Weekends and Holidays Adults $20; Mid-Week Adults $15, Under 21 $10, 3 and under Free. Visitor Fee Includes: aerial tram ride, self-paced, self guided tour, and complimentary tasting of five wines served by professional staff while seated at your own table.

A visit to Napa would not be complete without at least one visit to a winery–even with the kids in tow. Sterling Vineyards is a good choice for both adults and kids. Situated high on a hilltop, visitors must ride a tram to reach the tasting rooms. This is a fun and scenic ride for the whole family. Once you reach the winery, take a self-guided tour around the grounds, then choose from three tasting rooms where you can sit and taste a variety of wines. Children are provided for with a glass of sparkling juice.

Santa Rosa

Annadel State Park

6201 Channel Drive
Santa Rosa, CA 95409
www.parks.ca.gov

707-539-3911

Hours: Sunrise to Sunset

Price: Free

Annadel State Park is 60 miles north of San Francisco on the eastern edge of Santa Rosa. The park offers miles of trails for hiking, mountain biking, and trail riding. Annadel Park offers a great variety of flowers from early spring until early summer, especially around Lake Ilsanjo. The best months to see the park's wildflowers are April and May. Fishing Lake Ilsanjo offers excellent fishing for black bass and bluegill. A California fishing license is required for those 16 and older. Wear comfortable shoes and bring drinking water if you plan to hike.

Charles M. Schulz Museum

2301 Hardies Lane
Santa Rosa, CA 95403
www.schulzmuseum.org

707-579-4452

Bay Area Day Trips and Family Vacations

Hours: Labor Day–Memorial Day Weekdays 11 am–5 pm (except Tuesdays), Weekends 10 am–5 pm, Closed on Tuesdays. Memorial Day–Labor Day Weekdays 11 am–5 pm, Weekends 10 am–5 pm. Closed New Year's Day, Easter, Fourth of July, Thanksgiving Day, Christmas Eve, and Christmas Day.

Price: Adults $8, Youth and Seniors $5.

This museum is dedicated to memorializing the work of comic strip writer and artist, Charles M. Schulz, famous for creating the Peanuts characters. Children will enjoy winding their way through the Snoopy Labyrinth which is shaped to resemble Snoopy's head. Peanuts fans will not be disappointed to see original hand drawn comic strips drawn by Charles Schulz as well as tributes to the artist drawn by other famous cartoonists. Kids will have fun eating their lunch out of "Snoopy's dog bowl" at the café. This is a fun place to stop if you are driving through Santa Rosa or are visiting other attractions in the area.

Howarth Park

630 Summerfield Road near Montgomery Drive
Santa Rosa, CA 95404
www.ci.santa-rosa.ca.us

707-543-3282

Hours: Sunrise to Sunset

Price: Free

Located in Eastern Santa Rosa, Howarth Park is a great place to spend the day with the family. The park has miles of hiking, jogging, and biking trails, with many leading to Spring Lake Park and onto Annadel State Park. The Big K-Land Amusement Area features a narrated train ride that goes around over a bridge and through a tunnel. The carousel ride features thirty horses, two chariots and over one thousand lights. Along with the train and carousel ride, the amusement area also offers a Recreation Jump (weekends only); pony rides and Old Man Olson's Farm (summers only). The Playland Store has a variety of candy, ice cream, drinks and snacks available. In the Land of Imagination, children can dig for dinosaur bones in the sand, watch a volcano erupt, visit the Native American Village, climb up the Net-Climber, and explore the streets of the Old West Town or the new futuristic play structure. In the Climbing Wall area, children will have a great time challenging themselves on the climbing walls. The play area also has swings, picnic tables and other play attractions. The park also has access to Lake Ralphine where visitors can take boating lessons, go fishing or rent rowboats, paddleboats, canoes and sailboats.

Safari West

3115 Porter Creek Road
Santa Rosa, CA 95404
www.safariwest.com

707-579-2551
800-616-2695

Hours: Regular Safari Tour Schedule 9 am, 1 pm, and 4 pm daily; Winter Safari Tour Schedule 10 am and 2 pm daily. Please arrive 15 minutes prior to departure.

Price: Safari Tours: Adults $62, Children 3–12 $28. Reservations required. All reservations require a credit card and tours will be charged 100% at the time of booking. There is a 72-hour cancellation policy. Accommodations: Safari Tents: Saturdays: $245 double occupancy, $25 each additional guest and/or futon. Sunday–Fridays: $225 double occupancy, $25 each additional guest and/or futon. Children ages 2 and under are free. Continental breakfast included in price. Cottage: $350 a night for four people, each additional guest $25 .

Recommended occupancy: four to six guests. Continental breakfast included. Check website or call for special rates and packages.

Explore the 400 acres of Safari West in a three-hour adventure led by experienced guides in an open-air safari jeep. The experience includes a drive through a 12-Acre Extreme Africa Exhibit, where you can observe antelopes, gazelles, ostriches, and other animals in an exotic savannah setting. You may spy a wildebeest or see Cape buffalo and a zebra at the nearby watering hole. In the inner compound, you may spot a cheetah, primates, giraffes, lemurs, and birds. Wildlife drives are 2 1/2 to 3 hours long and are best for children over the age of three. The ride may also be uncomfortable for women who are pregnant. After a day out on safari, spend the night in one of the tent bungalows or cottages and experience what it might be like to spend the night in an African safari camp. Accommodations are far from rustic with wood floors, comfy beds, private bathrooms and hand-made furniture. Tents are imported from Africa and are built on high wooden platforms and feature decks where visitors have a close-up view of giraffes and the lake below.

Sonoma County Farm Trails

P.O. Box 6032
Santa Rosa, CA 95406
www.farmtrails.org/index.html

707-571-8288

Hours: Varies by farm.

Price: Most are free but may charge for special attractions or events.

Experience life on the farm! Sonoma County Farm Trails is a collective of farms that offers families a chance to visit and learn about farms and their products. Call or visit the website and request a free Farm Trails map and plan your visits. Many farms have seasonal events. Take the family berry-picking in the summer or pick apples and pumpkins in the fall. During the spring, visit the baby animals or see glorious fields of flowers. Purchase farm fresh fruit, honey, wine, flowers and cheese. Some farms allow farm stays where guests can spend a night or two. This is a fun way for city kids (and parents) to learn about life on a farm.

Bay Area Day Trips and Family Vacations

Spring Lake

391 Violetti Drive
Santa Rosa, CA 95409
www.sonoma-county.org/parks/pk_slake.htm

707-539-8092

Hours: Sunrise to Sunset. Campground is open 7 days a week from May 1 through September 30 and weekends and holidays the rest of the year. Call 707-565-2267 to make campground reservations.

Price: $6 per vehicle for day use from Memorial Day weekend through the Sunday after Labor Day; $5 at all other times. Campsites are $19 per night.

Spring Lake Regional Park is a 320-acre park offering many activities including camping, fishing, and picnicking. There are trails for walking, hiking, bicycling and horseback riding. The park includes a 3 acre swimming lagoon with a sandy shore and a concession stand. The lagoon is staffed with lifeguards and is open from Memorial Day weekend until Labor Day. The 72-acre lake is open year-round and is excellent for fishing, boating, windsurfing, paddle boating and canoeing. Paddle boat and canoe rentals are available. The Visitors Center at Spring Lake provides a wonderful educational experience for children and adults of all ages.

North Coast

Muir Beach

Muir Woods National Monument

Muir Woods National Monument does not have a street address. Refer to the website for specific directions.
www.nps.gov/muwo

415-388-2596

Hours: The Park is open from 8 am to sunset, including holidays.

Price: Adult (16+) $5, Children (15 and under) FREE, Annual Pass $20. Entrance fees are valid for same-day use at John Muir National Historic Site in Martinez. The pass is good for 12 months and admits the pass holder and accompanying passengers in a private vehicle to Muir Woods National Monument in Mill Valley, CA, and John Muir National Historic Site in Martinez, CA.

Muir Woods is located 12 miles north of the Golden Gate Bridge. Take Highway 101 to the Highway 1/Stinson Beach Exit. Follow the signs to Muir Woods. Muir Woods contains 6 miles of trails. There is a 1/2 hour loop, a 1 hour loop, and a 1 1/2 hour loop as well as longer hikes on trails that extend into surrounding parks. All of these walks afford views of thousands of old-growth coast redwoods, the tallest living things in the world. Kids can pick up a Junior Ranger booklet at the Visitor Center and learn what park rangers do to help protect nature. Picnicking, pets, bicycles, smoking, and camping are not permitted within the park. For your safety remain on established trails while visiting the Park. Poison oak and stinging nettles are common. The monument is busiest during the weekends and the middle of the day. It is best to visit during weekdays, morning hours and late afternoons. Parking space is very limited and fills quickly on most days.

Slide Ranch

2025 Shoreline Highway
Muir Beach, CA 94965
www.slideranch.org

415-381-6155

Hours: Hiking trails, beaches and tide pools are open to the public during daylight hours.
Price: Free to explore the trails and beaches. Additional fees for events and programs. Visit website for program schedules and fees.

Slide Ranch is a teaching farm located at a historic coastal dairy perched above the ocean in the Marin Headlands within the Golden Gate National Recreation Area. Visitors are welcome to explore hiking trails, beaches, tide pools, and observe the garden and animals at Slide Ranch. Interaction with the animals is only available to those who are registered in one of the programs. Slide Ranch offers a variety of educational programs to children and their families. Family Programs are offered on most weekends throughout the spring and fall and consist of Family Farm Days, Toddler Days, and Family Campouts. Under the guidance of experienced teachers, visitors can milk a goat, feed and collect eggs from chickens, rub a sheep's wool, plant seeds, and sample from the organic garden. Learn to make crafts and food just like the early farmers, and explore miles of wild trails and tide pools. Programs require pre-registration and fill up quickly. Food is not available for purchase except during special events, however, picnicking is allowed. A public parking lot is available down the hill from the main entrance as well as three public outhouse facilities with hand washing stations nearby.

Point Reyes National Seashore

Highway 1 (30 miles north of San Francisco)
Point Reyes Station, CA
www.nps.gov/pore/index.htm

415-464-5100

Hours: Open daily from Sunrise to Sunset
Price: Free for day use. Camping Fees $15/night/site for 1 to 6 people, $30/night/site for 7 to 14 people, $40/night/site for 15 to 25 people.

Point Reyes National Seashore comprises over 100 square miles, including 33,300 acres of coastal wilderness. Point Reyes is a thriving breeding ground for the once almost-extinct elephant seals and is an excellent place for seeing an amazing variety of land, sea, and sky creatures. It is also one of the best places for viewing the migrations of the California gray whale. There are many fun activities for families to enjoy including hiking, building sandcastles, watching for whales, seals and sea lions, visiting the lighthouse, and exploring the visitor centers where children can learn how to become junior rangers.

Bay Area Day Trips and Family Vacations

Bear Valley Visitor Center

Located half a mile west of Olema, CA along Bear Valley Road

415- 464-5100

Hours: Monday–Friday 9 am–5 pm; Saturdays, Sundays and holidays 8 am–5 pm. Closed Christmas Day.

Price: Free

The Bear Valley Visitor Center is the primary visitor's center located in the Point Reyes National Park and is a good place to get oriented to the trails and other points of interest within the park. Many trail heads are located just outside the center and several are short and easy enough to be managed by small children. The center provides a glimpse of the ecosystems and cultural heritage of the park and includes a seismograph, touch table, plant and animal exhibits, an auditorium, and a bookstore. Restrooms are available in the visitor's center and a picnic area is nearby. A half mile away from the visitor center is Kule Loklo, a replication of a Coast Miwok village. The Coast Miwok tribe once inhabited this area thousands of years ago and over 120 known village sites exist within the park. Make sure to visit Indian Beach where several Miwok houses have been reconstructed along the beach.

Kenneth C. Patrick Visitor Center

Located 30 minutes from Bear Valley on Drakes Beach off of Sir Frances Drake Blvd

415-669-1250

Hours: Open year round, weekends and holidays 10 am–5 pm; Closed Monday–Friday and Christmas Day.

Price: Free

Located at Drake's Beach, the Kenneth C. Patrick Visitor Center contains exhibits that feature Sir Francis Drake, marine fossils, a model of the lighthouse, a small aquarium, and a whale skeleton suspended from the ceiling. Have lunch at the café or at one of the sheltered picnic tables.

The Lighthouse Visitor Center and the Point Reyes Historic Lighthouse

Located 45 minutes west of Bear Valley on the Point Reyes Headlands, at the end of Sir Francis Drake Blvd.

415-669-1534

Hours: Open year round, Thursday–Monday from 10 am–4:30 pm; Closed Tuesdays and Wednesdays. Closed Christmas Day. Stairs to the lighthouse are closed when winds exceed 40 mph — check access availability at the Bear Valley Visitor Center.

Price: Free

The Lighthouse Visitor Center offers exhibits on whales, seals, sea lions, wildflowers and birds as well as the history of the Point Reyes Lighthouse. Once you've finished checking out the exhibits at the small visitor's center, prepare for the long descent down to the lighthouse itself which sits at the bottom of 300 steps near the edge of a rocky bluff. There is no need to worry about the safety of the little ones as the steps are well enclosed and there is little danger other than wearing them out. Once you reach the lighthouse, check out the spectacular view, visit the lens room, learn about the history of the lighthouse and its keepers and check out the equipment building next door.

Glass Beach

At the end of Elm Street
Fort Bragg, CA 95437
www.fortbragg.com
Hours: Sunrise to Sunset
Price: Free

Once upon a time the area around glass beach was used as a city dump. In 1967, this was banned but, as a result, the broken glass that remained has washed up over the years, creating a bejeweled shoreline. Visitors were once able to pick up the stones smoothed by the sea, but in order to preserve this unique beach, collecting glass is no longer permitted.

Russian Gulch State Park

Highway 1
Mendocino, CA 95460
www.parks.ca.gov
707-937-5804
Hours: Daily 6 am–10 pm
Price: $6 per car

Russian Gulch State Park is not a big park and thus has many short and manageable trails easy for adults and children alike. Along the coast, the park has access to a beach that offers swimming, tide pool exploring, skin diving and rock fishing. Inland, there is a 36-foot high waterfall. Hikers enjoy miles of hiking trails. The park also has a paved three-mile bicycle trail. The park also features the Devil's Punch Bowl, a collapsed sea cave with churning water caused by the constant pounding of waves against the headlands.

Skunk Train

100 West Laurel Street
Fort Bragg, CA 95437
800-866-1690
Hours: Call or check website for current schedule, tour options and to make reservations.
Price: Adults $45, Children (3–11) $20 for round trip ticket from Fort Bragg to Northspur. Additional cost for special tours and events. Call or check website for special events.

Hop on board the Skunk Train and take a 3 1/2 hour ride in an old-fashioned railroad car. Though the rail cars have been restored, the views on the coastal Redwood Route remain very much the same as they did since 1885 and are spectacular. Get a seat on one of the open observation cars to get a panoramic view of the scenery. Children will delight in riding through tunnels and over bridges. Food and snacks are not permitted on the train but there is a concession car that sells light snacks and drinks or you can order a box lunch ($14 for a deli sandwich, salad, cookie and beverage) when making your reservation. The trip starts in Fort Bragg and ends in Northspur where riders can disembark and stretch their legs at a grassy park. The Skunk Train holds a variety of events including a harvest train in the fall, a holiday ride in December and a train ride and barbecue during the warmer months.

Bay Area Day Trips and Family Vacations

Van Damme State Park

Highway 1 (3 miles south of the town of Mendocino)
Mendocino CA 95460
www.parks.ca.gov

707-937-5804

Hours: Sunrise to Sunset

Price: Day use is free. Campsites range from $15–$25 per night depending on the season. Go to www.reserveamerica.com to make reservations.

Van Damme State Park features ten miles of scenic trail along the lush fern-carpeted canyon of Little River. Park highlights also include a Pygmy Forest where fully grown miniature cypress and pine trees stand as little as six inches tall, a bog where skunk cabbages grow profusely, and 2,000 acres of beach. There is a small visitor center housed within an historic 1930's building. Kayak tours are available at a beach concession stand located at the beach parking lot. Other activities include hiking, camping, scuba-diving, abalone diving and fishing. Campsite amenities include food lockers, fire rings, comfort stations, barbecues and picnic areas and restrooms with showers.

Sierra Nevadas

The Children's Museum of Northern Nevada

813 North Carson Street
Carson City, NV 89701
www.cmnn.org

775-884-2226

Hours: Open daily from 10 am–4:30 pm

Price: Toddlers (1 & Under) Free, Children (2+) $3, Adults (14+) $5, Seniors (55+) $4.

The Children's Museum of Northern Nevada features interactive exhibits for children of all ages. Exhibits include an Archeological Dig where kids can don hard hats and goggles and pick and dig through stones to reveals bones and rocks. Children play doctor dress up in costumes, shop at the kid-size grocery store or play musical instruments at the Music Center. There are many other fun and educational exhibits at the museum that will provide hours of fun for little ones.

Rancho San Rafael Regional Park and the Wilbur D. May Center

1595 North Sierra Street
Reno, NV 89503

775-785-5961

Hours: Museum: Wednesday–Saturday 10 am–5 pm, Sunday Noon–4 pm. Arboretum: Wednesday–Saturday 8 am–5 pm, Sunday Noon–4 pm. The Great Basin Adventure: Memorial Day thru fall 10 am–5 pm. Closed during the winter months except for special events. Call for current schedule.

Price: Museum: Permanent Exhibits: Adults (18–60) $4.50, Seniors (60+) $3.50, Children (3–18) $2.50. Special Exhibits: Adults $6.50, Seniors $6.50, Children $5.50. Arboretum: Free for all visitors. The Great Basin Adventure: Adults $5, Seniors $3.50, Children $3.50.

Rancho San Rafael was once a working ranch and is now home to the Wilbur D. May Center which includes a museum, an arboretum and the Great Basin Adventure. The Museum houses a collection of artifacts collected by Wilbur D. May during his many travels. The museum also features the Garden Court, a lush garden with waterfalls, exotic plants and flowers, and ponds filled with koi and goldfish. The Arboretum and Botanical Garden has 12 acres covered with groves of trees, wetland habitats, outdoor courtyards, secluded gardens, and a labyrinth. The Great Basin Adventure is especially for kids and features a petting zoo, pony rides, a flume ride and a Discovery Room where youngsters can climb on dinosaurs, pan for gold, and explore. The Center is host to many special and seasonal events. Check the website or call for current schedule. Besides the attractions at the May Center, the park offers picnic areas with barbecue grills and a playground.

Lake Tahoe

Lake Tahoe has much to offer the entire family whether it's skiing in the winter or enjoying the activities on the lake during the summer. During the winter months, the ski resorts offer children's programs and there are many snow parks and sledding hills that the whole family can enjoy. During the summer families can spend the day windsurfing, snorkeling, jet-skiing, kayaking and sailing or just relaxing on one of the several beaches or picnicking at one of the many parks. There are many excellent trails for hiking and biking and enjoying the beautiful outdoors.

Boreal Mountain Playground

I-80 at Donner Summit
Truckee, California 96160
www.rideboreal.com

530-426-3666

Hours: 9 am–9 pm. Resort closes at 4 pm when night skiing is not in operation and on Christmas Eve.

Price: Any Time Lift Tickets (9 am–4 pm Adults $44, Teens (13–18) $39, Child (5–12) $12, Senior (60–69), Parent Shared $44, Over 70 $5. Children under 4 Free. Night Time Lift Tickets (3:30 pm–9 pm) Adults $25, Child (5–12) $12, Senior (60–69) $25, Over 70 $5, Children under 4 Free. College students with valid ID can ski for $15 on Fridays except on blackout dates. Prices are slightly more during the holidays. Check website for current holiday pricing. Playland Snow Tubing (over 42") $20, Playland Tube Carouse (under 42") $15, 4 and under Free.

Bay Area Day Trips and Family Vacations

Boreal offers many fun activities for the whole family including skiing, snowboarding, tubing, and sledding. The Boreal Kids Club offers kids ages 4–10 both ski and snowboard lessons giving them a chance to decide which sport they like best. Parents can purchase a Shared Pass, an affordable option, which allows each parent to take turns on the slopes while the other is supervising the children. Located at the far end of the Boreal parking lot, the resort now has a new tubing park aptly called Playland. Playland is equipped with a new moving carpet, groomed tubing lanes and a tubing carousel for children under 42"tall. Along with its great family atmosphere, Boreal is also well known for its night skiing.

The Gondola at Heavenly
Heavenly Mountain Resort
Corner of Wildwood and Saddle
South Lake Tahoe, CA 96150
www.skiheavenly.com
775-586-7000
Hours: Monday–Friday 9 am–4 pm. Saturday & Sunday 9:30 am–4 pm.
Price: Adults (19–64) $28, Senior (65+) $24, Teen ((13–18) $24, Children (5–12) $18, Children 4 and under Free.

Take a scenic 12-minute ride in an 8-passenger gondola and enjoy the breathtaking views of Lake Tahoe. The gondola delivers passengers mid-way to The Deck, a 14,000 square foot observation platform where visitors can enjoy a bite to eat at the café, enjoy a picnic at one of the picnic tables or enjoy the views from one of the high-powered telescopes. Guests can continue the journey to Adventure Peak where there are a host of activities including tubing, rock wall climbing, snowshoeing and cross country skiing.

Taylor Creek Visitor Center
Highway 89
Lake Tahoe, CA 96150
www.fs.fed.us/r5/ltbmu/recreation/visitor-center
530-543-2674
Hours: Weekends Memorial Day thru June 15 from 8 am–4:30 pm. Open daily June 16 thru September from 8 am–5:30 pm. 8 am–4:30 pm from 8 am–4:30 pm. The Stream Profile Chamber is open daily beginning Memorial Day weekend thru June 10th from 8 am until 4 pm and beginning June 16th from 8 am until 5 pm thru September. During the month of October, the Stream Profile Chamber is open daily from 8 am to 4 pm Closed for the winter months.
Price: Free

The Taylor Creek Visitor Center offers maps, brochures, wilderness permits, interpretive programs, and is the start of four fascinating self-guided trails. The Rainbow Trail will lead visitors to The Stream Profile Chamber, where visitors can study the stream environment through a panel of floor-to-ceiling windows. Children and family programs are available on Tuesdays and Fridays at 10 am and a naturalist led walk on the Rainbow Trail takes place at 10:30 am.

Northstar-at-Tahoe

Hwy 267 & Northstar Drive
Truckee, CA 96160
www.northstarattahoe.com

530-562-1010

Hours: Daily 8:30 am–4 pm from mid-November through mid-April weather and conditions permitting.

Price: Single Day Lift Ticket-Adult (23–64) $71, Young Adult (13–22) $61, Child (5–12) $27, Senior (65–69) $61, Super Senior (70+) $27, 4 and under Free. Parents' Predicament Ticket $71. Other ticket options are also available. Check website for current options and pricing.

Northstar-at-Tahoe is a short six-mile drive to Tahoe and is a resort that has all the bells and whistles. Along with the run-of-the-mill skiing and snowboarding, this resort also has ski bikes, snow scooters, a bungy trampoline and a huge transparent plastic sphere that allows thrill seekers to climb in and roll down the slopes. Parents can take turns skiing with the purchase of an interchangeable Parents' Predicament Ticket. The resort is well known for their highly rated kid's ski school. Northstar also offers tubing, ice-skating in a 9,000 square foot ice rink, cross-country skiing, snow-shoeing, an arcade, shopping, and several dining options.

Soda Springs Winter Resort

10244 Soda Springs Road
Soda Springs, CA 95728
www.skisodasprings.com

530-426-3901

Hours: Ski/Board chairlifts operate from 9 am–4 pm. Snow tubing tows operate from 10 am–4 pm.

Price: Lift Tickets Adults $25, Youth (8–17) $16, Child (7 and under) $10, Seniors (70+) $5. Snow Tubing (all ages) $15 includes snow tubes.

Soda Springs is one of the more affordable family winter vacation options and has lots to do for kids of all ages. There is skiing and snowboarding for the adults and, for the little ones, there is Planet Kids. Planet Kids is an area especially for children ages 10 and under. There are tubes, mini snowmobiles ($5 for 5 laps, including helmet), and a carousel. The Kids' X Park for little skiers and boarders has pint sized jumps so that even the youngest daredevils can catch some air.

SNO-PARKS

Various Locations
www.ohv.parks.ca.gov

916-324-4442

Hours: 7 am–7 pm

Price: Day permits are sold for $5 and are valid for one single day. Season permits are sold for $25 and are valid for the entire SNO-PARK season from November 1 through May 30. See website to learn how to purchase season permits.

Bay Area Day Trips and Family Vacations

For families who just want to play in the snow, the California Department of Parks and Recreation operates 21 SNO-PARK sites that provide snow-cleared parking lots with sanitation facilities and access to snow play areas, cross-country ski and snowmobile trails. Permits may be purchased at several outlets including drug stores, markets and sporting good stores. Check on-line to learn where to purchase a permit in your area and to print out a list and map of all SNO-PARK locations. Make sure to bring your own saucers, tubes, sleds, snow-shoes and snow toys. Call 1 (800) 427-7623 for a CALTRANS recording on highway conditions before your visit.

Yosemite

Badger Pass Ski Resort

Yosemite, CA 95389

www.yosemitepark.com/BadgerPass.aspx

209-372-8430

Hours: Open daily from 9 am–4 pm. Half-Day is Noon–4 pm. Tubing Sessions 11:30 am–1:30 pm and 2 pm–4 pm.

Price: Weekend and Holiday Lift Ticket Pricing Full Day Adult $38, Youth (13–17) $32, Child (12 and under) $15, Senior (65+) $32, Child (6 and under) Free with paying adult, One Ride Ticket $5. Half-Day Lift Tickets are $10 less than Full Day Tickets. Lift ticket rates are discounted during mid-week and non-holiday dates. See website for current rates. Tubing: $11 per person for a 2 hour session.

Located within beautiful Yosemite National Park, Badger Pass Ski Resort has many winter activities for the whole family. In addition to the downhill facilities, there are extensive cross country skiing and snowshoe trails. Other activities include ski tours, snowboarding, tubing and ice-skating.

Children's Museum of the Sierra

49269 Golden Oak Drive, Suite 104

Oakhurst, CA 93644

www.southyosemitemuseums.org

559-658-5656

Hours: Winter Hours (Mid-Sept.–Mid-June) Tuesday–Saturday 10 am–4 pm, Sunday 1 pm–4 pm. Summer Hours (Mid-June–Mid-Sept) Tuesday–Saturday 10 am–5 pm. Closed Sunday.

Price: $3 per person, Children under 2 Free.

Located 24 miles south of Yosemite National Park in Oakhurst is the Children's Museum of the Sierra. This 4,000 square foot museum is packed with hands-on exhibits that will delight children from ages 2–12. At one of the many interactive exhibits, children can be bankers, doctors, firefighters or artists. At the Dig Exhibit, children can dig for ancient artifacts. The Natural History Exhibit offers children a fun way to learn about animals, insects and minerals. There is a castle, a pirate ship, a pizza restaurant and more! The museum provides great indoor activity for the whole family.

Fresno Flats Historical Park

49777 Road 427
Oakhurst, CA 93644
www.southyosemitemuseums.org

559-683-6570

Hours: The Park is open for self-guided tours from dusk to dawn. The Museum is open Monday–Friday from 10 am to 3 pm. Guided tours of the grounds and buildings are available from Noon to 4 pm. Saturdays and Sundays. Closed during the months of January and February.

Price: Free

Fresno Flats Historic Park recaptures the lives of those who came to build their lives in the Sierra Nevada foothills and mountains of Central California. This museum complex consists of two restored and furnished 1870's homes, a pair of one-room school houses, two 19th century jail houses, and several farm buildings including a wagon shed, blacksmith and a log house. There are restrooms and picnic areas on the grounds.

Yosemite Mountain Sugar Pine Railroad

56001 Hwy 41
Fish Camp, CA 93623
www.ymsprr.com

559-683-7273

Hours: Hours vary according to steam train operation. Call to check for current schedule.
Price: Steam Train Adults $17, Children (3–12) $8.50, Children under 3 Free.
Jenny Rail Car Adults $13, Children $6.50, Children under 3 Free; Moonlight Special Adults $45, Children $22.50.

Located at Yosemite Park's South Gate on Highway 41 is the Yosemite Mountain Sugar Pine Railroad. Hop on board one of the refurbished railcars that were once used to provide transportation for logging and track repair crews and take an exciting 4-mile railroad ride through the majestic Sierra National Forest. There are several events and special excursions that occur throughout the year including a moonlight train ride which includes a barbecue dinner and music along with a ride under the stars. Also located at the Yosemite Mountain Station are a gift shop and a sandwich shop, the Thornberry Museum located inside a 140-year old log cabin where visitors get a glimpse of life at the turn of the century, and Gold Rush City Miners Camp where visitors can pan for gold.

Yosemite National Park

Yosemite, CA 95389
www.nps.gov/yose/index.htm

209-372-0200

Hours: Yosemite National Park is open 24 hours per day, 365 days per year, and no reservations are required to visit.
Price: Entrance fee is $20 per car and is valid for 7 days.

Yosemite is famous for its waterfalls, glaciers, and unusual rock formations. Millions of visitors visit the national park each year and it is a must see. There are many things to see and do in Yosemite including hiking, biking, camping, rock climbing, rafting, swimming, bird watching, stargazing and so much more. Highlights of the park include Yosemite Valley with its cliffs and waterfalls, Mariposa Grove and its magnificent giant sequoias, Tuolomne Meadows, a meadow surrounded by glorious mountain peaks, and Glacier Point which offers a spectacular view of the valley. Take advantage of the free shuttle buses that loop around Yosemite Valley and park your car at the free day-use parking lot and hop on the shuttle. The shuttle stops at 15 minute intervals and you can hop off, take a hike and hop back on when the kids are tired. There are a variety of free activities at the park geared especially for the kids, including story times, and learning programs such as Wee Wild Ones, an interactive program for kids 6 and under featuring stories, songs, games, crafts and other activities. Children of all ages can also become Junior Rangers or Little Cubs by picking up a booklet at the Visitors Center. The park also offers the Explore Yosemite Family Programs, which includes games, stories and activities during a short hike. The cost to join this program is $12.50 for the first child and $10 for each additional child, children 3 and under are free when participating with an older sibling. Parents are free. Check the Yosemite Today newsletter for current schedules. During the winter months, visit the Curry Village Ice Rink, an outdoor rink where skaters can skate under the stars or visit the Badger Pass Ski Resort. Yosemite offers various accommodations within the park including campsites, hotels, lodges, and cabins. Check on-line to explore the possibilities.

Bay Area Day Trips and Family Vacations

Chapter 3

Seasonal Events

W e have compiled a list of annual events that you'll definitely want to check out. Grab your family and try something new this month, you'll be glad you did!

Winter

Bah Humbug 5K Run/Walk

San Ramon, CA

www.ci.san-ramon.ca.us

When: December

Start the holiday season off right with a healthy fun run or walk through San Ramon. Participants receive a holiday long sleeve t-shirt, goodies provided by local sponsors and medals for the top three finishers in each age category.

City's Holiday Breakfast
Heather Farm Park Community Center

301 North San Carlos Drive

Walnut Creek, CA 94598

www.walnutcreekrec.org

When: December

Reindeer pancakes, seasonal music, arts and crafts, holiday videos and pictures with Santa.

Holiday De Lites

Downtown Antioch
Antioch, CA
www.art4antioch.org
When: December

Food and craft booths, a downtown street parade, community entertainment stage, lighted boat parade, holiday tree lighting ceremony, visit with Mr. & Mrs. Santa Claus, "snow" flurries and a Children's Toyland (small area of children's activities).

Holiday Frolic and Light Parade

www.cityofmartinez.org
When: November/December

Magically Martinez will become a wonderland of winter delights that includes lots of snow, kid's activities and hundreds of lights.

Walnut Creek on Ice

1375 Civic Drive
Walnut Creek, CA 94596
www.iceskatewalnutcreek.com
925-935-SNOW (7669)
When: November, December & January

Take your kids ice skating outdoors! See for yourself the magical transformation of Civic Park into what can only be described as a twinkling Winter Wonderland. Each year the dates, hours and prices change, so check the website before your visit. The website also offers parking and group reservation information.

Holiday Parade

Downtown Brentwood
Brentwood, CA
www.brentwoodchamber.org
When: December

Join in the fun as an observer or a participant. Parade ends at the City Park on Oak and Second Street with Santa Claus in the gazebo.

Moraga Women's Society Holiday Home Tour

Moraga, CA
925-376-3469
When: December

A tour of some of the most unique homes in Moraga. This event also features a tea, boutique and great raffle prizes.

Santa's Gold Rush 5 Mile
SF Marriott Courtyard Hotel (Across from Hilltop Shopping Center)

3150 Garrity Way

Richmond, CA 94806

When: December

One loop around beautiful Gold Lake. Gold medals to all that complete the scenic, semi-hilly 5M course. Registration includes many prizes from Santa's bag.

Chabot Space & Science Center

10000 Skyline Blvd.

Oakland, CA 94619

www.chabotspace.org

510-336-7373

When: New Years

Ring in the New Year at our Annual New Year's Eve Balloon Drop. Registration for this sold-out event starts in October. Immerse yourself in our state-of-the-art digital dome planetarium, giant screen MegaDome theatre and hands-on interactive exhibits and demonstrations. Marvel at the wonders of the Universe through the largest public telescopes in the Western United States.

Clayton Counts Down New Year's Eve Nite
Clayton Community Gym

700 Gym Court

Clayton, CA 94517

www.ci.clayton.ca.us

925-889-1600

When: January

Family and kids activities in an alcohol free environment with refreshments, food, games and prizes.

First Night Martinez

Downtown Martinez

Martinez, CA

www.firstnightmartinez.org

925-372-8295

When: January

An alcohol-free, community New Year's Eve celebration of the arts including live music, opera, ballet, magic, comedy, dance and more.

Martin Luther King Jr. Parade and Rally

El Cerrito, CA

www.el-cerrito.org

When: January

Parade begins at the El Cerrito DMV, continues on to the El Cerrito Community Center.

Pre-School & Parenting Fair

Pleasant Hill Community Center

320 Civic Drive

Pleasant Hill, CA 94523

www.pleasanthill.ca.gov

When: January

The only pre-school and parenting fair dedicated to the families of Contra Costa County. Over forty pre-schools are in attendance at this free event, plus parenting and family resources.

Concord Academy Valentines Day 5K/10K

El Dorado Park across from Concord High School

Concord, CA 94521

www.onyourmarkevents.com

209-795-7832

When: February

Concord Chocolate Festival

Crowne Plaza Hotel

45 John Glenn Drive

Concord, CA 94519

www.concordchocolatefestival.com

925-685-1181

When: March

Taste chocolate confections from bakeries, hotels, restaurants, chocolate manufacturers, pastry shops and candy shops. Also enjoy wine and cheese treats and plenty of demonstrations. Special half price children's tickets are available.

Easter Egg Hunt
Clayton Community Gym

700 Gym Court
Clayton, CA 94517
www.ci.clayton.ca.us
925-899-1600
When: March/April

Egg Hunt
Arlington Park

1120 Arlington Blvd.
El Cerrito, CA 94530
www.el-cerrito.org
510-215-4300
When: March/April
This is a traditional egg hunt with candy and eggs, and occurs rain or shine.

Liberty Gymnastics Training Center Easter Egg Hunt

2330-A Bates Avenue
Concord, CA 94519
www.libertygymtrainingcenter.com
When: March/April
This event features an egg hunt, tumbling, rope swing, trampoline, foam cube pit, crafts, games, music and prizes.

Lion's Club Easter Egg Hunt
Waterfront Park

Martinez, CA
www.cityofmartinez.org
When: March/April
Kids ages 2–9 are invited to attend this free event.

Lion's Club Easter Egg Hunt
O'Hara Park

Oakley, CA
www.oakleylions.com
925-625-7467
When: March/April

Pinole Egg Hunt
Fernandez Park
Pinole, CA
510-741-8554
When: March/Apri

Walnut Creek Spring Egg Hunts
Heather Farm Park
301 North San Carlos Drive
Walnut Creek, CA 94598

Larkey Park
2771 Buena Vista Avenue
Walnut Creek, CA 94596
www.ci.walnut-creek.ca.us
925-943-5858
When: March/April

Art Show
El Cerrito Community Center
7007 Moeser Lane
El Cerrito, CA 94530
www.el-cerrito.org
510-685-4747
When: April

Spring Clayton Cleans Up
City Hall Courtyard
6000 Heritage Trails
Clayton, CA 94517
www.ci.clayton.ca.us
When: April

Help pick up Clayton's trails, parks and open space.

Walnut Creek Downtown Fine Arts Festival
Main and Locust Streets
Walnut Creek, CA 94598
www.ci.walnut-creek.ca.us
When: April and September

Hundreds of arts and crafts dealers sell their wares.

West County Earth Day Festival
West County Recycling Center

101 Pittsburg Avenue

Richmond, CA 94801

www.recyclemore.com

510-215-3125

When: April

AAUW Garden Tour

www.danville.com

925-837-0826

When: May

Eight gardens in Alamo, Danville, Diablo and Blackhawk are featured. No children under 12 please.

Art and Wine Festival

Main Street

Clayton, CA 94517

www.ci.clayton.ca.us

925-672-2272

When: May

Arts and crafts, food and a Kiddieland.

Art on the Main

Main Street

Walnut Creek, CA 94596

www.ci.walnut-creek.ca.us

When: May

Features over 150 vendors and live music.

Bay Area KidFest
Todos Santos Plaza

Willow Pass Road and Grant Street

Concord, CA 94519

www.kidfestconcord.com

309-671-3287

When: May

Held on Memorial Day Weekend, KidFest is a place where kids and the community can come together. Kidfest is an alcohol and smoke free environment and showcases why Concord is a city Where Families Come First.

Cinco de Mayo Festival

Richmond, CA
510-620-6793
When: May

Enjoy Mexican art, music, dance, food exhibits, and classic cars on display.

Devil Mountain Run

Danville, CA
www.rhodyco.com/devilmtn.htm
When: May

The 5K/10K Devil Mountain Run remains a tradition for Children's Hospital & Research Center Oakland. Approximately 4,000 participants, including top competitive runners, walking enthusiasts, families and local businesses strut their stuff for fun and prizes. As the oldest continuous running event in the East Bay, it offers two flat and fast courses, 5K and 10K, that take advantage of Danville's beauty along a portion of the Iron Horse Trail.

Garden Study Annual Plant Sale
Winslow Center

2590 Pleasant Hill Road
Pleasant Hill, CA 94523
www.pleasanthill.ca.gov
When: May

Look for plants of all sizes at unbelievable prices. This is an annual fundraising event always held the day before Mothers' Day.

Heritage Rose Show
El Cerrito Community Center

7007 Moeser Lane
El Cerrito, CA 94530
www.el-cerrito.org
510-215-4300
When: May

Lafayette's Restaurant Walk

Lafayette, CA
www.lafayettechamber.org
925-284-7404
When: May

A tour of Lafayette's finest dining establishments and the opportunity to sample the signature cuisine of each restaurant.

MOM Day in the Park: Mother's Day
Todos Santos Plaza

Willow Pass Road and Grant Street

Concord, CA 94519

www.cityofconcord.org

925-671-3464

When: May

Calling all moms! Celebrate the day by dining at Todos Santos restaurants, and enjoy a special concert in the Park.

Music and Market Series
Todos Santos Plaza

Willow Pass Road and Grant Street

Concord, CA 94519

When: May-September

925-671-3464

Farmers' Market and free music concerts in the park with wonderful Bay Area musicians. Salsa, jazz, zydeco, blues and more.

San Ramon Art & Wind Festival

San Ramon, CA

www.ci.san-ramon.ca.us/parks/events/windfest/

925-973-3200

When: May

Featuring kite-making workshops, food, kid's activities, hot air balloon launch, live music and much more.

Taste of Pleasant Hill
Pleasant Hill Community Center

Pleasant Hill, CA 94523

www.pleasanthill.ca.gov

When: May

A great family event to benefit the Pleasant Hill Recreation & Park District Pre-School. Over 30 restaurants featuring food tasting, live music, and activities for children.

JF Kapnek Trust 5K Run/Walk
Miramonte High School

Orinda, CA

When: May

5K course for runners will be on the track, while joggers and walkers will have the option of utiliz-ing the cross country trails behind Miramonte. Course monitors will be stationed every kilometer with water available at the halfway point. There will be a 1K Kids Fun Run (under 10's welcome). This event will begin after the 5K event and will involve running approximately 2 laps around the track. Refreshments will be available to all runners. Brunch and music are featured after the event.

Festival of Greece

4700 Lincoln Avenue
Oakland, CA 94602
www.oaklandgreekfestival.com

510-531-3400

When: Third weekend in May
Hours: Friday & Saturday 10 am–11 pm, Sunday 11 am–9 pm, Free Friday 10 am–4 pm and Sunday 6 pm–9 pm.
Fee: $6 General Admission, Children under 12 Free

Bring the entire family and become Greek for the day at Ascension Cathedral's annual three-day festival. Held the third weekend in May on the beautiful Cathedral grounds overlooking the San Francisco Bay Area from the hills of Oakland. Experience traditional Greek food, pastries, and more. Greek folk dancing performances by award-winning dance troupes of all ages. School field trips available. Children's play area, face painting, balloons, exhibits, lectures, tours of the cathe-dral. Admission discount coupon available online.

Music at Noon
Todos Santos Plaza
Willow Pass Road and Grant Street
Concord, CA 94519
925-671-3464
When: May-July
Free lunchtime music series during the Tuesday Farmer's Market.

A Taste of El Cerrito
El Cerrito Community Center
7007 Moeser Lane
El Cerrito, CA 94530
www.tasteofelcerrito.com
510-215-4300
When: June

Black Diamond Blues Festival
Marina Blvd. between 3rd & 5th Streets
Pittsburg, CA 94565
www.bayareabluessociety.net/Black_Diamond1.html
925- 252-4842
When: June

City of Hercules Cultural Festival
Hercules, CA
www.ci.hercules.ca.us
When: June
Refugio Valley Park in Hercules comes alive in this citywide event. The festival is designed to provide the community with the opportunity to present its heritage through live entertainment, educational materials, arts and crafts, children's activities, and an exquisite selection of cultural foods.

Custom Car Show
Railroad Avenue between 3rd and 5th Streets
Pittsburg, CA 94565
925-252-4842
When: Each Thursday of the month, June through September
Featuring a unique display of custom cars, music and prizes. Fun for the whole family!

Danville Fine Arts Fair
Hartz Avenue
Danville, CA 94526
www.mlaproductions.com
925-837-4400
When: June

Dad Day in the Park: Father's Day
Todos Santos Plaza
Willow Pass Road and Grant Street
Concord, CA 94519
www.cityofconcord.org
925-671-3464
When: June
This event salutes Fathers with a special free concert in the park.

HALO'S Ramble 'Round the Reservoir
Homeless Animal's Lifeline Organization (H.A.L.O.)
Contra Loma Regional Park
Antioch, CA
www.eccchalo.org
925-998-0462
When: June
Dog walk, raffle prizes, doggie IQ tests, obedience course, vendor tables and more.

Juneteenth Parade & Festival
Richmond, CA
510-620-6793
When: June
Parade starts at Marina Way and Macdonald Avenue and marches to the Civic Center Plaza. Floats, bands and parade marchers will be judged in front of Nicholl Park. Enjoy entertainment, food, contests, children's activities and fun.

Walnut Creek Art & Wine Festival
Heather Farm Park
301 North San Carlos Drive
Walnut Creek, CA 94598
When: June
This festival features over 200 artists and craftspeople, fine food and wine, and two stages of live entertainment.

Antioch 4th of July Spectacular
Rivertown District

www.ci.antioch.ca.us

When: July

Brentwood CornFest

www.brentwoodchamber.org

When: July

Food, arts and crafts, fireworks, tractor races, carnival rides, corn eating contest, corn shucking contest, children's craft area, entertainment, farmers' market, and a car show.

Danville 4th of July Parade

San Ramon Valley Blvd. and Hartz Avenue

Danville, CA 94526

www.kiwanis-srv.org/parade.asp

When: July

This popular parade begins at 10am near San Ramon Valley High School. It features floats, vintage cars, community groups and sometimes even Clydesdale horses! A great family event.

Firecracker 5K Run/Walk

Crescent Drive

Pleasant Hill, CA 94523

925-680-4386

When: July

This fast 5K Run/Walk will make 3 loops of the downtown Crescent Plaza Area. All entry fees go to the Pleasant Hill School of your choice.

Fishing Derby
Martinez Marina

Martinez, CA

www.cityofmartinez.org

925-372-3510

When: July

Kids ages 5–12 are invited to participate at the Fishing Derby.

Fourth of July Festival and Parade
Todos Santos Plaza
Willow Pass Road and Grant Street
Concord, CA 94519
925-671-3464
When: July

Parade starts at noon from Willow Pass Road to Grant St. to Salvio St. Plus, enjoy an Old Fashioned Festival with Pancake Breakfast, live music entertainment, and crafts.

Historic Rivertown 5K Fun Run , 1 Mile Run and Family Scenic Walk
Corner of 2nd & East Streets
Antioch, CA 94509
www.antiochrivertown.com
925-754-8725
When: July

Benefits Antioch High School Cross Country Team. Prizes and age group medals. Featuring a 4th of July Parade, festival, food, arts and crafts, music and fireworks.

Independence Day Celebration
Richmond, CA
510-620-6793
When: July

The City of Richmond's Fireworks Celebration at Marina Bay Park. Bring a jacket, blanket and enjoy the show. Activities and entertainment begin at 6 p.m.

Pancake Breakfast, 4th of July Parade & Kiddieland
Downtown Clayton
Clayton, CA
www.ci.clayton.ca.us
925-673-7300
When: July

Pancakes at Endeavor Hall; parade on Main Street

Run San Ramon 5K/10K
San Ramon Park (Alcosta Blvd. and Bollinger Canyon Rd.)
San Ramon, CA
www.ci.san-ramon.ca.us
925-973-3200
When: July

T-shirts, refreshments, awards, and a raffle.

Saturday Summer Concerts & Events
www.art4antioch.org

When: July and August

Downtown Antioch, Antioch Historical Society Museum or Prewett Water Park and Community Center

Japanese Summer Festival
Diablo Japanese American Cultural Center

3165 Treat Blvd.

Concord, CA 94519

www.diablojaclub.com

925-682-5299

When: August

A variety of foods, children's game area, displays and exhibits featuring Japanese floral arranging, calligraphy demonstrations, a bonsai tree show, judo and kendo demonstrations and music and dancing. Shows by taiko drummers and bon odori (folk) dancing also are featured.

Pittsburg Scottish Renaissance Festival
Buchanan Park

4150 Harbor Street

Pittsburg, CA 94565

925-252-4842

When: August

Join in the excitement of Clan Campbell as they present the Renaissance Festival at Buchanan Park. This festival hosts over 65 vendors with products from hair braiding, costumes, jewelry, swords and tools to fortune telling. Strolling musicians, dancers and actors will entertain the masses through the day. Fun and games for the wee lads and lassies as well.

JVC Jazz Festival
Sleep Train Pavilion

2000 Kirker Pass Road

Concord, CA 94519

www.festivalproductions.net

925-676-8742

When: August

This signature event draws fans from all over the region and presents some of the best names in contemporary jazz.

Fall

Brentwood CityRead

www.brentwoodchamber.org

When: September and October

"Brentwoodians" are invited to read a chosen book and check out their copy using the honor system—a library card is not required. When you are finished with the book, you are to pass it on to a friend or return it to the Brentwood Library. Besides the library, various establishments in the area will also have copies available to read and pass on.

Children's Art and Literacy Festival

1035 Detroit Avenue

Concord, CA 94519

www.cocokids.org

925- 676-5442

When: September

The Contra Costa Child Care Council hosts this free family event which offers FREE books, hands-on fun and live entertainment.

Community Service Day

Throughout Pleasant Hill

www.pleasanthill.ca.gov

925-671-5229

When: September

Hundreds of volunteers work on community projects throughout the City of Pleasant Hill to improve the neighborhoods and quality of life.

Cultural & Heritage Day
Civic Square

San Pablo, CA

www.sanpabloevents.com

When: September

The Cultural & Heritage Day features vendors, live entertainment, children's activities, and food in celebration of the various cultural groups in the area of San Pablo.

Delta Blues Festival

Antioch, CA

www.deltabluesfestival.net

When: September

Lots of shade, kid-friendly, arts and crafts, food and refreshments and free parking. This is an alcohol-free event.

Fall Clayton Cleans Up
City Hall Courtyard

6000 Heritage Trail
Clayton, CA 94517
www.ci.clayton.ca.us

925-673-7308

When: September

Help pick up Clayton's trails, parks and open space.

Festival of Greece
St. Demetrios Greek Orthodox Church

1955 Kirker Pass Road
Concord, CA 94519
www.stdemetrios.ca.goarch.org/

When: September

Lafayette Art & Wine Festival

Lafayette, CA
www.lafayettechamber.org

925-284-7404

When: September

Featuring art, handmade crafts, sampling foods from top local restaurants, and enjoying quality wines and microbrews. Non-stop musical entertainment on three stages throughout the weekend.

Pear Festival
Moraga Commons Park

Moraga, CA
www.moraga.ca.us

When: September

Live Music, great food, delicious pear treats of all kinds, jumpies for the kids, and artist booths.

Richmond Homefront Festival

Richmond, CA
510-620-6793

When: September

Come and celebrate Richmond's Cultural Heritage at the Rosie the Riveter National Memorial Park located at the beautiful Marina Bay. Enjoy non-stop entertainment.

Shell/MEF Run for Education

Downtown Martinez
Martinez, CA
925-313-5613
When: September

All proceeds from this run benefit the Martinez Unified School District. Meet at the Plaza on Main Street at the corner of Estudillo. Don't forget the free Kids Run for children under 5 following the race.

Walnut Festival

Heather Farm Park
301 North San Carlos Drive
Walnut Creek, CA 94598
www.thewalnutfestival.org
925-935-6766
When: September

Orchard Nursery & Florist

4010 Mt. Diablo Blvd.
Lafayette, CA 94549
925-284-4474
www.orchardnursery.com
Hour: Open Daily 9 am–5 pm

Orchard Nursery & Florist, voted the Best Garden Center in the East Bay, is a delightful place for the whole family to enjoy and investigate the endless possibilities of growing a garden together. October's Harvest Festival brings charming barnyard animals (joining resident turtles Shelly & Scooter), piles of pumpkins, creative scarecrows and live music. And don't forget to visit the Lazy K Gift House—a great source for exceptional gifts and unique accessories. From brand new babies to brides & grooms or gifts for anyone on your list, you're sure to find the perfect thing to fit the bill.

Day at the Races on Iron Horse Trail

Hilton Concord and Adjacent Iron Horse Trail
Concord, CA
When: October

1K Race for Children and a 5K Race for Adolescents and Adults with Halloween Costumes optional. 10K Race for serious runners. Benefits literacy initiatives for elementary school students for whom English is a second language. Event co-sponsored by Concord Rotary Club. Entry fee includes spaghetti and meatballs lunch, and provides a $10 tax deductible donation.

Ghost Walk
Endeavor Hall
Clayton, CA
www.ci.clayton.ca.us
925-672-6171
When: October

Halloween Parade and Costume Contest
Todos Santos Plaza
Willow Pass Road and Grant Street
Concord, CA 94519
www.concordfirst.org
925-671-3464
When: October

Parade around the Plaza with treats for the kids. Event features entertainment and the Mayor's Mongrel Mash. Costume judging after the parade. Take a peek at the Todos Santos Scarecrow contest winner.

Hometown Halloween
Oak and First Streets
Brentwood, CA 94513
www.brentwoodchamber.org
When: October

Treats for all the trick-or-treaters in a safe and fun environment. The Brentwood Police Department hosts a "safety zone" teaching kids how to be visible during trick-or-treating. Also features fingerprinting, identifying contaminated candy, child seat inspections and face painting. AMR and the Contra Costa Fire Department will also be there.

Howe Harvest Festival
Howe Homestead Park
Walnut Creek, CA
When: October

Halloween activities for families including pumpkin carving, crafts, games, scarecrow making and a "Wicked Maze."

Indoor Flea Market
San Pablo Senior Center
1943 Church Lane
San Pablo, CA 94807
www.sanpabloevents.com
When: October

Pharaoh's Festival
Diablo Valley Lodge

4035 Treat Avenue
Concord, CA 94519
www.stmaryandstmina.org
When: October

A free event that's fun for all ages featuring ornaments, jewelry, clothing, gifts and delicious Egyptian food.

Primo's Run For Education 5K, Half Marathon
Iron Horse Middle School (Bishop Ranch/Alcosta)

San Ramon, CA
www.primosrun.com
925-820-9181
When: October

Lots of goodies and perks. A great family event.

Tarantula Run
Los Vaqueros Watershed

Brentwood, CA
www.rdysetgo.com
When: October

This event is a "trail run" with the majority of the course on dirt road and trail. All events wind through the beautiful Las Vaqueros Watershed. Special rates for youth under 14 and seniors over 60 in the 5K Run/Walk event. Costumes are encouraged.

Lafayette Reservoir Run

Lafayette, CA
www.lafayettechamber.org
When: October

The Lafayette Reservoir Run is the city's most popular "family affair," involving kids, parents, grandparents, and hundreds of serious runners from throughout the Bay Area. Over 2,000 participants compete in a 10k, 5k or 2 mile race through the heart of the downtown, around the reservoir and back. Sprinters, walkers, the "stroller brigade" and many of Lafayette's four legged residents share the streets on that festive Sunday morning.

Martinez Restaurant Tour

Martinez, CA
www.cityofmartinez.com
925-372-3510
925-370-8770
When: October

Oktoberfest

Downtown Clayton
Main Street
Clayton, CA 94517
www.claytonoktoberfest.com

925-672-2272

When: October

Arts, crafts, food and kids carnival rides

OktoberFest
Todos Santos Plaza

Willow Pass Road and Grant Street
Concord, CA 94519
www.concordfirst.org

When: October

Festivities include live music, a beer festival, food vendors, an activity area with games and activities for all ages, arts and craft vendors and a farmers' market. This is a free event.

City of Hercules Community Clean-Up Day
Hercules Middle/High School Parking Lot

Hercules, CA
www.ci.hercules.ca.us

When: November

Contra Costa Craft Faire
Contra Costa County Fairgrounds

Antioch, CA
www.ccfair.org

When: November

Unique booths including country and floral crafts, homemade candy, wood crafts and much more.

Gold Medal Turkey Trot
Pinole Valley High School

Pinole, CA

When: November

T-shirt and medals to all finishers. Turkey drawing for 5 turkeys.

Thanksgiving Community Breakfast

Lafayette, CA
www.lafayettechamber.org
When: November

Turkey Trot Run
Briones Regional Park

Orinda, CA
When: November

This is an 8.4 mile run at Briones Regional Park in Orinda and is not for beginning joggers—the course is hilly and entirely on trails.

Orchard Nursery & Florist

4010 Mt. Diablo Blvd.
Lafayette, CA 94549
925-284-4474
www.orchardnursery.com
Hour: Open Daily 9 am–5 pm

Orchard Nursery & Florist, voted the Best Garden Center in the East Bay, is a delightful place for the whole family to enjoy and investigate the endless possibilities of growing a garden together. Christmas offers a sparkling wonderland full of treasures collected from around the world. And don't forget to visit the Lazy K Gift House—a great source for exceptional gifts and unique accessories. From brand new babies to brides & grooms or gifts for anyone on your list, you're sure to find the perfect thing to fit the bill.

Here's a list of some great books to get you and your family started on some of your own traditions:

Everyday Traditions: Simple Family Rituals for Connection and Comfort

By Nava Atlas

I Love You Rituals

By Becky A. Bailey

Mrs. Sharp's Traditions—Reviving Victorian Family Celebrations of Comfort and Joy

By Sarah Ban Breathnach

The Book of New Family Traditions—How to create Rituals for Holidays and Everyday

By Meg Cox

Together: Creating Family Traditions

By Rondi Hillstrom Davis

The Intentional Family: Simple Rituals to Strengthen Family Ties

By William J. Doherty

New Traditions—Redefining Celebrations for Today's Family

By Susan Abel Lieberman

Little Things Long Remembered—Making Your Children Feel Special Every Day

By Susan Newmans

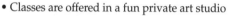

Parties and Gatherings

Whether you are planning a theme party at your home, or looking to move the party elsewhere, we think you'll find some of these local party resources helpful! Rent a "bounce house" or have a clown entertain. You'll find lots of ideas for the perfect party. Please see our chapter, "Places to Go" for locations that offer party packages.

Entertainers

1st Impressions Entertainment with Alan The Amazing and Friends

www.heyalan.com

510-65-PARTY

A few of their special activities for children ages 1–101 are magic shows, magic workshops, balloon animals, face painting, temporary tattoos, games, puppets, stories and arts & crafts.

An Awesome Entertainment & Party Company featuring Lovee'e the Clown

www.loveeetheclown.com

925-370-6108

Balloon animals, face painting, magic, games, story telling, train rides, juggling, puppeteers and more.

Ackerly Entertainment

www.ackerly-entertainment.com

408-246-8422

Phil's birthday party magic show (for kids ages 4 and up) makes your child the star of the party. The one-hour show incorporates age-appropriate magic with music, color, laughter and plenty of audience participation.

Add Some Fun

www.addsomefun.com

415-564-4981

Services include face painting, balloon sculptures, tattoo and henna, and magic. Services can be customized to fit your party/event needs. It is recommended that you book your party 4–6 weeks in advance (8 to be certain!).

Amazing Magic with Ric and Kara

925-787-6012

www.ricandkara.com

Three birthday party packages are available. The Pure Magic package is approximately one hour long and includes a 50 minute magic show that is extremely funny and highly interactive. They will magically float one child in the air, entertain with a funny puppet routine and for the big magic show finale, a live rabbit appears! The birthday child also gets a quick photo session holding the bunny in a top hat. The 30/30 Special is also an hour program and includes a 30 minute magic show and 30 minutes of balloon twisting. Finally, the 2 hour special features a one hour magic show and one hour of balloon twisting and face painting. Please call for pricing information.

Balloon Creations

www.ballooncreations.com

408-364-9633

Clowns, balloon entertainers, face painters, games specialists, fairy princesses, jugglers, cartoonists, magicians, mimes, impersonators, stilt walkers, themed characters, costumed characters and more!

Bay Area Magic Makers

www.bayareamagicmakers.com

415-333-3422

The husband and wife team of Naomi Caspe & Doug Kipping ("Duggy Wuggy") use the theatrical arts of clowning, mime, magic and storytelling to create a special event.

Boswick Turnstyle Jr., The Clown's Clown

www.boswick.net

415-665-1909

At a birthday party, the magic/comedy/juggling show will last from thirty to forty minutes depending on the attention span of the children. Performances include magic, juggling, physical comedy, audience participation, fire juggling, lots of "why did the chicken cross the road?" Jokes, acrobatic pratfalls, wily flirtations, and winsome tales that all lead to that great old Vaudeville feeling. All children will receive a balloon animal and Boswick is usually at the party for an hour.

Buki the Clown

www.bukitheclown.com

510-522-2229
800-352-8004

Buki provides face painting and Buki's Silly Magic Show, where the children perform the magic!

California Puppets

www.californiapuppets.com

707-552-4379

Three shows to choose from featuring Jungle Joe, a professional puppeteer and ventriloquist. His unique style makes his shows both educational and entertaining.

Carla Winter's Entertainment

www.c-winternet.com

925-937-5457

Face painting, henna tattoos, glitter tattoos, caricaturists, party psychics, graphology, balloon twisters, magicians, Santa and holiday acts, musicians and novelty acts.

Children's Delight

www.childrensdelight.com

408-267-7272

Character shows, including Cinderella, Anastasia and Prince Charming, balloon artists and face painters.

The Clown Co.

www.theclownco.com

415-621-2188
510-653-9450

Clowns, magicians, costume characters, magic and juggling, music and more!

Clowns 4 Less

www.clowns4less.com

866-227-5008

Magic, balloon animals, games and face painting. Party packages are ideal for birthday children ages 1–7 years old. All clowns are trained by a former Ringling Bros. Barnum & Bailey Circus clown.

Daffy Dave

www.daffydave.com

650-326-3711

Magic, slapstick comedy, cool goodie bags, kid-tested balloon sculptures, goofy juggling and plate spinning, fun audience participation, and funny ukulele songs.

Dan Chan the Magic Man

www.danchanmagic

415-244-2700

Magic, juggling, acrobatics, fire breathing, balloon sculptures, escapes and more.

Dennis Loomis

www.loomismagic.com

925-429-5201

Magical entertainment and balloon sculptures.

Dono the Clown

www.donotheclown.com

415-552-8104

Magic shows, balloon animals and hats.

Dreamstar Parties

www.dreamstarparties.com

866-516-7827

Magic, balloon twisting, storytelling with puppets, hula dancing, fairy dancing, games, face painting and bubble options. Party characters include fairy princesses, kid-friendly clowns, silly swashbuckling pirates, wise wizards and mermaids.

Everyday Sunny

www.everydaysunny.com

415-297-6845

Face painting, balloon twisting, magic making, songs and games, and creative crafts.

Family Fun Airbrush Tattoos

www.airbrush-tattoos.com

707-373-1863

From solid black tribal bands to multi-colored flowers, these tattoos can survive from a couple of days to 2 weeks with the proper care. While long-lasting, these tattoos can be quickly and easily removed with baby oil and/or rubbing alcohol. The water-based paints are incredibly durable yet easily removed and dry instantly and the paints will not come off on clothing.

Fire Pixie Entertainment

www.firepixie.com/parties

510-367-4517

Select a theme from Diva, Princess, Fantasy, Adventure and Simple and Seasonal parties or create your own party. Rates are hourly so you can choose as many activities as you want.

Flying Teapot Puppets

www.flyingteapot.com

Margaret@flyingteapot.com

Well-crafted puppet shows in your home. These gently shows are for children ages 2–6 and feature a full-size puppet stage, beautiful puppets, live music, interactive singing, and a variety of puppet styles and techniques.

The Fratello Marionettes

www.fratellomarionettes.com

925-984-3401

Current shows include The North Pole Review, The Vaudeville Follies, Peter and the Wolf, The Art of the Puppet and Pierre's Birthday Surprise. The Frog Prince will be available in April, 2008. See website for details.

Friendly Pony Parties and Barnyard Pals

www.friendlyponyparty.com

650-738-0248

Single pony parties, multiple pony parties, and pony carousels are available. Additional -features include pony photos, face painting, theme parties and a mobile petting zoo.

Funtastic Parties

www.funtasticparties.us

510-851-4577

Fairytale characters and fantastic face painting.

Ginger Snaps the Clown

925-829-6386

Jilliene Designs

www.jilliene.com

408-656-3522

Parties start at $150 and include an art, craft, scrapbook or card making project customized for the group's age, gender and occasion. Each child receives a complete class kit with everything they will need to complete the project. Set-up and clean-up is provided and games and prizes and lots of silliness can be incorporated into your party's theme.

Lee Curtis the Magical Wizard

www.magicalwizard.com

800-436-8749

Leo Luna the Magician

www.leoscolorfulmagic.homestead.com

925-846-3888

Live rabbits and doves.

The Lizard Lady

www.lizardladyreptiles.com

650-355-4105

Your child needs to be at least 4 years old for a birthday visit. The show is tailored to children from 4–12. Birthday boys or girls get to be the Lizard Lady's helper. For an optimum reptile petting experience plan an indoor location. The reptiles will be much more relaxed. The Lizard Lady does not present her program in parks. Each show includes 10 to 13 snakes, lizards and tortoise from the deserts, forests, grasslands and rainforest. Programs run 45 minutes to an hour. There is a limit of 20 children for this show, though less than 15 is recommended. A $15 fee is added per child over 20 if a large party is planned. Please call for East Bay prices.

The Magic of Chin Chin

www.chin-chin.com `

415-577-9345

Hilarious interactive magic. Balloon animals are also available.

Magic of Gerald Joseph

www.geraldsmagic.com

925-778-3757

Sleight-of-hand magic and state-of-the-art illusions.

Magic Dan

www.magicdan.com

415-337-8500

A blend of fast-paced magic and a whole lot of fun.

Magic Princess

www.magicprincess.com

888-5MAGIC

Price: $119 weekdays, $169 weekends for 90 minutes

Girl and boy themed parties that can include magic shows, face painting, fairy dancing, hula songs, puppet shows and balloons. For 12 children or less there is usually time for 3 activities. And, for $129 you can rent any one of their enormous jump houses.

The Magic of Norman Ng

www.nmagic4kids.com

800-307-8959

Norman's show includes his puppet sidekick Bob the Rabbit, his famous "Mystery of the Vanishing Knot," and children who make money fall from the sky! Two birthday packages to choose from... both include a 40 minute Komedy Magic Show and unique coloring books containing scenes from Norman's show. Please call for pricing information.

MagicMinis

www.magicminis.com

415-309-3689

Prices: Packages range from $125–$499

Balloon twisting, face painting, glitter tattoos and magic shows.

Miss Carol's Magical Puppet Time

www.magicalpuppetime.com

650-620-9280

Miss Carol features her own handcrafted marionette puppets in a cabaret variety show where puppets perform a vast array of acts referred to as vignettes (short skits). They sing, dance, play musical instruments, do comical things, tell stories and jokes, perform circus tricks like juggling, and perform magical illusions and more.

Most Unique Parties & Ponies

www.mostunique.com

831-338-9130

Face painting, magic with animals, twisty balloons, puppets, and mini-horse cart rides.

My Pony Party

www.myponyparty.com

408-847-6424

One hour parties that can include pony rides, petting zoos, pony led cart rides, and reptile shows. Please call for East Bay pricing.

National Puppet Theatre

www.nationalpuppets.com

408-309-2348

Price: From $100–$200

Parties can include puppets, sing-a-longs, games, crafts or stories. The puppets will sing a personalized birthday song with you child's name and age, and as a special gift, your child will receive a CD recording of the song.

Nature Connections

www.natureconnections.com

406-223-8066

Indoor and outdoor party packages for girls and boys, ages 4 and up. Party themes include bugs, rocketry, and wizardry. Parties are $99 for 8 children and $10 for each additional child plus mileage costs of $1/mile, for one way travel. Science discovery bags are $5 per child and include such items as magnifying glasses, observation boxes, petri dishes and pipettes for further discovery. They also contain chocolate, lollipops and 2 toys related to the theme of your party choice.

Nick Barone Puppets

www.nbpuppets.com

650-365-8070

Original and traditional tales, told in classic style and featuring superbly crafted puppets. A full puppet stage, lights and sound system, complete with a professionally recorded soundtrack featuring music, songs, and sound effects are brought to your home or event location. Current shows include Puss in Boots, Holiday Treats, Tales from the Enchanted Forest and T-Rex Thunderlizard's Wild West Revue. After the performance, Nick removes the stage curtains and demonstrates the puppets he designed and built specifically for each original production. Nick will demonstrate how he operated his puppets during the performance and explain a little about how he constructed them.

Noah's Ark Traveling "Stuff-N-Fluff" Animal Workshop

www.nohsarkworkshop.com

866-HUG-NOAH

This party comes to you! The birthday child gets a free stuffed animal in a birthday outfit and you are supplied with party invitations. You set the price of your party by selecting the un-stuffed animal, animal outfits and t-shirts. Each workshop guest will hand-stuff a cuddly friend. It's birthday party entertainment and a party favor in one!

Ponies R Us

www.partyponies.com

925-228-1734

Pony rides, sweet & gentle ponies.

Roy Porfido

www.magicshows.org

925-455-0600

The birthday child is used twice in the show; once near the beginning and once at the end. At the end of the show the birthday child becomes a magician (with a special little wizard hat) and he/she does the last magic trick in the show. There is ALWAYS a live bunny (Fluffy) in the show. The magic show itself runs forty-five minutes, then, depending on how many guests you have, another fifteen to twenty minutes for all the children to pet the rabbit, to give out a party favor and for the group to sing "Happy Birthday" in a very special manner. A typical birthday party show runs an hour to an hour and five minutes.

Sir Lantz

www.sirlantz.com

925-280-0112

877-611-6200

Perfect for children 5 years and older. Most magic shows average about 45 minutes and include live animals (bunny, bird, goldfish) and a candy toss. The birthday boy or girl will be Sir Lantz's assistant and star of the show.

Smiley Clown

www.smileyclown.com

510-305-5276

Balloon animals/sculptures, face painting with fun sparkles, great games, parachute fun, magic, music, prizes and more.

Spectrum of Science

www.spectrumofscience.com

925-820-2415

Provides customized, no mess, no fuss, high energy, interactive science parties for kids of all ages. The basic party ($200 + mileage) includes 15 participants (parents and grandparents are free), 15 science trading cards custom to birthday theme and a home-made, hands-on activity. Parties are 45 to 60 minutes.

Super Hero Station

www.superherostation.com

superherostation@yahoo.com

The show offers a variety of popular superhero scenes with special effects, choreography and props. At the end of each performance, the characters answer questions from the audience, pose for photographs and sign autographs.

Tickle Me Pony Rides

www.ponyparty.com

925-756-7335

925-447-7997

Pony parties, traveling petting zoo, mini-petting zoo, face painting, and cart and pony rides are available. See website for complete price list.

Tumble Express—A Gym on Wheels

www.tumbleexpress.com

650-654-2000

For children ages 2–6. The gym on wheels is equipped with tumble mats, rings, a zip line, balance beam, climbing ropes, a slide, trampoline, monkey bars, rock climbing wall and more. The cost is $225 for 1 hour of time on the bus. A Tumble Express Instructor will lead up to 15 children at a time, in a fun stretching warm-up exercise. Children will be lead through a series of obstacle courses and have an opportunity to try all of the equipment. Games and music will be incorporated as well. For groups that exceed 15 children, add $5 per additional child. The birthday child also receives a Tumble Express T-Shirt. Party Bags will be provided for the entire party. Please call for travel fees.

Tye the Magic Guy

www.tyethemagicguy.com

800-784-6064

The birthday child is declared the "Star of the Show" and is made to feel very special. Your "Star" will shine on stage with Tye and be the envy of all their friends. During one of the magical routines your child will become a magician and "make the magic happen." The Magic Show is thirty minutes and after the show you have a choice of all the children receiving animal balloons, or teaching the children easy-to-do magic tricks with everyday objects. Ideally this activity is for children 7 years and up, but age 6 is OK.

Zappo the Magician

www.zappothemagician.com

925-676-2776

Nearly 40 years of performing magic. Best suited for kids ages 4 and up.

Party and Event Planners

Bay Area Entertainment Network

www.entertainment-bayarea.com

408-945-7779

Specializing in providing quality talent for your event. Clients include balloon twisters and decorators, character entertainers, clowns, caricature artists, face painting, henna artists, jugglers, magicians, musicians, and more.

Fun with a Twist

www.funwithatwist.com

866-431-8708

Offering site selection, performers of all genres, catering, décor, event rentals, props, music, ponies/petting zoos, and more.

Laborfair.com

www.laborfair.com

Your FREE trusted solution for all your professional, household, personal and family care...get EVERYTHING and ANYTHING done for a fair price!

- FREE and direct access to thousands of quality local providers in 28 categories!
- Find Handymen, Housekeepers, Painters, Childcare, Private Lessons, and more!
- Find providers with specific skills such as CPR, Can Drive
- Trusted ratings, reviews and references
- Best of all, fair prices for everyone!

Learn what Bay Area Hip Mama's call a "necessity." Check us out today!

Social Butterfly Events

www.socialbutterfly-events.com

925-408-6627

High-end children's mobile theme parties and entertainment. Whimsical, magical and fun ideas Including Pink Princess, Rock with Hannah, Twinkle Toes, Garden Fairies, Barnyard, custom parties and more. They do all the planning, shopping, decorating, set-up and clean-up, entertainment and even host!

Sparkle Events

www.sparkle-events.com

408-464-2480

Themed children's parties include Darling Fairies (for ages 4–6 only), Princess for a Day (recommended for ages 5–8), Hawaiian Luau, Dazzling Diva (ages 6 and up), and more. Tween party themes can include a retro 60's party, a psychic sleep-over (ages 8 and up), and a Spa scent-sation (ages 8 and up). Refer to website for pricing.

Party Facilities

Best Little Barnyard

3280 Bixler Road
Brentwood, CA 94513
www.kalanacorral.com
www.bestlittlebarnyeard.com

925-628-4071

Hours: By reservation (typically parties are booked in 3 hour increments)
Price: Depends on activities chosen; please call for details

Pony rides, petting zoo, arts & crafts, games, and barn fun are all available. No kitchen facilities, but outside food is welcome.

Castle Rock Arabians

1350 Castle Rock Road
Walnut Creek, CA 94598
www.castlerockarabians.com

925-937-7661

Price: Three party packages to choose from, ranging in price from $265–$300

Magee, the birthday pony, will highlight your party for a day of fun. Magical Moments, Special Birthday, and Buckaroo Birthday packages available. All packages include a special option to "design your own party" for an additional $65. See website for details.

Chicz on the Go

www.chiczonthego.net

1-877-933-6644

Chicz on the go specializes in survival kits for young female athletes for weekend-long soccer tournaments to daylong swim meets. They offer bags for soccer, basketball, softball, volleyball, swimming/water polo, lacrosse, golf, chorus and dance all with specialized products that girls need before, during and after sports games. Having a birthday party chicz on the go can create custom party favors.

Children Theatre Party

2363 Boulevard Circle
Walnut Creek, CA 94595
www.thecleancomedycompany.com

925-943-6252

Hours: Generally on Sundays, but flexible

Price: $150 for 10 kids, 2 hour session

Acting/theme parties for children ages 6–12. On-site theatre, scripts, and costumes provided. Show is taped and birthday child will receive a video gift.

Clayton Valley Bowl

5300 Clayton Road
Concord, CA 94521
www.claytonvalleybowl.com

925-689-4631

Hours: Sun.–Thurs. 10 am–Midnight, Fri.–Sat. 10 am–1 am.

Clayton Valley Bowl is where families and friends come to play. This is the perfect place to hold a birthday party or event for up to 120 people. Everyone loves to bowl and the best part is, you don't have to worry about cleaning up the mess! Choose between three popular packages. All packages include plates, napkins, cups, balloons, free-bowling coupons, invitations, and a bowling souvenir for the birthday child. A party host supervises all this. Don't forget the very popular Digital Thunder for kids on Friday nights 4 pm–6 pm. Visit their website or call for more information.

Color Me Mine

1950 Mt. Diablo Blvd.
Walnut Creek, CA 94596
www.walnutcreek.colormemine.com

925-280-2888

Hours: Monday–Friday 11 am–9 pm, Saturday and Sunday 11 am–5 pm. May thru October, 11 am–8 pm weekdays, Saturday and Sunday 11 am–5 pm

Prices: Party packages are $7/person for one and one half hours and $10/person for a two hour party PLUS the price of the pottery.

There is an 8-guest minimum for all parties. Color Me Mine provides a staff member to assist your guests in the painting process. The party will be all set up for you and when your guests have finished painting, they will clean up and put down fresh table paper and turn your guests over to you for any other activities you would like to provide, i.e. cake, pizza, opening presents, etc. Party invitations are also available for an additional $1/each.

Diablo Gymnastics School

2411-J Old Crow Canyon Road
San Ramon, CA 94583
www.diablogym.com

925-820-6885

Hours: Call for availability

Price: Base price (up to 10 children) $170. $16 for each additional guest. Maximum of 16 children.

Games, relays, obstacle courses, trampolines... it's a healthy way to celebrate a special day! Basic party includes one hour and 45 minutes of fun, two party hosts, one hour of games and activities, tableware and decorations, set-up and clean up, free t-shirt for the birthday child and juice.

Earl Anthony's Dublin Bowl

6750 Regional Street
Dublin, CA 94568
www.earlanthonysdublinbowl.com

925-828-7550

Hours: Open at 9 am everyday

For birthday parties, family outings, play dates or youth and adult leagues, this is the place to be. Come for the Kids Afternoon Special Mon.–Fri. 2 pm–5 pm; one game of bowling, shoe rental, hot dog and soda all for one low price. Visit the website for information on birthday parties, reduced price offers, youth and adult leagues.

Encore Gymnastics

999 Bancroft Road
Walnut Creek, CA 94518
www.encoregym.com/wc/htm/wc_home.html

925-932-1033

Price: $220 for a maximum of 12 participants

You may choose from a Pirate, Princess, Hawaiian, or Superhero party theme (see website for details). The standard birthday party package is as follows:

The first 45 minutes of parties for children turning 1, 2, or 3 years old includes a super fun warm-up, gymnastic obstacle course, awesome jump house, and the famous trampoline and foam pit. The last 45 minutes are for cake and present opening. Each child must be accompanied by an adult, both with a signed waiver form.

The first hour of parties for children turning 4 or older includes rock climbing (for kids turning 6 and older), a gymnastic obstacle course, activities on the gymnastic equipment and the famous trampoline and foam pit. The last hour is for a super fun themed craft, cake, and present opening. Up to 14 participants is $250; each additional participant is $15 (20 person maximum).

A reservation deposit of $60 is non-refundable and required at time of booking for either package.

Sand Creek Crossing Center

2490 Sand Creek Road
Brentwood, CA 94513
www.encoregym.com/bw/htm/bw_aboutus.html

925-240-1133

Golden Gate Gymnastics

1441 C Franquette Avenue
Concord, CA 94520
www.goldengategymnastics.com/php/bday.php

925-674-9683

Hours: Call for availability

Price: Complete Birthday Party Package is $150

One and one half hours of fun and excitement includes 1 hour of fun in the gym and one half hour for cake and presents. Golden Gate will provide private use of the gym and party area, set-up of party area, decorations, tablecloth, plates, cups and utensils.

Parties and Gatherings

Gymboree Play & Music

1st Street Corner
3482 Mt. Diablo Blvd.
Lafayette, CA 94549
925-283-4896

Ages: 6 mos.–5 years
Hours: Call your local Gymboree location for party availability._
Price: Call for details

Make your birthday boy or girl feel extra-special with a party—Gymboree style! Kids will be wowed with colorful parachutes, tunnels and bridges. An enthusiastic teacher will lead the group in play and song with activities geared specifically for a first through fifth birthday.

Willows Shopping Center

1975 Diamond Blvd. #C-130
Concord, CA 94520
925-283-4896

Crow Canyon Commons

3191-A Crow Canyon Place
San Ramon, CA 94583
925-866-8315

Gymtastic

1901 Camino Ramon, #D
Danville, CA 94526
www.gymtastic.com
925-277-1881

Hours: Call for party availability
Price: Parties are $285 for up to 20 children–$10 for each additional child. Party price includes invitations and thank you cards, gift list, party instructions, set-up & clean-up, paper goods, juice and a helium balloon for each child. Party Favors available for $3.50 per child. A $100 non-refundable deposit is required to reserve a party date. Members receive a $25 discount.

Start with 19 of your child's friends, add an hour of instructed gymnastics and tumbling, group games, music and fun, mix with one half hour for cake, juice and presents, and top with a helium balloon for each child!

Liberty Gymnastics

2330 Bates Avenue
Concord, CA 94519
www.libertygymtrainingcenter.com
925-687-8009

Price: A $50 deposit to guarantee your spot is required. Parties are 1 hour 45 minutes long and cost $150 for a group of ten. Each additional person is $10.

Two safety certified gymnastics coaches will guide the birthday group through fun games and obstacle courses. Tables and chairs for the second part of the party are provided. Decorations and food are up to you. A refrigerator and freezer are provided in case you need things to stay cool. The seating area will hold up to 30 people, but if you need more space, let them know ahead of time so arrangements can be made. Invitations that include all the necessary information for your guests about your birthday party are also provided. It is recommended that you reserve your party one to two months in advance. You can book your party over the phone or in person.

The Little Gym of Brentwood... COMING SOON!

The Little Gym of Danville

3612 Blackhawk Plaza Circle
Danville, CA 94506
www.tlgdanvilleca.com

925- 736-3141

Hours: Parties are held on Friday, Saturday and Sunday afternoons. Ask a team member or call for available dates and times as reservations fill quickly.

Price: Call for details

Your fully supervised private party will be filled with music, games, and obstacle courses that your children will love. And they'll take care of everything—from invitations to clean-up.

The Little Gym of Pleasant Hill

115 Crescent Drive
Pleasant Hill, CA 94523
www.tlgpleasanthillca.com

925- 798-1800

Hours: Saturdays 2 pm, 4 pm, 6 pm and Sundays 11 am, 1 pm, 3 pm, 5 pm. All parties are 90 minutes long.

Price: Call for details

TLG parties include invitations (addressed, stamped and mailed for you!), a qualified birthday leader plus an assistant, all the set-up and clean-up, all the paper goods (plates, forks, cups, napkins), drinks for each child in the party room, a The Little Gym T-shirt for the Birthday Child and a gift registry (if you open your presents while you're there) The kids have the gym to themselves and the instructors facilitate games and activities! Please book early as parties book 4–6 weeks in advance.

Parties and Gatherings

My Gym

180 Market Place
San Ramon, CA 94583
www.my-gym.com/party_fran.asp?gymid=170

925-244-1171

Hours: Fridays 3 pm–7 pm, Saturdays 1:30 pm–6:30 pm, Sundays 10 am–6 pm

Price: 1 1/2 hrs (your package) $250/$275 for member/nonmember, 1 1/2 hrs (our package) $290/$315 for member/nonmember, 2 hrs (your package) $300/325 for member/nonmember, 2 hrs (our package) $340/$365 for member/nonmember. Please book in advance. $100 non-refundable deposit required.

Parties are 1.5 to 2 hours of nonstop fun. Their perfectly planned celebrations are created specifically for your child and include special song and game requests made prior to party. Games, gymnastics, space flight, puppets, rides, songs and exciting birthday events come with the package. All children participate in constant activity for the full length of the party and you have exclusive use of the facility! My Gym Party Packages include all set-up, decorations, plates, tablecloths, napkins, forks, invitations and thank you notes, cleanup and service of refreshments for 20 children with an extra charge for additional youngsters. Party favors available at an added cost.

2256 Oak Grove Road
Walnut Creek, CA 94598
www.my-gym.com/03.asp?page=5&gymid=50

925-952-9791

Hours: Friday parties can begin as early as 4:30 pm, Saturday parties begin at 1:30 pm and continue throughout the day, Sunday parties begin as early as 10 am and continue throughout the day.

Price: 2 hour party with their theme Members $340/Non-Members $365, 2 hour party with your own theme Members $300/Non-members $325, 1 1/2 hour party with their theme Members $290/Non-Members $315, 1 1/2 hour party with your own theme Members $250/Non-Members $275. A $100 non-refundable deposit is required. There is an additional $50 for 21–25 children.

Just Your Party

2411 Old Crow Canyon Road # T
San Ramon, CA 94583

925-837-2110

Hours: Call for availability

Price: Friday–Sunday $325. Monday–Thursday $275. Each additional child over 24 children is $10/child.

This is a 2-hour party that includes approximately 1 hour and 25 minutes in the game area for up to 24 kids to climb, bounce and slide and approximately 30 minutes in the private party room. The sports theme inflatable is used for most events but if your party is for kids 5 and under they are happy to switch it for animal land which is just for the little ones. Color invitations are provided upon booking. They will also provide paper plates, napkins and cups in the party room. All those using the games must sign a waiver to play and all guests must wear socks on the inflatable games and the climbing wall. Extras include pizza, goody bags and balloons.

Kids 'N Dance

www.kidsndance.com/birthday_parties.htm

Hours: House Party Saturdays and Sundays 1 pm–3 pm or 3:30 pm–5:30 pm, Studio Party Saturdays 1:10 pm–3:10 pm, Sundays 1 pm–3 pm or 3:30 pm–5:30 pm

Price: $175 for either House Party or Studio Party. $3 for each additional child

House Party—Includes 1 hour of dance adventures taught in your home. Costumes and music are supplied. Party package includes a Kids 'N Dance T-shirt for the birthday child. Studio Party includes the 1 hour of dance adventures plus an extra hour with your teacher. The teacher may fill your second hour of time by helping to organize cake and presents for you or play games with the children. This may include some of the equipment in the studio, games, more dancing, or simply be a way to help you organize and clean-up. The second hour is fashioned individually between the teacher and the family having the birthday. Party package includes a Kids 'N Dance T-shirt for the birthday child. Every one-hour adventure includes five or six dances that are first told as a story and then physically led by one of our teachers. There are costume changes that occur with each new dance! Parties may include 12 children. Refer to website for birthday party themes available.

Lafayette Dance Center

3369 Mt. Diablo Blvd.
Lafayette, CA 94549
925-284-7388

Oakland Studio

3841 Macarthur Blvd.
Oakland, CA 94610
510-531-4400

Mad Science Parties & Events

2337 Boulevard Circle
Walnut Creek, CA 94598
www.madscience.org/mtdiablo

925-941-1500

Hours: Saturdays and Sundays at 11:30 am, 1:30 pm and 4 pm. Weekday parties subject to instructor availability.

Parties and Gatherings

Mad Science parties entertain children of all ages (especially for boys and girls ages 4–10) with exciting, high-energy, interactive shows that come to you and can be held at your home, pizza place, park, etc. Turn your child into a Jr. Mad Scientist with a no-mess, hassle-free party where the birthday child receives a free Mad Science T-shirt and gets to be the assistant. You have the choice of a show theme as well as the option of Grand Finale extras like hovercraft rides, dry ice shows and laser shows. All party guests leave Mad Science parties with fun and educational take-home experiments like slippery slime, fantastic "floam," Mad Science putty, or super bouncy balls! All Mad Science Parties are approximately 45–60 minutes long. Call for pricing.

North Gait Equestrian Center

1101 North Gate Road
Walnut Creek, CA 94598
www.northgait.com/index/mn27106/Welcome

925-932-2282

Hours: Call for availability
Price: $35 per child. MINIMUM 17 kids; additional kids are also $35 per child

All parties are designed for boys and girls ages 6 and up. The Center has a fully covered area allowing for parties all year long. Sessions last approximately 2–3 hours and include interesting horse facts and safety rules, petting and handling the horse, and an instructional lead line riding around the arena. Riding instruction for each child will be provided either on or off a lead depending on the child's experience. Kids will also have fun painting the horse and learning anatomy, roping, tug-of-war, water balloon toss, a craft and a special gift. You must supply all food and beverages. Eight balloons are provided and additional balloons are added upon request at $1.50 per balloon. A mylar horse balloon is $15.

Picture Perfect Party

4564 Dublin Blvd.
Dublin CA 94568
www.pictureperfectparty.biz

925-828-3311

Hours: 9:30 am–5:30 pm Mon.–Sat. and 10 am–5 pm Sunday

Picture Perfect Party is a party facility that specializes in children ages 0–6. We host fun birthday parties in a child-safe, age-appropriate, interactive place and take digital party photos that parents can take home the same day! We also have drop-in play time, host playgroups and have special events for kids during the week. It is fun for kids, stress-free parents and memorable for all! Visit us at www.pictureperfectparty.biz.

Pixieland Amusement Park

2740 East Olivera Road
Concord, CA 94519
www.pixieland.com

925-689-8841

Hours: Vary by season

Pixieland Amusement Park is a hidden gem right here in our own backyard! Pixieland, located in Concord, has been one of the Bay Area's best kept secrets for more than 50 years! The Park features 7 rides that the tots will love including the famous G-16 Train, the "Dragon" Roller Coaster, Antique Cars, Frog Hopper, Red Baron Airplanes, Tea Cups and a Carousel. Visit for an hour, or stay the whole day with free admission and parking. Enjoy their famous hand dipped corn dogs, freshly spun cotton candy (two of many items) or bring your own snacks! Pixieland is the perfect setting for your special Birthday Party celebration! Open February through November. Please visit their website or call for more information.

Play Café

4400 Keller Avenue
Oakland, CA 94605
www.playcafewebsite.com
info@playcafewebsite.com

510-632-4433

Play Café was created by parents for parents and their children. The play area is a kid-sized town full of interactive and imaginative play elements. Whether it's cooking up some food in our Malt Shoppe, trying on costumes and putting on a show in our Theatre; or just taking a dip in our "Swimmin' Hole" ball pool, your children are sure to find plenty of activities to explore! Birthdays are our specialty at Play Café!

Pump It Up of Concord

1301 Franquette Avenue
Concord, CA 94520
www.pumpitupparty.com

925-969-9663

Jump, Climb, Slide, and Bounce your way into Pump It Up, America's #1 Inflatable Party Zone! Pump It Up, voted "Best Place to Have a Birthday Party," features giant, custom designed, fun-filled, interactive inflatable play structures.

You and your guests will love celebrating in our private, clean, safe, and climate-controlled inflatable play arenas and brightly decorated party rooms. Our friendly, trained staff will help ensure your party is one you and your guests will never forget!

Pump It Up is the perfect place to host your next birthday party, team party, field trip, club/group outing, fundraiser, corporate teambuilding, or other special event.

Pump It Up of Oakley

5351 Neroly Road
Oakley, CA 94561

Rancho Saguaro

1050 Pereira Road
Martinez, CA 94553
925-372-5867
Hours: Please call for availability
Price: Call or email laura@saguaroequine.com

No experience is necessary to have a great time riding at Rancho Saguaro. Each child is led on a ride by one of the staff and then allowed to brush or feed carrots to the horses. Picnic tables and a meeting room with tables and kitchen facilities are available. You can bring your own activities for after the ride, or they can supply all the fun, including the cake and party favors.

RKidz Club

11533 Dublin Canyon Road
Pleasanton, CA 94588
www.rclubif.com/html/rparties.html

925-463-1390

Hours: Party times are currently reserved only on Sundays between Noon and 5 pm. Please go to the RKidzClub calendar on their website for available times and dates.

Price: $120

Parties are for up to 12 kids between the ages of 6–17 and include 45 minutes of exclusive use of the fitness club. This includes a 25 minute structured fitness class led by a staff member and 20 minutes of exclusive use of entertaining fitness equipment such as Dance, Dance Revolution, GameBikes connected to Sony Playstations, PowerGrid Fitness Exerstations also connected to Playstation or Xbox. A decorated party room filled with balloons is yours for 45 minutes, where paper goods (plates, cups, napkins, forks) will be supplied. A dedicated party host will see to all of the details and will give the birthday child an RClub t-shirt and all of the guests a one week pass to RKidzClub Interactive Fitness. All participants must wear tennis shoes and socks. "Play clothes" are recommended. Pants, blue jeans or "nice clothes" should be avoided. Girls in dresses or skirts will not be able to participate in the fitness class. Remember this is a fitness club and the kids will get sweaty!

SewNow! Fashion Studio

960 Moraga Road
Lafayette, CA 94549
www.sewnow.com

925-283-7396

Hours: Monday–Saturday 9 am–5 pm (and during evening classes)

Price: $300 for up to 10 children

Little girls (ages 8+) will love to embellish their jeans, bling up their sneakers, make a scarf, or create a monogrammed tote or purse at this unique birthday spot. All parties include a sewing machine lesson and a hands-on project (supplies included).

Touchstone Concord

1220 Diamond Way, Suite 140
Concord, CA 94519
www.touchstoneclimbing.com/kids.html

925-602-1000

Hours: Please call for availability

Price: $100 for 5 children; $20 each additional child

Staff provides basic instruction and belaying for all party participants. Ratio of staff members to children is one to six or better. After climbing, celebrate in a private party area. Bring your own food and drinks or call for take-out. Parties start on the hour during regular gym hours and include two hours of rock climbing and use of a party area. You must reserve your event at least two weeks in advance. A deposit is required at the time of reservation.

Rentals & Party Supplies

A Tasty Freeze-Frozen Drink Machine Rentals
925-937-721

Aero Jump
925-674-0916

All Day Jumpers
925-977-9788

Amusement Warehouse
925-932-2515

Aromatherapy & Fairy Fun!
925-254-1122

Astro Jump Contra Costa
www.astrojump.com
925-687-5867
In addition to a great selection of inflatables, Astro Jump also rents cotton candy, popcorn and sno-cone machines.

Babaloons & Tunes
www.babaloons.com
888-339-7925
Singing Telegrams and balloon bouquets. Same-day delivery.

The Balloon Man
www.balloonmanonline.com
925-934-3186
Balloon decorating and bouquet deliveries.

Balloons for You
925-672-1432

Balloon Thrills
www.balloonthrills.com
www.balloonplanet.com
925-671-6961

Bay Area Jump

www.bayareajump.com

800-514-5867

Jumpers, entertainers, carnival games, tables, chairs, tents, and concession machines.

Best Bounce

www.bestbounce.com

925-833-8000

Bounce houses and party equipment.

Boswell's Discount Party Supplies

Mt. Diablo Blvd.
Lafayette, CA 94549
925-284-9150

5759 Pacheco Blvd.
Pacheco, CA 94553
925-676-3092

1901 Camino Ramon
Danville, CA 94526
925-866-1644

3160 Santa Rita Road
Pleasanton, CA 94583
925-461-3000

Bounceworld Rental Co.

925-363-5867

Bouncin Bins

www.bouncinbin.com

888-858-9258

Jump houses (wet and dry), water games, sports games, carnival games, food machines, etc. Over 300 units to choose from.

BYC Parties & Events

www.backyardcarnivals.com

925-945-1351

Parties and Gatherings

California Slush
925-828-2247

Chuck's Candy Park
925-682-8569

Do Me Favors
www.domefavorspartyfavors.com
925-2385

Face Painting
925-939-3744

Frozen Concoctions Frozen Drink & SnoCone Rental
925-935-6211

The Fun Factory
www.funfactoryparties.com
888-501-4FUN

Party characters, clowns, bounce houses, pony rides, petting zoos, balloons, costumes and accessories, decorations, refreshment machines, games, themed paper supplies, magicians, tents and furniture, piñatas, and super slides.

Jump For Fun
www.jumpforfun.com
800-281-6792

Various licensed jumpers, dunk tanks, sno-cone, cotton candy, and hot dog machines.

The Jumpy Company
www.jumpycompany.com
925-753-0597

In addition to jumpys, they offer slush, cotton candy, sno-cone hot dog and popcorn machines for rent. Free set-up and delivery.

Party America
545 Contra Costa Blvd.
Pleasant Hill, CA 94523
925-685-3500

Party Time Paper & Crafts
4511 Clayton Road
Concord, CA 94519
925-674-0565

Slush Connection
www.slushconnection.com
925-828-0655
Frozen drink machine rentals.

Sports Time Parties
www.sportstimeparties.com
925-787-7856
Games and house bouncers for all occasions.

Surprises
40 Adak Court
Walnut Creek, CA 94598
925-295-1280

Sweet Celebrations
170 Alamo Plaza
Alamo, CA 94507
925-855-1713

14 Crockett Drive
Moraga, CA 94556
925-631-9430

T Minus One
www.arcadeparty.com
925-932-3333
Pinball machines, video games, juke boxes, pool tables, air hockey and foosball rentals.

At Home Fun

The next time boredom strikes in your household try some of these fun and easy at home activities. Kick back and have fun with your kids! These ideas are also great for playgroups.

Tips for Working with Kids

- Encourage all art projects as a process, not product activity. What may be a mess to you could be a new planet, zoo or the next NASA spacecraft to your child. Allowing our children to explore on their own not only develops creativity, but also teaches problem solving, spatial relationships as well as cause and effect. These are skills they will need later for math and other academics.
- Refrain from showing examples of a completed project, especially one that has been completed by an adult. Provide the supplies and instructions and they will do the rest.
- Resist asking, "What is it?" Instead try, "Tell me about it."
- Avoid automatic praise such as "that's beautiful" or "very good." Asking your young artist how they feel about their creation and the experience of making it will build confidence and language arts skills.
- For easy cleanup when working with a group, rotate a bucket of warm soapy water for hand washing and be sure that they all have a clean paper towel for drying.

The Idea Box

Begin a new "Boredom Cure" with a tissue or shoebox. Have your little ones decorate it and when you come across an idea that strikes your fancy, write it on a slip of paper and place it in the box. Send them running to the idea box when they say they are bored. You can start by taking ideas from the Bay Area Mama's Handbook! It's best to select activities that can be accomplished independently.

At Home Fun

Make a Paper Bag Head

Put a happy face on a plain paper bag!
You will need:

- Colored Markers
- Plain lunch size paper bag
- White crayon or chalk
- Stapler
- Raffia

Use the markers to draw scarecrow-style facials feature on the bag. Use the white crayon or chalk for eyes and teeth. Once the bag is filled with goodies or lunch, staple the top closed and add a bundle of raffia for hair.

Pack a Costume Suitcase

To encourage hours of magic, masquerade and make-believe, pack old suitcases with dress-ups and disguises and store them under your child's bed. Stock up on Halloween costumes on the clearance rack a the end of the season to score some great deals on dress ups! We recommend scouring your closets, attic, dollar stores and local thrift store for some of the following items:

- Fancy old dresses, scarves and purses
- Hats—top, straw, witch, and cowboy hats; fedoras; Easter bonnets; baseball caps; chef's toques
- A feather boa
- A piece of sheer, velvet, or heavy fabric with a dress clip—an instant cape!
- Shoes of all kinds—cowboy boots, Chinese slippers, high heels
- A bathrobe or a kimono
- Wigs and fake fur for beards and sideburns
- A bandana
- Costume jewelry, including bangle bracelets and clip-on earrings
- Eyewear—nonprescription glasses, shades, and goggles
- Lipstick
- A black eye liner pencil for whiskers and mustaches
- Plastic fangs
- Wands
- A tiara
- Angel wings
- A tutu
- Masks
- Old neckties
- Silk flowers

- Sports jerseys
- Scrubs
- Fins, snorkel and a mask

Office Play

Children love to role-play their favorite adults. Create easy "themes" with things from around the house. Set up the kitchen table or some boxes, a child's imagination will do the rest.
You will need:

- Junk mail, flyers, coupons
- Office supplies
- Paper clips, tape, stapler
- Hole punch
- Boxes for incoming and outgoing mail
- Calculator
- Play phone

Around-the-World Dinners

For a real international learning experience, prepare a meal at home and get your kids in on the menu planning and cooking. You can even start the adventure with a family trip to your local library to check out an ethnic cookbook. After dinner, watch a video filmed in the country of choice.

Dinner Plate Portraits

Whether your kids are preschoolers or preteens, this mask-making project is a real crowd pleaser. The kids can cut out pictures of favorite rock stars, clothing and accessories from magazines to create plates that are part mask, part instant autobiography.
You will need:

- Paint stirrers
- Heavy duty paper dinner plates
- White glue and glue sticks
- Old magazines and catalogs
- Markers and crayons
- Colored construction paper or card stock
- Yarn and/or fun fur
- Scissors

At Home Fun

Attach a wooden paint stirrer as a handle to the bottom of each plate. To help the handle lie flat over the plate rim, cut a tab in the plate that is the same width as the stirrer. Then use white glue to attach the handle to the tab and to the back of the mask. Set out magazines, markers, crayons, construction paper, yarn, fun fur and other decorating supplies, along with glue sticks and scissors. Using the supplies set out to create hair, eyes, lips, noses, freckles and other features. These fun masks are great for parties and groups!

Leaf Birds
You will need:

- Heavy weight paper
- Cardstock or cardboard
- Shape of bird cut from a magazine or coloring book
- Different colored leaves
- White glue
- Paintbrush

Bust out your cardboard bird shape. Gather colored leaves of different sizes, shapes, and colors. Press leaves in a book to dry or flatten them (this may take a day or two). Glue leaves into place arranging different colors or textures for the beak, feathers, feet, etc.

Pine Cone Bird Feeder

This activity is perfect for most any season! Hang from a tree or near a window where your children can watch the birds feed.
You will need:

- Pine cones
- Paper plate
- Butter knife
- Smooth peanut butter
- Birdseed
- Ribbon or yarn
- Scissors

Cut a long length of yarn or ribbon to hang the bird feeder. Tie the ribbon in a knot around the pinecone near the top. Use a knife to spread peanut butter inside the pinecone and around the edges. Sprinkle birdseed over the pinecone. Spread some birdseed on a paper plate and roll the pinecone across it. Hang the bird feeder and watch for the birds to come and feed! You can check out a field guide at your local library to identify birds.

Hanging Bird Food Ornaments
You will need:

- Yarn or ribbon cut to 12 inch lengths
- A straw
- Some stale bread
- Cookie cutters
- Peanut butter
- Bird seed or sunflower seeds

Cut the stale bread into pretty shapes using a cookie cutter. Use a straw to poke a hole in the top of the shape. Thread the yarn or ribbon through the hole and tie both ends together to form a loop. If you like, put peanut butter or peanut butter and seeds on the bread. Hang the ornament from a tree branch, or you can hang pretzels or little donuts from the yarn if you like!

Little Bird Bowls
You will need:

- A small ice cream scoop
- Orange halves
- Shortening
- Bird seed or sunflower seeds

Cut the oranges in half, and scoop out the fruit. With the ice cream scoop, scoop out a ball of shortening. Roll the shortening ball in a tray of seeds. Place the seed ball inside the hollowed out orange half. Put the "bird bowl" in the crook of a tree.

Indoor Camp-Out

Answer the call of the wild with a retreat to the great indoors. You and your child can set up a basic fort (or grab a real tent of your own), grab a canteen, and unfurl some sleeping bags. Other props that enhance the encamped effect are marshmallows, a flashlight and your camper will no doubt require a compass to locate provisions. Finally a book of scary stories might sound the right note, and place a teddy bear outside of the tent for some growling.

At Home Fun

Smores

You will need:

- 1/2 cup light corn syrup
- 1 tablespoon butter
- 1–12 oz. package of chocolate chips
- 4 cups honey graham cereal
- 1 1/2 cups miniature marshmallows

Bring corn syrup and butter to boil. Lower heat and add chocolate. Stir until chocolate melts. Add cereal and marshmallows and stir. Put in square pan, covered with foil. Let set and cut into bars.

Shining Stars

With this handy stargazing device, your kids won't have to wait until nighttime to view their favorite constellations. Instead they can cast their own stellar images on a wall or ceiling in a darkened room.

You will need:

- Marker
- Large paper cup
- Pushpin or thumbtack
- Flashlight

Draw a constellation, such as the Northern Cross, or the Big or Little Dipper, on the bottom of a large paper cup. Then use the pushpin to make a small hole in the center of each star. Now turn of the lights and hold the cup so that the bottom is pointing toward a wall. Shine the flashlight into the open end of the cup, angling it a bit to diffuse the rays, and enjoy a starry view.

Make Your Own Jigsaw Puzzle

Have your child draw a picture or find one in a children's magazine. Glue the picture onto pieces of heavy paper or cardboard. After the glue dries, carefully cut or tear the picture into five or six large pieces and have your child put it back together again.

Build a Skyscraper

Start by collecting cardboard boxes in various shapes and sizes. Tape the boxes shut with packing tape, then stack and tape them on top of each other. Using markers or crayons your kids can decorate the boxes with windows, columns, gargoyles and mailboxes. They might add some 3-D touches such as tissue paper flowers and bushes or paper flags. (If you don't have plain brown boxes, wrap yours with butcher paper or turn them inside out and tape them back together.) You can also do a "mini" version by using old cereal boxes, oatmeal containers and shoeboxes!

Whats In the Bag?

Fill a bag with ordinary household items. Reach into the bag. How many items can be identified without looking? Ask your child to describe the object; is it smooth to the touch, cold like metal, soft? Increase the challenge by putting objects that are similar to each other in the bag. This is a simple activity that will also help encourage your child's language development!

Look at Me!

Have your child observe you for a minute. Leave the room. Return to the room, having changed a small detail in your appearance. Remove an earring, put on some lipstick or change your hair. Can they guess?

Indoor Snowball Fight

Wad up newspaper balls and have a snowball war indoors!

Paper Snowflakes

You know the drill, fold up your paper and see what you can produce with a pair of scissors in hand.For some original snowflake ideas check out:
www3.ns.sympatico.ca/dstredulinsky/links.html

Rose-Colored Windows

On a gray day or in the middle of the winter satisfy your longing for flowers and springtime with this fun activity. Use washable paints to create a flower garden on your window. Use paintbrushes and fingers to create stems, leaves and different flower blossoms. You can also try Crayola Window Writers. This will add a splash of color and fun to a gray day.

Color Your World

Got a snowy fort to decorate? Or the blank slate of a snow bank? Go ahead and paint it. Fill spray bottles with food coloring and water (about six drops per bottle) and let the troops run wild. Thinking of a more precise look? If the surface is solid and smooth try working with regular tempera paint and paintbrushes.

Winter Photography

Take pictures of nature, such as icicles, birds and trees.

At Home Fun

Sugar-Cube Igloo

Build an igloo, a pyramid or a skyscraper! Start by laying a base row of sugar cubes for your project. You can make mortar of two egg whites mixed with three cups confectioners' sugar; add subsequent layers of cubes one row at a time. Stop at increments to let some of the mortar dry. Sprinkle with a blizzard of sugar, use food coloring to brighten up the landscape.

Homemade Bowling

Use empty water bottles as the pins and find a spare ball to roll.

Endless Roll of Paper

What can you do with a large roll of white or butcher paper? Anything you like!

Draw an imaginary roadway and city for toy cars, or a magical landscape for figurines. Illustrate a running story with panels you add to daily. All you need is a roll of paper, some crayons or markers, and your imagination.

Paint to Music

For a quick and soulful project, let your kids put on some tunes, grab a paintbrush, and paint what they hear. Does the mood of the music suggest a color? How about painting the shape of the slow melody or moving the brush along with the energy of the rhythm? Try classical music

No-Peeking Sketches

With its potential for silliness, this fun drawing game is a great thing to try with your kids. To begin write the names of a dozen simple items, such as house, dog, plane, and so on, on strips of paper. Place the strips in a hat and have each person take one. Without showing their word to anyone else, players take turns sketching the object with their eyes closed, while the others attempt to guess what is being drawn.

Finger Paint

With a batch of this quick and easy paint (which keeps in airtight containers), you can turn your young artist loose on newsprint or in the bathtub at a moments notice.
You will need:

- 2 tablespoons sugar
- 1/2 cup cornstarch
- 2 cups cold water
- 1/2 cup clear dishwashing liquid
- Food coloring (for vibrant colors, use food coloring paste)

Mix the sugar and cornstarch in a small pan, then slowly add the water. Cook over low heat stirring until the mixture becomes a smooth, almost clear gel (about 5 minutes). When the mixture is cool, stir in the dish washing liquid. Scoop equal amounts into several containers and stir in the food coloring. This paint contains dish soap, so it dissolves in water, which makes it perfect for bathtub finger painting. (Test to be sure bright paints won't leave a residue; most come clean with a powdered cleanser.)

Marble Painting

Marbles, paint and some "Rock and Roll" are used to create a beautiful picture, worthy of any refrigerator gallery.

You will need:

- Poster or tempera paint
- Paper
- Muffin tins
- Container (gift box, shoebox, Pringles or tennis ball can, or 13x9 baking dish)

Place the paint into the muffin tins. Drop a few marbles in each color. Lay the paper into the bottom of box or roll it up for round container. Place marbles from one color into the container and roll around by moving the box from side to side. Remove that color and continue with the other colors. This painting style can be used to create unique Holiday decorations. Cut your paper into the desired shape (i.e. heart, shamrock, Easter egg). Then continue with painting process.

Straw Painting

Children of any age will enjoy this art discovery. Aim your straw at the paint and BLOW! Maneuver the paint to go in any direction, by moving your straw.

You will need:

- Straws
- Poster or tempera paint
- Paper

Place drops of paint onto the paper, and blow! Remind children to take a break, to avoid dizziness. Combine with a Ping Pong ball blowing game, and you have a science lesson that is really FUN!

Colored Rice

Colored rice is a non-toxic alternative to glitter and sand for the young artist. Use with white glue on paper.

You will need:

- Uncooked white rice
- Flour
- Food coloring

At Home Fun

• Vinegar

Place 1/2 cup rice into a bowl. Add 5 drops of coloring and 1/2 teaspoon vinegar to set the color. Spread flat onto a baking sheet. Bake at 200° for 45 minutes to dry. You may want to make more than one color at a time. Be sure to keep them on separate trays when baking.

Make a Potato Picture

Cut a potato in half and carve a simple shape or design into it. Let your child dip the potato into finger paint and press it on a clean piece of paper, aluminum foil, or on a paper bag. Use the finished masterpiece for a homemade card, wrapping paper, or trick-or-treat bag.

Best Ever Play Dough Recipe

When it comes to busting boredom, play dough always does the trick. Store it in airtight containers for weeks of hands on fun.

You will need:

• 1 cup all purpose flour
• 1 cup water
• 1/2 cup salt
• 1 teaspoon vegetable oil
• 1/2 teaspoon cream of tartar
• Food coloring

Mix the flour, salt, cream of tartar, water, and oil in a saucepan. Cook over medium heat until it holds together (keep mixing or it will stick to the bottom of the pan). When the dough is cool enough to touch, knead it on a floured surface, divide it into smaller balls, and add a different shade of food coloring to each ball.

Edible Play Dough

Create critters and things from edible play dough!

You will need:

• 1/2 cup peanut butter
• 1/2 cup honey
• 1 cup dry non-fat milk solids
• 1 1/2 cup graham cracker crumbs

Combine all ingredients in bowl and mix well. For eyes, ears, tails, hair, and other finishing touches, try using grated coconut, chocolate chips, banana or apple slices, carrot curls, celery slices, etc. For easy clean up, eat the results!

Tabletop Hockey

If you want to score some instant fun on a rainy day, cut a plastic berry box in half. Invert one half and set it at one end of a table. Now your kids can line up at the opposite end and try to score by flicking button pucks into the net.

The Foil Family

You will need:

- Rectangular sheet of aluminum foil (about 10x15 inches)
- Scissors

Make two cuts down from the top of the sheet and one from the bottom. Now scrunch together the center of the sheet to form a torso and pinch and mold the upper corners into arms and the lower corners into legs and feet. Finally, shape the upper midsection into a head and neck. Make them strike any pose your child likes!

Spin a Marker Spiral

Have your kids ever seen anything so archaic as a record player? While you dig out your old one, have them choose a few washable markers. Poke a hole in the center of a paper plate, set it on the phonographs as you would a record and turn on the player. Have your kids hold the tips of one or more markers on the plate and repeat on the other side. If you like, use scissors to cut around the spiral until you reach the plate's middles, then string up one end of the strip and let it hand down in a colorful curlicue.

Grow a Sweet Potato

The perfect indoor gardening project, this sweet potato vine is quick and easy to grow
You will need:

- Sweet potato that has begun to sprout
- 2 toothpicks
- Glass jar
- Terra-cotta pot and potting soil

Pierce the middle of the sweet potato with toothpicks, one on each side, and suspend over the jar. Fill the jar almost to the top with lukewarm water and set it on a bright windowsill. Be sure that the root end of the potato called the pointier faces downward. In 7–14 days, you'll see whiskery rootlets growing under the water. In a week or two, you should see tiny red sprouts at the top, which will soon open into red-veined green leaves.

When growth is about 6–8 inches high, transplant the potato to a flowerpot. Fill the pot about a third of the way with soil, put in the tuber, and add soil up to the growth. Cover the tuber completely to discourage rotting. Water often to keep the soil lightly moist.

At Home Fun

Trains, Boats and Cars

Use a large box for the main body of the vehicle. Make sure your child can sit in it comfortably. With child-safe paper fasteners, attach paper plates for wheels and steering, or cut circles from cardboard and attach with a length of yarn taken through the center. Cut out a windscreen from another box or piece of cardboard, with a window, and glue to the main body. Add extra "carriages" on a train by tying smaller boxes behind the main one. These carry the passengers (teddies or other favorite toys). Draw symbols or pictures with a thick marker and finally color or paint.

Shamrock Prints

You will need:

- Bell pepper
- Paper
- Paint

Cut a bell pepper in half through the middle. (Not end to end from the stem, but from the center). This will make a shamrock shape out of the cut section of the bell pepper. Clean out the seeds. Dip the cross sections of the pepper into some paint and press the shamrock print onto paper.

Wind Bags

Throw your grocery bag to the wind with this kite-flying feat. First tie together the handles of a plastic shopping bag with the end of a ball of string. Staple a few 2-foot lengths of ribbon to the bottom of the bag for kite tails. Now find a windy spot outdoors and start running. As the bag fills with air, slowly let out the string and the kite should begin to soar and dive.

Wind Chimes

Make wind chimes for children to hang outside. Wind chimes can be made of many different things. See what materials the children suggest. You could try forks, spoons, shells, sticks, pieces of metal, or pie tins. Hang them outside and see how they sound!

Worms in Dirt

Make instant chocolate pudding according to package directions. Pour into individual clear plastic cups to set. Sprinkle the top of the pudding with cocoa powder and add chocolate sprinkles if desired. Drop in a few gummy worms.

Make Tiny Bubbles

For a slew of miniature bubbles, tape together a bunch of plastic drinking straws. Dip one end in the bubble solution, hold the other about 1 inch from your mouth (do not put your lips on the straws) and blow. Learn how to blow all kinds of bubbles at www.bubblemania.com.

Homemade Wonder Wands

Here are a few good bubble wands:

Miniature Paper Clip Wand
How to make it: Bend a paper clip into a bubble wand shape.
Dipping container: Cap from a small jar.
What you'll get: A single baby bubble.

Flyswatter Bubblette Wand
How to make it: Grab a clean flyswatter.
Dipping container: Frisbee turned upside down.
What you'll get: Cumulus-cloud like masses of mini bubbles.

Classic Coat Hanger Wand
How to make it: Bend hanger into a circle and handle. Wrap the circle with string.
Dipping Container: Upside down trash can lid.
What you'll get: A very long bubble!

Giant Hula Wand
How to make it: Dig out your hula-hoop.
Dipping container: Kiddie pool.
What you'll get: The biggest bubbles ever!

Bubble Recipe

You will need:

- 3 cups water
- 1 cup dishwashing liquid
- 1/2 cup light corn syrup

In a large plastic container stir the water, dishwashing liquid, and corn syrup. (Although you can use any brand of dish detergent, we found that Joy and Dawn produce the best bubbles.) Store the homemade soap in a covered container. Tip: The best time to blow bubbles is when the air is calm and muggy, such as after a rain shower (bubbles last longer when there is more humidity).

Mock Chalk

This tough version is ideal for sidewalk use. Mix 2 parts plaster of paris with 1 part warm water and add powdered tempera paint to get the desired color. For each stick, line a toilet paper tube with waxed paper, seal one end with tape, and pour in the mixture. Tap the tube to release bubbles. Allow to harden.

At Home Fun

Watercolor Chalk Painting

During a gentle rainfall, hand your kids some colored chalk and let them create an impressionistic masterpiece. They can draw rainbows, family portraits, and nature scenes on the driveway, then watch the rain blur the edges (big, simple images produce the best results). To help the rain along, "paint" over the picture with a large, damp paintbrush.

Listen to a Rain Stick

Your child can make a rain stick of his own from a cardboard mailing tube and dry rice or beans.
You will need:

- 1/2 pound of finishing nails and a hammer
- Cardboard mailing tube
- 1–2 cups of small beans or rice
- Tape
- Acrylic paint and paintbrushes

Randomly hammer nails into the sides of the cardboard mailing tube. Ideally the nails should be almost as long as the tube is wide. With one end of the tube securely capped (tape if necessary), pour the beans or rice into the cylinder. Then place a hand over its open end and tilt the tube to test the sound. You can pour out some of the filler or add more until you achieve the sound you like. (If you want a slower-sounding fall, hammer in more nails.) Cap the open end and tape. Now decorate the outside of the rain stick with acrylic paint. Once the paint dries completely, tilt the stick, close your eyes, and listen to the rainfall.

Pet Rocks

This is a fitting project to do after a nature hike. Encourage your kids to look for natural features in the rocks that resemble noses, chins, ears and so on. Help little kids stick pebbles, googly eyes and pom-poms in place with double sided tape or glue. Kids can use fun fur for hair, mustaches, and beards or apply additional features with acrylic paint.

Sand Art

This is an easy, inexpensive project with great results and is easy for all ages.
You will need:

- Construction paper
- Glue
- Sand

Give each child a piece of paper to draw a picture or write words with glue. Before the glue dries pour some sand over the page. Let is sit for a few minutes and then shake off the excess sand. This can also be done with colored sand.

Dive for Correct Change

Young swimmers love the challenge of diving for coins. Now, with goggles and a fistful of change, you can test their underwater dexterity and their math skills at the same time.

You will need:

- Swimming pool
- 1–4 players
- Coins

Throw the change into the pool and ask your aquanauts to bring back, say, 17¢. For older kids, challenge them with a figure like $1.27.

Grease a Watermelon

This silly pastime is a hallowed tradition at summer camps. To play, divide everyone into two teams. Each defends a goal, either a dock or one side of a swimming pool. Players enter the water, and the melon (made slippery with vegetable shortening) is floated out into the center of the playing area. At a signal, each team attempts to maneuver the melon toward the other team's goal and heft it up onto dry land. The winners get to split the melon!

The S.S. Juice Box

Hot weather invariably leads to two things: piles of empty juice boxes and thoughts of water. This craft lets you combine the two, as your young shipwrights head out to chart the depths of the backyard kiddie pool.

You will need:

- Scrap plastic (like an old report cover or milk jug)
- Permanent markers or stickers
- Hole punch
- Drinking straws
- Scissors or craft knife
- Empty juice box

Cut a rectangular sail from the scrap plastic and decorate it with markers or stickers. Punch a hole at each end and thread the straw through. With the scissors or craft knife, cut a small X in the center of the empty juice box and insert the straw and sail. Float your boat in the wading pool, and blow through another straw to send it sailing.

At Home Fun

Beach Lights

A day at the beach means mayonnaise jars full of salty treasures. Why not put them to beautiful use? Your kids can sift through the day's loot and festoon these sparkling candleholders. They will be ready just in time to light at the table. Use tacky glue to stick assorted shells and sea glass onto a glass votive candleholder (these cost less than a dollar at craft stores). Allow it to dry, add a votive candle, and light! (For a quicker drying time a parent can use hot glue to affix the treasures).

Start a Book Club

A kid's book club can relieve the boredom on two fronts. First, it offers a fun weekly (or monthly) occasion to look forward to. Second, it is a great incentive to read stories that jumpstart the imagination. Before each club meeting have all the kids read the same book (or specified chapters). Then, when members get together, they can share their thoughts and some snacks to. To get things started, the host child might want to make a list of five or so discussion questions. If the readers are younger, you can read aloud while they listen or draw along to the story.

Frozen Fish Popsicles

Make blue gelatin according to package directions. Pour it into popsicle molds and drop in a few gummy fish. Add the sticks and freeze. For variation, put the gelatin in individual clear plastic cups. When it is soft-set, add several gummy fish to each one.

Play Four Square

No keeping score, no winner and still the best darn game at recess! Draw a four square court on your driveway with chalk and let the games begin. Just like the good ol' playground!
You will need:

- Red playground ball
- Chalk
- 4 Players

Ball Catchers

These are great for children that are too young to catch a small ball. They may have better luck with these larger containers.
You will need:

- 2 plastic milk cartons or laundry detergent bottles
- Sharp scissors
- Colored electrical tape or painters tape
- Markers
- Ball

Wash out the milk cartons and let them dry before starting. Use sharp scissors to cut the milk carton or detergent bottle. First cut off the bottom, then cut a U shape under the handle. Make sure you don't cut into the handle. Use colored electrical tape or painters tape to decorate the milk cartons. Have fun playing catch with these fun toys!

Clothes Hanger Tennis

You will need:

- Balloon
- Two wire hangers bent into an oval shape
- One pair of old pantyhose

Bend coat hangers into an oval shape. Cut pantyhose in half, put one leg over one coat hanger and tie a knot at the end. Do the same for the other coat hanger. They become tennis rackets! Blow up balloons and use as a tennis ball. This is great fun to play and can be played inside or outside.

Make Paper Airplanes

Check out www.bestpaperairplanes.com for 10 original flying designs. A fun activity for a group of kids to try different designs and see which one works best!

More Great Resources

Mylilpicasso.com

My Lil' Picasso offers arts and crafts kits for children ages 3 through 10. Kits are sold individually or on a subscription basis for a 6 or 12 month period. The kits are delivered to your home in a fun, colorful, hand-painted package addressed to your child so that he/she is sure to recognize the package as his/her own. Each themed bi-monthly kit features 2–3 art projects with materials, 3–5 crafts, stickers, stamps, and an assortment of fun activities to provide hours of enjoyment for your lil' Picasso. A newsletter is included with each kit and packed full of teacher inspired ideas, lesson plans, and lesson objectives designed to help you make the most of the kit contents.

FamilyFun Boredom Busters

Edited by Deanna F. Cook

Find 365 creative, inventive and expertly chosen projects that will ensure there is always something fun to do every single day of the year. Features bright, full color photographs.

The Little Hands Big Fun Craft Book: Creative Fun for 2-6 Year Olds
By Judy Press

Make a hearts and flowers necklace, a handprint family tree, a noodle nametag, or a tooth fairy pouch. Over 70 fun arts and crafts projects encourage creativity.

FamilyFun Crafts
Edited by Deanna F. Cook

The perfect resource for busy families in search of creative and exciting ways to turn free time into fun family time, Disney's FamilyFun Crafts nurtures a child's creativity through painting, drawing, paper crafts, kitchen crafts, nature crafts, homemade toys, and much more. Color illustrations. You can find any of these books online and in bookstores. If you're looking for a great deal try www.half.com, or buy "used" from www.amazon.com.

In the garden

Life Lessons of Gardening

Along with the fun of getting dirty, gardening helps children learn valuable lessons about patience as they wait for vegetables to grow, responsibility as they see how necessary their care is to the garden and even loss when flowers die at the end of a season. "They learn about nurturing a life and what it takes to keep something alive," says Amy Gifford, an education associate for the National Gardening Association. Gifford also extols the value of exercise as children physically work in the garden, that families learn to work together and share and that gardening helps to build a child's senses.

The garden can teach us and our children profound lessons about life and the world around us. Below are just a few of the many benefits of gardening with your family.

Science
It teaches them about the lifecycle and the wonder of nature, not to mention earth science and the effects we have on our environment. Kids also get a first hand account into the miracle of life trapped inside a single seed, something to be discovered and cherished.

Life 101
Gardening offers a great opportunity to connect with nature on a deeper level, by touching it, caring for it and watching it grow. Gardening teaches the rhythms of the seasons and the life cycle. The garden is life's lessons in action; there is no telling or listening, only doing. If they don't water the plants, they'll die. If they don't tend the weeds, they'll take over. Though the lessons seem small, it is the first step toward larger ideas and responsibilities.

Relaxation

Gardening has also been shown to reduce stress, no matter what your age. The quiet, calming effect of gardening can soothe the stressed out or over-stimulated child. Even better, the garden appeals to all five of our senses, we can see, touch, smell, hear and even "taste" our garden. The healing effects of gardening are well documented, and are even being used in programs to help children of abuse and/or broken homes to rebuild their self-esteem.

Family Time

It's also a great time to connect with your kids. Talk together, or work quietly along side each other. You never know, you may rediscover your child in the backyard pumpkin patch.

Other benefits of gardening for children include:

- Improvement in fine and gross motor skills
- Improved social skills
- Enhanced self-esteem
- Enhanced sensory perception and creativity

Garden Tips

Gardening can be made easy and fun for children of all abilities by keeping mind a few things:

- Caring for their own section of the garden can give children a great feeling of accomplishment as they watch their plants grow and change.
- Let kids have their own spot. If they want to toss 10 seeds in one hole, let them and they will see what happens. Learn from experience.
- Have drinks and snacks available
- Provide small or child-sized tools for better grip
- Use larger seeds for easier handling; place smaller seeds into a spice jar and sprinkle for easier planting
- Allow for frequent rest breaks
- Plant plants that grow quickly and easily
- Modify the garden using raised beds, containers or trellis to make gardening easier for a child with special needs

Create Your Own Grass Man

Paint a silly face on a medium size terra cotta pot. Place some gravel at the bottom of the pot, fill it with soil, and sprinkle a handful of grass seeds on the surface. Keep it damp and in a light place. In a few weeks, the grassy hair will grow. But if you don't take control, it will grow and grow and grow. Give it a trim and create your own grassy hairstyle.

At Home Fun

Magic in a Pot

Place some pebbles at the bottom of a bucket or a 9-inch planting pot. Fill the pot to the brim with potting compost. Sprinkle about 20 seed on the top, cover them with a bit of compost, and water them. Leave the pot in a warm, light place. After a couple of weeks, seedling will begin to show. When you have good growth from your seedlings, you can put the pot outside. Place little plastic figures or tiny gnomes among the little plants.

Seed Starter Ideas

Flowers

Fill an empty egg carton with compost. Push one seed into each sup so that it is covered by the soil. Water to make the soil damp. Shoots should appear after about a week or two. When the shoots are strong enough, transfer them into the garden.

Vegetables

Use empty yogurt containers (from a six pack of yogurt). Fill with compost and plant your vegetable seeds. Tape a picture of what you have planted to the side of the container. When the plant is big enough, transfer it to the garden.

Catnip Sock Toy

Catnip is simply irresistible to cats. Fill a bag or a sock with catnip and watch your kitty go crazy! Create a face on a colorful sock with buttons and beads, and fill the sock with catnip. Add rice or dried peas to make it heavier. Tie a knot and let your cat loose on it.

Picture Pots

Give your plants a personality by decorating their pots. Paint bugs, flowers, polka dots, zebra stripes or create a spooky castle.
To paint pebbles and pots, use acrylic or poster paint. To make sure they are shiny and waterproof mix the paints with PVA glue. Use one dollop of PVA to every two dollops of paint.

Ping Pong Ball Plant Labels

Plant curious ping-pong labels all over your garden. Simply make a hole in a ping-pong ball and stick it on top of a plant cane. Use waterproof pens or markers to decorate them and write the name of the plant.

Air Plants

This plant needs no soil, barely needs water, and doesn't even like too much sunlight! This is an air plant. They can perch on rocks, tees and even telephone wires! They hardly demand any attention but will certainly attract it.
Pop the air plant in a vase or perch it on a surface and give it a good, allover spray with cooled, boiled water about once a week. Sit back and watch it grow!

Great Gardening Books

The Gardening Book

DK Publishing

Colorful photographs and step by step instructions show you how to create over 50 projects from a miniature garden that fits into the palm of your hand, to grass people with heads you can groom. Perfect for budding gardeners who want to get growing.

Kid's Gardening

By Kevin Raftery, Kim Gilbert, Jim M'Guinness

Now young readers will know from whence those carrots came. This full-color extravaganza contains nearly a hundred pages of wipe-clean cardstock, hundreds of illustrations, dozens of growing activities, plus 15 varieties of vegetable, flower and herb seeds.

National Gardening Association Guide to Kids' Gardening

National Gardening Association

This is the official youth gardening guide of the 250,000 member National Gardening Association. It combines more than 70 gardening project ideas with practical how-to advice on starting and maintaining a youth garden. Included with the purchase of each book is a free six-month membership in the National Gardening Association.

Roots, Shoots, Buckets & Boots: Gardening Together With Children Sunflower Houses: Inspiration from the Garden-A Book for Children and Their Grown-Ups

By Sharon Lovejoy

The pictures and illustrations alone are enough reason to buy these books. The author keeps a young child's attention span in mind and emphasizes the small wonders a garden brings. The projects are not only kid-friendly but also give a child reason to stick it out from planting to harvest. These books go one step further in skillfully weaving in science, folklore and practical gardening information.

Helpful Websites

National Gardening Association

www.kidsgardening.com

The National Gardening Association is a nonprofit organization established in 1972 to help gardeners, and to help people through gardening. This site is one of the best resources we have found. It includes helpful gardening tips, activities, books and more. Excellent educational and family resource.

Miscellaneous

Kiddie World Center

1899 West San Carlos Street

San Jose, CA 95128

408-279-5437

www.kiddieworldcenter.com

Hours: Mon.–Sat. 10 am–6 pm, Sunday 11 am–5 pm

Since 1948, the helpful, friendly staff at Kiddie World Center has offered attentive service to its customers, young and old.

We're here to help customers with personalized service based on their needs, and to work with their budget. Customers will find unique, stylish items with good lines, from the ultramodern to the classic, which can serve children from infant & toddlers to teens. Popular furniture names like Young America,D.L. Mayra, Glenna Jean Lea, Dozydotes and Dwell are here. For outdoor fun, Kiddie World Center offers custom play sets from Backyard Adventures and top of the line trampolines from Alley Oop. "When we do a backyard, we always ask the ages of the children," Lopez says. The staff at Kiddie World Center then uses their knowledge and expertise to build what he calls "the "the dream set" for each family based on the children's ages, desires, and space requirements, and budget. We will give you the "the biggest bang for their buck."

The Great Outdoors

Today American families spend more than 90% of their time indoors. A national study released by the Outdoor Industry Foundation found that Americans who participate in at least one outdoor activity on a regular basis reap mental and physical health benefits. The outdoors enriches our lives by reducing stress levels and connecting people with family and friends. It also shows that people are more likely to be active throughout their lives if they start outdoor activities at a young age. Even more, they cited that parent-organized activities were among the most effective ways of getting their children more active. So what are you waiting for? Enjoy the many opportunities from biking to hiking with your family!

General Resources

The following are some general outdoor websites for Bay Area Mamas to use in their search for great family activities. Any of these websites will provide you with a wealth of knowledge concerning the outdoors. Find information on biking, bird watching, camping, canoeing, climbing, fishing, hiking and more.

California Department of Fish and Game

www.dfg.ca.gov

This is the place to find information about hunting, freshwater fishing, marine fishing, and wildlife viewing. You can access information on public lands and hatcheries, as well as apply for fishing and hunting licenses.

California State Parks

www.parks.ca.gov

Find everything you need for a great family getaway in the beautiful state of California. You can make reservations at the state park campgrounds either on the Internet or through the reservation line.

National Park Service

www.nps.gov

The National Park Service has a great website that takes you to wonderful maps and detailed information about the national parks in California. Start by searching through the Parks and Recreation area and you will be able to compare different locations for great outdoor family vacations.

National Wildlife Federation

www.nwf.org/kids

This link is the "Just for Kids Ranger Rick" information area for children ages 1-18. You can find all sorts of great activities to do in your own backyard that are fun and educational. There is an area just for parents or just for educators about the wildlife information and activities that are happening.

Recreation.gov

www.recreation.gov

This extensive website has an organized way to help you look through each state's outdoor recreation opportunities. You can find almost every outdoor activity category here and then find locations and information about that activity in your state.

REI

1975 Diamond Blvd., Suite B100
Concord, CA 94520
www.rei.com

925-825-9400

There are three REI locations in the Bay Area. Through these businesses your family can find out when local hikes, outdoor introduction classes and other wonderful events are taking place. Go to the website or stop by your local store for a current calendar of events.

1338 San Pablo Avenue
Berkeley, CA 94702
510-527-4140

43962 Fremont Blvd.

Fremont, CA 94538

510-651-0305

San Francisco Bay Trail

www.abag.ca.gov/bayarea/baytrail

The Bay Trail currently has 288 miles of trail throughout nine counties in the Bay Area. When the entire trail is complete, there will be 500 miles of hiking and biking trails. This website has numerous trail maps available that are downloadable and available for purchase.

Biking

East Bay Regional Park District

www.ebparks.org

This is a great resource for bike trail information. Both paved and unpaved trails are listed in separate sections. There is a section that features descriptions of the top ten bike trails. You can also access links to biking organizations in the area. Be sure to check out the listing of parks that do not permit bikes as well.

Mountain Biking in the San Francisco Bay Area

By Lorene Jackson

www.globepequot.com

This book covers over 80 mountain bike trails in the Bay Area. Sections include tips for riding with kids, local attractions, maps and thorough ride descriptions. Also included are ratings and technical difficulty for the rides.

Bird & Wildlife Watching

Diablo Audubon Society

P.O. Box 53

Walnut Creek, CA 94597

www.diabloaudubon.com/index.php

Look on this website for DAS sponsored bird watching outings that are great for families. You can also sign your family up to participate in a bird counting day that helps the DAS track bird populations.

John Muir National Historic Site

www.nps.gov/jomu

Located as part of this historic site is Mt. Wanda, where you can take a ranger-led bird watching hike and see anything from hawks and owls to hummingbirds and woodpeckers.

Mount Diablo Interpretive Association

www.mdia.org/Home.htm

This website provides links to wildlife viewing opportunities on Mt. Diablo. Visit the Mitchell Canyon Interpretive Center on the North side of Mt. Diablo State Park for exhibits about wildlife, trails, geology and plant life. Interpretive materials about the wildlife found on Mt. Diablo and trail maps are available for purchase here. There is also a museum and observation deck at the summit of Mt. Diablo. The stunning view from the observation deck is a must-see.

Big Break Trail

www.ebparks.org

1-888-EBPARKS

1-888-327-2757

Hours: 5 am–10 pm unless otherwise posted

Fees: None–parking is also free

The Big Break Trail is a great place for bird watching and nature study. The 6.5 mile paved, multi-use trail goes from Creekside Park in Brentwood to the Delta shores of Big Break.

Beaches

Contra Loma Regional Park

1200 Frederickson Lane

Antioch, CA 94509

www.ebparks.org

925-757-0404

Fees: $3 age 16–61, $2 age 1–15, $2 seniors 62+ or disabled, FREE under 1 year

The lake's swim lagoon, staffed with lifeguards in the summer, has a sandy beach with restrooms and a concession stand. Swimming is allowed only when lifeguards are on duty.

Miller/Knox Regional Shoreline

Keller Beach

900 Dornan Drive

Richmond, CA 94801

www.ebparks.org

510-235-1631

Keller Beach is at the north end of Miller/Knox. There, visitors can wade and swim in San Francisco Bay. No lifeguards are on duty. Picnic tables and restrooms are nearby. There are no beach access fees.

The Great Outdoors

Crown Memorial State Beach
Eighth Street and Otis Drive
Alameda, CA 94501
www.ebparks.org

510-521-7090

Hours: 5 am–10 pm unless otherwise posted
Fees: There are no beach access fees, but there is a $5 parking fee and a $2 fee per dog

Visit the 2.5 mile Crown Memorial State Beach and enjoy warm, shallow water, sand dunes and a bicycle trail. Facilities at the beach include a bathhouse with changing rooms. Swimming is permitted during park hours year round. No lifeguards are on duty. Beach wheelchairs are available free of charge on a first-come, first-served basis

Cull Canyon Regional Recreation Area
18627 Cull Canyon Road
Castro Valley, CA 94546
www.ebparks.org

510-537-2240

Fees: $3.50 age 16–61, $2.50 age 1–15, $2.50 seniors 62+ or disabled, FREE under 1 year

Cull Canyon boasts a swim complex with a bathhouse, vending machines and lifeguard service. The swim complex is open during the warm weather season. This white, sandy beach is shallow and therefore perfect for families with small children. No swimming allowed without lifeguards on duty.

Del Valle Regional Park
7000 Del Valle Road
Livermore, CA 94550
www.ebparks.org

925-373-0332

Hours: 6 am–6 pm

East and West Beach are available for swimming at Del Valle Regional Park. Swimming is permitted year round north of the boat ramp, even when lifeguards are not on duty. Check the East Bay Parks website for lifeguard schedule if you wish to go when lifeguards are on duty. There are no beach access fees.

Don Castro Regional Recreation Area
22400 Woodroe Avenue
Hayward, CA 94541
www.ebparks.org

510-538-1148

Hours: Swim hours are 11 am–6 pm, and only when lifeguards are on duty
Fees: $3 age 16–61, $2 age 1–15, $2 seniors 62+ or disabled, FREE under 1 year

The swimming lagoon is open from May to September. Amenities include bathhouse with shower, vending machines, and a sandy beach. Beach wheelchairs are available free of charge on a first-come, first-served basis.

Quarry Lakes Regional Recreation Area

2100 Isherwood Way
Fremont, CA 94536
www.ebparks.org

510-795-4883

Fees: $3 age 16–61, $2 age 1–15, $2 seniors 62+ or disabled, FREE under 1 year

Swimming at Horseshoe Lake is permitted year round, even without lifeguards on duty. Year round amenities include a sandy beach, a bathhouse, sand volleyball courts, boat launch, vending machines and lifeguard service in spring and summer. Swimming is allowed in swimming area only. A beach wheelchair is available free of charge on a first-come, first-served basis.

Shadow Cliffs Regional Recreation Area

2500 Stanley Boulevard
Pleasanton, CA 94566
www.ebparks.org

925-846-3000

Fees: $6 parking fee per vehicle and $2 per dog fee

The bathhouse and refreshment stand are open on the weekends in spring and fall, and daily during summer months. Lifeguards are on duty only during the summer months. Beach wheelchairs are available free of charge on a first-come, first-served basis. There are no beach access fees. Swimming is allowed throughout the year in the designated area, at the swimmer's own risk. Pets and glass containers are not allowed on the sand portion of the swim area.

California Splash Waterslides at Shadow Cliffs

2500 Stanley Boulevard
Pleasanton, CA 94566
www.shadowcliffs.com

925-829-6230

Hours: 10:30 am–5:30 pm, weather permitting

There are waterslides, picnic areas facing the slides, BBQ's, and lockers. It is located at Shadow Cliffs Regional Recreation Area, but is privately owned and operated. Riders must be at least 42 inches tall.

Temescal Regional Recreation Area

6502 Broadway Terrace
Oakland, CA 94610
www.ebparks.org

510-652-1155

Fees: $3 age 16–61, $2 age 1–15, $2 seniors 62+ or disabled, FREE under 1 year

Temescal Recreation Area has a beach house with changing rooms, vending machines and showers. Swimming is allowed without lifeguards. Swimming is allowed from approximately April to October. Check website for exact dates. Beach wheelchairs are available free of charge on a first-come, first-served basis.

Tilden Regional Park

Lake Anza Road at Central Park Road
Berkeley, CA 94708
www.ebparks.org

510-843-2137

Fees: $3.50 age 16–61, $2.50 age 1–15, $2.50 seniors 62+ or disabled, FREE under 1 year

Lake Anza has a wonderful sheltered, sunny, sandy beach that is great for families. Lifeguards are on duty during the swim season. Swimming is allowed without lifeguards on duty. Swimming is usually allowed from April to October.

Camping

Recreation One-Stop

www.recreation.gov

This website is a great resource for all national park camping opportunities. Now you can look for information about Federal recreation sites and make campsite and tour reservations on the same website.

Great Family Campsites

Anthony Chabot Campground

9999 Redwood Road
Castro Valley CA 94546
www.ebparks.org Information
www.reserveamerica.com Reservations

510-635-0135

This campground overlooks Lake Chabot. Amenities include 75 trailer, tent, or walk-in campsites, hot showers, naturalist-led campfire programs, an amphitheater and hiking/fishing access to Lake Chabot. Youth group campsites are available and can be reserved as well.

Carnegie State Vehicular Recreation Area Campground

18600 Corral Hollow Road
Tracy, CA 95376
www.parks.ca.gov

925-447-9027

Hours: 8 am–Sunset seven days a week

Carnegie has 23 campsites which are available on a first-come, first-served basis. Amenities include fire rings, restrooms, showers and water faucets. Water and electrical hook-ups are not available. Picnic tables are located throughout the valley floor; however, fires are restricted to the fire rings provided in the campground. Visit the website for more information.

Del Valle Family Campground

Del Valle Regional Park

7000 Del Valle Road
Livermore, CA 94550
www.ebparks.org

510-562-2267

This campground has 150 sites, 21 of which have water and sewage hookups (no electrical). The sites are served by centrally located toilet and shower facilities. There are also seven group campgrounds. Reservations can be made at least 12 weeks in advance.

Mount Diablo State Park

96 Mitchell Canyon Road
Clayton, CA 94517
www.parks.ca.gov

925-837-2525

Hours: The park kiosk is open from 8 am–Sunset

Mt. Diablo has three campgrounds with a total of 56 campsites. Amenities include picnic tables, fire pits or stoves, water and restrooms. The Juniper and Live Oak campgrounds also have showers available free of charge. The campgrounds are ideally for tent camping, but there is enough room to fit an RV up to 20 ft. in length. There are no hook-ups or dumping stations at Mt. Diablo.

Juniper Campground (36 sites, elevation 3000 ft)

Juniper is located approximately 2 miles below the summit on Summit Road. Juniper has great views. Reservations are available.

Live Oak Campground (22 sites, elevation 1450 ft.)

Live Oak is one mile above the Southgate entrance station, off Southgate Road. Live Oak is near Rock City. Check out the fascinating rock formations while in Rock City. Reservations are available.

Junction Campground (6 sites, elevation 2200 ft.)

Junction Campground is between Southgate and Northgate at the Ranger Station. This campground is in an open woodland location. It is available on a first-come first-served basis only.

Stewartville Backpack Camp
Black Diamond Mines Regional Preserve

www.ebparks.org

888-EBPARKS

888-327-2757

This camp, located at Black Diamond Mines Regional Preserve, is accessible by hiking 3.2 miles from Preserve Headquarters. This campground is a good bet for families with older children. There are picnic tables and pit toilets. The camping fee is $5 per night and per person. There is a two night maximum stay during spring, summer, and fall.

Canoeing, Rafting & Kayaking

All-Outdoors California Whitewater Rafting

1250 Pine Street, Suite 103
Walnut Creek CA 94596

www.aorafting.com

800-24-RAFTS (247-2387)

925-932-8993

This rafting company has 3/4, 1, 2 and 3-Day California river rafting trip options. There are trips designed for beginner, intermediate and expert rafters. A great trip for families with small children is the easy beginner Tom Sawyer Section/South Fork float trip for $124, which includes lunch. The trips on the South Fork of the American River range from $109 to $144, depending on whether you pick the 1/2 day or the full day trip. Book a trip Sunday-Friday from April–October. Visit the website for a listing of other rafting trip options for older children.

Cal Adventures, at UC Berkeley

www.oski.org

510-642-4000

Cal Adventures offers classes, trips, and rentals for sea kayaking, river kayaking, and rafting. Youth sea-kayaking classes are available in the spring and summer. River rafting trips are available on the South Fork of the American River. Sea kayaking trips include San Francisco Bay, Tomales Bay, Monterey Bay/Elkhorn Slough, Mono Lake and others.

Del Valle Reservoir

7000 Del Valle Road
Livermore, CA 94550
www.ebparks.org
888-EBPARKS
888-327-2757

Hours: Park hours are 6 am–9 pm
Fees: Parking fee is $6 per vehicle

The Del Valle Reservoir is five miles in length. There are two companies that rent boats for use on the reservoir: Rocky Mountain Recreation Company and Sunrise Mountain Sports. Sunrise Mountain Sports also offers lessons.

Rocky Mountain Recreation Company

www.rockymountainrec.com/lakes/lake-delvalle.htm
925-449-5201

Features motorboats, pontoon boats, canoes, rowboats and paddle boats. Call for rate and rental information

Sunrise Mountain Sports
Del Valle Kayak Center

www.sunrisemountainsports.com
925-245-9481 For rentals
925-447-8330 For lessons

Offers kayak, Hobie and sea kayak rentals and kayak lessons

Lake Chabot

17600 Lake Chabot Road
Castro Valley, CA 94546
www.ebparks.org
888-EBPARKS
888-327-2757

Hours: 5 am–10 pm unless otherwise posted or permitted
Fees: $5 per vehicle for parking and $2 fee per dog

There are rental boats available including rowboats, canoes, pedal boats, kayaks, Duffy boats, and boats with electric trolling motors. Visit the marina to the rent boats and go for tour boat rides. For more information regarding boat rentals, contact Urban Park Concessionaires online or call (510) 247-2526

The Great Outdoors

Climbing

Touchstone Climbing and Fitness

1220 Diamond Way Suite 140
Concord, CA 94519
www.touchstoneclimbing.com

925-602-1000

Hours: Monday–Friday 5:30 am–10 pm, Saturday and Sunday 9 am–6 pm

The rock walls at Touchstone are substantial. There are classes for kids ages 6 and up. Moms who are members can enjoy climbing the rock wall while the kids are at the free childcare.

Rocktopia at Encore Gymnastics

999 Bancroft Road
Walnut Creek, CA 94518
www.encoregym.com/wc/htm/wc_climbing.html

925-932-1033

Rocktopia is open seven days a week for parties, groups and events. They also offer free climb gym hours.

Fishing & Boating

Pier Fishing in California, 2nd Edition

By Ken Jones

The most comprehensive book ever published on fishing California piers.
Featuring:

- Detailed instructions on how to fish more than 100 different California piers
- Detailed information of the 100 most common fish caught from California piers
- Environment and in-depth history of California
- Tackle and equipment
- Bait and artificial lures
- Cleaning and cooking your catch
- In-depth history of California piers

2nd Edition Paperback, 528 pages
List Price: $29.95

Pier Fishing In California

www.pierfishing.com

This website is an excellent resource for locating fishing piers in the Bay Area and is filled with useful information about each one.

Urban Park Concessionaires

www.norcalfishing.com

925-426-3060

This company runs the fishing/boat rentals for Comanche, Chabot, Los Vaqueros, and San Pablo Parks. Visit the website for comprehensive information on rental rates and fishing licenses.

Antioch/Oakley Regional Shoreline

Bridgehead Road at Wilbur Avenue

Antioch, CA 94509

www.ebparks.org

888-EBPARKS

888-327-2757

Hours: Park is open 5 am–10 pm; Pier is open 24 hours daily, year round

This park boasts great fishing on a 550-foot pier in the San Joaquin River. Some of the fish caught from the pier include striped bass, channel catfish, Sacramento pike, sturgeon, steelhead and salmon. All anglers aged 16 or older are required to hav a fishing license. There is no entrance or parking fee.

Lafayette Reservoir

Mt. Diablo Boulevard

Lafayette, CA 94549

www.ebmud.com

www.lafayettechamber.org/pages/reservoir.htm

925-284-9669

Fees: The fishing access fee is $4 per day and the usual state license requirements and bait restrictions apply

Fishing is allowed year round during daylight hours. Opening and closing times are posted at the gate. Fish species found at the reservoir include rainbow trout, largemouth bass, channel catfish, bluegill, black crappie, redear sunfish, yellow perch, brown trout, and brook trout.

Los Vaqueros Reservoir

LV Marina Center

9990 Los Vaqueros Road

Byron, California 94514

www.norcalfishing.com

925-371-2628

The marina has fishing supplies, snacks, hot food and ice cream. Anglers can rent the electric boats that are docked at the marina. You can now rent fish finders on some of the boats. The lake has been stocked with more than 300,000 game fish of 12 types, including rainbow trout and largemouth black bass.

Hiking

East Bay Trails: Hiking Trails in Alameda And Contra Costa Counties

By David Weintraub

www.wildernesspress.com

This book is packed with great trails in both Alameda and Contra Costa Counties. Included are maps and trail descriptions of 56 trails along with a listing of favorites. You can also use this book to find a great waterfall or an easy hike for the kids.

Bay Area Hiker

www.bahiker.com

Bay Area Hiker is a great resource filled with tips on hiking in the area. There are detailed descriptions of hike difficulties and available resources.

EBMUD

www.ebmud.com

510-835-3000

Visit this website, click on the Services category and then on Recreation. Once there you can print out trail maps and find info on trail fees/permits.

A Few of Our Favorite Hikes

Canyon View Trail to Little Yosemite
Sunol Regional Wilderness

www.ebparks.org

This hike is three miles in length. It takes you to an area known as "Little Yosemite" which is aptly named because terrain is reminiscent of Yosemite, with its giant granite boulders and fast moving water. The hike takes approximately two hours, and can be hiked year round. It is of moderate difficulty for children. There are wonderful places to stop along the way for the kids to explore, as well as a large and varied bird population. Kids will also enjoy climbing the giant moss covered rocks along the way. Make sure to bring a lunch with you, as there is a wonderful spot to have a picnic near the granite boulders. Be aware that the East Bay Parks District prohibits wading in the creek. Visit the website for a good detailed map that outlines the hike. Restrooms are available by the parking area.

Directions: Traveling on I-680, take the Calaveras Road, South exit. Continue for about five miles and turn left on Geary Road. Stay on Geary until it ends at the entrance to the park. Find parking near the park headquarters.

Boardwalk/Muskrat Trails Loop
Coyote Hills Regional Park

www.ebparks.org

This hike is located at the Coyote Hills Regional Park. The 1.5 mile hike is easy for children and can be completed in about an hour. The ground is level and can be hiked year round. Your children can enjoy the sights and sounds of a marsh while looking for dragonflies and water birds that call the park home. There is a long boardwalk over portions of the cat tailed packed marsh.

Directions: Traveling on CA 84, take the Paseo Padre Parkway exit for 1.5 miles. Turn West on Patterson Ranch Road, continue 1 mile to Visitor Center.

East Shore Trail
Anthony Chabot Regional Park

www.ebparks.org

The East Shore Trail is a great moderate day hike for kids. It is three miles in length and will take approximately three hours to complete. It's fun to walk the perimeter around the lake, and a lot of the trails are paved, so this is a good place to take a stroller. There are great opportunities to view various birds along the way.

Directions: Access the trail by taking the Fairmont Drive exit off I-580 and head east. Follow Fairmont until it turns into Lake Chabot Road and then all the way to the park entrance.

Huckleberry Path Nature Trail
Huckleberry Botanic Regional Preserve

www.ebparks.org

The Huckleberry Path Nature Trail is a great place to visit especially in the early spring, which is why the trails are often crowded in the month of February. This 1.75 mile day hike is easy for children and will take approximately one hour to complete. One of the features of this trail is the plant species that can be found, including two plants that are found in only two places in the world. The climate of this particular location lends itself to a host of varied fauna and plants. Be aware that there is poison hemlock along the trail, so it is a good idea to be able to identify it before you go on the hike. Make sure to get a trail map that has the plants pictured and listed. A great activity for the kids is to try and identify the different plant species as they hike.

Directions: Take Highway 24 and exit Fish Ranch Road. Take a left onto Grizzly Peak Blvd. Travel 2.5 miles, then turn left on to Skyline Blvd. Go about .5 miles, past the entrance to Sibley Volcanic Regional Preserve, to the park entrance.

The Great Outdoors

Carquinez Overlook Loop Trail
Carquinez Strait Regional Shoreline

www.ebparks.org

Hike along the bluffs and shorelines of Carquinez Strait. This hike is great to take in the fall and winter, because it has good sun exposure. The kids can also enjoy watching the many boats of all shapes and sizes that pass by. Have the kids keep an eye out for birds such as hawks, vultures, and the smaller Loggerhead Strike, a small grey and white bird with a hooked beak.

Directions: Take I-80 and I-680 to Crockett. Once in Crockett, follow Carquinez Scenic Drive east to the Bull Valley Staging Area. When you get to the parking lot, take the hiker's gate to the trail-head.

Lafayette Reservoir Trail
Mt. Diablo Boulevard
Lafayette, CA 94549
www.ebmud.com
www.lafayettechamber.org/pages/reservoir.htm

925-284-9669

Fees: There are two parking options. If you stay no longer than 2 hours, bring your quarters and make use of the $.50 per 1/2 hour metered parking. If you plan to stay longer, use the $6 pay parking inside the gate.

You can enjoy this hike whether you have a couple of hours or the better part of a day. It is a great place to take the dogs and the kids. There is a loop paved trail around the perimeter of the lake. It is a great trail for strollers, but some of the hills can seem a little challenging for small children on bicycles. If your children do want to bring a bike, scooter or roller blades, there are some day restrictions—Tuesdays and Thursdays from noon to closing and Sundays from opening to 11 am. There are several play structures and restrooms located along the path. If you stay through the lunch hour, there are some nice places for a picnic at one of the picnic areas as well. If you have time, there are also canoes and pedal boats available for rent at the activity center. Check the website for more details.

Contra Costa Canal Trail
Iron Horse Trail

Briones to Mt. Diablo Trail
Mt. Diablo Boulevard
Lafayette, CA 94549
www.ebparks.org

888-EBPARKS

Hours: 5 am–10 pm unless otherwise posted

There are three main paved, multi-use trails that are run by East Bay Parks. These trails have many access points throughout the East Bay. They also interconnect with each other, which makes them ideal for traveling long distances with kids on bikes or scooters. If possible, you can plan to stop along the way at a park such as Heather Farms or Larkey Park along the way. Visit the East Bay Parks for detailed trail maps. If you bring the family dog, remember to pick up after your dog, and make sure to keep bags with you at all times.

Horseback Riding & Lessons

Castle Rock Arabians
Heritage Trails

1350 Castle Rock Road
Walnut Creek, CA 94598
www.castlerockarabians.com

925-937-7661

Open 7 days weekly from 9 to 5 Private lessons by appointment. Special classes for Tiny Riders, ages 4 to 6. *An Equestrian Lifestyle for the entire family Castle Rock Arabians*

Horseback riding lessons are available for kids ages three and up. Diablo Magazine voted it the best of the East Bay for riding lessons. They also offer birthday party plans and summer camp opportunities as well. There are classes available in English, Western and trail riding.

The Great Outdoors

New Heights Training Stables, LLC
Trainer: David Acord

10970 Crow Canyon Road
Castro Valley, CA 94552
www.davidacordequestrian.com

lifeline37@yahoo.com
925-858-6843

New Heights is committed to serving riders and horses of all levels. They offer a systematic train-ing program customized to meet the individual needs of each horse and rider, positive instruction and educational clinics. Visit their website for more information.

Chabot Equestrian Center
Anthony Chabot Regional Park

14600 Skyline Blvd.
Oakland, CA 94619
510-569-4428

www.chabotequestriancenter.com

There are trainers available for all skill levels in Western, Hunter/Jumper, Therapy Riding and Dressage. There are also clinics and boarding available.

Las Trampas Wilderness Equestrian Center

18015 Bollinger Canyon Road
San Ramon, CA 94583
925-838-7546

Hours: Open daily from 9 am–5 pm

This stable offers lessons, pony rides, horse boarding, and day camps. The stable also has night rides and BBQs during daylight savings hours. While on the trail rides, you can enjoy views of San Francisco, Mt. Diablo, Marin and San Jose.

Skyline Ranch Equestrian Center

5750 Redwood Road
Oakland, CA 94619
www.skyline-ranch.com

510-336-0850

Fee: Lessons range in price from $25 to $55 for a 1 hour lesson, and price varies depending on what type of horse and how many riders are in the lesson

Skyline Ranch offers riding lessons, boarding and has a therapeutic riding program. Lessons are available for beginners, intermediates and advanced riders.

Piedmont Stables
Redwood Regional Park

6525 Redwood Road
Oakland, CA 94619
www.skyline-ranch.com/Piedmont.htm

510-336-0850

Piedmont Stables is the sister stable of Skyline Ranch, and they are just down the street on Redwood Road Visit the Skyline Ranch website for basic information regarding the programs offered at Piedmont.

Western Trail Riding
Sunol Regional Park

Geary Road
Sunol, CA 94586
www.westerntrailriding.com

925-862-9044

Fees: Range from $25/person for a half hour to $80/person for a 4 hour ride

They feature numerous trail riding options. Visit their website for detailed descriptions about trail ride options.

Hunting & Marksmanship

Concord Sportsmen's Club

4700 Evora Road
Concord, CA 94519
www.concordsportsmensclub.org

925-431-8979

This club offers a rifle range, skeet shooting, and pistol range.

Briones Archers Range
Briones Regional Park

www.archeryweb.com/briones

510-785-2501

It is accessible off the Crescent Ridge Trail from the park's Bear Creek Road entrance. Visit the website for detailed directions.

Sailing

City of Oakland Parks and Recreation
Lake Merritt

568 Bellevue Avenue

Oakland, CA 94610

www.oaklandnet.com/parks/programs

510-238-2196

Fees: $2 parking fee on weekends, $2 fee to launch boats. Free on Mondays during the winter when the boathouse is closed

The City of Oakland/Lake Merritt offers an extensive sailing program, which includes a sailing team and sailboat club. Visit the website for a detailed listing of current program offerings. Several kinds of sailboats are available for rent, as well as other types of watercraft. There is parking adjacent to the sailboat house. Personal flotation devices required.

Richmond Yacht Club

351 Brickyard Cove Road

Richmond, CA 94801

www.richmondyc.org

510-237-2821

The Richmond Yacht Club offers a Junior Sailing Program for kids ages 8-18. Kids are required to join as a Junior member of the RYC in order to participate in the sailing program.

Sea Scouts
Island Yacht Club (Sponsor)

Alameda Marina

1815 Clement Avenue

Alameda, CA 94501-1376

www.seafox9.com

www.seascout.org/ships/state.php3?statein=Ca

The Sea Scout Program focuses on a combination of boating skills and citizenship. Some of the boating skills that are taught include rowing, steering at the helm, sail trimming and safety in the proper handling of boats. There are regattas, excursions and seamanship contests. The Sea Scout Program has a ship, sailboats and power vessels. There are also courses available in swimming, lifesaving, first aid, Coast Guard Auxiliary Sailing and Seamanship and cardiopulmonary resuscitation.

Vallejo Yacht Club
485 Mare Island Way
Vallejo, CA 94590
www.vyc.org

707-643-1254

Kids must be at least nine years old and must be able to pass a swim test before they can take lessons. Membership in the club is not required to participate in the sailing program.

Scouting

Boy Scouts of America Mt. Diablo Silverado Council
800 Ellinwood Way
Pleasant Hill, CA 94523
www.bsa-mdsc.org

925-674-6100

The Boy Scouts of America was incorporated to provide a program for community organizations that offers effective character, citizenship and personal fitness training for youth.

Specifically, the BSA endeavors to develop American citizens who are physically, mentally, and emotionally fit; have a high degree of self-reliance as evidenced in such qualities as initiative, courage and resourcefulness; have personal values based on religious concepts; have the desire and skills to help others; understand the principles of the American social, economic and governmental systems; are knowledgeable about and take pride in their American heritage and understand our nation's role in the world; have a keen respect of the basic rights of all people; and are prepared to participate in and give leadership to American society.

Boy Scouting, one of three membership divisions of the BSA (the others are Cub Scouting and Venturing), is available to boys who have earned the Arrow of Light Award or have completed the fifth grade, or who are 11 through 17 years old and subscribe to the Scout Oath and Law. The program achieves the BSA's objectives of developing character, citizenship, and personal fitness qualities among youth by focusing on a vigorous program of outdoor activities.

Call the Mt. Diablo Silverado Council to find a den or troop in your area.

Girl Scouts of San Francisco Bay Area
Mailing address
P.O. Box 2249
Oakland, CA 94621-0149

Physical Address
7700 Edgewater Drive Suite 340
Oakland, CA 94621
www.girlscoutsbayarea.org

510-562-8470
800-447-4475

The Great Outdoors

The Girl Scouts organization has been a pioneer throughout history. The organization became integrated even before the civil rights movement occurred. They had a conservation program before Earth Day was established. Before women wore trousers, the Girl Scouts hiked in the wilderness. Girls Scouts of the San Francisco Bay Area is committed to helping California's girls grow strong. Call the Girl Scouts of San Francisco Bay Area to find out about a troop in your area.

Recycling

Recycling saves energy, natural resources and our environment. Though curbside recycling is available, many items still need to be taken to local recycling facilities. Below is a list of companies and organizations that offer recycling for items such as paint, batteries, and E-waste. Did you know that it is illegal to throw regular household batteries and fluorescent light bulbs into the garbage? There are many businesses, such as Ikea and Walgreens, that also collect batteries throughout the Bay Area. Check the following websites for more information.

California Integrated Waste Management Board

1001 I Street
P.O. Box 4025
Sacramento, CA 95812-4025
www.ciwmb.ca.gov

916-341-6000

The California Waste Management Board website lists the items that are not allowed to be placed in household garbage. You can also locate recycling facilities for things like cell phones, household batteries and latex paint.

eRecycle

www.erecycle.org

This website explains the laws regarding ewaste recycling and provides any links to different recycling options.

West Contra Costa Integrated Waste Management Authority

One Alvarado Square
San Pablo, CA 94806
www.recyclemore.org

510-215-3125

Central Contra Costa HHW Collection Program

4797 Imhoff Place
Martinez, CA 94553
www.centralsan.org

1-800-646-1431

Chapter 7

Community Recreation

There are so many opportunities for children of all ages to participate in youth sports and recreation. Most of the sports programs offered through these community recreation programs are recreational and non-competitive in nature, although some recreation programs offer competitive leagues. This section was created as a quick reference to compare each center and what they have to offer. We tried to include as many programs as possible, but many centers offer more programs than are listed in this section. Please contact your local recreation center for complete information. Please note that programs and activities are changing constantly, and most programs are seasonal, or could be terminated due to lack of enrollment, changing program coordinators, etc.

Program Fees

Fees differ throughout each recreation program and each department. Many departments offer reduced rates for those with a lower income. Some programs also offer early registration discounts if you sign your kids up by a certain date.

Countywide Recreation

East Bay Regional Park District

2950 Peralta Oaks Court, Box 5381
Oakland, CA 94605
www.ebparks.org
510-635-0135

Amenities: 29 Regional Inter-Park Trails, 11 Freshwater Swimming Areas, Boating and/or Stocked Fishing Lakes and Lagoons, Handicapped-Accessible Swimming Pool, 40 Fishing Docks; 3 Bay Fishing Piers, 235 Family Campsites; Youth Camping Areas, 2 Golf Courses, 9 Interpretive & Education Centers, and 18 Children's Play Areas

Classes/Activities: Swimming, Summer Day Camps for Children, Horseback Riding, Camping, Special Events for Kids with Disabilities

City and YMCA Programs

City of Antioch Leisure Services

P.O. Box 5007
Antioch, CA 94531
www.ci.antioch.ca.us/LeisureSvcs/LeisureGuide

925-776-3070

Amenities: Water Park, Theater, Multi-Use Room, Skate Park, Gallery, Golf Course, Soccer Fields, Softball Fields, Basketball Courts, Tennis Courts, Baseball Fields, Volleyball/Sport Courts

Youth Sports: Basketball, Indoor and Outdoor Soccer, Flag Football, Junior Giants Baseball

Classes/Activities: Ballet, Hip-Hop, Tumbling/Gymnastics, Salsa, Cheerleading, Tap, Jazz, Self-Defense, Karate, Swimming, Tennis, Golf

Brentwood Parks & Recreation

740 3rd Street
Brentwood, CA 94513
www.ci.brentwood.ca.us/department/pr/cob_par/parks/home.cfm

925-516-5444

Amenities: Baseball Fields, Soccer Fields, Basketball Courts, Volleyball Courts, Bocce Ball Courts, Tennis Courts, Equestrian Staging Area, Aquatic Center with water slide, Skate Park

Youth Sports: Swim Team, Soccer, Basketball

Classes/Activities: Dance, Karate, Horse/Pony Camps, Self-Defense, Gymnastics, Water Polo

Concord/Clayton YMCA

700 Gym Court
Clayton, CA 94517
www.mdrymca.org/loc_concord_clayton.php?sid=21

925-889-1600

Youth Sports: Basketball, Soccer, Indoor Soccer, Flag Football, Cheerleading

Classes/Activities: Sports Clinics, Teen Leadership, After-School Enrichment Programs, Childcare, Monthly Art Activities for Preschoolers

Concord Parks and Recreation

2974 Salvio Street
Concord, CA 94519
www.ci.concord.nc.us/pkrec

925-671-3404

Amenities: Soccer Fields, Golf Course, Swimming Pool, Tennis Courts, Skate Park, Basketball Courts, Baseball Fields, Batting Cages
Youth Sports: None
Classes/Activities: Martial arts, Bumper Bowling, Gymboree (fitness/music), Gymnastics, Dance, Hip-Hop, Karate, Soccer, Swimming

Danville Recreation Services

420 Front Street
Danville, CA 94526
www.ci.danville.ca.us

925-314-3400

Amenities: Baseball, Softball & Soccer Fields, Basketball & Volleyball Courts, Bocce Ball Courts, Swimming Pools
Youth Sports: Volleyball, Indoor and Outdoor Soccer, Basketball
Classes/Activities: Tae Kwondo, Bumper Bowling, Hip-Hop, Cheerleading, Ballet, Gymnastics, Tennis, Swimming, Dance, Cooking, Soccer, Tap, Spanish, Carpentry, Jazz, Voice, Theater Workshops

San Ramon Valley YMCA

1029 LaGonda Way
Danville, CA 94526
www.mdrymca.org

925-831-1100

Youth Sports: Soccer, Basketball, Football
Classes/Activities: Summer Camps, Enrichment Program

El Cerrito Parks & Recreation

7007 Moeser Lane
El Cerrito, CA 94530
510-559-7006
www.el-cerrito.org

Amenities: Tennis & Basketball Courts, Kickball Areas, Playground Equipment, Swim Center, Jogging Track, Picnic Area, Community Center
Youth Sports: Swim Team, Baseball, Soccer, Basketball
Classes/Activities: After school Programs, Summer Day Camps, After school Enrichment Programs, Sunday Soccer and Baseball, Junior Giants Sports, Peewee sports, Gymnastics, Cheerleading, Music, Dance and Story Time in Hungarian, Polynesian Dance, Dance, Art and Natural Science, Clay and Crafts, Print Making Class, Belly Dancing, Baby Signs, Sign Say and Play, Carpentry, Sewing, Quilting, Crochet

Hercules Recreation & Community Services

2001 Refugio Valley Road
Hercules CA 94547
www.ci.hercules.ca.us/New/Rec/parks.htm

510-799-8291

Amenities: Tennis Courts, 3 Baseball Fields, Soccer Fields, 5 Outdoor Basketball Courts
Youth Sports: Basketball, Youth Swim Team
Classes/Activities: Tahitian Dance, Oil Painting, Martial Arts (Karate, Tae Kwon Do, Modern Arnis de Mano), Tumbling/Gymnastics, Cardio Kick Boxing, Belly Dancing, Swimming /Lessons, Basketball Camps, Tennis, (Toddler Sports Camps, Basketball, Soccer, Football and Baseball)

Lafayette Parks & Recreation Community Center

500 St. Mary's Road
Lafayette, CA 94549
www.lafayetterec.org

925-284-2232

Amenities: Multi-Sports Facility, Soccer and Baseball Fields, Pirate Ship Play Area
Youth Sports: Dodge Ball League, Indoor Floor Hockey, Roller Hockey League, Remix Basketball, Little Lacrosse League
Classes/Activities: Critters N Clay, Busy Bee Cooks, Kids Klay Play, Kinderdance, Kindergym, Kindermusik, KinderTots, Let's Make Music, Music Together, Mad Science, Piano and Me, Spanish for Kindergarteners, Engineering Fundamentals with Legos Workshop, Carpentry, Show Biz Kids, and Spanish for Children. Aikido, Babysitting for Beginners, Beginning Guitar, Chess, Digital Filmmaking, Robotics, Tennis Clinics, Soccer, Basketball, Fencing, Tumbling/Gymnastics

Martinez Recreation & Community Services

525 Henrietta Street
Martinez, CA 94553
www.cityofmartinez.org/depts/recreation/

925-372-3510

Amenities: Playground Areas, Soccer Fields, Ball Fields, Tennis Courts, Bocce Ball Courts, Grass Volleyball and Basketball Courts (some lighted), Picnic Areas, Swimming Pools, Horse-Shoe Pits, Skateboard Park, Sand Volleyball Court, Jogging Track
Youth Sports: Flag Football League, T-Ball
Classes/Activities: Swimming Lessons, Karate, Tumbling/Gymnastics, Dance, Bowling, Tai Chi, T-Ball, Soccer, Special Seasonal Events

Moraga Recreation Hacienda de Las Flores

2100 Donald Drive
Moraga, CA 94556
www.moraga.ca.us

925-376-2520

Amenities: Volleyball, Amphitheater, Picnic Areas, Tot Play Area, Water Play, Sand Volleyball Court, Horseshoes Pit, and Half Court Basketball, Skate Park, Disc Golf Course
Classes/Activities: Music Together, Chess Camp, Carpentry, Kids Cooking, Juggling, Pre-Ballet, Theater

Oakley Recreation Division

3231 Main Street
Oakley, CA 94561
www.ci.oakley.ca.us

925-625-7041

Amenities: Tot lots/Play Structures, Youth Playgrounds/Play Structure Areas, Soccer fields, Baseball and Softball Fields, Basketball & Tennis Courts, Exercise and Fitness Apparatus Area, Swimming Pool, Tetherball Courts
Youth Sports: Intramural Youth Soccer
Classes/Activities: Pre Ballet, Kinder Ballet, Pre Tap, KinderTap, Aikido for Kids, Hands on Nature, The World Around You, Hands On Science, Summer and Winter Camps, After School Programs, Youth Core Summer Camp

Delta Family YMCA

1250 O'Hara Avenue
Oakley, CA 94561
www.mdrymca.org

925-625-9333

Amenities: Cardio Theatre, Cardiovascular Equipment, Strength Training Equipment & Personal Training, Free Childwatch
Youth Sports: T-ball, Soccer, Flag Football, Basketball, Cheerleading
Classes/Activities: Drama, Illustration, Childcare, Teen Leadership, Swimming, Gymnastics, Summer Camp

Orinda Parks & Recreation

28 Orinda Way, Mail Box 2000
Orinda, CA 94563
www.ci.orinda.ca.us/parksandrec
925-254-2445

Amenities: 3 Lighted Tennis Courts, Amphitheater, Water Play Area, Picnic and Barbecue Areas, Game Fields, Volleyball Area, Horseshoe Pit

Youth Sports: Tennis, Basketball, Volleyball, Soccer, Orinda Youth Association (OYA) sports, Sports Camps, Snowboarding and Skiing

Classes/Activities: Arts and Crafts, Dance, Foreign Language Spanish/French, Music, Babysitting Skills, Carpentry, Movement/Drama/Musical Theater, Fitness/Self-Defense/Yoga, Gymnastics, Mad Science, Cooking, Aquatics, Acting, Rock and Roll, Chess, Mad Science, Holiday Classes

Pittsburg Recreation Dept.

65 Civic Avenue
Pittsburg, CA 94565
www.ci.pittsburg.ca.us
925-252-4842

Amenities: Picnic Areas, Soccer fields, Tennis Courts, Basketball Courts, Bocce Ball Courts, Baseball Fields, Swimming Pool, Rental Facility

Youth Sports: Flag Football, Soccer

Classes/Activities: Basketball, Soccer, Flag Football, Dance, Art, Golf, Swimming, Karate & Self-Defense, Dance, Music, Bowling

Pleasant Hill Recreation & Park District

147 Gregory Lane
Pleasant Hill, CA 94523
www.pleasanthillrec.com
925-682-0896

Amenities: Children's Play Structures, Sand Volleyball Courts, Ball Fields, Bocce Ball Courts, Swimming Pools, Sprayground, Lighted Surface Courts, Teen Center, Picnic Areas, Room Rentals

Youth Sports: Flag Football, Basketball, Soccer

Classes/Activities: Swimming Lessons, Pre-School Program, Golf, Bowling, Music, Dance, Ballet, Mad Science, Soccer, Martial Arts, Arts & Crafts, Sports, Fitness and Music. Kinder-Kare, Parent-Tot Time, and Tours for Tots, Summer and Holiday Camps, Tennis Seasonal Events

Irvin Deutscher Family YMCA

350 Civic Drive
Pleasant Hill, CA 94523
www.mdrymca.org
925-687-8900

Amenities: Swimming Pool, Fitness Equipment, Locker Rooms Shower Facilities
Youth Sports: Swim Team
Classes/Activities: Swimming Lessons, Yoga for Kids, Youth Sports Training, Child Watch Center, Teen Center

Pinole Parks & Recreation

2131 Pear Street
Pinole, CA 94564
www.ci.pinole.ca.us/recreation

510-724-9062

Amenities: Picnic Tables, Play Areas, Basketball Courts, Baseball Fields, BBQ Pits, Playhouse, Youth Center, Swim Center
Classes/Activities: Tiny Tots, Summer Camps, Holiday Camps for Middle Schoolers

Richmond Parks & Recreation

3230 MacDonald Avenue
Richmond, CA 94804
www.ci.richmond.ca.us

510-620-6793

Amenities: Ball Fields Nichol Park Complex, Stage, Lighted Ball Soccer and Baseball Fields, BBQ picnic tables, Basketball Courts Tennis Courts, Community Center, Indoor Gym Multi-purpose Room w/ Stage, Fitness Center, Recreation Complex, Gym, Tennis Courts, Bocce Ball Court, Putting Green
Youth Sports: Basketball Flag Football, Softball, Junior Giants Baseball, Tennis Aquatics Volleyball, Street Hockey, Track and Field, Little League, Soccer, Basketball Tournament
Classes/Activities: Seasonal Sports Clinics, After School Programs, Enrichment Classes

Hilltop Family YMCA

4300 Lakeside Drive
Richmond, CA 94806
www.ymcaeastbay.org/hilltop

510-222-9622

Amenities: Two Racquetball Courts, Massage Center, Basketball Courts, Indoor Swimming Pool, Group Exercise, Strength Training Equipment, Free Weights, Cardiovascular Equipment, Dry Sauna
Youth Sports: Basketball, Tae Kwon Do, Indoor Soccer, T-Ball, Volleyball
Classes/Activities: Lap and Family Swim Times, Child Watch, Tot Exercise, Swim Lessons, Gymnastics, Cheerleading, Kid Fit Day Camp

San Ramon Parks & Community Services

12501 Alcosta Blvd.
San Ramon, CA 94583
www.ci.san-ramon.ca.us/parks/index.htm

925-973-3200

Amenities: Tennis Courts, Basketball Courts, Volleyball Courts, Bocce Ball Courts, Baseball/Softball and Soccer Fields, Playground Areas, Aquatic Park, Skateboard Park, BMX Area, Community Center Gyms, Performing Arts Centers, Trails, Gardens, Historic Properties

Youth Sports: Flag Football, Tennis Basketball Indoor Soccer

Classes/Activities: Aquatics, Arts and Craft, Cooking, Enrichment Classes, Music, Dance, Library Programs, Preschool, Sports, Fitness Activites, Theater

Walnut Creek Recreation Division

301 North San Carlos Drive
Walnut Creek, CA 94598
www.walnut-creek.org/recreation.asp?OgId=4

925-943-5858

Amenities: Swim center with three Pools, Tennis Court, Basketball Courts, Volleyball Courts, Walking Trails, Man-Made Pond, Baseball/Softball Fields, Soccer Field, Children's Playground, Picnic Tables, Barbeques

Youth Sports: Diving Team, Swim Team, Synchronized Swim Team

Classes/Activities: Adventures with Toddlers (nature outings), Cooking, Gymnastics, Ice Skating, Dance, Karate, Ski & Snowboard, Cooking, Computer Game Creation, Ice Hockey, Martial Arts, Carpentry, Acting, Science Classes, Kidz Love Soccer, Aquatics, Golf, Bowling, Gymnastics, Special Needs Indoor Sports League, Karate and Summer Day Camp

Sports and Children's Fitness

W e definitely understand how hard it is to find information about leagues for your kids! Information is constantly changing so be sure to call each league for more details. Remember to check the "Community Recreation" chapter to find leagues sponsored by your local community recreation center.

Benifits of Sports

As we've researched the different opportunities in our community we've come across a lot of helpful information about the benefits of sports participation for kids. Did you know that participating in sports

- Teaches cooperative play
- Good sportsmanship
- Fair play
- Social competence
- The ability to give and receive feedback
- Teamwork

There are sports out there for everyone whether they are solo, team, competitive or recreational. Just remember to choose a sport that best fits your child and keep it a positive experience. Play ball and have a great time doing it!

Team Sports

City Sports, County Sports & Youth Programs

Depending on what type of sport or activity you're looking for, a good place to begin your search will be on local city or county government websites. Most counties provide sports, fitness, and recreation activities that boys and girls can enjoy all year long. You can find instructional, recreational and competitive leagues for all levels of interest and ability. Most city and county sites are independently managed so there isn't one magic word or phrase to look for on each site. Look for terms like "Parks and Recreation," "Community Sports" and "Youth Sports/Programs."

Bay Area Outreach & Recreation Program

www.borp.org

This website focuses on sports programs designed for children with disabilities. Several sports leagues are available for both girls and boys.

Cal Youth Sports & Recreation

Berkeley, CA

www.oski.org

This website provides information about all youth sports programs at UC Berkeley.

Walnut Creek Youth Athletic Association

www.wcyaa.com

925-933-4884

The Walnut Creek Youth Athletic Association offers recreational sports for boys and girls ages 4 through 8th grade, including Flag Football, Basketball, T-Ball/Baseball/Softball, and Summer Soccer. The emphasis is on fun, good sportsmanship and team play. Coaches are volunteers or team parents.

Walnut Creek Sports League

www.walnutcreeksportsleague.com

Visit the Walnut Creek Sports League website for information regarding basketball, baseball, flag and tackle football, t-ball, baseball soccer camp and windsurfing camp.

Baseball

John Skilton's Baseball Links

www.baseball-links.com/links/Youth_Baseball/California

This is a link listing every type of baseball league in California. Scroll through the various links to find your local league or baseball association.

Little League California District 57

www.eteamz.com/ca57

California District 57 consists of 13 different Little League organizations throughout Danville, San Ramon, Livermore, Pleasanton and Dublin. Click on "Leagues" to see the specific list for your area. There is also a listing for clinics, camps and tournaments.

Junior Giants

www.sanfrancisco.giants.mlb.com/sf/community/gcf/juniorgiants.jsp

The Junior Giants program is available throughout Bay Area recreation centers. It is available free of charge for kids ages 5-18. It is a non-competitive program. Visit the website for links to the cities participating in the program. Click on "Find a League Near You" to get contact names and phone numbers for those in charge of your local program.

Rob Andrews Baseball Camps

1280 Mountbatten Drive
Concord, CA 94518
www.robandrewsbaseball.com
925-935-3505

Rob Andrews Baseball Camps are offered in 7 cities throughout the Bay Area. There are regular camps for children ages 7 and up. There is also an advanced training camp. The camp is open to both boys and girls, but there are usually no more than 5 girls attending any given session.

Pinole-Hercules Little League

www.phllca4.org

The Pinole-Hercules Little League offers the following programs: Tee Ball (ages 5–8), Baseball (ages 8–16) and Girls Softball (ages 8–16).

Tara Hills Recreation Association

P.O. Box 37
Pinole, CA 94564
www.tarahillsbaseball.net
510-724-2105

Tara Hills Recreation Association offers leagues that can accommodate ages 4 to 16 year olds. The program is competitive, but also emphasizes sportsmanship.

Pleasant Hill Baseball Association

3100 Oak Park Blvd.
Pleasant Hill, CA 94523
www.phba.org
925-933-7950

Pleasant Hill Baseball Association offers teams for girls and boys ages 5–15.

Sports and Children's Fitness

Walnut Creek Little League
P.O. Box 3235
Walnut Creek, CA 94598
www.wcbaseball.org

The Walnut Creek Little League offers baseball and softball programs for boys and girls ages 8–16.

Basketball

Junior Warriors Program
www.nba.com/warriors/community/junior_warriors_basketball_league.html

The Junior Warriors program is offered throughout Bay Area community centers. Visit the website to find the program nearest to your neighborhood.

Junior NBA/WNBA
www.nba.com/jrnba

The Junior NBA/WNBA is offered throughout recreation centers and other facilities. The website has listings for participating locations.

National Jr. Basketball Association
www.njbl.org
714-917-3565

This website has links to all of their local chapters. Go to the Divisional section and select chapter/division list. Then click on the link for your city.

NorCal Preps
www.norcalpreps.rivals.com/content.asp?SID=985&CID=27576

This is a listing for all the boys' club teams in the area.

Football

NFL Flag Youth Football
eteamz.active.com/nflflag

There are numerous NFL flag football programs throughout the Bay Area. Type in your zip code to locate participating organizations in your area.

San Ramon Valley Thunderbirds Youth Football and Spirit Leader Organization
Danville, CA
www.srvtbirds.com

The San Ramon Valley Thunderbirds offer football and spirit programs for boys and girls from age 8 to 14.

USA Football

www.usafootball.com

877-5-FOOTBALL (1-877-536-6822)

NFL Flag is a national program that teaches kids about football and encourages participation and sportsmanship. Go to the Youth Football section and select directory. Then input some basic information, and the website will find leagues in your area. All of the league listings will also be sent via e-mail. Many of the leagues have home pages and online registration available.

Gymnastics

American Academy of Rhythmic Gymnastics

San Ramon, CA 94583
www.arclub.net

925-828-6177

Beginner, advanced and competitive team programs.
Children ages 4 and up are taught the Olympic sport of rhythmic gymnastics, combining the elegance, grace and beauty of a dancer with the strength and coordination of an athlete. Tumbling, yoga, pilates, flexibility, muscle tone, balance, concentration skills together with music appreciation are emphasized. Girls will enjoy ribbons, hoops, balls and ropes. Your child will learn to be fit for life and love it!

Encore Gymnastics

999 Bancroft Road
Walnut Creek, CA 94518
www.encoregym.com

925-932-1033

There are two locations in the Bay Area. Visit their website for more information.

Golden Gate Gymnastics

1441C Franquette Avenue
Concord, CA 94520
www.goldengategymnastics.com

925-674-9683

Classes are offered for pre-school age, recreational competition and open gyms.

Liberty Gymnastics

2330-A Bates Avenue
Concord, CA 94520
www.libertygymtrainingcenter.com

925-687-8009

Liberty Gymnastics offers programs for toddlers all the way up to adults. There are recreational classes, rhythmic classes, and a competitive program as well.

Sports and Children's Fitness

Gymtastic
1901 Camino Ramon #D
Danville, CA 94526
www.gymtastic.com
925-277-1881
There are classes for children ages 1–9 and summer camps as well.

Hockey
East Bay Hockey League
www.ebayhockey.com

The East Bay Hockey League provides youth roller hockey leagues in Alameda, Danville, Dublin, Alamo and San Ramon.

Lacrosse
Diablo Scorpion Lacrosse
www.scorpionlacrosse.com
925-648-7845

The Diablo Scorpion Lacrosse Team offers lacrosse programs for children in Danville, Alamo and San Ramon. Both girls and boys programs are available. There are 18 club teams ranging from Kindergarten through 8th grade.

Rugby
Diablo Youth Rugby Club
Pleasant Hill, CA
www.diabloyouthrugby.org

The Diablo Youth Rugby Club offers a youth team for children ages 5 to 15. Sign-up is available online.

Lamorinda Youth Rugby Football Club
www.lamorugby.com
925-295-1043

The Lamorinda Youth Rugby Football Club has teams for children in 1st through 8th grade. There are both intramural and league play teams.

Soccer

Contra Costa County is home to a large number of soccer clubs, both competitive and recreational. There are so many, in fact, that the listing below only includes a few of the clubs, as well as some general resources to help you in your search for the ideal soccer experience for your child. As far as recreational soccer programs go, check the AYSO website listed below to find a league in your area. If you and your child are ready to jump to the next level and try competitive soccer, most of the competing leagues in Contra Costa County are members of the Golden State Soccer League. Check that website for a listing of competitive leagues in your area.

American Youth Soccer Association

www.soccer.org
1-800-872-2976

The AYSO is a recreational soccer organization that focuses on giving kids equal playing time. Visit the website to locate a soccer organization in your area.

Golden State Soccer League

www.goldenstatesoccer.com

Visit the Golden State Soccer League for a comprehensive resource of leagues in the area. Once on the website, go to the Member Clubs/links section for a complete listing of teams and the links to their websites.

Mt. Diablo Soccer Association

P.O. Box 21111
Concord, CA 94521
www.mdsoccer.org

Mt. Diablo Soccer Association is a member of the AYSO. There are teams for children ages 4 1/2 to 18. There is also a select winter soccer program for children in U-10, U-12 and U-14 divisions.

Delta Youth Soccer League (DYSL)

P.O. Box 2085
Antioch, CA 94531
www.deltasoccer.org
925-439-4396

DYSL provides recreational and competitive soccer programs for boys and girls ages 4 to 19 years in the Antioch, Pittsburg, Bay Point and adjacent unincorporated areas.

Sports and Children's Fitness

Diablo Valley Soccer Club

P.O. Box 27665
Concord, CA 94527
www.dvsc.com
925-229-DVSC

DVSC offers competitive soccer for girls and boys. Children must tryout in order to join the team. Visit the website for tryout information.

Lamorinda Soccer Club Inc.

www.lamorindasoccer.com

This soccer club offers a competitive program for children ages 7 to 19.

Mustang Soccer League

www.mustangsoccer.com
925-831-1323

The Mustang Soccer League encompasses Alamo, Danville, Diablo, Blackhawk and parts of South Walnut Creek. There is a large competitive program for children ages 6–19

West Contra Costa Youth Soccer League

Pinole, CA
www.wccysl.com

There are recreational and competitive programs through this league.

Walnut Creek Soccer Club

Walnut Creek, CA
www.wcsc.org
925-930-0210

The Walnut Creek Soccer Club offers recreational and competitive teams for children ages 6–18. Season starts the first week in September.

Softball

San Ramon Valley Girls Athletic League

www.srvgal.org
925-838-2694

San Ramon Valley Girls Athletic League has teams for girls between the ages of 5 and 18.

Swim Teams

There certainly is no shortage of swim clubs in the Bay Area. Below you will find a listing of some of the clubs in Contra Costa County, but it is by no means comprehensive. If you don't see a nearby swim club listed, check out the Club Swim website listed below. It's an excellent resource for finding a club or team in your area.

Aquatic Times

www.aquatictimes.com

This website provides a comprehensive listing of swim teams in the area, as well as links to each team's website.

Club Swim

www.clubswim.com

Club Swim is a well organized website that includes resources about area swim teams, swimming instruction, diving, synchronized swimming and water polo information and listings.

Aquanuts Synchronized Swimming Team

P.O. Box 3068
Walnut Creek, CA 94598
www.aquanuts.org

925-934-4792

Aquanuts is one of the top synchronized swimming organizations in the country. There is a team for young girls up to teens, and summer camps for girls to try out the sport. They practice at Heather Farm Park in Walnut Creek.

Blackhawk Swim Team

www.hoxswim.com

925-736-6500

The Blackhawks Swim Team, also known as the Hox, offers a recreational swim program. The season usually consists of 10–12 meets and goes from June to August. There are programs for children ages 4 to 18 years. They also offer a program called Pre-Hox, which is for swimmers ages 4 and older to prepare to move to the swim team the following swim season. Membership at the Blackhawk Country Club is required in order to be involved in either of the swim team programs.

Dana Hills Swim Team

P.O. Box 698
Clayton, CA 94517
www.danahillsotters.com

The Dana Hills Swim Team offers both recreational and competitive swim team programs. There are programs for children ages 4 to 18 years.

Sports and Children's Fitness

Danville Sea Devils Swim Team

www.sea-devils.org

Danville Sea Devils Swim Team offers a swim team program for children ages 4 to 18. Their practices take place at the Danville Station Pool. New swimmers usually register in February.

Livorna Swim Team

P.O. Box 334
Alamo, CA 94507
www.livornadolphins.com

The Livorna Dolphins practice at the Livorna Estates neighborhood pool, located in South Walnut Creek on the border of Alamo. They offer a Junior Dolphin program for younger children and a competitive program for swimmers up to 18 years old. Visit their website for registration information.

Martinez Community Swim Team

P.O. Box 2098
Martinez, CA 94553
www.gototters.org

The Martinez Community Swim Team offers programs for children ages 4 to 18 years. Registration is usually held in March. The team practices at Rankin Pool Park.

Pleasant Hill Aquatics

468 Boyd Road
Pleasant Hill, CA 94523-3209
www.phaquatics.org
925-932-9595

The Pleasant Hill Aquatics Swim Team offers a family-oriented and parent supported recreational program. There are programs for children ages 5 to 18 years.

Pinole Seals Swim Club

Pinole Swim Center
2450 Simas Avenue
Pinole, CA 94564
www.pinoleseals.org
510-758-7566

The Pinole Seals offers swim training for kids age 5 to 18. Swimmers of age four and under are allowed if they have an older sibling on the team.

Orinda Moraga Pools Association

P.O. Box 451
Orinda, CA 94563
www.ompaswim.com

925-455-5952

The Orinda Moraga Pools Association offers a summer recreational swim league for children of all abilities aged 3-18.

Terrapins Swim Team

Concord and Brentwood, CA
www.terrapinswim.com

925-680-8372 x208

The Terrapins Swim Team offers a comprehensive program for novice through Olympic hopeful athletes. The competitive team competes year round. Other programs include a summer recreation competitive swim team, winter water polo, training programs, and fall/summer stroke programs. The Terrapins train at Heritage High School Pool and Liberty School Pool in Brentwood, and Cowell Pool in Concord.

Solo Sports

Aircraft and Aviation

Pacific States Aviation

www.pacificstatesaviation.com

925-685-4400

Pacific States Aviation offers ground training only for children under 16. For in plane training, kids must be 16 or older.

Sterling Aviation

145 John Glenn Drive
Concord, CA 94520
www.sterling-flight.com

925-687-2850

Sterling Aviation offers ground training only for children under 16. For in plane training, kids must be 16 or older.

Cycling

P & R Sports—Sand Hill Ranch

Mailing Address:
601 Fourth Street
Brentwood, CA 94513

Track Address:
50 Camino Diablo
Brentwood, CA 94513
www.prsports.com

925-240-6247

The Bicycle Area is open every Saturday and Sunday10am to 5 pm year-round, weather-permitting. There is also a weekly e-mail newsletter you can sign up for so they can send you weather reports and news of closed days (for races or events). Helmets are mandatory. The fee is $10 per person to ride. Kids under the age of 18 cannot be dropped off without a signed waiver from their parents. The waiver is available on the website. Honor students, with copy of a recent report card, and a GPA of 3.75 or better, can ride free for one practice day. There is a Biker Cross (mountain cross) track, Dual Slalom, car jumps, a teeter-totter, and training sections over rocks and logs.

Fencing

Sport Fencing Center

5221 Central Avenue #9
Richmond, CA 94804
www.sportfencingcenter.com

510-528-5110

Sport Fencing Center features nine fencing strips with electronic scoring machines. Sport Fencing Center offers programs for children age five through adult

Sword Play Fencing

1061 Shary Circle, #A1
Concord, CA 94518
www.swordplayfencing.net

925-687-9883

Sword Play Fencing Academy offers group lessons and private instruction in foil, épée, and sabre for men and women of all ages. Sword Play is open to everyone.

Golf

Junior Golf Association of Northern California

700 Center Court
Morro Bay, CA 93442
www.jganc.com

The JGANC website is a great resource for learning information pertinent to the junior golfer.

Boundary Oak Golf Course

3800 Valley Vista Road
Walnut Creek, CA 94596
www.BoundaryOak.com

925-934-6211

Boundary Oak offers both private and group golf instruction classes.

Grayson Woods

400 Iron Hill Street
Pleasant Hill, CA94523
www.golfgraysonwoods.com

925-935-7277

Grayson Woods is the ideal golf course for families. Kids and adults love the beautiful 18 hole putting course, with a stream and waterfall traveling throughout. The nine hole par 3 course is also great for practicing on a full size course. Golf gear, as well as golf carts, are available for rent. You can also book golf lessons with one of the instructors. They have state-of-the-art swing analysis available. Treat the kids afterwards with an ice cream bar at the onsite snack shack.

Karate

The Bay Area has so many karate gyms that there are too many to mention here. Below you will find a few karate schools as well as one general resource to help you in your search.

San Francisco.com

www.local.sanfrancisco.com

This website is an excellent resource for finding all karate classes in your area. It is also useful to find other classes and activities in your area.

America's Best Karate of Danville

321 Hartz Avenue, Suite 1
Danville, CA 94526
www.abkdan.com

925-838-3820

This Karate School teaches both Olympic style sparring, and point sparring.

Danville Karate International

105 Town and Country Drive, Suite E
Danville, CA 94526
www.karateintl.com

925-820-9612

Danville Karate has limited class sizes. They focus on teaching life skills such as self-discipline, respect, propriety, leadership and perseverance. They do not have contracts.
Blackbelts are offered in Kenpo Karate and Tae Kwon Do/Moo Duk Kwan (Korean Karate).

East Bay Karate-Do

1365 Buchanan Road
Pittsburg, CA 94565
www.Eastbaykarate-Do.com

925-439-0964

East Bay Karate-Do has karate programs for all ages. The Little Ninjas program is for 3 to 6 year olds, the Little Dragons are for 7–11 year olds, and there is also a teen and adult program.

Family Martial Arts of America

984 Howe Road
Martinez, CA 94553
www.fmaakarate.com

925-370-6000

Pee Wees classes are for Children 4–6 years old. This program is designed for the very young in mind. We teach children to follow directions and to learn coordination in a fun and exciting environment.
Children 7–12: Our focus is confidence and discipline. Students are taught that they can reach their goals, no matter the obstacle, whether it is in karate, school, or other aspects of their life. These lessons are remembered even into adulthood.

Hamilton Martial Arts Academy

6271 Lone Tree Way, Suite K
Brentwood, CA 94513
www.reksuitswest.com

925-884-3800

The Hamilton Martial Arts Academy offers a trial class for prospective students.

Sports and Children's Fitness

Kang's Taekwondo Academy

1368 Sunset Drive
Antioch, CA 94509
www.kangstkd.com

925-978-9999

Kang's Taekwondo Academy features classes for children of all ages.

1251 Arroyo Way
Walnut Creek, CA 94598
925-933-6647

Karate For Kids

1839 Ygnacio Valley Road
Walnut Creek, CA 94598
www.maakarate.com

925-932-9000

There are gyms in San Ramon and Walnut Creek. There are classes for children ages 3 1/2 and up.

Richard Lee's East West

140 Alamo Plaza Suite C
Alamo, CA 94507
www.bokfudo.com

925-831-0292

Richard Lee's offers martial arts training for children as young as 3 1/2 years old. Your child can take a complimentary class to give him/her the opportunity to see if there is an interest, and to give the instructor the chance to determine your child's readiness.

Satori Academy of Martial Arts

2720 Pinole Valley Road
Pinole, CA 94564
www.satoriacademy.com

510-758-2007

This school has many locations. The website offers information on all of the locations, including the Pinole location. They offer a Little Samurai program (5-6 year olds) and a Junior Program (6-12 year olds).

Motocross

Club Moto

Livermore, CA 94551

www.clubmoto.com

925-443-MOTO

Club Moto offers individual and group riding lessons for all skill levels of riders. The group lessons are $50 per rider. The track is located off of Highway 580 west over Altamont pass. Exit at the Altamont Pass/Greenville Road exit in Livermore. Club Moto is open for general practice Saturdays 9 am–3 pm, Sundays 9am-5pm and Wednesday nights 3 pm–9 pm. Club Moto admission is $20 per rider, which includes a spectator pass and $35 for parents and their children. Monthly Passes are $125 for individuals and $200 for parents and their children.

P & R Sports—Sandhill Ranch

601 Fourth Street

Brentwood, CA 9451

Track Address:

50 Camino Diablo

Brentwood, CA 94513

www.prsports.com

925-240-6247

There is a certified instructor for the MSF (Motorcycle Safety Foundation) at Sand Hill.

Classes are a one-day, approximately 5 hour session. Classes cover the basics of learning to ride with a focus on safety. They are grouped according to age, with 6 years old being the minimum. Classes are four students at a time and are usually taught on Saturdays. Classes fill up approximately 2 months in advance. Loaner bikes, helmets and boots are available.

Running

Youth Runner Magazine

www.youthrunner.com

Visit the Youth Runner Magazine to learn more about the sport of running, as well as upcoming youth running events in your area.

Kids Running

www.kidsrunning.com

This is an excellent resource for parents of kids who are interested in running. There is a useful chart that gives recommendations for how much running is appropriate for kids of different ages. There are also some running games, fun run calendars and healthy eating tips.

Sports and Children's Fitness

Pacific Association Youth

www.pausatf.org/indexyouth.html

Pacific Association Youth is a cross country and track and field association that offers programs for kids starting as young as 8 years old.

Scuba Diving Instruction

Advanced Diving Technologies

625 California Avenue
Pittsburg, CA 94565
925-432-2111

Advance Diving Technologies offers classes in all levels of training, including both recreational and technical training.

Anchor Shack Dive & Travel

5775 Pacheco Blvd.
Martinez, CA 94553
www.anchorshack.com
925-825-4960

The Anchor Shack has an on-site heated pool and offers classes for open water beginners to Master Scuba Diver.

Skateboarding

Antioch Skatepark

4701 Lone Tree Way
Antioch, CA 94509
www.ci.antioch.ca.us
925-779-7070

Enjoy two rails, a volcano, a pyramid with box, a vertical wall, a big and small twinkie, some hips, a double bowl and stairs. Skateboarders must wear helmets, knee and elbow pads at all times while using the park.

San Ramon Sk8 Park

Central Park at the corner of Bollinger Canyon Road and Market Place
San Ramon, CA 94583
www.srteen.org
925-973-3362

On weekends prior to 11 am, priority is given to children ages 11 and under. An adult must accompany children under the age of 7. Skateboards and in-line skates only—no bicycles allowed. All users are required to wear helmets, knee and elbow pads.

Swimming Instruction

All-Star Academy of Danville

5800 Camino Tassajara
Danville, CA 94506
www.allstardanville.com
925-967-0900

All-Star Academy of Danville offers both a swimming program and a daycare program. Visit the website for contact information.

Carson Swim School

2601 Anderson Lane
Brentwood, CA 94513
www.carsonswimschool.com
925-634-7946

Carson Swim School has two locations, one in Antioch and one in Brentwood. They offer lessons for infants 6 months old to competitive lessons for older kids.

801 East 18th Street
Antioch, CA 94509
925-755-AQUA

Canyon Swim School

21 Campbell Lane
El Sobrante, CA 94803
www.canyonswimschool.com
510-223-4600

This swim school offers lessons for infants all the way up to older competitive swimmers. Visit their website for more information.

Fremont Swim School/American Swim Academy

Locations in Dublin, Livermore, Fremont & Newark
www.FremontSwimSchool.com
www.AmericanSwimAcademy.com
1-800-810-7946 (SWIM)

Hours: Open daily and year round
Prices: Vary

Fremont Swim School has been the authority on swim instruction for 35 years. Indoor, heated pools make learning to swim comfortable and small class size combined with quality instruction make these schools the #1 choice for swim lessons. All ages and abilities—6 months to adult.

Sports and Children's Fitness

Little Dipper Swim School

552 Boyd Road
Pleasant Hill, CA 94523
www.littledipperswimschool.com

925-932-5861

The Little Dipper Swim School offers lessons for infants (3 months & up) to older children.

Sherman Swim School

1075 Carol Lane
Lafayette, CA 94549
www.shermanswim.com

925-283-2100

Sherman Swim School features an outdoor pool and offers lessons from late spring through fall. They also offer springboard diving lessons for kids 7 and up.

Sue's Swim School

2701 Stone Valley Road
Alamo, CA 94507
www.sueswimschool.com

925-837-2428

Sue's Swim School offers private, group and Parent and Me classes.

Tennis

Youth Tennis League

youthleaguetennis.org/california/NCAL/ncal.html

The Youth Tennis League offers lessons throughout Alameda and Contra Costa Counties. The website has listings of lesson sites as well as online registration.

Rancho Colorados Swim and Tennis Club

3016 Rohrer Drive
P.O. Box 246
Lafayette, CA 94549
925-299-6993
www.ranchocolorados.com

There are tennis camps available after school for children ages 5 and up, as well as summer tennis camps. Check the website for upcoming events and programs.

Moraga Tennis & Swim Club

1161 Larch Avenue
Moraga, CA 94556
www.moragatennisandswimclub.com

925-376-1622

Moraga Tennis and Swim Club has a competitive tennis team and also offers clinics and private lessons throughout the fall and summer.

Sleepy Hollow Swim and Tennis

1 Sunnyside Lane
Orinda CA 94563
www.golegends.org

925-254-1126

There are spring and summer programs for children ages 5-18.

Walnut Creek Tennis Center

at Heather Farm Park
Walnut Creek, CA 94598
925-945-0105
www.werent.com/happyvalleytennis.htm

Walnut Creek Tennis Center provides a full service tennis program. This includes a racquet demonstration program and a variety of lessons and programs for adults and juniors.

Wakeboarding & Waterskiing
Golden Gate Water Ski Club

www.ggwsc.org

Visit the website to find opportunities for kids to compete in waterskiing.

Yoga
World Yoga Healing Arts Center

1530 South Main Street
Walnut Creek, CA 94596
www.world-yoga.com

925-274-9642

The World Yoga Healing Arts Center offers a kids' yoga program for 4-8 year olds.

General Resources

Chicz on the Go
www.chiczonthego.net
1-877-933-6644

Chicz on the go specializes in survival kits for young female athletes for weekend-long soccer tournaments to daylong swim meets. They offer bags for soccer, basketball, softball, volleyball, swimming/water polo, lacrosse, golf, chorus and dance all with specialized products that girls need before, during and after sports games. Having a birthday party chicz on the go can create custom party favors.

Spectator Sports

Baseball

Oakland Athletics (American League)
Oakland/Alameda Coliseum
Highway 880 & Hegenberger Road
Oakland, CA 94621
510-638-0500

San Francisco Giants (National League)
SBC Park
San Francisco, CA 94107
www.giants.mlb.com

Golden State Warriors
Oakland/Alameda Coliseum
Highway 880 & Hegenberger Road
Oakland, CA 94621
www.nba.com/warriors

Football

Oakland Raiders
Oakland/Alameda Coliseum
Highway 880 & Hegenberger Road
Oakland, CA 94621
www.raiders.com
1-800-RAIDERS

San Francisco 49ers
Candlestick Park

Giants Drive and Gilman Avenue
San Francisco, CA 94124
www.sf49ers.com

415-656-4900

Hockey
San Jose Sharks

www.sharks.nhl.com

408-999-5757

Horse Racing
Golden Gate Fields

1100 Eastshore Highway
Berkeley, CA 94710
www.goldengatefields.com

510-559-7300

Soccer
San Jose Earthquakes

www.sjearthquakes.com

408-556-7700

Visit the San Jose Earthquake's website for ticket information.

College Sports

California Golden Bears
University of California at Berkeley
www.calbears.cstv.com

Diablo Valley College Vikings
Diablo Valley College, Pleasant Hill
www.dvc.edu/athletics
925-685-1230 ext. 260 Information
925-687-4445 Tickets

St. Mary's College Gaels
St. Mary's College, Moraga
www.stmarys-ca.edu
925-631-4000 Information
925-631-4392 Tickets

Chapter 9

Music

Beyond the enjoyment of learning a new skill and appreciating what they can produce, music offers a myriad of positive benefits to our kids. The following research indicates that music increases a child's abilities giving them skills such as:

- Creative and Analytical Thinking
- Concentration
- Discipline
- Self-Esteem
- Self-Expression

- Coordination
- Imagination
- Problem Solving
- Fine Motor Skill Development
- Increased Intelligence

Music Studies

Students of the arts continue to outperform their non-arts peers on the SAT, according to reports by the College Entrance Examination Board. In 2006, SAT takers with coursework/experience in music performance scored 57 points higher on the verbal portion of the test and 43 points higher on the math portion than students with no coursework or experience in the arts. Scores for those with coursework in music appreciation were 62 points higher on the verbal and 41 points higher on the math portion. The Student Descriptive Questionnaire, a self-reported component of the SAT that gathers information about students' academic preparation, gathered data for these reports. Source: The College Board, Profile of College-Bound Seniors National Report for 2006; www.collegeboard.com

Nearly 100% of past winners in the prestigious Siemens Westinghouse Competition in Math, Science and Technology (for high school students) play one or more musical instruments. This led the Siemens Foundation to host a recital at Carnegie Hall in 2004, featuring some of these young people, after which a panel of experts debated the nature of the apparent science/music link. The

Music

Midland Chemist (American Chemical Society) Vol. 42, No. 1, Feb. 2005

Young children who take music lessons show different brain development and improved memory over the course of a year, compared to children who do not receive musical training. The brains of musically trained children respond to music in a different way than those of untrained children, and that the musical training improves their memory. After one year the musically trained children performed better in a memory test that is correlated with general intelligence skills such as literacy, verbal memory, Visio spatial processing, mathematics and IQ.

-Dr. Laurel Trainor, Prof. of Psychology, Neuroscience, and Behaviour at McMaster University, Director of the McMaster Institute for Music and the Mind; Canada; published 9/20/06; www.sciencedaily.com/releases/2006/09/060920093024.htm

Read on to find resources to get your children involved in music so they can reap these benefits!

National Suzuki Music Association

www.suzukiassociation.org

The Suzuki Association of the Americas (SAA) provides programs and services to members throughout North and South America. Go to the "parents" icon and click on the "teacher location." Follow instructions to view a list of teachers in your area.

Summer Suzuki institutes are special camps that provide an intensive musical experience for families with children who currently study an instrument through the Suzuki Method. Institutes are located in all regions of the U.S. and Canada, offering activities for students, parents and teachers in one-week sessions throughout the summer. For more information on summer institutes visit their website under the "Parent's Link" and then click on "Summer Institutes."

Suzuki Music Association of California

www.suzuki-ca.org

The Suzuki Music Association of California (SMAC) is a professional organization for teachers and families who are involved with Suzuki Music education. Instruments involved are piano, bass, flute, guitar, harp, oboe, recorder, violin, cello and viola. Their website has a comprehensive list of teachers, the instruments they teach, where they are located and how they can be reached.

Suzuki Association of Northern California

www.suzukinorcal.org

Suzuki Association of Northern California (SANC) provides members with motivating and inspiring events, including the Annual Graduation Concert, the Advanced Suzuki Institute for violin, viola and cello students, the Peninsula Play-In, Suzuki Family Overnight Camp Campbell and Teacher workshops, and short intensive courses.

Music Teachers Association of California

www.mtac.org

The music Teacher association of California offers a variety of benefits and services to professional music teachers and students. This site has a comprehensive database of instructors searchable by zip code and instrument.

Musika

www.musikalessons.com

Instruments: Cello, clarinet, drums, flute, trumpet, guitar, piano, saxophone, trombone, violin and voice.

The Musika Teacher Group is the nation's premiere music lesson organization. They offer the creative stimulation and structure offered in a music school setting in the privacy of your own home or one of their teachers' studios.

California Bluegrass Association

www.cbaontheweb.org

The California Bluegrass Association (CBA) is a Non-Profit Corporation which is dedicated to the furtherance of Bluegrass, Old-Time, and Gospel Music in California. The organization was formed to promote, encourage, foster, and cultivate the preservation, appreciation, understanding, enjoyment, support, and performance of traditional instrumental and vocal music of the United States. Their website has a comprehensive list of instructors in California.

Craigslist

www.craigslist.us (for an overview)
www.craigslist.org

You can search Craigslist for music teachers in your area. Craigslist.org is an especially good resource for finding a music teacher, for a not so common instrument. Simply enter the type of lesson you are looking for and you will get a list of matches in your area.

Gymboree Play & Music

Ages: 6 mos-5 years
Hours: Call your local Gymboree location for party availability._
Price: Call for details

Designed by child development experts, each of Gymboree's seven levels focus on and support the specific developmental milestone your child is working on at his/her age--from sensory explorations for young babies to cause and effect, two-way communication, "motor planning," imaginary play, to early listening and language skills. Each program level incorporates fundamental, engaging activities that help to build your child's cognitive, social and physical skills. "Sibling Solutions" are available for families with multiple children who wish to experience a variety of classes at Gymboree. Contact your local Gymboree for classes and times. Gymboree Play & Music centers also offer art and music classes as well as Mommy and Baby Fitness classes. For specific information on classes in Oakland, El Cerrito or Lafayette, you may also call (510) 834-0982.

Music

<u>The following locations offer Gymboree Classes:</u>

1st Street Corner

3482 Mt. Diablo Blvd.
Lafayette, CA 94549
925-283-4896

Willows Shopping Center

1975 Diamond Blvd. #C-130
Concord, CA 94520
925-283-4896

Crow Canyon Commons

3191-A Crow Canyon Place
San Ramon, CA 94583
925-866-8315

Kindermusik

www.Kindermusik.com

www.eastbaykindermusik.com

Kindermusik is one place to dance, sing, play and learn about instruments, share a story, create, compare, explore, and more. Each class level is carefully designed to enhance your child's musical, language, mental, physical, social and emotional development, and to pave the way for each new developmental step. Family involvement lets you learn and enjoy with your child --from dancing with your baby to reading the notes of your child's first musical composition.

Go to **www.Eastbaykindermusik.com** to find a qualified Kindermusik instructor near you.

<u>The following listings are Kindermusik affiliates:</u>

Lindsay Levin

Walnut Creek, Danville, San Ramon, and Dublin, CA
dghende865@comcast.net
925-866-8055
Ages: newborn to 7 years old

Joanne Finn

Pleasant Hill, CA 94523
jcfinn@phch.org
925-708-1604
Ages: newborn to 7 years old

The Crossings

Concord, CA

www.eastbaykindermusik.com

missjaneb@sbcglobal.net

925-706-8827

Ages: newborn to 7 years old

Terri Knight

El Cerrito, CA94530

knights5@scglobal.net

510-528-12290

Ages: 3 to 5 years old

Joanna Mina

Hercules, CA

musikwithjojo@yahoo.com

Ages: newborn to 3 years old

Cristy Aday

Pinole, CA

kmwithkristy@yahoo.com

510-508-6356

Ages: newborn and up

Wildflower Pool Clubhouse

Antioch, CA

www.eastbaykindermusik.com

missjaneb@sbcglobal.net

925-706-8827

Ages: newborn to 7 years old

Kindermusik with Miss Jane

Brentwood, CA

www.eastbaykindermusik.com

missjaneb@sbcglobal.net

925-706-8827

Ages: newborn to 7 years old

Music Together

www.musictogether.com

Music Together is an internationally recognized early childhood music program for babies, toddlers, preschoolers, kindergarteners, and the adults who love them. First offered to the public in 1987, it pioneered the concept of a research-based, developmentally appropriate early childhood music curriculum that strongly emphasizes and facilitates adult involvement.

Music Together classes are based on the recognition that all children are musical. All children can learn to sing in tune, keep a beat, and participate with confidence in the music of our culture, provided that their early environment supports such learning.

The following listings are Music Together affiliates:

Music Together in the Tri-Valley

www.musictogether.net

925-551-7722

Danville: Tao Sports

Livermore: Livermore Valley Tennis Club
Livermore: Triple Threat Performing Arts
Pleasanton: Ingram and Brauns Musik Shoppe
San Ramon: Dougherty Station Community Centre
Walnut Creek: Contra Costa Ballet Centre
Walnut Creek: Giggle

East Bay Music Together

www.eastbaymusictogether.com

510-843-8641

Alameda: Alameda Yoga Station
Alameda: Rhythmix Cultural Works
Albany: Vara Healing Arts
Berkeley: Berkeley Jewish Community Center
Berkeley: Crowden Center
Berkeley: Julia Morgan, Yoga Room
Berkeley: St. John's Berkeley
Lafayette: Lafayette Community Center NEW!
Montclair: St. John's Montclair
Moraga: Hacienda De Los Flores
Oakland: Glenview Performing Arts Center
Oakland: Lake Merritt United Methodist Church
Rockridge: Danspace
Walnut Creek: Tice Valley Community Gymnasium

Music Together of Concord

www.mucictogetherofconcord.com

925-946-2990

Concord: Touchstone Climbing and Fitness
Concord: Willow Pass Community Center
Clayton: O'Hara's Martial Arts
Martinez: California Academy of Ballet

Music Together of Tracy

www.mttracy.com

866-663-2615

Brentwood: Dance Dynamics Suites
Brentwood: Expressions Dance Academy
Tracy: Studio Jazz

More Music Classes

ABC's of Singing

1545 Arbutus Drive
Walnut Creek, CA 94595

925-943-5408

With over 30 years of teaching music in local schools, Marian Steinbergh now offers private voice instruction to all ages . Students are coached in voice building in a variety of musical styles including classical, popular, operatic and musical theatre. Pupils have an opportunity to participate in 5 to10 recitals a year, state competitions, baroque festivals and scholarship programs. Marian's credentials include an MFA, years of performing and musically directing six productions at Diablo Valley College.

Andrea's Musical Adventures

www.musicwithandrea.com
andreagaspari@sbcglobal.net

925-280-7364

Andrea's Musical Adventures will take your child from their first musical exploration as baby/toddler, through their preschool & pre-piano musical stages, and into group piano lessons that teach music reading & performance as well as composition skills preparatory to private piano lessons. Birthday party packages available.

<u>Classes are held at:</u>
Encore Gymnastics
999 Bancroft Road
Walnut Creek, CA 94596
Contact Andrea to register for all music classes at Encore.

Lafayette Community Center
500 Saint Mary's Road
Lafayette, CA 94549
925-284-2232

Renaissance Clubsport
2805 Jones Road
Walnut Creek, CA 94596
925-942-6344

Home Studio
3103 Diablo View Road
Lafayette, CA 94549
925-280-7364

Stores That Offer Music Lessons

Countrywood Music
2058 "B" Treat Blvd
Walnut Creek, CA 94598
www.countrywoodguitars.com
925-818-6026 Rick Cittar
510-326-3083 Lenny Gill
925-285 4977 Ron Quesada
Instruments: Guitar and bass

The instructors offer lessons in guitar and bass to students at the Beginning, Intermediate, and Advanced Levels of ability in all popular styles, such as Blues, Folk, Finger-Style, Classical, Indie Rock, Punk Rock, Heavy Metal, Classic Rock, Nu Metal, Ska, Worship, Pop, Soul, Funk, and Jazz. The instructors are professional entertainers as well, and offer individual private one-on-one instruction.

Danville Music

3 Railroad Avenue
Danville, CA 94526
www.danvillemusic.com

925-743-0788

Instruments: Piano, brass, woodwinds, drums, guitar, violin, viola and cello
Hours: Monday through Friday 11 am–8 pm, Saturday 10 am–5 pm, Sunday Noon–4 pm.

Danville Music offers private lessons as well as a full line of musical instruments and accessories to purchase or rent. A complete selection of sheet music, instructional materials and music supplies are available.

East Bay Music/Cue Productions

1835 Colfax Street
Concord, CA 94520
www.eastbaymusic.com

925-687-4220

Instruments: Brass, woodwinds, guitar, bass and percussion.
Hours: Monday through Friday 2 pm–7 pm, Saturday Noon–5 pm, Closed Sunday.
Ages: 7 years old and up

East Bay Music offers private music lessons, instrument rentals, repairs, and theater sound design. Carole Davis is the brass and woodwind specialist at East Bay Music, with over 25 years of teaching experience. Students are accepted from ages 10 years and up. Chris Meek is the fretted instrument specialist, covering guitar and bass. Chris teaches both acoustic and electric instruments to adults and teens, and will work with motivated children as young as seven years old. Nick Fishman is the resident percussion specialist.

F.A.M.E. Yamaha Music Center

1630 Contra Costa Blvd. Suite 210
Pleasant Hill CA 94523
www.fameymc.playkeyboard.net

925- 691-5220

Instruments: Piano, guitar, bass guitar, keyboard, theory, ear training, composition, improvisation, sight singing
Ages: 3 years–Adults

They offer group piano lessons for ages 3 and up through the world-renowned Yamaha teaching method. They also offer private lessons in piano, guitar and voice and art classes. During the summer, they offer camps specializing in music composition, art, and voice.

Gill's Music

331 Sunset Drive
Antioch, CA 94509
www.gillsmusic.net

925-757-2323

Hours: Monday through Friday 10:30 am–6 pm, Saturday 10:30 am–4 pm.
Brentwood Studio Hours by appointment. Closed Sundays
Instruments: Piano, guitar, bass, drum, voice, violin, woodwind, brass, and group classes.

Gill's Music has a terrific in-house staff of very patient music teachers who offer private music lessons as well as occasional small group classes. Visit their website or call for instructors and fees.

House of Woodwinds

2205C San Ramon Valley Blvd.
San Ramon, CA 94583
www.houseofwoodwinds.com
lrdouglas@rcn.com

925-831-8341

Hours: Monday Noon–8 pm, Tuesday thru Friday 11 am–8 pm, Saturday 10 am–5 pm
Instruments: Clarinet, flute, piano, saxophone, trumpet, trombone, guitar, drums, oboe, voice, jazz bass and jazz piano.

House of Woodwinds offers a large list of qualified instructors at their San Ramon store. Please call to have your name placed on the list for upcoming instruction.

Legacy Piano Resales

38 Beta Court, Suite B8
San Ramon, CA 94583
www.legacypiano.com

925-735-8625

Lessons: Piano, violin, voice and guitar.
Ages: 6 years old and up.

Legacy Piano has a good selection of pre-owned Steinways and other brand name pianos.

Lynda McManus Piano Company

2100 San Ramon Valley Blvd., Ste 1
San Ramon, CA 94583
www.lyndamcmanuspiano.com

925-743-3787

Instrument: Piano

The Lynda McManus Piano Company supports a wide range of music programs to enhance the appreciation and love of music.

Music Schools

Bay Area Academy of Music

5460 Sunol Blvd., #I
Pleasanton, CA 94566
www.bayareaacademyofmusic.com

925-398-8683

At Bay Area Academy of Music, we realize that most of our students will not become profession-al musicians. Our mission is to provide people of all ages and abilities the skills they need to enjoy music for life. We thoroughly screen and hire only highly educated, experienced and skilled pro-fessional instructors. We operate on a 10-month fall session, from September through June, and offer a 2-month summer session to further advance your skills.

Galileo Music Academy

2100 San Ramon Valley Blvd. #5
San Ramon, CA 94583
www.galileomusicacademy.com

925-914-0516

Lessons: Violin and viola

Fees: Registration $50 per family, 30 minutes $30, 45 minutes $45, 60 minutes $60

Galileo Music Academy brings a unique music education experience to Tri-Valley students of all ages and levels. Their approach to music education is modeled on the country's most prestigious music conservatory preparatory programs to educate the complete musician. They offer private and group lessons in a safe, fun and stimulating learning environment where students' musical knowledge and creativity can flourish.

Lamorinda Academy of Music and Arts

3381 Mt. Diablo Blvd.
Lafayette, CA 94549
www.musicandart.org
925-299-1240

Instruments: Piano, keyboard, organ, violin, viola, cello, voice, guitar, bass and flute.

They have highly qualified teachers for their instrumental lessons. Private lessons are offered on various popular instruments, voice, and composition. They also offer a preschool musical program, Singing is Fun Children's Ensemble, and musical theatre programs.

Music One Studios

1268 Pine Street
Walnut Creek, CA 94596
www.musiconestudios.net
925- 932-4458

Instruments: Piano, flute and voice.

Music One Studios has been providing quality music instruction in Walnut Creek, California and the East Bay since 1980. They offer small group classes as well as private instruction.

Singingwood Music

Walnut Creek, CA
www.singingwood.com
925-935-9295

Instruments: Violin, fiddle, guitar, mandolin and bodhran (Irish hand drum)

Singingwood is the music studio of John Blasquez, located in Walnut Creek. He teaches private lessons, workshops, group classes, and coaches musical groups. His website has many valuable resources and information about local events.

Under The Sun Studios

2956-H Treat Blvd.
Concord, CA 94518
www.utsstudios.com
info@utsstudios.com
925-465-6131

Instruments: Electric guitar, acoustic guitar, classical guitar, electric bass, piano, rock and pop keyboards, violin and voice.

Under The Sun Studios is Contra Costa County's destination for music and theater education and performance. Located on the Walnut Creek/Concord border on Treat and Oak Grove, their 3000 square foot facility houses practice studios/lesson rooms, a well outfitted music classroom, and a performance area complete with stage lighting and sound, and music instructors, acting coaches, directors, entertainers, and artists. They have improvisational acting or "Improv" and musical theater classes, and groups and troupes to perform with when your child wants to get on stage.

Choruses

If your child enjoys singing, a good place to start looking for instruction is at their school chorus or at church. Churches often have a children's mass or service where a children's choir will sing.

San Francisco Bay Area Chorus Directory

www.choralarchive.org

The purpose of the SF Bay Area Choral Archive is to provide both current and historical information relating to choral activity in the SF Bay Area. You will find a comprehensive list and many entries with links to choruses in Northern California. You're sure to find a chorus in your area to fit your child's musical interests.

Contra Costa Children's Chorus

Campuses in Walnut Creek, East County and San Ramon
www.childrenschorus.org

925-945-7101

Fees: Tuition varies with level

CCCC is celebrating its 24th year in providing choral music education to children. Offering several levels of instruction, it develops musical competence, provides performance opportunities and educates students in several languages. Care is taken to maintain the health of the young voice as students attend weekly rehearsals to practice and perform masterpieces from a wide variety of choral repertoire. Performance skills are honed through concerts, tours and a summer musical theatre program.

Rehearsal Sites:

Walnut Creek Chorus

1963 Tice Valley Boulevard
Walnut Creek, CA 94596

San Ramon Chorus
Dougherty Station Community Center
17011 Bollinger Canyon Road
San Ramon, CA 94583

East County Chorus
Brentwood Elementary
200 Griffith Lane,
Brentwood, CA 94513

Metro Gnomes™
Ages: 3–6 year old

This is a program focused on early childhood musical training.

Danville Girls Chorus
P.O. Box 665
Danville, CA 94526
www.danvillegirlschorus.com

925-837-2624
Ages: 3rd–8th grade

The Danville Girls Chorus (DGC) is a non-profit, independent music education organization. DGC offers a complete program of choral music education through a variety of learning experiences and performance opportunities. Singers are taught the basics of vocal production and learn the fundamentals of musicianship and note-reading. They are exposed to a variety of musical styles ranging from classical and folk tunes to contemporary and pop music. Participation in this program develops a sense of responsibility, confidence and self-esteem in the singers.

Pacific Boychoir
410 Alcatraz Avenue
Oakland, CA 94609
www.pacificboychoir.org

510-652-4722

The Pacific Boychoir is one of the country's leading boys choirs, performing in concerts with orchestras, at sporting events, around the country and around the world. Over 120 boys from four Bay Area counties, aged 5–18, are taught by teachers who are experts on boys' voices. Auditions are held monthly for boys age 5–10. No experience is necessary for this once-in-a-lifetime opportunity for boys. Boys age 11–18 with previous musical experience can also audition.

Do You Like To Sing?

If you are between 6-15, become part of an organization which has received acclaim as one of the nation's top children's choruses! Offering several levels of instruction, our program provides music education & vocal training for the proper development of young voices. Children learn music in several languages and from a wide variety of choral repertoire. *No prior experience is necessary.*

★Campuses in <u>Walnut Creek</u>, <u>East County</u> & <u>San Ramon</u>!

For the 3-6 yr old, choose *METRO♪GNOMES™* - a program designed especially for them. It will develop your child's music ability with 3 different music focuses: singing, rhythm & movement. Classes in Walnut Creek.

Theatre Arts For Kids™ is our summer program; a challenging musical theatre arts program focusing on vocal technique, musicianship, dance, dramatics and technical theatre. Each session ends with a staged and costumed performance.

For Information: **925-945-7101, x200**
frontdesk@childrenschorus.org
www.childrenschorus.org

CONTRA COSTA
Children's
Chorus

...Celebrating 24 years of providing choral music education to children.

"Astonishing"
—Los Angeles Times

After school music
for boys age 5-18

The Pacific Boychoir

A distinctive musical experience

www.pacificboychoir.org

Music

San Francisco Girls Chorus

44 Page Street, Suite 200
San Francisco, CA 94102
www.sfgirlschorus.org

415- 863-1752

Ages: 7–18 years old

The San Francisco Girls Chorus has become a regional center for choral music education and performance for girls and young women. More than 300 singers from 160 schools in 44 Bay Area cities participate in this internationally recognized program, deemed "a model in the country for training girls' voices" by the California Arts Council. The organization is comprised of five choruses. The East Bay program meets on Wednesdays and Fridays at the Mormon Temple, 4770 Lincoln Avenue, in Oakland, from 4 pm to 6 pm.

Music Programs

Blue Devils

The Blue Devils

4065 Nelson Avenue
Concord, CA 94520
www.bluedevils.org

925-689-2918

Ages: 7 to 21 years old

The Blue Devils offer young men and women between the ages of 7 and 21 quality educational and performance experiences in the areas of musical and dance performance. Founded in 1957, The Blue Devils' objective is to develop personal character through challenging physical, emotional, mental, and social activities while promoting the values of dedication, hard work, and commitment to a team effort. The Blue Devils organization currently offers seven youth programs. They have won numerous local, national and international titles.

Guitars Not Guns

www.guitarsnotguns.org

Contact: Patty Maloney

hearttouch@mindspring.com

Their mission is to provide guitars and lessons to foster kids, at risk youth and other deserving children in a classroom setting with qualified teachers. They teach boys and girls ages 8 to 18 how to play in weekly classes, starting with the basics like the parts of the guitar, how to tune it and the right way to hold it.

Music-Parks & Recreation

Many cities have a Parks and Recreation department which offer music classes. Contact your local city's Park and Recreation Department for more details.

City of Concord Parks and Recreation

2974 Salvio Street
Concord, CA 94519
www.concordreg.org

925-671-3404

Hours: Monday–Friday 9 am–5 pm

The City of Concord offers a variety of classes in music starting from Music Together classes for preschoolers, to buddy piano and guitar, voice training, and hip hop for youth and teens.

City of Lafayette Recreation Programs

Lafayette Community Center

500 Saint Mary's Road
Lafayette, CA 94549
www.lafmor-recreation.org

925-284-2232

Hours: Monday–Friday 9 am–5 pm

They offer Kindergym for children ages 1–4 years old and Kinderdance for children ages 3–5 years old. They also offer beginning guitar for students 8 and up, and drums for ages 9 and up.

Pleasant Hill Recreation and Park District

Pleasant Hill Community Center

320 Civic Drive
Pleasant Hill, CA 94523
www.pleasanthillrec.com

925-676-5200

Registration Hours: Monday–Friday 9 am–3 pm

Pleasant Hill Recreation and Park District offers Kids in Tune, Music for Kids (Yamaha Music System) and Kindermusik with Joanne for Preschoolers. They offer guitar, Yamaha keyboard prep, keyboard, and hip hop youth and teen music activities.

Music

Town of Moraga Recreation Programs

2100 Donald Drive
Moraga, CA 94556
www.ci.moraga.ca.us/moraga-recreation-programs.php

925.376.2520

They offer Music Together for children ages newborn to 5 years old.

Walnut Creek Civic Arts Education

P.O. Box 8039
Walnut Creek, CA 94596
artsed@walnut-creek.org

925-943-5846

Instruments: Baritone horn, bass, guitar, cello, clarinet, coronet, flugelhorn, flute, viola, French horn, guitar (acoustic & electric), harp, piano, percussion, recorder, saxophone, steel drums, string bass, Suzuki violin, trombone, trumpet, tuba, violin and voice.

Fee: Starts at $30 per half hour

In addition to lessons on specific instruments, Civic Arts Education offers music classes in ear training, sight singing, jazz improvisation, and music theory/therapy.

Chapter 10

Theatre, Dance and Creative Arts

The arts are so much more than just fun "extra" activities for kids. Participation in the arts opens up children's worlds and minds, and offers them the skills they need for a bright future.

Did you know that...

- The arts teach kids to be more tolerant and open
- The arts allow kids to express themselves creatively
- The arts promote individually, bolster self-confidence, and improve overall academic performance.
- The arts can help troubled youth, providing an alternative to delinquent behavior and truancy while providing an improved attitude towards school.

Young artists as compared to their peers are likely to:

- Attend music, art, and dance classes nearly three times as frequently
- Participate in youth groups nearly four times as frequently
- Read for pleasure nearly twice as often
- Perform community service more than four times as often
- More likely to be class officers and excel in academic achievement

-Living the Arts through Language + Learning: A Report On Community-based Your Organizations, Shirley Brice Heath, Stanford University and Carnegie Foundation for the Advancement of Teaching, American for the Arts Monograph, November 1998

Encourage your child to try new things and explore new interests continually. You may stumble upon a passion for acting, dance, art or even sewing! The arts in its many forms enriches our children's lives and broadens their horizons.

Theatres

Concord

City of Concord Parks and Recreation

2974 Salvio Street
Concord, CA 94519
www.concordreg.org

925-671-3404

Hours: Monday–Friday 9 am–5 pm

The City of Concord offers a variety of classes such as Young People's Performing Arts, You're a Star Theatre Party, Voice Training, Jazz Dance, Ballet and Tap Dance.

Under The Sun Studios

2956-H Treat Blvd,
Concord, CA 94518
www.utsstudios.com

925-465-6131

Ages: Teen-Adult

Under The Sun Studios is Contra Costa County's destination for Music and Theater education and Performance. Located on the Walnut Creek/Concord border on Treat and Oak Grove, their 3000 square foot facility houses practice studios/lesson rooms, a well outfitted music classroom, and a performance area, complete with stage lighting and sound, not to mention some of the best and brightest music instructors, acting coaches, directors, entertainers, and artists in the area. They have Improvisational Acting or "Improv" and Musical theater classes, and groups and troupes to perform with when you want to get on stage

Willows Theatre Company

1975 Diamond Avenue
Concord, CA 94520
925-798-1300 Box Office
925-798-1824 Admin Office
Hours: Call for details
Prices: Call for details

The Award winning Willows Theatre Company is a non-profit professional theatre company that develops and produces contemporary American plays and musicals. Willows Theatre Company maintains its own facilities, employs professional administrative staff and provides related services. The goal of the Willows Theatre Company is to ensure that the art of live theatre is accessible and relevant to the audience of the San Francisco East Bay Area.

The Belasco Theatre Company

P.O. Box 1117
Danville, CA 94526
www.belasco.org
925-256-9516
Ages: 7–18 years

Belasco Theatre Company is a unique program for young people, providing instruction in the basic components of performing arts (drama, improvisation, auditioning, projection, staging, voice and dance) and allowing students to experience the rigors of musical comedy theatre. Well-qualified choreographers and vocal instructors provide additional training and collaborate with the director during auditions and productions.

Contra Costa Civic Theatre

951 Pomona Avenue
El Cerrito, CA 94530
www.ccct.org
510-524-9132
Ages: 7 and up

Their mission is to provide affordable, high quality entertainment to residents throughout the East Bay and provide training in live performing arts for children and adults. They offer Musical Juniors on Mondays from 4pm-6pm and summer camps. Musical Juniors rehearses an entire show over ten weeks while teaching drama skills including ensemble work, vocal projection, character creation, and choreography.

Kids 'N Dance

3369 Mt. Diablo
Lafayette, CA 94549
925-284-7388
Ages: 6–18 years
Cost: Varies—approximately $299 a show

Musical Theater at Kids'N Dance teaches vocal, dance and acting skills in a creative, supportive and FUN environment, culminating in stage performances for each level of study.

Town Hall Theatre Company of Lafayette

3535 School Street at Moraga Road
Lafayette, CA 94549
www.townhalltheatre.com
925-283-1557

Town Hall Theatre Company believes in a theater that is an artistic focal point in the community, that serves the community in a socially and educationally responsible manner, and that provides creative opportunities for performers, designers, technicians, directors, writers, educators and students, both within and outside of the Lamorinda community, as well as in the greater Bay Area. The Town Hall Theatre Company of Lafayette is a non-profit theater organization promoting education in the arts for members of the local community and beyond. Town Hall Theatre provides innovative education programs to over 600 young actors every year.

Town of Moraga Recreation Programs

2100 Donald Drive
Moraga, CA 94556
www.ci.moraga.ca.us/moraga-recreation-programs.php
925-376-2520

The Town of Moraga offers hip hop and a High School Musical song and dance class. They offer drama classes through the California Youth Theatre for ages 4-18 years.

Pleasant Hill

Pleasant Hill Recreation and Park District
Pleasant Hill Community Center

320 Civic Drive
Pleasant Hill, CA 94523
www.pleasanthillrec.com
925-676-5200

They have a theatre group called S.T.A.G.E. Troupe for 3rd graders to college. They also offer ballet, hip hop, hula, creative dance, tap and jazz.

Walnut Creek

Center Rep

1601 Civic Drive
Walnut Creek, CA 94598
www.centerrep.org
925-295-1400

Center REPertory Company is the resident professional theatre company of the Lesher Center for the Arts. The Young REPertory Theatre Workshop, now in its 34th year, trains and develops students interested in the theatre arts as a vocation or a serious avocation.

Civic Arts Education Program
Youth Theatre Company

P.O. Box 8039
Walnut Creek, CA 94598
www.youththeatrecompany.org

925-943-5846

Ages: 5–18 years

Youth Theatre Company offers four stepping stones for young performers. The Youth Theatre Company engages children, kindergarten through high school age in musical theatre performance and theatre education.

Contra Costa Children's Chorus

P.O. Box 2518
Walnut Creek, CA 94598
www.childrenschorus.org

925-945-7101

Ages: 4–17 years

They offer TheaTricks programs throughout the year as well as summer camps and music camps for children.

Diablo Light Opera Company

P.O. Box 5034
Walnut Creek, CA 94598
www.dloc.org

Ages: 7–20 years

Starstruck Saturday (ages 7–15) introduces children to the magic of musical theater. No auditions are required to participate in the program, and students of all experience levels are encouraged to register. Director Barrett Lindsay Steiner and professional staff guide the students in character development, vocal techniques, dance-choreography, audition techniques, and other theater skills, as well as team building and leadership training.

Starstruck Teens (ages 12–18) This program offers musical comedy training to both middle and high school teens. Weekly classes teach students about dance, singing and acting and develop skills such as vocal projection, teamwork and self-confidence in a warm and supportive environment. The program culminates in a staged musical production. No audition necessary.

Stars 2000 (ages 12-30) was created to provide teens with an opportunity to participate in theater workshops and performance. This program gives young performers a chance to work with an experienced production staff and perform in a professional theater—the Lesher Theater at the Dean Lesher Regional Center for the Arts. The program offers an excellent training ground for future participation in a major theater company.

Tri Valley

smARTSunlimited

53 Wright Brothers Avenue, Suite D
Livermore, CA 94551
www.smARTSunlimited.com

925-245-0283

SmARTSunlimited is a one-stop talent development for children between the ages of 2–17. They teach children workable skills in the arts, which can be utilized in artistic endeavors now, and in the future. They are the largest full service talent organization in the Tri-Valley. Offering specialized programs in music, theater, acting and film. Whether your child is interested in music, film, theater, or perhaps you're not quite certain, SmARTSunlimited makes a terrific starting point for parents looking to develop artistic talent and skills in their children.

Local Theatre

There are many wonderful local theatre groups in the Bay Area and occasionally they may have parts for younger children and teens. It's also a great opportunity to take your budding actor or actress to see a live professional performance.

East Bay

East Bay Children's Theatre

www.childrens-theatre.org

510-537-9957

510-834-4077

East Bay Children's Theatre (EBCT) is the oldest continuously performing theatre group in the San Francisco Bay Area. EBCT is a non-profit organization supported by over 45 active volunteers. Since 1933 EBCT's main purpose has been to bring the heritage of traditional folk tales in the form of musical theatre free of charge to economically disadvantaged elementary schools in Oakland and surrounding areas. Through their productions they strive to highlight important moral lessons that promote positive values and strengthen self-esteem of children.

Walnut Creek

CTA Crossroads

1277 Boulevard Way
Walnut Creek, CA 94595
www.ctacrossroads.org

925-944-0551

Their mission is to provide family-oriented theatre of the highest quality by producing shows with artistic integrity, which are designed to educate, enrich, ennoble, enlighten, and entertain audiences.

Contra Costa Christian Theatre

P.O. Box 3025
Walnut Creek, CA 94598
925-939-3200

Contra Costa Christian Theatre is a non-profit professional quality theatre company/ministry. Participants are from many different churches and backgrounds (Christian and non-Christian), coming together to produce plays with a good moral message. They may have parts for children.

Contra Costa Musical Theatre

P.O. Box 4446
Walnut Creek, CA 94598
www.ccmt.org
925-210-0268

Contra Costa Musical Theatre, Inc. (CCMT) was founded in August 1961, for the express purpose of producing Broadway musicals. They have performed at the Dean Lesher Regional Center for the Arts since its opening in 1990. CCMT produces two productions a year and combines with Diablo Light Opera Company's two productions to offer a four-show season.

Vallejo Music Theatre

823 Marin Street
Vallejo, CA 94590
www.vallejomusictheatre.org
707-649-ARTS (2787)

The Company now produces three musicals a season opening in July with a large family-oriented full-scale Broadway show; a Young Audiences Production in December; an adult oriented musical in February; a large concert or cabaret series and has many fundraising activities throughout the year. In 2007, they added an opera production in October. Beginning in 2002 the Company began a Young Audiences Program, producing an original musical based on well-known fairy tales. The program has continued to grow from a small budget production to a full-scale production held each December for children of all ages.

Dance

Antioch

Doreen's School of the Dance

520 Third Street
Antioch, CA 94509
925-757-8981
Ages: 3 and up
Classes: Ballet, Jazz and Tap

Offering a friendly family environment for students of all ages, we encourage respect for the efforts of each dancer. The art of dance teaches discipline of the body and mind, provides healthy exercise and promotes a knowledge and appreciation of music.

Concord

Da Island Way

960 Detroit Avenue
Concord, CA 94518
www.daislandways.com
925-677-5057
Ages: 5 and up
Classes: Tahitian

They maintain a family atmosphere, while also keeping a very high caliber of expectation out of their students. Da Island Ways has multiple top awards in Tahitian dance and music dating back to their beginnings. They have open enrollment and take applications every June.

D'Ann's Academy of Dance

1301 Franquette Avenue, Suite C
Concord, CA 94520
www.dannsdance.com
925-827-0733
Age: 3 on up
Classes: Hip Hop, Tap, Jazz, Ballet and Yoga

D'Ann's Accademy of Dance offers small class sizes, hassle free recitals, competition and performing teams.

Dance Connection Performing Arts Centre

2956 Treat Blvd., Suite I
Concord, CA 94518
www.danceconnectionpac.com

925-676-5678

Ages: 2.5 up thru Teens & Adults

Classes: Jazz, Ballet, Tap, Hip Hop, Modern, Lyrical, Tumbling, Flamenco, & Jazzercise* New Vocal Training Program

DCPAC is the East Bay's largest dance training center with five state of the art studios. They have a distinguished faculty of 12 highly-qualified instructors. Most are full-time and exclusive to DCPAC. They have an annual holiday show at the Dean Lesher Regional Center for the Arts in Walnut Creek. They have a boys only program and offer special scholarships.

Moving Arts Dance Center

2355 Whitman Road, Suite D
Concord, CA 94519
www.movingartsdance.org

925-825-8399

Ages: 3 and up

Classes: Ballet, Modern Dance, Tap, Jazz and acting

With a non-competitive philosophy of dance, the distinguished faculty of Moving Arts Dance develops dancers with a strong professional and emotional base. One of the greatest joys of teaching dance is to impart an understanding of the value of dance as an art form, which enhances one's personal growth. Through studying this art form, one develops a powerful tool for self-expression, and enhances everyday life skills such as problem solving, critical thinking, and teamwork.

The Tumbling Company

930 Detroit Avenue, Suite B
Concord, CA 94518 94519
www.tumblingcompany.com

925-674-1405

Ages: 3 and up

Classes: Tap, Ballet, Jazz and gymnastics

The Tumbling Company believes that movement exploration, dance and gymnastics provide the best opportunity for children to develop their maximum physical potential, increase self-confidence and self-awareness, and have fun in the learning process. Their classes are taught in a positive, noncompetitive, organized environment. Their professional staff is highly qualified and devoted to helping children grow through physical fitness.

Danville

The Next Step Dance Studio

109-A Town & Country Drive
Danville, CA 94526
www.nextstepdance.com

925-831-0777

Ages: All ages

Classes: Ballet, Funk Jazz, Hip Hop, Jazz, Tap, Performance Teams

The Next Step Dance Studio offers dance instruction and performance opportunities for children and teens. They offer classes for all ages and dance levels. They offer accelerated programs for students who want more serious training and performance opportunities. In all their classes students will be exposed to technique, musicality and artistic expression. They have three locations in Danville.

Village Shopping Center

109-A Town & Country Drive

Grange Hall

743 Diablo Road

Bally Total Fitness

3464 Blackhawk Plaza Circle

Dublin, Livermore, Pleasanton & San Ramon

Dance Fusion

2217 North San Ramon Valley Blvd.
San Ramon, CA 94583
www.dancefussionco.com

925-831-2882

Ages: 3 and up

Classes: Creative Movement, Jazz, Ballet, Hip Hop and Pilates

Dance Fusion Company aims to provide a fun yet focused work environment in which all of our students are challenged to realize their full potential as dancers and as people. They offer competition and performing teams.

Jazz n Taps

P.O. Box 1600
1270 Quarry Lane
Pleasanton, CA 94566
www.jazzntaps.com

925-484-0678

Ages: 3 and up

Classes: Tap, Jazz, Ballet, Modern, and Hip-Hop

Jazz n Taps provides opportunities for intensive dancers on their competitive

Let's Dance

6635 Dublin Blvd.

Dublin, CA 94568

925-895-1488

Ages: 12 and up

Classes: Ballroom, Latin and Swing

Kurt Senser teaches Ballroom classes and provides private lessons.

Livermore Area Recreation and Park District

4444 East Avenue

Livermore, CA 94550

www.larpd.dst.cs.us

925-373-5700

Ages: 18 months and up

Classes: Dancin' Bogie Babies, Ballet, Hawaiian, Tap, Hip Hop, Break Dancing, Jazz and Cheerleading

The San Ramon Valley Dance Academy

101 Ryan Industrial Court

San Ramon, CA 94583

www.srvda.com

925-837-4656

Ages: 3 on up

Classes: Pre-Ballet, Ballet, Jazz, Tap, Hip Hop, Modern, Special needs, and Gymnastics/Acro

The 9,000 square foot facility houses four studios, one equipped to provide a complete gymnastic program, plus a Dance Shoppe to supply every dancer's needs. The Academy offers a diverse curriculum to students of all ages and abilities (beginner through professional). The Academy's "Color Me Dance" program for children ages 3–6 provides an excellent introduction to dance for the young, creative mind. Students trained at the Academy have danced professionally in many diverse venues, including ballet companies, musical theatre, dance companies, television and more.

Spotlight Arts Academy

6979 Sierra Court

Dublin, CA 94568

www.spotlightaa.com

925-828-9722

Ages: 2 and up

Classes: Ballet, Jazz, Tap, Hip-Hop, Kinder-dance, Lyrical, Modern, Musical Theater, and Specialty Classes in Pilates, Ballroom and Break-dance.

With an experienced faculty of qualified instructors, their goal is to provide the San Francisco Bay Area with the finest dance instruction in the greatest variety of styles in the area. For the more serious student they have two performance teams that perform in competitions, festivals and showcases. Their philosophy is to train and strengthen individuals through artistic expression, technique and terminology. With limited class sizes, students at Spotlight Arts Academy will receive specialized attention in an enjoyable and healthy environment.

Studio Eight

3420 Fostoria Way, Suite A-100
San Ramon, CA 94583
www.studio8pac.com

925-876-1556

Ages: 4 and up

Classes: Hip Hop, Jazz, Ballet, Tap, Cheerleading, Performing Teams, Pilates and Yoga

Studio 8 teaches technical skills while also building confidence. They want the student to learn artistry, technique and self expression. Studio 8 strives to provide a healthy and positive experience.

Tiffany's Dance Academy

Pleasanton, San Ramon & Livermore
www.tiffanydance.com

925-447-5299

Ages: 2 and up

Classes: Ballet, Jazz, Tap and Creative Movement and Hip Hop

Tiffany's Dance Academy believes that learning dance technique is extremely important. They are committed to providing superior, professional training in ballet, tap, jazz and hip-hop. At the same time, they try to create a balanced environment for all of their dancers.

Valley Dance Theatre School

20 South "L" Street
Livermore, CA 94550
www.valleydancetheatre.com

925-243-0925

Ages: 3 1/2 and up

Classes: Creative Movement, Ballet and modern Dance

The Valley Dance Theatre is a non-profit ballet company formed in 1980 by Betsy Hausburg and Penny Tomasello with the goals of providing performance opportunities for talented local dancers and bringing affordable, quality dance performances to the valley. The company offers semi-annual performances in December of the "The Nutcracker" with the Livermore-Amador Symphony and in May, the company chooses from a variety of classical and contemporary repertoires and collaborations.

El Cerrito & Richmond

East Bay Center for the Performing Arts
339 11th Street
Richmond, CA 94801
www.eastbaycenter.org
510-234-5624
Ages: 4 and up—Varies by class
Classes: West African Dance, Richmond Jazz Collective, Iron Triangle Urban Ballet, Ballet, Mexican Music and Dance, Jazz Dance and Hip Hop

El Cerrito Ballet Center
6712 Portola Drive
El Cerrito, CA 94530
510- 235-1734

Katie's Dance Studio and Company
10311 San Pablo Avenue
El Cerrito, CA 94530
www.katiesdancestudio.com
510-524-1310
Ages: 3 1/2 and up
Classes: Ballet, Jazz, Tap, Acrobatics and Hip Hop

Katie's Dance Studio is renowned for producing students who are well-trained. Many of Katie's students have gone on to dance professionally throughout the world. Students who take lessons at Katie's Dance Studio learn dance technique, how to work together as a group and how to achieve self confidence through the joy of dance.

Emeryville

Allegro Ballroom

5855 Christie Avenue
Emeryville, CA 94608
www.allegroballroom.com
510-655-2888

Ages: 7–21 years

Classes: Youth Dance Program

The Allegro Ballroom is a California non-profit public-benefit educational corporation to promote ballroom dancing and other dance art forms. They are a multi-cultural ballroom dance school open to all, and maintain a non-discrimination policy. They offer a free Youth Dance Program on Saturdays from 2 pm–3 pm. Parent or guardian is also welcome to participate in the class.

Lafayette

Kinderdance

3527 Mt. Diablo Blvd., Suite 374
Lafayette, CA 94549
www.kinderdance.com
925-788-1020

Ages: 2–6 years

Classes: Kinderdance, Kindergym and Kindertot

Kinderdance® is the original nationwide dance, motor development, gymnastics, and fitness program that combines academic readiness skills which are specifically designed for children ages 2 to 12. What makes Kinderdance® unique is that all of the programs incorporate educational concepts in a developmentally designed curriculum that teaches to the total child. We place special emphasis on building "Self Confidence" and "Self-Esteem" in young children.

Kids 'N Dance

3369 Mt. Diablo Blvd.
Lafayette, CA 94549
www.kidsndance.com
925-284-7388

Rhythm Room Dance and Movement Center

3330 Mt. Diablo Blvd., Suite 101
Lafayette, CA 94549
www.rhythmroomdance.com
925-283-4801

Ages: 5 on up

Classes: Acting, Ballet, Jazz, Jazz Funk, LA Jazz, Latin Jazz, Boys technique, Hip Hop, Break Dancing, Cheerleading and Choreography

The Rhythm Room is known for its welcoming, non-competitive atmosphere, beginner friendly classes, pre-professional program, "all adult" classes, and it's unique "all boys" program.

Martinez

California Academy of Ballet

6635 Alhambra Avenue, Suite 105
Martinez, CA 94553
www.californiaacademyofballet.com

925-945-0397

Ages: 3 to adult

Classes: Classical Ballet, Tap, Jazz, Modern Dance, Tone and Stretch

The California Academy of Ballet offers high quality comprehensive programs emphasizing a professional and positive learning environment. Students are taught by an outstanding artistic staff consisting of accomplished instructors. The studio is equipped with fully floating floors that are designed especially for dance. Many of their advanced students have been accepted into nationally and internationally recognized professional ballet intensive summer programs.

In Motion Dance Center

835 Arnold Drive Suite 5
Martinez, CA 94553
www.inmotiondancer.com

925-229-5678

Ages: 2 1/2 to Adult

Classes: Jazz, Ballet, Tap, Hip Hop, Tumbling, Ballroom and Cheerleading

Perfect your dance skills in two state of the art dance studios, both with sprung floors and full-length mirrors.

Moraga

California Academy of Performing Arts

P.O. Box 6147
Moraga, CA 94570
www.capadance.net

925-376-2454

Age: 2 years 9 months and up

Classes: Ballet, Jazz, Tap, Pointe, Hip Hop and Pilates

CAPA was founded in 1981 by Joan Robinson and Ronn Guidi, then Artistic Director of the Oakland Ballet. They wanted to create a place in the beautiful Moraga Valley where the "children of the suburbs" could have access to the finest professional training. Joan and Ronn realized their dream, and though Ronn soon found the demands of the Oakland Company too demanding to do both, he was confident that Joan would continue the integrity of their joint plan.

Lamorinda Ballet Center

370 Park Street, Suite D
Moraga, CA 94556
www.lamorindaballet.com

925-376-0661

Ages: 3 and up
Classes: Tiny Tot, Pre-Ballet, Pre-Professional

Lamorinda Ballet Center was developed to enhance the technical training of students and help them to develop the strong training that a professional career or dance degree demands. Students work intensively to develop their Classical Ballet Technique, instructed by a staff of highly-trained former and current professional dancers.

Pleasant Hill

Fearon O'Connor School of Irish Dance

Union City and Pleasant Hill

www.fearon-oconnor.com

415-401-6015

The Butler-Fearon-O'Connor School of Irish Dance is one of the top Irish dance schools in the world. Classes are offered for all levels of dancers, from very beginner to championship. They strive to make each child the very best Irish dancer that they can be.

Pleasant Hill Recreation and Park District

Pleasant Hill Community Center

320 Civic Drive
Pleasant Hill, CA 94523
www.pleasanthillrec.com

925-676-5200

Pleasant Hill Recreation and Park District offers Kids in Tune, Creative Movement, Pre-Ballet, Ballet, Hip Hop, Hula, Jazz and Tap

Studio A

2245A Morello Avenue
Pleasant Hill, CA 94523
www.studioadance.net

925-691-0505

Ages: 3 to Adult

Classes: Jazz, Tap, Ballet and Hip Hop

Providing classes for the recreational as well as the pre-professional dancer, the studio creates an environment that fosters the confidence and self-esteem of each of the students. As a result of this positive reinforcement, their dancers develop into strong, expressive young artists.

Civic Arts Education Program

111 North Wiget Lane
Walnut Creek, CA 94598
www.arts-ed.org

925-943-5846

Ages: 3–18 years

Classes: Diablo Valley Apprentice Program, Pre-Ballet, Ballet, Tap, Jazz and Hip Hop

ClubSport

See listing in Just for Moms chapter under Workout Facilities

Contra Costa Ballet Centre

2040 North Broadway
Walnut Creek, CA 94596
www.contracostaballet.org

925-935-7984

Ages: 3 1/2 and up

Classes: Pre-Ballet, Ballet, Pointe, Ballet Technique

The Contra Costa Ballet Centre's program serves the development of students from their first encounters with music and movement to becoming accomplished professional dancers. There are three separate divisions, which are carefully designed to introduce the correct technique and instruction appropriate for the age and physical development of the student. The three separate divisions are the Children Division, the Student Division, and the Adult Division. There are two sessions a year: a fall session (coinciding with the normal school year; beginning of September to mid-June) and a summer session (beginning of July to mid–August).

Diablo Ballet

P.O. Box 4700
Walnut Creek, CA 94598
www.diabloballet.org

925-943-1775

Ages: 11–18 years

Classes: Ballet Technique, class, Repertory and Pointe

Diablo Ballet's Apprentice Program is a highly competitive program offering intense training to young dancers who have outstanding potential. This program, which is open only by audition, offers participants extensive preparation for the working world of professional dance by providing ballet instruction taught by professional dancers, professional performance experience in conjunction with Diablo Ballet, and the opportunity to participate in regional and international competitions. Apprentice dancers appear annually in a highly popular production of the Nutcracker, presented jointly by Diablo Ballet and Walnut Creek Civic Arts Education. In addition to rigorous training, participants in the Apprentice Program enjoy the excitement of close contact with a professional company, a unique and invaluable experience in preparation for their professional careers.

Encore Gymnastics

999 Bancroft Road
Walnut Creek, CA 94598
www.encoregym.com

925-932-1033

Ages: 3 and up

Classes: Ballet, Jazz, Hip Hop and Gymnastics

Encore develops a child's fitness and self esteem through fun, quality programs where safety comes first! They accomplish this through positive teaching and encouragement in a creative environment.

Lareen Fender The Ballet School

1357 North Main Street
Walnut Creek, CA 94596
www.theballetschool.org

925-934-2133

Ages: 3 1/2 and up

Classes: Ballet, Jazz, Tap Yoga and Theatre

At Lareen Fender's The Ballet School, there are few limits to when dance training can begin and no limits to where it can lead. The Ballet School has helped both children and adults take their first steps into the world of ballet, jazz and theatre. On the other end of the spectrum, the school has trained many fine professional dancers for professional companies throughout the world.

Creative Arts

Lafayette

The Art Room

50 Lafayette Circle
Lafayette, CA 94549
www.theart-room.com

925-299-1515

Ages: 4 and up

Classes: Drawing, Pastels, Cartooning, Watercolor, Pottery and more

The Art Room is a studio offering art instruction to children and adults in downtown Lafayette. Students experience and enjoy the creative process while learning the skills needed to create a work of art with pride. Their goal is to achieve a balance between process and result.

Lafayette Studio

3506 Mt. Diablo Blvd.
Lafayette, CA 94549
www.laa4art.org/lafayettestudio.html

925-284-5143

Ages: Mature Teenagers and up

Classes: Paint and Draw from a Model and Figure Drawing Class

Lafayette Studio offers art classes for adults and mature teenagers taught by distinguished local artists.

Lamorinda Academy of Music

3381 Mt. Diablo Blvd.
Lafayette, CA 94549
www.musicandart.org

925-299-1240

Ages: 3 and up

Classes: Drawing ,Painting, Mixed Media and Clay

Livermore

Livermore Area Recreation and Park District

4444 East Avenue
Livermore, CA 94550
www.larpd.dst.cs.us

925-373-5700

Classes: Cartooning, Beading

Oakland

California College of Arts

5212 Broadway
Oakland, CA 94610
www.cca.edu

510-594-3600

Ages: Middle School, High School Programs

California College of Arts (CCA) offers three summer programs for young adults. The Young Artist Studio Program (YASP) at California College of the Arts provides an exciting, intensive studio art experience for students interested in exploring the visual arts in a professional art school setting. The program is designed for students who have completed the sixth, seventh, or eighth grade. Check their website for an extensive list of classes.

The Summer Atelier program is for students who have completed the ninth grade. Participants explore drawing, alternative photographic processes, and screen-printing.

Pre-College provides an opportunity for high school students to study art or creative writing in an art school setting while earning three college credits. The program also enables participants to develop strong portfolio pieces for college admissions. Check their website for current course list.

The Crucible

1260 7th Street
Oakland, CA 94612
www.thecrucible.org
510-444-0919
Ages: 8–18 years
Classes: Blacksmithing, Foundry & Moldmaking, Neon & Light, Welding, Ceramics, Glass, Paper Works, Woodworking, Jewelry and More

The Crucible is the Bay Area's only nonprofit sculpture studio, educational foundry and metal fabrication shop offering classes in fine and industrial arts. From cast iron to neon, and from large-scale public art to the most precise kinetic sculpture, The Crucible is fast becoming the best-equipped public industry and arts education facility on the West Coast.

Pleasanton

Monart School of the Arts
Tri Valley Monart

3037-D Hopyard Road
Pleasanton, CA 94566
www.monart.com
925-484-0126

Monart is the only nationally-based drawing program whose "progressive" curriculum is taught in its own studio environment.

Richmond

Richmond Art Center

2540 Barrett Avenue
Richmond, CA 94804
www.therichmondartcenter.org
510-620-6772
Ages: 3 and up
Classes: Painting, Drawing, Clay, Cartooning and Sculpture

The Richmond Art Center is a nonprofit visual arts center that offers a variety of classes from well trained artists, many of whose work is exhibited or sold nationally.

San Ramon

Art 'n Play

21001 San Ramon Valley Blvd.
San Ramon, CA 94583
www.artnplay.com

925-479-0222

Ages: 18 months and up

This studio offers children painting, clay and a place for imaginative play.

Walnut Creek

Civic Arts Education Program

111 North Wiget Lane
Walnut Creek, CA 94598
www.arts-ed.org

925-943-5846

Ages: 3–18 years

Classes: Drawing, Painting, Ceramics, Cartooning, Watercolor, Acrylics, Sewing and Paper Crafts

For over 40 years the City of Walnut Creek's Civic Arts Education program has been the regional center of arts learning—promoting new visions, supporting exploration, stimulating creative thought and encouraging personal self-expression. It brings high quality visual and performing arts instruction and educational experiences to participants of all ages.

Color Me Mine

1950 Mt. Diablo Blvd.
Walnut Creek, CA 94596
www.walnutcreek.colormemine.com

925-280-2888

Ages: All

Color Me Mine is a paint-your-own ceramic studio that's fun for the whole family.

First 5 Contra Costa

www.firstfivecc.org
www.firstfivecc.org/onlinenews/09_07/news.htm#6

925-943-5899 ext. 471 Central CC Counter
510-234-5624 ext. 24 West CC County

First 5 Contra Costa has allocated approximately $100,000 to provide free interactive performing and visual art workshops for children ages 3 to 5 years old and their parents. The City of Walnut Creek's Fine Arts Preschool is offering classes in Antioch, Concord, and San Ramon. Space is limited to 16 children per class. To register for these classes, contact Cynthia Schultz at the central county number listed above.

In West County, parents can contact the East Bay Center for the Performing Arts for more information on free classes starting soon. Information is available at the West County number listed above.

Antioch

Queen B's Quilt Shop

720 West 2nd Street
Antioch, CA 94531
www.queenbquiltshop.com
925-978-4587

This is a nice and friendly quilt shop with classes for the Moms. No classes for the kids at this time.

Berkeley

Stonemountain & Daughter

2518 Shattuck Avenue
Berkeley, CA 94703
www.stonemountainfabric.com
510-845-6106

Ages: 9 and up

Classes: Youth Summer Camps and After School Classes

While taking a three or four day class you will make a pair of comfy pj pants or shorts. In the process you'll be learning basic machine sewing skills and safety, readying and interpreting a commercial sewing pattern, and learning basic information about fabrics and cutting. Machines provided. Small classes for lots of personal attention. Lots of quality fabrics and notions at a great price.

Brentwood

Michaels

5501 Lone Tree Way
Brentwood, CA 94513
www.michaels.com

925-308-7335

Michaels is the nation's largest specialty retailer of arts and crafts materials. They offer a Kids Club every Saturday morning to make fun and creative projects with an instructor. Visit their website or contact a store for specific projects and times.

Concord

Beverly's Fabric and Crafts

4677 Clayton Road
Concord, CA 94520
www.beverlys.com

925-686-1886

Beverly's is an industry leader in crafts with 22 stores in operation in California. It's a great place to find supplies for all your sewing and crafting projects. Their website has demos and projects.

Jo-Ann Fabric & Craft Superstore

1675 B Willow Pass Road
Concord, CA 94520
www.joann.com

925-671-7141

Classes: Sewing, Quilting, Jewelry, Home Décor Sewing, Wilton Cake Decorating, Knitting, Crochet, Scrapbooking, Sewing and Quilting Classes for Kids. Call stores for current classes and times

Superstores offer a larger selection of products as well as classes from Jo-Ann Creative University™.

Thimble Creek

1150 D Burnett Avenue
Concord, CA 94519
www.thimblecreek.com

925-676-5522

They offer a beginning quilting class for teens. Check their website for schedule and new classes.

Danville

The Quilter's Inn

125-F Railroad Avenue
Danville, CA 94526
www.thequilters-inn.com

925-837-8458

They offer fun beginning quilting classes for children in the summer.

Dublin

Michaels

7890 Dublin Blvd
Dublin, CA 94568
www.michaels.com

925-829-2268

Lafayette

The Cotton Patch

1025 Brown Avenue
Lafayette, CA 94549

925-284-1177

Ages: 9 and up

Classes: Beginning Quilting, Kid's Christmas Stocking and Kids Christmas Pajamas

Their class schedule comes out 3 times a year and they offer classes for children. Please refer to their website for the current class offerings. Durring the summer they offer a week long Camp on beginning quilting.

Livermore

In Between Stitches

2033 Railroad Avenue
Livermore, CA 94550
www.inbetweenstitches.com

925-371-7064

Ages: 9 and up

They offer a week long summer camp for beginning quilting.

San Ramon

Jo-Ann Fabric & Crafts

2425 San Ramon Valley Blvd
San Ramon, CA 94583
www.joann.com
925-831-8880

Pinole

Michaels

1450 Fitzgerald Drive
Pinole, CA 94564
www.michaels.com
510-222-4947

Pleasant Hill

Michaels

60 Gregory Lane
Pleasant Hill, CA 94523
www.michaels.com
925-521-1081

Memories, Photography and Keepsakes

We've given you plenty of ideas on how to make memories with your family, now the trick is to preserve them! We have included a list of scrapbook stores and some of their most popular classes to get you organized and preserving those stacks of pictures. We have even found people who will make your scrapbook for you and also put together video montages. Still looking for the perfect photo of your child? A list of photographers who specialize in children's photography is also included. Want to photograph your child yourself? Helpful hints on selecting a digital camera, taking photos and obtaining printed photos are also included.

Beverly's Fabric and Crafts

4677 Clayton Road
Concord, CA 94521
925-686-1886
www.beverlys.com

Beverly's is an industry leader in crafts with 22 stores in operation in California. They have a large selection of scrapbooking supplies, including albums, paper, punches, stickers, embellishments, tools, storage, books and more. They offer classes in scrapbooking.

Jo-Ann Fabric & Crafts

www.joann.com

Supplies for all your scrapbooking needs, including albums, embellishments, stickers, organizers, die cuts, paper and much more. Superstores offer a larger selection of products as well as classes from Jo-Ann Creative University™.

Memories, Photography and Keepsakes

Jo-Ann Fabric & Craft Superstore

1675 B Willow Pass Road
Concord, CA 94520
925-671-7141

2425 San Ramon Valley Blvd
San Ramon, CA 94583
925-831-8880

Michaels

60 Gregory Lane
Pleasant Hill, CA 94523
www.michaels.com

925-521-1081

Michaels is the nation's largest specialty retailer of arts and crafts materials. They offer a large selection of scrapbooking products including albums, paper, punches, scissors, die cutters, tools, storage, books, the Martha Stewart Crafts™ line and more.

1450 Fitzgerald Drive
Pinole, CA 94564
510-222-4947

5501 Lone Tree Way
Brentwood, CA 94513
925-308-7335

7890 Dublin Blvd
Dublin, CA 94568
925-829-2268

Scrapbook Stores

B Simple Scrapbooking

2222 Second Street, Suites 1 & 3
Livermore, CA 94550
www.bsimplescrapbooking.com

925-215-5424

Hours: Saturday Noon–5 pm. Monday, Tuesday, Thursday, Friday, Saturday 10 am–6 pm, Wednesday 10 am–10 pm.

This new store offers supplies and classes in traditional scrapbooking, digital scrapbooking and digital photography. They have a spacious room to host birthday parties, wedding showers and special events.

California Stampin & Scrapbook

5480-2 Sunol Blvd.
Pleasanton, CA 94566
www.castampin.com

925-417-842

Hours: Monday–Wednesday 10 am–5 pm, Thursday 10 am–8 pm, Friday 10 am–6 pm, Sat 10 am–5 pm, Sunday Noon–5 pm. California Stampin and Scrapbooks is an online/retail store

It's Scrapbook Time

2348 Buchanan Road
Antioch, CA 94509
www.itsscrapbooktime.com

925-778-8922

Hours: Monday–Saturday 10 am–7 pm, Sunday Noon–5 pm

They offer a large selection of products and a diverse class schedule. Their goal is to provide a vast selection of archival quality scrapbooking supplies at reasonable prices. During store hours they offer free crop time in their bright and cheery workshop space, provided there is no class scheduled.

Jordan's Village Books

3324 Village Drive
Castro Valley, CA 94546
www.jordansvillagebooks.com

510-538-2249

Hours: Monday–Friday 10 am–6 pm, Saturday 10 am–5:30 pm, Sunday Noon–5 pm.

They have everything from papers to cutters. You'll enjoy their huge selection of scrappin' products. To locals, they're known as "the sticker store." They carry an awesome array of stickers, including holiday and Disney stickers.

My Daughter's Wish

2835 Contra Costa #E
Pleasant Hill, CA 94523
www.mydaughterswish.com

925-952-4437

Hours: Monday 10 am–5 pm, Tuesday–Thursday 10 am–6 pm, Friday & Saturday 10 am–8 pm, Sunday Noon–5 pm

My Daughter's Wish is a scrapbook store geared toward the paper artist. They carry unusual items and have classes that teach unusual techniques. They always have a great selection of artistic papers. They have crop nights on Friday and Saturday. Check their class schedule, which changes monthly.

Memories, Photography and Keepsakes

Pleasant Memories Scrapbook

4247 Rosewood Drive #14
Pleasanton, CA 94588
www.pleasant-memories.net

925-227-0113

Hours: Monday, Wednesday, Friday, Saturday 10 am–6 pm, Tuesday and Thursday 10 am–7 pm, Sunday Noon–5 pm.

They sell many types and styles of scrapbook and stamp supplies. Every Thursday you save 25% off the selected product of the day.

Remember When

607 Gregory Lane Suite 150
Pleasant Hill, CA 94523
www.rememberwhenph.com

925-938-1700

Hours: Monday–Saturday 10 am–8 pm.

They like to carry the latest and greatest in papers and supplies. They like to find the new and emerging lines from different artists and feature their products. They offer a variety of classes and one of the most popular is a Disney class. They have crop nights on Friday and Saturday and they bring in pizza.

Richard's Crafts

225A Alamo Plaza
Alamo, CA 94507
www.richardsartsandcrafts.com

925-820-4731

Their memory department offers scrapbooking papers, stickers, albums and supplies. Classes are available. They carry a large selection of arts and crafts supplies.

Scrapbook Territory

1717 4th Street
Berkeley, Ca 94710
www.scrapbookterritory.com

510-559-9929

Hours: Tuesday–Sunday 10 am–6 pm, Friday 10 am–8 pm, closed Mondays

They are the largest scrapbooking store in the Bay Area with over 4,000 square feet. They have free cropping all day and Fridays until midnight. They offer the latest and greatest in papers and products. Their class schedule changes monthly offering classes in new techniques and the latest papers. If you are new to scrapbooking and you're not quite sure where to start, Intro to Scrapbooking could be the class for you.

Memories, Photography and Keepsakes

ScrapDiva

1185 Second Street, Suite J
Brentwood, CA 94513
www.scrapdivabrentwood.com

925-516-6910

Hours: Monday–Friday 10 am–6:30 pm, Saturday 10 am–5 pm, Sunday Noon–5 pm.

ScrapDiva is a hip place to crop and shop. They carry a wide range of products, have a room for you to crop, and lots of fun and educational classes.

Scrappin' With Mommie & Me

2401-A San Pablo Avenue
Pinole, CA 94564

510-742-2010

They carry a variety of papers, stickers and embellishments. One of their most popular classes is a Disney scrapbooking class.

Stamper's Warehouse

101-J Town and Country Drive
Danville, CA 94526
www.stamperswarehouse.com

925-362-9595

Hours: Monday, Tuesday, Wednesday, Friday 10 am–6 pm, Thursday 10 am–9 pm, Saturday 9:30 am–5:30 pm, Sunday Noon–5 pm.

This store offers a large selection of scrapbooking supplies as well as a huge selection of rubber stamps. Their class schedule is published every four months and they have many experienced teachers as well as nationally-known teachers.

The Paper Source

740 Hearst Avenue
Berkeley, CA 94710
www.paper-source.com

510-665-7800

Hour: Monday–Wednesday 10 am–6 pm, Thursday–Saturday 10 am–7 pm, Sunday Noon–6 pm. Holiday hours may vary.

Paper Source is the premiere seller of fine, handmade papers from around the world. Their spectacular selection is sold in a wide range of forms—large sheets, pre-cut and packaged letter sized sheets, envelopes and accessories. Their palette is uniquely Paper Source—with colors developed by and exclusively manufactured for them.

Memories, Photography and Keepsakes

Scrapbooking Resources

CK Media Family

www.primediascrapbooking.com

Ninety-seven percent of scrapbookers use scrapbooking magazines as a resource and CK Media Family publishes three great magazines: Creating Keepsakes, Simple Scrapbooks and Paper Crafts. Go to their website to see the latest issues as well as to find out about special issues and their newest books on scrapbooking.

Creative Memories

www.creativememories.com

This direct sales company offers traditional scrapbooking with paper, albums and stickers as well as digital scrapbooking software. You can go to their website to find a consultant near you.

Scrapbooking.com Magazine

5900 La Place Court Suite 105
Carlsbad, CA 92008
www.srapbooking.com

760-929-7090

This is an online magazine with page layouts and step by step instructions, online shopping links, product demos, a store locator and much more. This site has some fun projects and useful information.

Scrapbook EXPO

P.O. Box 7474
Norco, CA 92860
www.scrapboolexpo.com

360-897-6032

Scrapbook EXPO is a traveling scrapbook show that offers you the opportunity to learn the newest and hottest scrapbooking techniques as well as top-notch workshops and basic classes taught by experts. They have exciting events, make and takes, contests, crop nights and more. Visit their website to find the date of an EXPO near you. Cities in or near the Bay Area that hold Scrapbook Expos are Pleasanton, Sacramento and Santa Clara.

Stampin' Up

www.stampinup.com

This company has an awesome selection of stamps to order by mail or online. Whether you want to purchase a catalog, host a workshop or become a demonstrator, check out their website for more information or to find a demonstrator in your area.

Stampington & Company

22992 Mill Creek, Suite B
Laguna Hills, CA 92653
www.stampington.com

949-380-7318

Stampington & Company are the makers of fine art stamps and the publisher of Somerset Studio®, The Stampers' Sampler®, Stampington Inspirations™, Belle Armoire®, Legacy™, Art Doll Quarterly™, Take Ten™ and Somerset Memories which is dedicated to scrapbooking and heritage arts. This is a great website that has something to offer everyone.

Digital Scrapbooking

www.cottagearts.net

CottageArts.net product line, Simply Digital™, currently offers themed CDs and a huge variety of downloadables of custom designed layout templates, background papers, and embellishments to help you create stunning digital scrapbooking layouts, or to print for use in traditional scrap-books.

Creative Memories

www.creativememories.com
(See reference above)
They offer software for digital scrapbooking.

Shutterfly

www.shutterfly.com

Shutterfly does more than deliver award winning digital prints right to your door. They offer solutions to digital photo storage and organizational needs as well as offering services to create photo books.

Digital Scrapbooking Magazine

www.digitalscrapbooking.com

This is a monthly magazine that is devoted to digital scrapbooking. They offer education, product information, contests and more.

How Fast They Grow

howfasttheygrow.com

The digi-scrapbook featured on this site makes it easy to create your own page with digital photos, creative titles and journaling. Drag, drop, type and you're on your way.

Great Photographers

These photographers have been recommended by Mamas like you. We selected these photographers because other parents have had great experiences with them. We hope you find someone you'll love to work with, and more importantly, someone who will provide you with those priceless portraits that you will treasure for years to come.

Avalon Arts Studio

Benicia, CA
www.avalonarts.com

707-751-0190

Fairy Portraits are by far the most popular request—but they are a full service photography studio. Also available are photographs of families and adults, senior photos, formal portraits, personal portrait Storybooks of your child and Belly and Baby portraits.

Cantrell Portrait Design

421 Kahrs Avenue
Pleasant Hill, CA 94523
www.cantrellportrait.com

925-934-1994

Bambi Cantrell's cutting edge style has attracted many and her images have been published in numerous magazines such as Martha Stewart Living, American Photo and Time Magazine to name a few. Check out her website to see her stunning images of children, family, and seniors. Her associate, Michael Van Auken, is also an award winning photographer whose images of babies and children are not to be missed.

Chett K Bullock Fine Photography

www.chettbullock.com

925-673-0357

Chett Bullock's blend of traditional and photojournalistic style is to capture spontaneous moments in an artistic and creative way. He shoots on-location in color or black and white. His black and white studio photos of babies are priceless.

Craig Merrill Photography

1205 Pacific Avenue
Alameda, CA 94502
www.merillphotographic.com

510-865-3629

Craig's style is fun and relaxed with an eye for something different. It can be traditional or very untraditional. His photography experience runs almost 30 years, including everything from weddings, special events, families, children, and professional headshots. Grace McHugh, Craig's wife, is a professional hair and makeup artist. They collaborate, or work independently. She has 22 years of experience in the beauty business, mainly working in the medium of photography.

Dana Smith Photography

Brentwood, CA

www.danasmithphotograpy.net

925-516-2216

As a mom to four little girls, she realizes how fast children grow and how quickly those special times go by. Dana specializes in outdoor location portraits of children and families using natural light. She also has indoor studio sessions available for little babies. She strives to make your portrait session a comfortable, fun and memorable experience.

Darlene Tom Photography

San Ramon, CA

www.darlenetomphotography.net

925-866-2805

Families come from all over the Bay Area to have their children photographed by Darlene. Darlene specializes in maternity, baby, children, and family photography. She captures a child's expression and personality to show "who" they are, not just "what" they look like. Her portrait style is usually simple, close up and full of everything a parent wants.

Gretchen Adams Photography

www.gretchenadams.com

925-676-7036

As a mother of two, Gretchen understands the need and desire for images of your family that speak to the heart. She is able to put her subjects at ease creating a comfortable and relaxed environment.

Imagine That... Photography
Penny Porter

www.imaginethatphotography.net

925-299-0251

Imagine That...specializes in maternity, children and family portraiture. Creating the portraits at the family's home or favorite outdoor space is a great way to make sure everyone is happy. Penny creates fun and original ways to capture the magic of each family. She is one of the last real photographers using film to create black/white and color photos. Ask about "Through the Year" portrait plans.

Memories, Photography and Keepsakes

Jennifer Scog Photography

Walnut Creek, CA
www.jenniferscogphotography.com

925-9307734

She incorporates her bold sense of fashion and unique style to create classic, timeless images. Capturing the true spirit of her clients, Jennifer creates a comfortable, candid atmosphere allowing subjects to relax and be themselves.

Judy Host Photography

www.judyhost.com

925-736-2344

Judy Host is one of Northern California's leading photographers. As an accomplished artist, her portraits are at once both magical and mystical. Judy has that rare ability to create a special rapport with her clients that ultimately tells a story or reflects feeling in that one-of-a-kind portrait.

Kevallyn Marie Photography

Walnut Creek, CA
www.kevallynmariephoto.com

925-766-3121

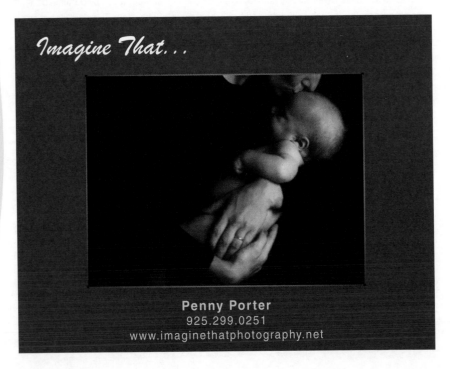

Imagine That...

Penny Porter
925.299.0251
www.imaginethatphotography.net

Kevallyn emphasis is in photographing children and nature. She uses an artful eye and attention to detail to capture images unique to a subject's personality and style. Her specialty is catching candid and definitive moments whether that be an exuberant expression, a quite glance or beautiful scene.

Kouns Photography

2575 Dreby Drive
San Ramon, CA 94583
ww.kounsphoto.com

925-365-1036

Kouns Photography is a family owned business that specializes in baby, children and family photography. They do both on location and studio portraits. For studio portraits they believe less is more, and therefore limit props to very simple, classic items such as luxury fabrics and greenery accents. Their style is relaxed and informal. They like to capture your family in its true spirit with all their natural expression and charisma.

Lani Allen Photography

327-A St. Mary's Street
Pleasanton, CA 94566
www.laniallenphotography.com
admin@laniallenphotography.com

925-216-9826

Lani Allen Photography located in a cute cottage in the heart of downtown Pleasanton was voted "Best Photographer" for a reason. Lani enjoys capturing your precious growing belly, the tiny toes in the new miracle of life or the song dancing in a child's eyes. She is committed to making your photo session enjoyable! Either on location or in studio, Lani will capture the true essence of the moment...the ones you never want to forget.

Lasting Images Photography

22 Cobblestone Court
San Ramon, CA 94583
www.lastingimagesfoto.com

925-837-8080

Danielle Jess of Lasting Images Photography specializes in capturing candid, creative and timeless portraits of expecting mothers, newborns, infants and children in a variety of settings. As a mother of three young children, Danielle understands the importance of patience, flexibility and the need to create a fun and comfortable environment for you and your child/children.

Many options available—black & white portraits, coffee table books, canvas and fine art prints, selective coloring of portraits—please inquire for additional information.

Memories, Photography and Keepsakes

Linda Johnson Photography

510 West Third Street
Antioch, CA 94509
www.lindajohnson.com

925-779-1325

Linda Johnson specializes in creating wall portraits that are unique and highly personal. Her fanciful, award winning images of children playing in a storytelling setting will capture your heart. Each photograph is individually designed, together with the client to create a concept that incorporates symbols of meaningful endeavors and remembrances of people and places important to the family.

Meritage on Main

4615 First Street, Suite 110
Pleasanton, CA 94566
www.meritageonmain.com

925-462-9364

Michael Gan is an accomplished award winning photographer. Leslie Artis is an artist that has always worked closely with her clients to create art that expresses their spirit and soul. This has carried over into her photography. Together they make up Merritage on Main.

Pam Biasotti Photography

www.pambiasotti.com

925-556-1529

Pam works as an on-location photographer, specializing in natural light portraiture of children and expectant mothers. Her style can be described as editorial, lifestyle photography. There is something about the little people in our lives that Pam feels is important to document. Every picture is a story.

Photographic Images by Deidre Lingenfelter

2499 Diablo Ranch Place
Danville, CA 94526
www.imagesbydeidre.com

925-837-0232

As the mother of three sons, she realized and embraced the importance of photographing children as they grow. Her newest subjects are her grandchildren! Her goal for each new client is to capture a moment, an expression and to create a piece of art that will be cherished for generations to come. Deidre and her husband have built a studio on their property including old gates from Europe, weathered doors, an English garden and a stone stairway.

Photography by Jill

3093 Citrus Circle, Suite 125
Walnut Creek, CA 94598
www.photojill.com

925-324-2972

Jill specializes in photography for babies, children, families and maternity. She loves photographing a life being lived. Children's portraits are usually taken at a playground, where kids can just be
kids. Nothing stiff and posed. Just little lives happening.

Portrait Originals by Shel Najera

www.shelnajeraportraits.com

925-229-3665

Shel specializes in timeless portraits of babies, children, and families. Her black and white or color
photos are a unique work of art created in studio or on location. Antique color portraits are printed on archival rag paper, and then intricately hand painted with oils. No two are exactly alike.
Hand painted color portraits create an antique essence with a painterly feel.

Susan J Weiand Photography

www.susanjweiand.com

408-996-1933

Her specialty is candid photography of children and families. Parents like the natural look of her
portraits and she is adept at making small children feel at ease during the photography session.

Tamiland, Inc.

150 Cole
San Francisco, CA 94117
www.tamiland.com

415-668-5930

Tami DeSellier is a Bay Area photographer specializing in babies, toddlers, children and families
since 1986. She is directly involved with every client and prefers to shoot in black and white with
minimal props to capture each child's natural expressions and personality. Her clients will tell you
that she has an astonishing ability to anticipate each child's expression and knows exactly when
to trip the shutter to get the shot... that's the skill that separates her from her peers. She's known
for her energetic disposition and passion for photography.

Memories, Photography and Keepsakes

Wentling Studio

1804 Colfax Street
Concord, CA 94520
www.wentlingstudio.com

925-685-7760

Wentling's Studio is a 3rd generation, award winning, professional photography studio. They specialize in children's portraiture and are Home of the Original Watch Baby Grow and Kids Klub Programs. The studio staff love children and it shows in their portraits. Their private camera room sessions are innovative, fun, and interactive. They will capture your child's special charm in portraits that you and your family will treasure for generations come. This same expertise, creativity and enthusiasm are brought to their family, event and location shoots as well. See ad in the back.

Selecting a Digital Camera for YOU

Many mamas have taken photos for so long that the issue is not taking a photo, but instead it is how to select a digital camera as technology is continually improving. Here are a few key questions to ask yourself:

What "mega" does this mama need?

As with everything bigger is better, but do you really need the best? For 8x10 photos and smaller you would want a 3 mega pixel or higher camera but if you will use the photos for the internet or won't be printing larger than 4x6, a 1 to 2 mega pixel camera will do. Just remember that photos are made up of a whole lot of little dots—each dot is a pixel. The more pixels you have, the more detailed your photo will be! And it is easy to reduce a photo from 8x10 to 4x6 but when you try to take a 4x6 photo and make it an 8x10 you lose quality because the dots separate a little more. So, get a camera that provides you high enough quality for the largest size photo you plan to print.

Do I need to zoom?

Despite the variety of zooms available, it really is best to get as close to your subject as possible. When buying a camera you will note an optical zoom and a digital zoom. Optical zoom refers to the same zoom from your 35mm camera. It does not reduce the quality of your photo. If you are often far from your subject, than you would want a high optical zoom. Digital zoom lowers the pixels in photos—the closer you zoom, the fewer pixels your photo will have.

Is a camera that fits in the diaper bag good enough?

Yes. Digital cameras come in all shapes and sizes, but the smaller the camera, the fewer features it will probably offer. Make a list of features you really need and see if you find them in the small camera, if yes, then small is for you!

Can I use rechargeable batteries?

Each camera has it's different battery requirements but most cameras use batteries that can be recharged and if you want to save money in the long run, make sure you buy one of these because digital cameras use of batteries FAST.

Is the memory card that comes with my camera enough?

Maybe, maybe not. If you upload photos daily, a small memory card will be sufficient, but if you ever plan to travel with your kids, you may not have enough space to take as many photos as you may like. The type of memory card used by the camera is another factor to consider. If you want your camera for traveling, a higher-capacity memory card is very handy for storing photos until you can download them to a computer. If you use a camera at work or frequently carry it with you, you may want a more durable card. Many variables determine how much memory space is taken including image content, file types and compression. Be sure to ask your retailer for the manufacturers table which shows how many images you can save on their included memory card or visit the manufacturer's website.

Does it matter how big the screen (LCD monitor) is?

Only to you...try it out and see if the resolution on the screen is comfortable for you.

Take the time when making an investment in a digital camera. Look around; visit various retailers even if you ultimately buy your camera online. Ask questions and ask more questions! The most expensive camera may not be the best camera for you so don't feel pressured by the price of the camera. Just make sure it will do what you need it to do.

Photography Basics

Everyone enjoys a great photograph of their family, but we know that when the family budget is tight a professional session may be a luxury you have to skip. That doesn't mean have to pass up the opportunity to capture your family on film, use these simple tips and you'll be snapping frame-worthy photos in no time!

Make eye contact.

"Look at me when I'm talking to you!" That concept is as important for taking a photograph as it is for communicating. Direct eye contact is very engaging and translates well to film. Hold the camera at the eye level of your subject to capture their magnetic gazes and killer smiles. Remember, your children don't always have to be staring at the camera. The eye level angle will create the personal feel that you are looking for in a photograph.

Get close.

Fill the picture with your subject. Zoom in to capture those small, meaningful details on the faces of your children. But don't get too close, most cameras get burry if you get closer than about three feet. Remember, this is a good rule of thumb if you are looking to create a portrait photograph. If you are trying to create a memorable vacation or holiday photo, scenery elements will be key.

Memories, Photography and Keepsakes

The flash is your friend.

Sunny days can be deceptive. While a nice bright day provides plenty of light for your photograph it can also create deep shadows on the face of your subject. A flash can be helpful on a cloudy day too. The flash will brighten up people's faces and make them stand out in the photograph. A key to using your flash effectively is knowing the range. For most cameras the flash range is about fifteen feet.

Be aware of the background.

It is easy to get so focused on the face of your subject that you overlook the fact your great photo is set against a distracting background. A simple background will show off your family. As you look through the camera lens pay special attention to the scenery and activities behind your children to make sure that no one looks like they have a tree growing out of the back of their head!

Watch the light

If you are interested in capturing your family outside, some of the best natural light can be found early and late in the day. The soft light of a cloudy day is also very flattering on facial features. If the light doesn't suit your fancy, move yourself or your subject until you are satisfied.

Get the picture you want.

Don't just take pictures, make it happen! Ask your subjects to "squeeze together," "sit over here" or "lean toward the camera."

Get down!

Most babies and infants will be more comfortable and act more naturally if you let them lay down. You can capture your babies smile best if you are willing to perch over him or her and be patient!

Keep your camera with you.

No, not at all times, but if you know you want to get some good photos of the family boating or working on an art project, turn them loose and keep your camera handy to capture candid moments that you'll treasure for a lifetime!

Uploading Websites

Once you buy your camera and take your photos, what's next? Printing your photos! You may choose to invest in a photo printer or find an online site to upload your photos to. Below is a quick summary of just a few of the many online options. Most sites also offer photo cards, calendars and much more.

Creative Memories Photo Center

www.cmphotocenter.com

Specializing in printing digital photos and StoryBooks, a digital scrapbook that is printed and bound and shipped to you! The Perfect Print is Creative Memories' name for the image created from most digital cameras, typically referred to as the 4xD print. 4xD is the industry term for a print that is 4 x 5.33-inches, a unique printing option. Pricing starts at $0.19 for either 4xD or 4x6 prints, but a pre-paid card finds pricing as low as $0.12 a print! Shipping not included in pricing. See website for more details.

Costco Photo Center

www.costco.com

At Costco Photo Center you have the ability to upload prints and have them either shipped or listed for pick up at a Costco Wherehouse near you.

CVS Online

www.cvs.pnimedia.com

You get 10 free prints on Kodak paper when you sign-up but any order under $5 incurs a $1.49 service charge. 4x6 prints are about $0.19, 5x7 $1.49 and 8x10 $3.99. Shipping is about $5.99 for two day and $9.99 for next day.

Kodak EasyShare Gallery

www.kodakgallery.com

You get 10 free prints on Kodak paper when you sign-up. 4x6 prints are about $0.15, 5x7 $0.99 and 8x10 $3.99. Shipping is about $4.99 for 76 or more prints.

Ritz — Wolf Camera

www.ritzpix.com

4x6 prints on Fuji paper are about $0.19, 5x7 $0.99 and 8x10 $3.89. Photo pick up available at your local Wolf store. Shipping cost is standard postal delivery charges.

Shutterfly

www.shutterfly.com

You get 15 free prints on Fuji paper when you sign-up. 4x6 prints are about $0.19, 5x7 $0.99 and 8x10 $3.99. Prepaid plans are available and reduce prices significantly. Shipping is about $4.99 for 76 or more prints. You can also save money on shipping and have your photos printed at your local Target.

SnapFish

www.snapfish.com

You get 20 free prints on Kodak paper when you sign-up. 4x6 prints are about $0.12, 5x7 $0.79 and 8x10 $2.99. Prepaid plans are available and reduce prices significantly and there are discounts for large quantity orders. Shipping is about $1.97 for 25 and $0.49 for each additional 10 prints ordered.

Memories, Photography and Keepsakes

Walgreens

www.photo.walgreens.com

You get 10 free prints on Kodak paper when you sign-up. 4x6 prints are about $0.19, 5x7 $1.99 and 8x10 $3.99. Shipping is about $4.99 for 76 or more prints. Shipping is about $1.97 for 25 and $0.49 for each additional 10 prints ordered or pick up in store.

Wink Flash

www.winkflash.com

Looking to save a buck? You get 50 free prints on Fuji paper when you sign-up. 4x6 prints are about $0.12, 5x7 $0.29 and 8x10 $1.99. Shipping is only a $0.99 flat rate.

Chapter 12

Just for Mom

The responsibilities that come with motherhood are extensive but it's important not to neglect one's own needs. Whether your needs have to do with employment concerns, meeting fellow mamas or getting in shape, this chapter offers resources for you. Do you want to continue working? Have you considered becoming an entrepreneur? There are so many employment options for mothers whether it be part time, full time or work whenever you want time.

You'll also find a list of moms groups where you can connect with other women and find some great playmates for your kids. Join a workout facility or program that caters to females and keep your body happy and healthy.

Beauty & Day Spas

In the unselfish world of motherhood, there seems to be a notion that going to a spa is a lavish, self-indulgent affair. That taking time out to be pampered, spoiled and thoroughly looked after is over-indulgent.

If it will make you feel any better, we are including some of the benefits of what you'll get from a little pampering once in awhile so that you can feel like you've got a legitimate excuse to go and take some time for yourself. Going to a spa can actually have therapeutic effects. These include:

- Sooth tense and sore muscles
- Clean, tone and nourish the skin
- Detoxify the body to enhance the immune system
- Stimulate circulation to ease conditions like arthritis and rheumatism

* Relieve anxiety, anger and depression
* Calm allergies and ease symptoms of diabetes, migraines and asthma
* Improve flexibility
* Increase the body's energy flow
* Heal emotional distress
* Enhance body-mind awareness
* Improve spiritual focus and clarity.

Now you have the perfect excuse! If you can't find one that fits listed above, make one up! Don't know where to go? Try any of these local spas and we're sure you'll be glad you did!

Changes Salon & Day Spa

1475 North Broadway
Walnut Creek, CA 94596
www.changessalon.com

925-947-1814

Price Range: Massages start at $60 and up

Features: Variety of Massages including a Pregnancy Massage, Spa Body Treatments and Wraps, Wellness Assessment, Creating Health Workshop, Facials, Makeup Instruction, Permanent Make-up, Laser Hair removal, Waxing, Manicure, Pedicures, Haircuts, Color and Styling

Château de Sable

551 Hartz Avenue
Danville, CA 94526
www.chateaudesablespa.com

925-831-8568

Price Range: Massages start at $95/hour

Features: Customized massage packages and pregnancy Massages, Duo Massage Retreat, Facials, Spa Body Treatments, Waxing and Brows Hair Design, Makeup, Lashes and Hair Extensions

Claremont Resort & Spa

41 Tunnel Road
Berkeley, CA 94705
www.claremontresort.com

800-551-7266 ext. # 2 Claremont Spa

Price Range: Massages start at $80/25 minutes

Features: This is a full service spa offering Massages (including a Pre-Natal Massage), Water Therapy, Body Wraps, Waxing Services, Brows, Facials, Nail Care, Hair Care, Acupuncture, Pilates, Yoga and Nutrition Therapy

Entourage Spa

Two Theatre Square, Suite 148
Orinda, CA 94563
www.entouragespa.com

925-254-9721

Price Range: Massages start at $85/50 minutes

Features: Massage Therapy including Pregnancy Massage, Facials- European and Domestic, Waxing, Hair Services, Nail Care, Body Treatments/Body Wraps, Make up, Med Spa Services, Café and Wine Bar

Jerol Beauty Salon

301 Hartz Avenue
Danville, CA 94526
www.jerolsalon.com

925-820-6044

Price Range: Facials start at $38/30 minutes

Features: Massages, Facials, Hair Care, Hair Extensions, Nail Care, Waxing Services, Makeup and Skin Treatments

LA European Mobile Spa

780 Main Street, Suite #206
Pleasanton, CA 94566
925-846-8891

"Blink" and you're in Paris! Let us take you away from the day to day grind and replace it with a little Ooo la la! Bay area Mama's are selective and savvy that's why they choose La Lu European Mobile Spa for their "Home Pampering Party experience."

Services: We provide spa services at any location in the Tri-valley and the greater Tri-valley areas. You and your guests can choose from massage, facials, hand and foot treatments and body treatments too! Please don't forget to ask about our special gift for the hostess. Call today to schedule your in home spa!

Le Jardin at the Spa

1603 Oak Park Blvd.
Pleasant Hill, CA 94523
www.lejardinatthespa.com

925-935-4247

Price Range: Facials start at $75/hour

Features: Massages including a Pregnancy Massage, Facial, Skin Care Treatments, Cosmetic Peels, Waxing Services, Make-up, Nail Care, Haircut, Color, Perms and Extensions

Lily Pad Day Spa

2347 Willow Pass Road
Concord, CA 94520
www.lilypaddayspa.net

925-825-1101

Price Range: Massages start at $70/hour

Features: Massages, Facials, Acne Treatment, Microdermabrasion, Glycolic Resurfacing Peel and Waxing

Miracullum

1355 North Main Street
Walnut Creek, CA 94596
www.miracullum.com

925-943-6146

Price Range: Facials start at $85

Features: Age Defying Facials, Rosacea & Sensitive Skin Facials, Acne, Problem, Oily Skin Facials, Brightening Facials, Microdermabrasion, Photo Light Treatment, Lymphobiology, Peels, Massages, Body Treatments, Foot Treatments, Hair Removal, Eyelash Enhancements and Permanent Makeup

Remedy Skin Care Center

264 Spring Street
Pleasanton, CA 94566
www.remedyskincarecenter.com

925-461-1400

Price Range: Massages start at $1/minute

Features: Massages including a Pre/Post Natal Massage, Reflexology, Lactic Lightening Facial, Rosacea Cooling Facial, Microdermabrasion, Peels, Waxing and Tinting

Renaissance ClubSport Walnut Creek

2805 Jones Road
Walnut Creek, CA
www.renaissanceclubsport.com

925-938-8700

Price Range: Massages start at $95/50 minutes

Features: Massages including a Prenatal Massage, Facials, Face and Body Treatments, Microdermabrasion, Makeup and Special Body Treatments

Royale Image Day Spa

3500 Clayton Road, Suite C
Concord, CA 94519
www.royaleimagespa.com

925-682-8881

Hours: By appointment

You deserve nothing but the "Royale treatment," so come escape into this beautiful upscale day spa located in Concord, California. Offering unique Air Brush Tanning services as well as European facials, body waxing, massage therapy, manicure & pedicures, body treatments, make-up application and spa get-away packages. All spa services are administered by California licensed professionals, who provide beneficial treatments, using the highest quality products designed to cater to each client's specific needs and total body wellness. Please visit their website or call for more information.

The Spa at Club Sport

350 Bollinger Canyon Lane
San Ramon, CA 94583
www.clubsportsr.com

925-735-1182

Price Range: Massages start at $35/20 minutes

Features: Massages including Prenatal Massage, Facial Treatments, Microdermabrasion, Peels, Body Treatments, Waxing Services, Permanent Cosmetics, Nail Services and Hair Services

Just for Mom

Soft Touch Skin Care

1401 Cypress Street
Walnut Creek, CA 94596
www.softtouchskin.com

925-785-8877

Price Range: Massage start at $55/30 minutes

Features: Facial Treatments, Peels, Microdermabrasion, Red Light Rejuvenation, Waxing and Threading, Lash Tinting, Makeup, Massage Therapy, Prenatal Massage and Body Wraps

Beauty Enhancement

The East Bay Laser & Skin Care Center, Inc.

1479 Ygnacio Valley Road, Suite 209
Walnut Creek, CA 94598
www.eastbaylaser.com
eastbaylaser@aol.com

925-932-9389

Hours: Monday–Friday 10 am–5 pm

Dr. M. Christine Lee is a noted laser expert, published author and board-certified dermatologist with advanced fellowship training in lasers, cosmetic surgery, skin cancer surgery and reconstruction. "I received the best training possible, and I'm able to offer the widest, most expansive array of technological options," Dr. Lee says. "With over 40 different lasers, I can always choose the most appropriate treatment based upon the individual needs of each and every patient."

Isagenix Cleansing and Fat Burning System
Linda Ehrich, Consultant

www.cleansedforlife.com
www.isadelight.com
www.yoursuccess-yes.isagenix.com

925-698-1452

Would you like to gain optimum health, renewed energy and mental clarity and to release unwanted pounds and inches safely and easily and keep them off? Isagenix will help you achieve your goals! We have toxins in our body from pollutants, pesticides, insecticides and impurities in our water. Toxins attract fat as a protective layer. Let me show you how Isagenix can help you lose the fat quickly while building lean muscle.

Jumpstart Medicine

710 South Broadway, Suite 110
Walnut Creek, CA 94596
www.jumpstartmedicine.com

925-277-1123

Just for Mom

Jumpstart Medicine offers a physician-supervised weight loss program individually designed for women and men looking to lose weight safely and effectively. On average, our patients lose 25 to 60 pounds in 3 months. We work with everyone from new mothers to post-menopausal women. Most patients feel great, have no cravings, and stay highly motivated due to quick results, which they can see and feel. How much do you want to lose?

Bishop Ranch 11

2301 Camino Ramon, Suite 290
San Ramon, CA 94583
925-277-1123

Kristin Walker M.D., Inc.
General and Cosmetic Dermatologist

89 Davis Road, Suite 180
Orinda, CA 94563
925-254-1080

Dr. Walker, board certified dermatologist, offers care in general adult and pediatric dermatology, laser surgery, skin cancer surgery, and cosmetic dermatology. Her friendly and supportive staff can help return the glow to your skin with the most advanced skin care lasers and technologies. Dr. Walker is proud to announce the addition of a Nutritionist and Aesthetician to her practice.

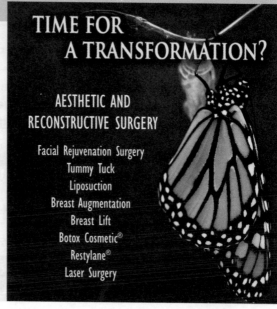

Michelle J. Place, M.D., F.A.C.S.

919 San Ramon Valley Blvd., Suite 255
Danville, CA 94526
www.michellejplacemd.com

925-837-1347

Hours: Monday through Friday 9 am–5 pm, Call for a complimentary consultation

Dr. Place's practice is primarily Aesthetic or Cosmetic Surgery. She provides complete patient care with an experienced and friendly staff. Dr. Place and the Aesthetic Skin Care Center offer a complete service beginning with conditioning treatments for the skin, laser and intense pulsed light treatments, and extending to Botox, collagen and Restylane. Surgical procedures include facelifts, eyelid lifts, brow lifts, body contouring, liposuction, tummy tucks, arm lifts, and breast surgery.

Timothy Leung, MD

905 San Ramon Valley Blvd., Suite 110
Danville, CA 94526
www.elegantsurgery.com

925-831-1317

From your first consultation-through the decision making process, procedure, recovery, and admiring results-you feel confident and secure with Dr. Leung. His specialties include aesthetic plastic surgery of the face and body, and comprehensive skin care solutions.

Vivian Ting, MD, FACS

Plastic and Cosmetic Surgery
Clinical Assistant Professor, University of California (UCSF)
Veritas Plastic Surgery
1776 Ygnacio Valley Road, Suite 108
Walnut Creek, CA 94598
www.viviantingmd.com

925-939-9200

Harvard trained and board certified, Dr. Vivian Ting practices at John Muir Medical Center in Walnut Creek. She combines state-of-the-art technique with the highest level of patient care in procedures for facial rejuvenation, eyelid and and nose reshaping, breast surgery, and body contouring. Mommy makeovers are a popular request of her clients. She is described by patients as an "honest and gifted surgeon," and is committed to refining the elegance, confidence and well being of her patients.

Business Resources

Have an invention or a desire to run a small business? From national to local organizations, support is right at your fingertips.

Business and Professional Women/USA

www.bpwusa.org

BPW/USA fosters the success of working women by providing career advancement resources, worklife strategies and personal and professional connections.

Career Transitions Group

Janet Keller

atcallbackcom@earthlink.net

510-547-3704

If you are considering a career transition or thinking about returning to work, you may want to join this group for support, brainstorming, or simply for a little encouragement.

Contra Costa Small Business Development Center

2425 Bisso Lane, Suite 200
Concord, CA 94520
www.contracostasbdc.com

925-646-5377

The Contra Costa Small Business Development Center provides professional consulting services and a wide variety of educational programs for all small businesses owners in Contra Costa County. The Small Business Development Center is the largest management and technical assistance program serving the small business sector in the US.

Just for Mom

Entrepreneur Center

84 West Santa Clara Street
San Jose, CA 95113-1815
www.ecenteronline.org

408-494-0210

Want to enter the world of entrepreneurship? The mission of the Entrepreneur Center is to provide entrepreneurs with a full range of support services, in one convenient location, to help them succeed in today's competitive economy. The services include financing programs, technical assistance, training, technology and procurement.

Flexperience

www.flexperiencestaffing.com

Flexperience is a boutique firm in the Bay Area that connects experienced marketing, human resources, finance, and legal professionals with opportunities for part-time, flex-time, or project based work with their clients. They understand the desire of many people to balance a rewarding professional life with an enriching personal life.

Ladies Who Launch

Allie Covarrubias

www.ladieswholaunch.com

415-730-3159

Fee: $325 Incubator Workshop (price subject to change)

Ladies Who Launch was designed with a network building mentality where you're given tools and inspiration to put your vision into action. To become an "Incubator" you attend workshops that will help you launch a new idea, expand a current venture or simply explore ideas for success.

Mom Inventors, Inc.

P.O. Box 830
Alamo, CA 94507
www.mominventors.com

866-376-1122

This is a free community where you can obtain tools and resources to help you put an idea into action, launch and grow your business. You can obtain information on licensing, forms, instructions on how to share your ideas without others taking them, product safety regulations, and so much more.

Mommy Track'd

www.mommytrackd.com

Mommy Track'd is the working mother's guide to managed chaos. They offer busy stay-at-work moms a smart and entertaining resource to help manage the daily tug of war between work and family.

National Association of Women Business Owners
San Francisco Bay Area Chapter

1500 Franklin Street
San Francisco, CA 94109
www.nawbo-sf.org

415-333-2130

Dues: $125

The National Association of Women Business Owners-San Francisco Chapter meets particular challenges. Sharing their resources, expertise and experiences benefits everyone. Greater networking opportunities and strategic alliances give an advantage to individual businesswomen. Their events and programs also provide the means to learn and earn more.

National Association of Women Business Owners - California
(a consortium of all of California's Chapters)

888-NAWBO.CA

www.nawbo-ca.org

714-832-5012

NAWBO California was created as the "senate" of all nine (9) chapters, whose volunteer board members convene quarterly to share knowledge, build business relationships and form lasting partnerships with corporations and governmental entities. They are part of the National Association of Women Business Owners (NAWBO), a nationwide women's business organization with 80 chapters throughout the United States and an affiliation with Les Femmes Chefs d'Entreprises Mondiales (World Association of Women Entrepreneurs) in 33 countries

East Bay SCORE

492 9th Street, Suite 350
Oakland, CA 94607
www.score.org

510-273-6611

Want to start a small business but don't know where to begin? Have you already started a business but have questions about running it? SCORE offers free and confidential small business advice for entrepreneurs. You can go to their website and email questions, call to schedule a face-to-face small business counseling session or attend a low-cost workshop. They also offer "How To" articles and business tools. The local chapter knows the market, local rules and regulations, and can help you with your business needs.

U.S. Small Business Administration—San Francisco District Office

455 Market Street, 6th Floor
San Francisco, CA 94105-2420
www.sba.gov

415-744-6820

The U.S. Small Business Administration (SBA) is an independent agency of the federal government that aids, counsels, assists and protects the interests of small businesses. The mission of the SBA is to help Americans start, build and grow businesses.

WomanOwned.com Business Networks for Women

www.womanowned.com

This is an organization that helps women who are starting or growing a business.

Works For Me

worksforme@yahoogroups.com

Works For Me is a network of mothers in the Bay Area who are in career transition. Members include stay at home moms, working moms, and entrepreneur moms, who want to manage their careers while being the mom they want to be. The group sponsors networking events in addition to this online presence in order to create a community of support.

Local Moms Groups

Everyone needs a way to plug into the community. If you're feeling isolated, cooped up, wishing you could meet more moms to relate to or are simply looking for a great way to be involved in your community, try joining a local mom's group. You can meet amazingly diverse people and form lasting relationships. From support groups to playgroups, you can find just about anything through a mom's group.

East Bay Moms

www.eastbaymoms.com

East Bay Moms' mission is to provide support, companionship, and networking for members. They provide an avenue for parents to meet, exercise and enjoy the outdoors. All interested parents of infants and toddlers are welcome to join.

East County Mothers Club

www.eastcountymothersclub.org

The East County Mothers' Club serves the East Contra Costa County communities of Antioch, Bay Point, Bethel Island, Brentwood, Byron, Discovery Bay, Knightsen, Oakley, and Pittsburg.

Holistic Moms Network

www.holisticmoms.org

At the Holistic Moms Network (HMN) members share a common bond: a desire to be the best parents possible by providing their children with a physical, psychological, and spiritual environment that will nourish them and allow them to reach their greatest potential. Meet other moms who are interested in natural health and holistic therapies or following an "alternative" parenting style. They have an East Bay Chapter which meets in Oakland the last Tuesday of each month.

Hoot Owls

www.groups.yahoo.com/group/HOOTOWLS_EBCA

HOOT OWL stands for Husbands Out Of Town Or Working Late. This group recognizes that it can be hard when your husband works late or is out of town, so they get together in the day, evening and/or weekends with their kids and offer camaraderie.

International MOMS Club

www.momsclub.org

The International MOMS Club is a support group designed just for the at-home mothers. If you are interested in the world around you, want a variety of activities for you and your children, and are proud of your choice of at-home mothering for your family, this club could be for you. Go to the website to find a local chapter. If there isn't one, they can help you start one.

MOMS Club of Antioch
www.MOMSClubAntiochCA.homestead.com

MOMS Club of Antioch and Oakley
www.antiochoakleymoms.org

Moms Club of Discovery Bay
discobaymoms@yahoo.com

MOMS Club of San Ramon, Danville Dublin
momsclubsanramon@yahoo.com

Iron Horse Mothers Club

www.ironhorsemothersclub.com

The IHMC is a support network for their members. Many moms join the mother's club in order to find a playgroup for their child(ren); however, the mother's club has much more to offer. They plan many different activities throughout the year for kids, moms and kids, and the whole family.

Just for Mom

LaMorinda Moms Club

www.lamorindamomsclub.org

The Lamorinda Moms Club is a social and support club for parents with children under five years of age in the greater Lamorinda, area including the cities of Lafayette, Moraga and Orinda.

Their organization strives to help members enrich their lives through cultivating new friendships, personal and professional growth, and community involvement. They have become one of the largest parenting organizations in the San Francisco Bay Area, with approximately 570 members. The club hosts dozens of activities and special events each month, and provides valuable resources to parents in the Lamorinda area.

Mocha Moms

www.mochamoms.org

Mocha Moms Online is a site for stay at home mothers of color. Mocha Moms is a support group for stay at home mothers of color who have chosen not to work full-time outside of the home in order to devote more time to their families. Visit their website to find a local chapter.

Meetup

Meetup.com

Come to a Moms Meetup to share experiences, find advice, give support and make new friends. From mom groups to play groups, you have access to various groups that fit your needs. Go to their website, type in your zip code and find a Meetup group near you with your similar interests.

www.sahm.meetup.com Stay at Home Mom groups
www.moms.meetup.com Mom groups
www.playgroup.meetup.com Playgroups
www.singleparents.meetup.com Single Parents

MOPS (Mothers of Preschoolers)

www.mops.org

MOPS recognizes that the years from infancy through kindergarten are foundational in a mother-child relationship and are filled with unique needs. MOPS helps moms through relationships established in the context of local churches that provide a caring atmosphere for today's mother of young children. Go to their website and find a group location near you.

Mothers and More

www.mothersandmoresv.homestead.com

Mothers & More is an international not-for-profit organization supporting sequencing women— mothers who have altered their career paths in order to care for their children at home. They meet regularly in parks for playgroups, have moms' night out, and publish a bi-monthly newsletter.

Mothers in Balance
Yvonne Lefort, M.A.

Moraga, CA 94556
www.mothersinbalance.com
yvonne@mothersinbalance.com
925-376-5885

Yvonne Lefort founded Mothers in Balance to meet the needs of today's working and stay-at-home moms. She offers career counseling and coaching to stay-at-home mothers wishing to re-enter the workforce as well as working mothers who want to change careers. Being a mother herself, she understands the needs and issues of mothers, and supports them in their search for a balanced lifestyle. Check out her website for a list of classes she offers.

Mount Diablo Mothers Club

www.mdmcmoms.org

The Mt. Diablo Mother's Club is a social and support group for expectant families and families with infants and young children. They openly welcome parents of all situations: working, at home, single and adoptive. The Mt Diablo Mothers Club is based out of Walnut Creek and serves Walnut Creek, Pleasant Hill, Martinez, Concord and Clayton.

Moxie Moms

www.moxie-moms.com/bayareaeast/indx.php

Moxie Moms is a network of moms for friends, fun and fitness. Moxie Moms facilitates outdoor and indoor social events throughout the week for moms to get together with their little ones. They also have fitness partners to help moms get back into shape or gain a greater fitness level. And, perhaps most importantly, they organize involvement with local charities and work with local retailers and service providers to provide discounts for Moxie Moms members.

Pleasant Hill/Walnut Creek Mothers Club

www.mom4mom.org

The Pleasant Hill/Walnut Creek Mother's Club is a network of parents and parents-to-be, encompassing all areas of the East Bay. They are dedicated to helping one another achieve their greatest parental abilities and to serving as a resource to those seeking interaction and education within their communities.

Additional Resources

Berkeley Parents Network

www.parents.berkeley.edu

This web site contains thousands of pages of recommendations and advice contributed by members of the Berkeley Parents Network, a parent-to-parent email network for the community of parents in the Berkeley, California area. Formerly called "UCB Parents", this network is run by a group of volunteer parents in their "spare" time. Many busy parents have taken the time to enlighten and inform with their suggestions, their wisdom, and their experience, archived here for all who wish to view it. They also send out 10–12 email newsletters each week to 19,824 local parents.

ComeUnity

www.comeunity.com

ComeUnity provides hundreds of definitive articles, resource directories, expert interviews and exclusive book reviews on parenting, adoption and children with special needs.

Contra Costa Parents of Multiples

www.ccpom.homestead.com

Contra Costa Parents of Multiples is a non-profit organization that provides support, information and the sharing of experiences on the birth, care and raising of twins, triplets and higher order multiples. They have monthly meetings as well as activities.

DoubleTalk

www.doubletalkfortwins.com

DoubleTalk is a resource for parents of twins. For more than 10 years Karen Pollack has been an educator at the Women's Health Center for John Muir Medical Center, facilitating the "Adjustments to Life; Tips From the Experts" component of the nationally acclaimed Marvelous Multiples®. She offers workshops for mothers and their twins for newborns through 6 months and 6 months through 12 months. She also offers consultation services for scheduling and sleeping.

La Leche League

www.lllnorcal.org

Fee: $40/year

La Leche League is a source of education, information, encouragement and support for mothers who want to breastfeed. Benefits include a one year subscription to New Beginnings magazine. Visit their website for local meetings in your area.

MOST for Moms (Mothers Outreach Support Team)

www.mostformoms.com

MOST strives for a world where new mothers feel nurtured and valued. They facilitate support and discussion groups for pregnant women and new moms, as well as provide birth and postpartum doula services.

Online Play Group

www.onlineplaygroup.com

Internet resource for finding, starting and managing playgroups, moms' clubs and other organizations for parents and caregivers.

Parents Resources and More

www.pram.net

Parents, Resources and More (PRAM) is an inclusive, community-driven, non-profit organization formed in 1999 to support families with young children (birth through age 5) in the greater Richmond area.

Support Group for Mothers

www.supportgroupformothers.com

If you are a new mom, or a mom with older children and you want to talk with other mothers just like you with a facilitator leading the discussion, this could be the group for you. Small groups are set up with weekly meetings or individual consultations are available as well.

Triplet Connection

www.tripletconnection.org

The Triplet Connenction is an international network of caring and sharing for multiple birth families. They have a fantastic packet of information which helps parents know exactly what they're up against, and specifically what they can do to enhance and promote the best possible outcomes for their pregnancies.

Twins by the Bay

www.twinsbythebay.org

Twins by the Bay is a non-profit support group for parents of multiples in Oakland, Berkeley and the surrounding area. Its mission is to educate, support and assist parents in the raising of multiple-birth children. Member benefits include a Preemie Closet, the use of loaner equipment and costumes, the New and Expectant Parent Support Group, newsletter, national and regional club membership, information sharing and much more.

Workout Facilities & Classes

Nothing is better than looking and feeling your best. To meet the demands of motherhood, exercise is essential to maintain a physical and emotional balance. Studies have shown that regular exercise reduces stress and can alleviate the symptoms of depression. There are so many facilities designed for women, so have fun choosing one!

ABsolute Center

3658 Mt. Diablo Blvd., Suite 101
Lafayette, CA 94549
www.absolutecenter.net

925-299-9642

Discover the source of intelligent fitness. Absolute Center 's approach to reconditioning is based on helping clients achieve their goals by integrating Resistance Training, Pilates and Yoga. The full-service studio offers a personal and professional environment, perfect for those seeking knowledge to better understand and implement their full potential.

Bally Total Fitness

800-515-2582

www.ballyfitness.com

Bally Total Fitness is the largest chain in North America and offers cutting edge classes as well as comprehensive core classes. Go to their website to find a club near you.

The Bar Method

1946A Mt. Diablo Blvd.
Walnut Creek, CA 94596
www.barmethod.com

925-933-1946

The Bar Method™ exercise system creates a uniquely lean, firm, sculpted body by reshaping and elongating muscles while maintaining an intense pace that burns fat and increases stamina.

Birkram Yoga

www.bikrameastbay.com

The Bikram Method of Hatha Yoga is a series of twenty-six poses and two breathing exercises designed to provide a total body workout. Check their webite for their locations in San Ramon, Orinda and Walnut Creek.

Club One

www.clubone.com

Club One offers state-of-the-art equipment, top-flight instructors, comprehensive programs, and personal amenities. They have clubs in Brentwood and Oakland.

Just for Mom

Club Sport

www.clubsports.com

Club Sport brings you the latest and most innovative ways to achieve total health and fitness. Locations in Pleasanton, Fremont, and two locations in Walnut Creek.

Fitness 19

www.fitness19.com

Fitness 19 is a family-friendly health club that has everything you need to get fit. Check their website for a location near you.

Mt Diablo Region YMCA

925-609-9622

www.mdrymca.org

Six locations in the Bay Area offer fitness programs and camps for adults and children.

Pilates

www.pilates.com

800-745-2837

Your one stop shop for selecting a Pilates studio.

24 Hour Fitness

www.24hourfitness.com

800-432-6348

Visit their website to find a club near you.

Touchstone Climbing

1220 Diamond Way, Suite 140
Concord, CA 94519
www.touchstoneclimbing.com

925-602-1000

Touchstone Climbing Inc. is dedicated to the creation and operation of superior quality indoor rock climbing and fitness facilities. It is their goal to create a friendly, supportive, fun and safe environment where participants of all ages and ability levels can participate in athletic and social activities.

Fitness Centers & Groups Designed Just for Women

Baby Boot Camp

www.babybootcamp.com

Baby Boot Camp stroller-based fitness classes are designed specifically to help moms get fit. Classes combine strength-training exercises with cardiovascular drills. Pilates, yoga and abdominal exercises help improve core strength. The stroller, resistance tubes (and even your child!) are used as an integral part of the workout.

Butterfly Life

www.butterflylife.com

The Butterfly Life experts have developed simple and effective programs to help women succeed at weight management and healthy living. Butterfly Life provides a nurturing and supportive environment where members can exercise using state-of-the-art fitness equipment designed specifically for women, as well as gain insight into nutrition, psychology, beauty and fashion.
Go to their website to find a club near you.

Curves, Contra Costa County

www.curves.com

Curves offers a 30-minute total body workout equivalent to a 90-minute workout using hydraulic engineering that is specifically designed for women. The program is flexible allowing the member to achieve their fitness goals within busy schedules. The program is efficient, effective, affordable and fun. The facility offers weight loss/nutritional counseling and offers women's nutritional products. Hours vary according to location. Please check the website for the Curves nearest you.

Jazzercise
800-348-4748

www.jazzercise.com

Find a local class and get jazzercising.

Ladies Workout Express
800-833-LADY

www.ladiesworkoutexpress.com

Ladies Workout Express is an interval circuit training program that provides a full strength and aerobic workout in just 30 minutes. Go to their website to find a club near you.

More energy in 30 minutes. Perfect for new moms.

JOIN NOW
ONE WEEK
FREE*

Our total body workout combines strength training and cardio to boost your metabolism and your energy level. With the total support of our trainers to help make sure you achieve maximum results, you'll have that baby weight off in no time.

YOUR CURVES WILL AMAZE YOU."

curves.com

Over 10,000 locations worldwide.

Antioch	Moraga
925-777-9787	925-376-0110
El Cerrito	Pittsburg
510-558-3485	925-427-4525
Emeryville	Walnut Creek South
510-601-6161	925-945-7484
Lafayette	Concord North
925-962-0206	925-603-7555

*Free week may be redeemed on first visit or exchanged for special membership discount. Not valid with any other offer. Valid only at participating locations. New members only. ©2008 Curves International

See Mommy Run

www.seeMOMMYrun.com

seeMOMMYrun.com is a non-profit organization dedicated to improving the health and well-being of mothers and children by providing easy access to family-friendly fitness groups. It is their mission to help moms in every community, no matter their social status, cultural background, or income level build lifelong social networks, maintain active lifestyles and be positive role models for their families and friends.

Tri Valley Adventure Boot Camp

www.trivalleybootcamp.com

info@TriValleyBootcamp.com

925-518-3434

Challenge your potential...It's your fitness, make it an adventure! Tri Valley Adventure Fitness Boot Camp is a 4-week outdoor fitness program that offers fitness instruction, nutritional counseling and motivational training-packed with fun and energizing activities designed to help you reach your fitness goals. Do you want to lose weight, tone your body, and feel great? Then Tri Valley Adventure Fitness Boot Camp is for you! We offer women-only and coed fitness camps along with other health & fitness programs to help you jump start your fitness. Log on to our website today for more information.

Mom's Night Out

Being a mother is very rewarding, and we all love being around our children, but lets face it, we all need some time alone or adult interaction. Take some time out for yourself to reenergize and regroup, so the daily tasks of motherhood don't become too overwhelming. One idea is to form a group of friends who meet regularly, on a monthly basis, just to get together to have fun and interact. Hire a babysitter or get Dad involved so that you can take a break and have some much deserved time to yourself. Here are some fun ideas to do with your friends:

- Go see a movie
- Host a monthly game night
- Have a dessert night
- Schedule a package deal at the spa
- Go to a dinner theater
- Go bowling
- Meet friends at the gym
- Have a craft/scrapbook night
- Host a party

Time for You!

How often do we find ourselves busy with the many tasks of raising a family, most of which are not easy, that we forget how important it is to take care of ourselves? Don't be afraid to take some time out for YOU. Have Dad take the kids for an afternoon or evening—it will be beneficial for him to spend some one-on-one time with them too. If some alone time is something you crave, take a break and try a few of these suggestions:

- Bubble bath; lots of bubbles, and soft music or candles
- Go to a bookstore or library and get comfy with a good book
- Take a walk
- Go to the gym
- Go see a movie
- Catch up on your favorite TV show
- Pamper yourself at the spa or salon
- Go shopping for yourself
- Take a nap
- Start a hobby like sewing or scrapbooking
- Take a road trip

Special Interests

Acc'sentials, LLC

520 Main Street
Pleasanton, CA 94588
ww.accsentials.com

925-931-9130

Acc'sentials—the one stop shop for contemporary men's apparel with accents and gifts for women. Creating a unique personal shopping experience; be it at our downtown Pleasanton location or your private home or office. Specializing in custom shirts, made-to-measure suits, footwear, denim, resort wear...also providing healthy skin care needs. Introducing Bennie's Backyard! Located in the Backyard of Acc'sentials, Bennie's Backyard is the ideal location for your next event!

Alameda Towne Centre

Corner of Park Street & Otis Drive
Alameda, CA 94501
www.AlamedaTowneCentre.com

510-521-1515

As Alameda's premiere shopping destination, Alameda Towne Centre (previously known as South Shore Center) is completing redevelopment to provide an experience like no other, including open air promenades with lush greenery and a central fountain area create a relaxing atmosphere to shop, eat or just a place to unwind. Designed as a neighborhood community center with over 60 stores including—Trader Joe's, TJ Maxx, Borders, Children's Place, Safeway, Old Navy, Color Me Mine, Massage Envy and more.

Knit This, Purl That!

205A Main Street
Pleasanton, CA 94566
www.yourknittingplace.com
yourknittingplace@sbcglobal.net

925-249-9276

Knit This, Purl That, is the only store of its kind between Walnut Creek and San Jose, offering not only a wide selection of yarn and accessories but classes, special events, and a relaxing environment where customers can work on projects and get advice from other knitters.

Laborfair.com

www.laborfair.com

Your FREE trusted solution for all your professional, household, personal and family care...get EVERYTHING and ANYTHING done for a fair price!

- FREE and direct access to thousands of quality local providers in 28 categories!
- Find Handymen, Housekeepers, Painters, Childcare, Private Lessons, and more!
- Find providers with specific skills such as CPR, Can Drive
- Trusted ratings, reviews and references
- Best of all, fair prices for everyone!

Learn what Bay Area Hip Mama's call a "necessity." Check us out today!

Savvy Seconds

560 Main Street
Pleasanton, CA 94566
www.savvyseconds.com
savvyseconds@sbcglobal.net

925-846-6600

A resale boutique on Main Street in Pleasanton's downtown shopping district, Savvy Seconds offers an assortment of new and used designer clothing for women. This upscale consignment boutique makes it fun to buy trendy designer fashions at great prices. If you are looking for Channel or Gucci shoes, cute bags from Michael Kors, or tops from INC, Banana or Bebe, you will find them all at Savvy Seconds for 50–60% off the original retail prices.

Now We're Cooking

148 East Prospect Avenue
Danville, CA 94583
Between Starbuck's and Father Nature's.
www.NowWereCooking.com

925-743-1212

Hours: Open Tuesday–Thursday 9 am–9 pm, Friday 9 am–6 pm, Saturday 9 am–3 pm. Additional times available upon request

Price: Average $16 for meals serving 2–3 people and $26 for meals serving 4–6 people

Now We're Cooking makes it easy to enjoy terrific dinners any night of the week. We take the challenge out of making dinner so you can spend time with your family. Assemble your meals, or we'll assemble, and leave with 6 or more ready-to-cook meals. Try our Fresh & Ready for Tonight meals, and have dinner on the table in 30 minutes. We also have gourmet cooking parties, wine tastings, and delivery services.

<u>To My Friend—Reflections on Motherhood: Wit and Wisdom on Raising Toddlers to Teenagers</u>

By Michele Sbrana

www.Michelesbrana.com

Written by Danville author Michele Sbrana, this book has been summed up by reader Abby Anderson as "A delightfully entertaining book! It's one of my greatest treasures since becoming a mother. Michele addresses the joys and obstacles of parenting in ways that warm my heart and makes me laugh out loud. This book is packed with wonderfully creative advice for every step of the way. Keep it out where you can see it—you'll want a daily dose!"

Tommy T's Comedy & Steakhouse

5104 Hopyard Road
Pleasanton, CA 94566
www.tommyts.com

925-227-1800

Hours: Open Nightly

Tommy T's has been synonymous with comedy for four decades, offering first-rate headline entertainment and good food. From special mom-favorite acts such as the Three Blonde Moms and Anjelah Johnson to a night out with such headliners as Craig "The Lovemaster" Shoemaker, Tommy T's is the place to catch great comedy seven nights a week. Enjoy tasty appetizers, salads, burgers, seafood, chicken and steak specialties. Perfect for a girls night, special event, school fundraiser or sports fundraiser.

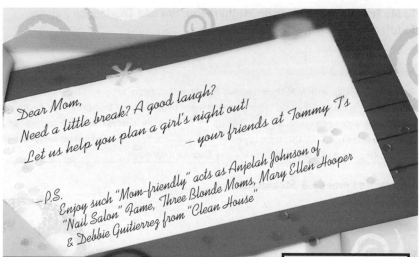

Childcare and Preschools

Childcare

There are many different styles of childcare available, from in home nannies to home daycares to center based care run by national companies. Caregiver ratios and services can very widely so visit many different daycare facilities to find what works for your family.

National Association for the Education of Young People

www.naeyc.org

Whether you're looking for a quality Child Care program, preschool, or school for your child, or you're interested in activities you can do at home to encourage your child's development, NAEYC can help.

General Resources

Contra Costa Childcare Council
Administrative Office and Central/South Area Resource and Referral Office

2280 Diamond Boulevard, Suite 500

Concord, CA 94520

www.cocokids.org

Central@cocokids.org

925-676-KIDS (5437)

925-830-0506 South Area

Hours: Monday–Thursday 9–4, Friday 9–12

Serving: Alamo, Concord, Danville, Lafayette, Martinez, Moraga, Orinda, Pacheco, Walnut Creek, San Ramon

West Area Resource and Referral Office

3065 Richmond Parkway, Suite 112
Richmond, CA 94806
West@cocokids.org

510-758-KIDY (5439)

Hours: Monday–Thursday 9–4, Friday 9–12

Serving: Crockett, El Cerrito, El Sobrante, Hercules, Kensington, Pinole, Richmond, Rodeo, San Pablo

East Area Resource and Referral Office

3104 Delta Fair Blvd..
Antioch, CA 94509
East@cocokids.org

925-778-KIDS (5437)

Hours: Monday–Thursday 9–4, Friday 9–12

Serving: Antioch, Bay Point, Pittsburg

Far East Area Resource and Referral Office

1181 Central Boulevard, Suite A
Brentwood, CA 94513
www.cocokids.org
Brentwood@cocokids.org

925-513-7900

Hours: Monday–Friday 8–12 & 1–4

Serving: Brentwood, Discovery Bay, Oakley

The Contra Costa Child Care Council helps parents find the best child care placement for their child and family. To make referrals, the Child Care Council maintains information on more than 1,800 licensed caregivers, including Licensed Family Child Care Homes and Child Care Centers. Trained Resource and Referral Counselors assist parents in need of child care by identifying child care programs near the parent's desired area, providing information on the different types of child care options, and equipping parents with information to make an informed child care selection. The Council assists parents with consultation on specific parenting concerns, maintains resource libraries for parents and develops parent support and leadership groups.

Community Care Licensing Division Child Care Office

Bay Area Regional Office

1515 Clay Street, Suite 1102
Oakland, CA 94612
510-622-2602

After interviewing different child care providers be sure to get their license number and call the Licensing Division's number above. They can tell you if any problems have been reported regarding this child care provider and/or if the licensing division has noted anything wrong from their visits.

Insider Pages.com

www.insiderpages.com

Insider Pages was created to help people find the best local businesses through recommendations from their friends and neighbors. At InsiderPages.com, people share reviews of local businesses and find great services they can trust. This is a good resource for all kinds of childcare and educational needs.

Laborfair.com

www.laborfair.com

Your FREE trusted solution for all your professional, household, personal and family care...get EVERYTHING and ANYTHING done for a fair price!

- FREE and direct access to thousands of quality local providers in 28 categories!
- Find Handymen, Housekeepers, Painters, Childcare, Private Lessons, and more!
- Find providers with specific skills such as CPR, Can Drive
- Trusted ratings, reviews and references
- Best of all, fair prices for everyone!

Learn what Bay Area Hip Mama's call a "necessity." Check us out today!

Town and Country Resources

www.tandcr.com

Town and Country is a comprehensive website for families searching for nannies as well as other domestic help.

Stanford Park Nannies

www.spnannies.com

Stanford Park Nannies is a full service Nanny agency serving the Bay Area.

Au Pair Care

www.aupaircare.com

Au Pair Care is a national site providing information and services for families seeking an Au Pair.

Childcare and Preschools

Antioch

Alice In Wonderland Day Care

1224 West 7th Street
Antioch, CA 94509
925-754-3712

Alice's Montessori

2032 Hillcrest Avenue
Antioch, CA 94509
925-754-6771

Bridgeway Preschool

3415 Oakley Road
Antioch, CA 94509
www.bridgewaychurch.org
925-779-4700

Child Day Schools

112 East Tregallas Road
Antioch, CA 94509
www.tcdschools.com
925-754-0144

Kids Clubs

800 Gary Avenue
Antioch, CA 94509
www.kidsclub-batc.com
925-706-1669

Kinder Care Learning Center

2300 Mahogany Way
Antioch, CA 94509
www.kindercare.com
925-778-8888

Kinder Care Learning Center

4308 Folsom Drive
Antioch, CA 94531
www.kindercare.com
925-754-3137

Kindercare
4108 Lone Tree Way
Antioch, CA 94531
925-754-1236

LA Petite Academy
1350 East Tregallas Road
Antioch, CA 94509
925-779-0110

Little Darling Angels Preschool
4504 Farallon Court
Antioch, CA 94509
925-779-0567

Nay's Play Place
1400 Sycamore Drive #4
Antioch, CA94509
925-755-4900

Starlight Academy
508 West Tregallas Road
Antioch, CA 94531
925-755-4543

Y Child Care At Kimball
1310 August Way
Antioch, CA94509
925-778-8652

YMCA
4550 Country Hills Drive
Antioch, CA 94531
925-778-1258

615 Greystone Drive
Antioch, CA 94509
925-778-9622

Childcare and Preschools

4600 Appaloosa Way
Antioch, CA 94531
925-778-1258

1711 Mission Drive
Antioch, CA 94509
925-756-1637

Ywca Of Ccc Mary Rocha
931 Cavallo Road
Antioch, CA 94509
925-778-6234

Bay Point

Little People's Childcare
2875 Clearland Circle
Bay Point, CA 94565
925-709-1772

Sunnybrook Learning Center
3255 Willow Pass Road
Bay Point, CA 94565
www.sunnybrooklearningcenter.com
925-709-6000

Brentwood

Aim High Child Care
200 Griffith Lane
Brentwood, CA 94513
www.aimhighchildcare.org
925-513-9326

Aim High Child Care Center Inc
2010 Shady Willow Lane
Brentwood, CA 94513
www.aimhigh.com
925-634-0998

Aim High Child Care Center Inc.
601 Grant Street
Brentwood, CA 94513
925-513-6429

250 1st Street
Brentwood, CA 94513
925-516-7257

1755 Central Blvd.
Brentwood, CA 94513
925-516-9006

190 Crawford Drive #37
Brentwood, CA 94513
925-516-1760

Apple Dumpling Day Care Center
780 Minnesota Avenue
Brentwood, CA 94513
925-516-6433

Bright Star Christian Preschool
2200 Ventura Drive
Brentwood, CA 94513
925-516-4001

Contra Costa County Child Care
8385 Brentwood Blvd.
Brentwood, CA 94513
925-513-7900

Little Handprints Preschool
1100 Fairview Avenue
Brentwood, CA 94513-2625
925-513-1757

Montessori School Of Brentwood
1191 Balfour Road
Brentwood, CA 94513
925-516-2111

Childcare and Preschools

Stay & Play Family Child Care
771 Griffith Lane
Brentwood, CA 94513
925-516-6940

Sunshine House
3700 Walnut Blvd.
Brentwood, CA 94513
925-516-9100

Sunshine House
401 Chestnut Street
Brentwood, CA 94513
925-634-5678

Wee Care Children's Center
1275 Fairview Avenue
Brentwood, CA 94513
925-634-5180

Clayton

Children's Center Clayton Valley
1578 Kirker Pass Road
Clayton, CA 94517
925-672-0882

Children's World Learning Center
6095 Main Street
Clayton, CA 94517
www.knowledgelearning.com
925-672-9370

Clayton Hills Child Care Center
80 El Portal Drive
Clayton, CA 94517
925-672-5217

Kindercare
6760 Marsh Creek Road
Clayton, CA 94517
925-672-0717

Concord

Angels Montessori Preschool

1566 Bailey Road
Concord, CA 94521
925-686-5621

Ayers Day Care Center

5120 Myrtle Drive
Concord, CA 94521
925-671-4922

Building Blocks Infant Preschool

1011 Oak Grove Road
Concord, CA 94518
925-671-2979

Calvary Chrisitan School

3425 Concord Blvd.
Concord, CA 94519
925-682-6728

Cambridge Community Center

1187 Meadow Lane
Concord, CA 94520
925-798-1078

Champions

2448 Floyd Lane
Concord, CA 94520
925-680-1344

Champions At Wren El

3339 Wren Avenue
Concord, CA 94519
www.knowledgelearning.com
925-363-5300

Child's Place & Play

4412 Sugar Maple Court
Concord, CA 94521
925-676-5870

Concord Child Care

1360 Detroit Avenue
Concord, CA 94520
www.concordchildcare.org

925-689-5151

Dianne Adair Day Care

1862 Bailey Road
Concord, CA 94521
www.dianneadair.org

925-429-1432

Early Beginnings

2009 Risdon Road
Concord, CA 94518

925-689-7388

El Monte Day Care Center

1400 Dina Drive
Concord, CA 94518

925-682-5060

Highlands Day Care Center

1326 Pennsylvania Blvd.
Concord, CA 94521

925-672-6144

Kid's Choice

5100 Clayton Road #36
Concord, CA 94521
www.kindercare.com

925-687-0983

Kinder Care Learning Center

1551 Bailey Road
Concord, CA 94521
www.kindercare.com

925-682-9560

Kinder Care Learning Center

2898 Concord Blvd.
Concord, CA 94519
925-827-9939

Kinder Care Learning Center

4347 Cowell Road
Concord, CA 94518
925-680-8707

Kinder Morgan

5625 Imhoff Drive
Concord, CA 94520
925-798-8587

Knowledge Beginnings

3201 Salvio Street
Concord, CA 94520
925-676-0161

LA Petite Academy

4304 Cowell Road
Concord, CA 94518
www.lapetiteacademy.com
925-676-4416

Lads' & Lassies' Latch-Key

1649 Claycord Avenue
Concord, CA 94521
925-687-4550

Monte Gardens Day Care Center

3841 Larkspur Drive
Concord, CA 94519
925-356-2343

Montessori School Of Concord

3039 Willow Pass Road
Concord, CA 94519
www.montessorischoolofconcord.com
925-682-8067

Mt Diablo Community Child

2750 Parkside Circle
Concord, CA 94519
www.mdccca.org

925-798-5021

Mt Diablo Community Child Care

3333 Ronald Way #A
Concord, CA 94519

925-685-7950

Nisha's Kids World Childcare

4101 Nulty Drive
Concord, CA 94521

925-435-5949

Pumpkin Patch Preschool & Chld

900 Mohr Lane
Concord, CA 94518

925-685-2227

Street Agnes School Extended Day Care

3886 Chestnut Avenue
Concord, CA 94519

925-689-0711

Street Francis

850 Oak Grove Road
Concord, CA 94518

925-685-7931

Sun Terrace Preschool

3585 Port Chicago Hwy
Concord, CA 945200

925-676-4373

Super Kidz Club

2140 Minert Road
Concord, CA 94518

925-682-0143

Westwood Day Care Center
1748 West Street
Concord, CA 94521
925-969-1784

Ygnacio Valley Christian
5353 Concord Blvd.
Concord, CA 94521
925-798-3151

YMCA
1705 Thornwood Drive
Concord, CA 94521
925-689-1170

YWCA Shadelands
1860 Silverwood Drive
Concord, CA 94519
925-825-9195

Danville

Acorn Learning Center
816 Diablo Road
Danville, CA 94526
925-837-1145

Autumn Creek Learning Center
14 Osborn Way
Danville, CA 94526
www.autumncreek-lc.com
925-743-4187

Bianchi Schools Preschool
909 Camino Ramon
Danville, CA 94526
www.knowledgelearning.com
925-838-8541

Childcare and Preschools

Children's Academy Of Danville

2425 Camino Tassajara
Danville, CA 94526
925-736-3336

Danville Montessori School

919 Camino Ramon
Danville, CA 94526
www.danmont.com
925-838-7434

Diablo Hills Country School

1453 San Ramon Valley Blvd.
Danville, CA 94526
925-820-8523

Growing Room

4675 Camino Tassajara
Danville, CA 94506
www.growingroom.com
925-648-9093

Kids Country

1531 Saint Helena Drive
Danville, CA 94526
www.kidscountry.org
925-831-8591

667 Diablo Road
Danville, CA 94526
925-837-0330

741 Brookside Drive
Danville, CA 94526
925-831-3530

2200 Holbrook Drive
Danville, CA 94506
925-736-3638

1001 Diablo Road
Danville, CA 94526
925-820-3646

120 Town And Country Drive #A
Danville, CA 94526
www.kidscountry.org
925-743-9108

300 Quinterra Lane
Danville, CA 94526
925-820-3101

Kinder Care Learning Center

730 San Ramon Valley Blvd.
Danville, CA 94526
www.kindercare.com
925-552-9825

Larson's Children Center

920 Diablo Road
Danville, CA 94526
www.larsonschildrencenter.com
925-837-4238

Starlight Montessori School

989 San Ramon Valley Blvd.
Danville, CA 94526
www.starlightschool.com
925-314-1706

Sycamore Valley Day School

1500 Sherburne Hills Road
Danville, CA 94526
925-736-2181

Childcare and Preschools

Discovery Bay

Y Child Care

1700 Willow Lake Road
Discovery Bay, CA 94505
www.mdrymca.org
925-634-5495

El Cerrito

Del Norte Childcare

6883 Cutting Blvd.
El Cerrito, CA 94530
510-970-7965

Hug A Bug Preschool

8637 Don Carol Drive
El Cerrito, CA 94530
510-559-9479

Keystone Montessori Preschool

6639 Blake Street
El Cerrito, CA 94530
www.keystonemontessori.org
510-236-7479

Tati's Family Daycare

2011 Junction Avenue
El Cerrito, CA 94530
510-215-0683

El Sobrante

Busy Bodies Learning Programs

3143 Keith Drive
El Sobrante, CA 94803
510-243-1942

Heidi's Little Angels

Appian Way
El Sobrante, CA 94803
510-222-3732

Childcare and Preschools

Hope Preschool

2830 May Road
El Sobrante, CA 94803
510-222-9222

Kid's Corner Preschool

716 Appian Way
El Sobrante, CA 94803
510-758-5532

Kinder Care Learning Center

3240 San Pablo Dam Road
El Sobrante, CA 94803
www.kindercare.com
510-222-1144

Sonja's Preschool & Childcare

3500 El Portal Drive
El Sobrante, CA 94803
510-222-9282

We Care Daycare

3301 Morningside Drive
El Sobrante, CA 94803
510-222-6202

Yani's Child Home Care

715 Renfrew Road
El Sobrante, CA 94803
510-669-0474

Hercules

Hansel & Gretel Family Daycare

124 Hemlock Court
Hercules, CA 94547
510-799-0830

Learning Star Preschool

343 Grenadine Way
Hercules, CA 94547
510-245-8100

Little Munchkins Daycare
P.O. Box 5810
Hercules, CA 94547
510-245-0678

Mother Goose Day Care
109 Quail Court
Hercules, CA 94547
510-245-2067

Nayna's 24 7 Childcare
166 Bobolink Way
Hercules, CA 94547
510-799-4777

Sweet Blessing Child Care
1883 Redwood Road
Hercules, CA 94547
510-245-7216

Lafayette

Center-Arts Technology & Science
961 1st Street
Lafayette, CA 94549
925-283-4500

Child Day Schools
1049 Stuart Street
Lafayette, CA 94549
www.tcdschools.com
925-284-7092

First Steps Learning Center
3201 Stanley Blvd.
Lafayette, CA 94549
925-933-6283

Husky House Child Care
3855 Happy Valley Road
Lafayette, CA 94549
925-283-7100

Kids Hideout

3301 Springhill Road
Lafayette, CA 94549
925-283-7808

Old Firehouse School

984 Moraga Road
Lafayette, CA 94549
www.oldfirehouseschool.com

925-284-4321

Martinez

Bianchi Schools Preschool

1285 Morello Avenue
Martinez, CA 94553-4710
www.knowledgelearning.com

925-372-7701

Cherub Child Care

853 Center Avenue
Martinez, CA 94553
925-228-5800

Childtime Learning Center

6635 Alhambra Avenue # 300
Martinez, CA 94553
www.childtime.com
925-947-6800

Forest Hills Preschool

5834 Alhambra Avenue
Martinez, CA 94553
www.foresthillsschool.com
925-370-1601

Helping Hands Christian Preschool

1865 Arnold Drive
Martinez, CA 94553
925-229-2975

Rising Stars Learning Center

127 Midhill Road
Martinez, CA 94553
925-228-0116

Sunshine House

4950 Pacheco Blvd.
Martinez, CA 94553
925-372-8242

They Grow So Fast Children Center

5309 Degnan Drive
Martinez, CA 94553
925-957-0807

Woodbridge

4955 Alhambra Valley Road
Martinez, CA 94553
925-228-7540

Woodbridge Children's Center

205 Vista Way
Martinez, CA 94553
925-229-5767

Woodbridge Children's Center

1200 Morello Park Drive
Martinez, CA 94553
925-228-4166

Woodbridge Children's Center

4105 Pacheco Blvd.
Martinez, CA 94553
925-228-0672

YWCA

www.ywca.org
1320 Arnold Drive #170
Martinez, CA 94553
925-372-4213

Moraga

Child Day Schools

372 Park Street
Moraga, CA 94556
www.tcdschools.com
925-376-5110

Oakley

A Child's Place

3405 West Main Street
Oakley, CA 94561
925-625-9795

Delta Kids Center

61 Delta Road
Oakley, CA 94561
925-625-6127

Childcare and Preschools

Flo's Childcare & Preschool
4307 Bordeaux Drive
Oakley, CA 94561
925-625-1140

Joyland Preschool & Daycare
132 Ohara Avenue
Oakley, CA 94561
925-625-3921

Sunshine House
875 West Cypress Road
Oakley, CA 94561
925-625-5600

YMCA
1000 Vintage Pkwy.
Oakley, CA 94561
www.ymca.org
925-679-0422

1141 Laurel Road
Oakley, CA 94561-5906
925-625-8490

Orinda

Street John Preschool Daycare Center
501 Moraga Way
Orinda, CA 94563
925-254-4470

Pinole

Deuel's Day Care & Preschool
2499 Simas Avenue
Pinole, CA 94564
510-758-1355

Fresh Start Child Care
1044 Marlesta Road
Pinole, CA 94564
510-724-9795

Mama Bear's Playcare
2594 Emma Drive
Pinole, CA 94564
510-741-8336

Missette's Day Care
1839 Sarah Drive
Pinole, CA 94564
510-222-4130

Montessori Children's House
2281 Johanna Court
Pinole, CA 94564
510-758-1301

Pittsburg
First Baptist Head Start
2240 Gladstone Drive
Pittsburg, CA 94565
www.firstbaptistheadstart.org
925-473-2000

Kids First Daycare & Learning
497 Windwood Drive
Pittsburg, CA 94565
925-709-5437

Kinder Care Learning Center
150 East Leland Road
Pittsburg, CA 94565
www.kindercare.com
925-432-8800

Childcare and Preschools

Railroad Junction School
2224 Railroad Avenue
Pittsburg, CA 94565
925-427-2000

There's No Place Like Home
1 Way
Pittsburg, CA 94565
925-427-2889

Words-Life Christian Day Care
543 Silver Saddle Drive
Pittsburg, CA 94565
925-432-4788

Pleasant Hill

Discoveryland Preschool
800 Grayson Road
Pleasant Hill, CA 94523
925-935-3520

Kidstop
1 Corritone Court
Pleasant Hill, CA 94523
www.pleasanthillrec.com
925-680-5298

Play & Learn School
1898 Pleasant Hill Road
Pleasant Hill, CA 94523
925-947-2820

Pleasant Hill Day Care Center
2097 Oak Park Blvd.
Pleasant Hill, CA 94523
www.dianneadair.org
925-938-3043

Sequoia Day Care Center

277 Boyd Road
Pleasant Hill, CA 94523
925-939-6336

Small World Infant & Toddler

1641 Oak Park Blvd.
Pleasant Hill, CA 94523
925-944-3528

Stepping Stones Learning Center

2750 Pleasant Hill Road
Pleasant Hill, CA 94523
925-933-6520

Sunrise Children's Center

1715 Oak Park Blvd.
Pleasant Hill, CA 94523
925-946-0111

YMCA

395 Civic Drive
Pleasant Hill, CA 94523
www.mdrymca.org
925-609-9639

530 Kiki Drive
Pleasant Hill, CA 94523
925-827-4743

Richmond

A World Of Learning Montessori

1472 San Joaquin Street
Richmond, CA 94804
510-233-5574

AFU Day Care

2105 Macdonald Avenue
Richmond, CA 94801
510-435-2802

B B Day Care
4330 Roosevelt Avenue
Richmond, CA 94805
510-541-9239

Brenda's Kidz Kare
227 17th Street
Richmond, CA 94801
510-234-2528

Early Years Learning Center
600 S 16th Street
Richmond, CA 94804
510-758-3952

Eden's Garden Child Care
2210 Lincoln Avenue
Richmond, CA 94801
510-965-0798

Felts Family Day Care
2914 Gilma Drive
Richmond, CA 94806
510-223-7801

LA Petite Academy
3891 Lakeside Drive
Richmond, CA 94806
510-222-3070

LA Petite Academy
1221 Nevin Avenue
Richmond, CA 94801
510-970-7100

Lawson Babysitters
311 Marina Way South
Richmond, CA 94801
510-235-7879

Lil' Angels Learning Center
2842 Moyers Road
Richmond, CA 94806
510-262-0737

Little Cherubs Christian Care
2906 Obrien Road
Richmond, CA 94806
510-758-8715

Magic Years Children's Center
1221 Nevin Avenue
Richmond, CA 94801
510-215-7369

N Y Learning Center
4908 Kirk Lane
Richmond, CA 94805
510-236-2146

Odyssey School
1800 Barrett Avenue
Richmond, CA 94801
510-235-4825

Robinson Daycare
4229 Florida Avenue
Richmond, CA 94804
510-965-0001

YMCA
485 Lucas Avenue
Richmond, CA 94801
510-412-5639

Rodeo

Valley Preschool & Daycare
1477 Willow Avenue
Rodeo, CA 94572
www.valleybible.org
510-245-2273

Childcare and Preschools

YMCA
200 Lake Avenue
Rodeo, CA 94572
510-412-5644

San Pablo

Sonja's Preschool & Childcare
1420 Amador Street
San Pablo, CA 94806
510-232-9282

Tasha's Childcare
1300 Rumrill Blvd.
San Pablo, CA 94806
510-215-7207

Triple P's Come Learn With Me
2816 Gonzaga Avenue
San Pablo, CA 94806
510-758-8777

San Ramon

Acorn Learning Center
5075 Crow Canyon Road
San Ramon, CA 94582
925-735-7900

Acorn Learning Center
17025 Bollinger Canyon Road
San Ramon, CA 94582
925-560-6488

Afsania's Day Care
12220 Toluca Drive
San Ramon, CA 94583
925-556-5448

Bears Cuddliest Day Care

33 Andover Place
San Ramon, CA 94583
925-833-8157

Evie's House

10092 Nantucket Drive
San Ramon, CA 94582
925-634-0997

Growing Room Golden View Site

5025 Canyon Crest Drive
San Ramon, CA 94582
www.thegrowingroom.org
925-735-0730

Growing Room Neil Armstrong

2849 Calais Drive
San Ramon, CA 94583
925-833-9166

Growing Room Twin Creeks Site

2785 Marsh Drive
San Ramon, CA 94583
www.thegrowingroom.org
925-820-5808

Joyful Noise Preschool Center

19901 San Ramon Valley Blvd.
San Ramon, CA 94583
925-828-5596

Kids Country

2300 Talavera Drive
San Ramon, CA 94583
925-275-0574

Kids Country

7534 Blue Fox Way
San Ramon, CA 94583
925-829-4630

Childcare and Preschools

Kids Country

3250 Pine Valley Road
San Ramon, CA 94583
925-552-4489

Kids Country

8700 Northgale Ridge Road
San Ramon, CA 94582
925-735-4468

Kid's Country Montevideo Site

13000 Broadmoor Drive
San Ramon, CA 94583
925-828-6717

LA Petite Academy

1001 Market Place
San Ramon, CA 94583
925-277-0626

Little Angels School

157 Shadowhill Circle
San Ramon, CA 94583
925-837-2859

Teddy Bears Children's Center

210 Porter Drive #110
San Ramon, CA 94583
925-838-4148

Tristar Chinese School

2001 Omega Road
San Ramon, CA 94583
www.archnet.com
925-314-0476

Walnut Creek

Bancroft Day Care Center

2200 Parish Drive
Walnut Creek, CA 94598
www.dianneadair.org

925-938-4063

Buena Vista Club

2372 Buena Vista Avenue
Walnut Creek, CA 94597

925-930-0272

David & Pari's Family Day Care

2893 Grande Camino
Walnut Creek, CA 94598

925-930-7319

Family Care

2496 Warren Road
Walnut Creek, CA 94595

925-930-6564

Kid Time Inc

1547 Geary Road
Walnut Creek, CA 94597

925-930-6550

Kids Only Club

551 Marshall Drive
Walnut Creek, CA 94598

925-943-7957

Kinder Care Learning Center

2875 Mitchell Drive
Walnut Creek, CA 94598
www.knowledgelearning.com

925-935-5562

Childcare and Preschools

Kindercare

2850 Cherry Lane
Walnut Creek, CA 94597
925-943-6777

Love & Care Learning Center

1985 Geary Road
Walnut Creek, CA 94597
925-944-2880

Murwood KEY Spot Inc

2050 Vanderslice Avenue
Walnut Creek, CA 94596
www.murwoodkeyspot.com
925-932-8118

Parkmead Keyspot

1920 Magnolia Way
Walnut Creek, CA 94595
925-939-1543

Saybrook Learning Center

1355 Walden Road
Walnut Creek, CA 94597
925-937-8211

Step Ahead Learning Center

1338 Las Juntas Way
Walnut Creek, CA 94597
www.stepaheadlearning.com
925-943-6199

Sunny Town Family Daycare

3133 Manor Avenue
Walnut Creek, CA 94597
925-947-1215

Sunrise Childcare

570 Walnut Avenue
Walnut Creek, CA 94598-3731
925-939-9920

Susie Fox Family Day Care Home

134 Hall Lane
Walnut Creek, CA 94597
925-934-0967

Trinity Lutheran Preschool

2317 Buena Vista Avenue
Walnut Creek, CA 94597
925-935-3360

Valle Verde Children's Center

3275 Peachwillow Lane
Walnut Creek, CA 94598
www.vvchildrenscenter.org

925-944-5255

Walnut Creek Kinder World Center

1029 Homestead Avenue
Walnut Creek, CA 94598
925-935-8560

Walnut Heights Club

4064 Walnut Blvd.
Walnut Creek, CA 4596
925-930-8458

Wee Care

2210 Oak Grove Road
Walnut Creek, CA 94598
925-210-1091

Preschool

Choosing a preschool can be difficult even for the experienced parent. Other parents are often the best source of information. Some community centers, places of worship, YMCA's and Jewish Community Centers offer preschool.

Preschool California

www.preschoolcalifornia.org

This is a preschool advocacy site with information on statewide preschool initiatives.

General Resources

Fountainhead Montessori School
Danville Campus

939 El Pintado Road
www.fountainheadmontessori.org

925-820-6250

925-820-1343 Administrative Office

Fountainhead Montessori is dedicated to the education of children in an environment designed to stimulate and develop the child's love of learning. The Montessori philosophy leads to the development of a child's strong sense of self-esteem, dignity, independence, self-direction, and awareness of the community. Social and emotional development is fostered in a nurturing atmosphere. Class schedules can be customized to fit individual needs. Ratios run anywhere from 1:5 to 1:12 depending on the program. No toilet training, work commitments, or fund raising required. No hidden fees. Fountainhead has been serving children since 1972 and offers flexible programs for children ages 18 months through Kindergarten depending on location.

Dublin Campus

6665 Amador Plaza Road
925-829-2963

Livermore Campus

949 Central Avenue
925-579-0110

Orinda Campus

30 Santa Maria Way
925-254-7110

Pleasant Hill Campus

490 Golf Club Road
925-685-2949

Growing Light Montessori Schools

1450 Moraga Road
Moraga, CA 94556
www.growinglight.net

925-377-0407

Growing Light Montessori celebrates the individual in your child. Age-appropriate curriculum is designed to foster independent work skills and engage the child's interests to develop intellectual curiosity and a genuine love for learning. Students are encouraged to express themselves confidently and explore new concepts and ideas in a nurturing environment. Reflecting diverse cultures and backgrounds, Growing Light Montessori teachers are specifically trained in the Montessori Method of Education. Morning, Mid-Day and Full Time Programs available year-round. Healthy, organic snacks provided. Elective enrichment programs also available.

4700 Lincoln Avenue
Oakland, CA 94602
510-336-9897

52 Arlington Avenue
Kensington, CA 94707
510-527-1278

Rising Stars Montessori Learning Center

127 Midhill Road
Martinez, CA 94553
925-228-0116

High quality childcare with a Montessori curriculum creates a fun and enriching learning environment. Our philosophy, and teachers promote confidence, responsibility, respect, independence and a love of learning. In addition to mathematics, phonetic reading and writing, the curriculum includes music, art, science and cultural geography. Children explore the sciences with hands-on experiences designed to inspire curiosity and wonder.

Saybrook Learning Center

1335 Walden Road, at Civic Drive
Walnut Creek, CA 94597
925-937-8211
Ages: 2 through 6
Hours: 6:45 am to 6:15 pm

Our year round curriculum includes: math concepts, reading readiness, arts, crafts, music, language development, gymnastics and large/safe playgrounds. We offer breakfast, hot lunch and snacks. We also offer potty training.

Super Kidz Club

2140 Minert Road
Concord, CA 94518
925-682-0143

Hours: Open Monday–Friday 6:30 am to 6 pm, Flexible days and affordable rates.

"A family's home away from home." We are a licensed childcare center providing a nurturing environment for your infant, preschooler or kindergartener, with potty training assistance if needed. We also offer before and after schoolcare with transportation to and from school, emphasizing homework assistance, social skills and art project creation. During vacation break, we involve the children in field trips to various locations, including the pool, movies, miniature golf and local parks.

Walnut Avenue Christian Community Preschool

260 Walnut Avenue
Walnut Creek, CA 94598
www.waccp.com
925-937-7063

Hours: Monday–Friday 9 am–3 pm

We offer part time preschool programs for children 15 months to 6 years of age. Our program is highly individualized, offering a wide range of materials and utilization of ideas and experiences from several schools of educational thought. There are learning stations for a broad range of science, music, art, creative drama, pre-math and pre-reading on sequential levels. Our teaching staff is well educated and experienced. The school was established in 1976.

Alamo

Alamo Country School

1261 Laverock Lane
Alamo, CA 94507
www.alamocountryschool.com

925-939-0779

Creative Learning Center

120 Hemme Avenue
Alamo, CA 94507
www.clcalamo.com

925-837-4044

Evergreen Montessori Day Care

10 Christopher Lane
Alamo, CA 94507
925-934-6331

Merriewood Children's Center

2964 Miranda Avenue
Alamo, CA 94507
www.meadowlarkchildrenscenter.com

925-837-8792

Methodist Preschool

902 Danville Blvd.
Alamo, CA 94507
925-837-2788

Antioch

Busy Kids Christian Child Care

620 East Tregallas Road
Antioch, CA 94509
925-777-9055

Covenant Christian Preschool

1919 Buchanan Road
Antioch, CA 94509
925-757-5016

Hilltop Christian Preschool
2200 Country Hills Drive
Antioch, CA 94509
925-779-9297

Little Angels Preschool
3905 Rocky Point Drive
Antioch, CA 94509
925-754-7885

Little Lu Lu's Christian
2725 Minta Lane
Antioch, CA 94509
925-754-7771

Sonshine Home Christian Preschool
1324 Putnam Street
Antioch, CA 94509
925-706-2403

Brentwood

Andi's Little Angels
349 Sherwood Drive
Brentwood, CA 94513
www.andislittleangels.com
925-634-5389

Apple Dumpling
833 2nd Street
Brentwood, CA 94513
925-513-1177

Celebration Christian School
624 Anderson Avenue
Brentwood, CA 94513
www.celebrationschools.com
925-240-5437

Childcare and Preschools

Dainty Center
1265 Dainty Avenue
Brentwood, CA 94513
925-634-4539

Loma Vista Kid Zone
2110 San Jose Avenue
Brentwood, CA 94513
925-513-1113

Montessori School & Edu Fndtn
1191 Balfour Road
Brentwood, CA 94513
925-240-1191

Clayton

Wee Three Bears Play Center
411 Wright Court
Clayton, CA 94517
925-672-5214

Concord

A White Dove School
1850 2nd Street
Concord, CA 94519
925-689-5067

Bright Stars Learning Center
3036 Clayton Road
Concord, CA 94519
925-363-4933

First Lutheran Preschool
4006 Concord Blvd.
Concord, CA 94519
www.firstlutheranconcord.org
925-798-5330

First Presbyterian Preschool
1965 Colfax Street
Concord, CA 94520
925-676-6244

Myrtle Farm Montessori School
4976 Myrtle Drive
Concord, CA 94521
925-356-2482

Street Michael's Episcopal Day
2925 Bonifacio Street
Concord, CA 94519
925-685-8862

Walnut Country Preschool
4498 Lawson Court
Concord, CA 94521
925-798-9686

World Of Adventure Preschool
3764 Clayton Road
Concord, CA 94521
925-798-7364

Danville

Community Presbyterian Preschool
222 West El Pintado
Danville, CA 94526
www.cpcdanville.org
925-837-3316

Garden Montessori School
495 Verona Avenue
Danville, CA 94526
www.gardenschool.net
925-837-2969

Childcare and Preschools

Noah's Ark Preschool
1550 Diablo Road
Danville, CA 94526
925-362-8565

Rainbow Montessori School
101 Sonora Avenue
Danville, CA 94526
925-831-6199

SAB Ramone Valley Christian
222 West El Pintado
Danville, CA 94526
www.srvca.org
925-838-9622

Stratford School
3201 Camino Tassajara
Danville, CA 94506
925-648-4900

Discovery Bay
All God's Children Christian
1900 Willow Lake Road
Discovery Bay, CA 94505
925-513-8006

El Cerrito
Children's Garden Montessori
2335 Tulare Avenue
El Cerrito, CA 94530
510-232-3089

El Cerrito Preschool Co-Op
7200 Moeser Lane
El Cerrito, CA 94530
www.ecpckids.com
510-526-1916

Montessori Learning Center

7200 Schmidt Lane
El Cerrito, CA 94530
510-525-4500

Ocean View Montessori Day Care

717 Clayton Avenue
El Cerrito, CA 94530
510-527-3294

Piccoli Preschool

1532 Richmond Street
El Cerrito, CA 94530
510-234-3230

Pride & Joy Preschool

1342 Lawrence Street
El Cerrito, CA 94530
510-232-3121

Rising Sun Motessori School

10 Ramona Avenue
El Cerrito, CA 94530
510-528-6041

Sycamore Christian Preschool

1111 Navellier Street
El Cerrito, CA 94530
www.sycamore-preschool.org

510-527-9522

El Sobrante

Patty's Montessori School

801 Park Central Street
El Sobrante, CA 94803
510-223-4520

Childcare and Preschools

Small World Montessori School
4555 Hilltop Drive
El Sobrante, CA 94803
www.smallworldmontessori-school.com
510-222-6059

Hercules

Pillow Preschool
1702 Pheasant Drive
Hercules, CA 94547
510-799-5426

Lafayette

Happy Days Learning Center
3205 Stanley Blvd.
Lafayette, CA 94549
925-932-8088

Joyful Beginnings Preschool
955 Moraga Road
Lafayette, CA 94549
925-284-1143

Merriewood Children's Center
561 Merriewood Drive
Lafayette, CA 94549
www.merriewood.org
925-284-2121

Michael Lane Preschool
682 Michael Lane
Lafayette, CA 94549
925-284-7244

Seedlings Preschool
49 Knox Drive
Lafayette, CA 94549
www.lopc.org
925-284-3870

Martinez

Creekside Montessori
1333 Estudillo Street
Martinez, CA 94553
www.creeksidemontessori.com
925-228-5718

Lasting Impressions
244 Morello Avenue
Martinez, CA 94553
925-228-8715

Martinez Early Childhood Center
615 Arch Street
Martinez, CA 94553
925-229-2000

Morello Hills Christian Preschool
1000 Morello Hills Drive
Martinez, CA 94553
www.morellohills.org
925-372-7155

Moraga

Creative Playhouse Inc
1350 Moraga Way
Moraga, CA 94556
925-377-8314

Growing Light Montessori
1450 Moraga Road
Moraga, CA 94556
925-377-0407

Growing Tree Preschool
1695 Canyon Road
Moraga, CA 94556
925-376-8280

Childcare and Preschools

Moraga Bright Beginnings
1689 School Street
Moraga, CA 94556
925-376-2600

Mulberry Tree Preschool
1455 Saint Marys Road
Moraga, CA 94556
925-376-1751

Saklan Valley School
1678 School Street
Moraga, CA 94556
www.saklan.org
925-376-7900

Oakley

Just Kiddin Around
309 Stratford Place
Oakley, CA 94561
925-625-2409

Little Sandbox Daycare
4169 Cherry Court
Oakley, CA 94561
www.littlesandboxdaycare.com
925-625-2658

My Turn Learning Center
5300 Main Street
Oakley, CA 94561
925-625-1804

Sweet Beginnings Preschool
1433 West Cypress Road
Oakley, CA 94561-1980
925-679-9642

YWCA Freedom Childcare Center
1050 Neroly Road
Oakley, CA 94561
925-625-5181

Orinda

Holy Shepherd Christian Preschool
433 Moraga Way
Orinda, CA 94563
www.holyshepherd.org

925-254-3429

Orinda Preschool
10 Irwin Way
Orinda, CA 94563
www.topsonline.org

925-254-2551

Street Marks Nursery School
451 Moraga Way
Orinda, CA 94563
925-254-1364

Pinole

Happy Lion School & Day Care
2612 Appian Way
Pinole, CA 94564
510-222-2416

LA Casita Bilingual Preschool
592 Tennent Avenue
Pinole, CA 94564
www.la-casita.org

510-724-1724

Nicki's Quality Day Care
2411 Kyer Street
Pinole, CA 94564
510-758-4092

Childcare and Preschools

Pittsburg

Little Promises Preschool

1210 Stoneman Avenue
Pittsburg, CA 94565
www.ccenterschool.org

925-432-3800

Street Peter Martyr Extended Care

455 West 4th Street
Pittsburg, CA 94565
925-432-3586

Pleasant Hill

Kidz Planet Inc

2245 Morello Avenue
Pleasant Hill, CA 94523
www.kidz-planet.org

925-825-3012

Mary Jane's Preschool

2902 Vessing Road
Pleasant Hill, CA 94523
925-935-3084

Peter Pan Preschool

399 Gregory Lane
Pleasant Hill, CA 94523
www.peterpanpreschool.org

925-685-2275

Pioneer Montessori School

2702 Pleasant Hill Road
Pleasant Hill, CA 94523
925-947-2340

Street Mark's Christian Preschool

3051 Putnam Blvd.
Pleasant Hill, CA 94523
925-934-6114

Richmond

El Nuevo Mundo-National

1707 Pennsylvania Avenue
Richmond, CA 94801
510-233-2329

Happy Brown Bears Preschool

2225 Gaynor Avenue
Richmond, CA 94801
510-236-9101

Jean's Small World Nursery

3411 Center Avenue
Richmond, CA 94804
510-233-7575

Marie Omonike Learning Envrnmt

324 37th Street
Richmond, CA 94805
510-232-6129

Noah's Ark Preschool

555 37th Street
Richmond, CA 94805
510-235-8989

Nystrom College Prep Preschool

217 South 11th Street
Richmond, CA 94802
510-620-9961

Pacific Academy

1615 Carlson Blvd.
Richmond, CA 94804
www.pacificacademy.com
510-528-1727

Pacific Academy Preschool

1711 Carlson Blvd.
Richmond, CA 94804
510-526-7847

Childcare and Preschools

Richmond Children's Academy

2900 Cutting Blvd.
Richmond, CA 94804
510-232-2236

San Ramon

Growing Room

10701 Albion Road
San Ramon, CA 94582
www.thegrowingroom.org
925-556-0383

Happy Days Preschool Learning

20801 San Ramon Valley Blvd.
San Ramon, CA 94583
925-828-8007

Montessori School Of San Ramon

2400 Old Crow Canyon Road #A3
San Ramon, CA 94583
925-855-7434

Stepping Stones Learning Center

2691 Crow Canyon Road
San Ramon, CA 94583
www.kidswonder.com
925-820-8820

Walnut Creek

Alice's Montessori Learning

3158 Putnam Blvd.
Walnut Creek, CA 94597
925-947-0603

Creative Play Center

2323 Pleasant Hill Road
Walnut Creek, CA 94596
925-932-3173

Garden Gate Montessori School
63 Sandy Lane
Walnut Creek, CA 94597
www.gardengatemontessori.com
925-943-7484

Grace Cooperative Preschool
2100 Tice Valley Blvd.
Walnut Creek, CA 94595
925-935-2100

Jewish Community Center
2071 Tice Valley Blvd.
Walnut Creek, CA 94595
www.ccjcc.org
925-938-7800

Lafayette Nursery School
979 1st Street
Walnut Creek, CA 94596
www.lafayettenurseryschool.com
925-284-2448

Morning Star Preschool Inc
2131 Olympic Blvd.
Walnut Creek, CA 94595
925-947-2952

My School
535 Walnut Avenue
Walnut Creek, CA 94598
925-947-1399

Old Firehouse School Walnut Creek
55 Eckley Lane
Walnut Creek, CA 94596
925-934-1507

Pied Piper Preschool
2263 Whyte Park Avenue
Walnut Creek, CA 94595
www.piedpiperpreschool.com
925-932-3816

Childcare and Preschools

Sunflower Creative Learning

637 Dapplegray Court
Walnut Creek, CA 94596
925-939-9929

Valley Parent Preschool

935 Camino Ramon
Walnut Creek, CA 94596
925-837-5401

Walnut Avenue Church Community

260 Walnut Avenue
Walnut Creek, CA 94598
www.waccp.com
925-937-7063

Walnut Creek Presbyterian School

1801 Lacassie Avenue
Walnut Creek, CA 94596
www.wcpres.org
925-935-1669

Chapter 14

Schools and Educational Resources

Parents are their children's first and most important teachers and advocates, but all adults have a stake in raising a generation of well-educated children. Environmental, social and economic factors have a powerful effect on student performance. Read on for valuable information for your child's education.

Some Helpful Tips

Parents' willingness to contact teachers on a regular basis about their child's progress is perhaps the first step to becoming involved in their child's education. Armed with good information about a child's performance, parents can proceed in both direct and indirect ways to influence the child's progress. Mothers and fathers can become directly involved in a child's education by:

- Overseeing the child's homework time;

- Setting a time each day for homework to be done, and checking the child's work for completeness and understanding;

- Limiting time spent with friends and watching television;

- Providing support for educators, essential leadership for programs, and ideas for improvements in the education system.

- Taking advantage of opportunities to become involved with school administration and policy development—for example, attend school board meetings and join the PTA.

General Resources

California Department of Education

www.cde.ca.gov

They have information about Specialized Programs such as Charter and Private Schools, Curriculum and Instruction, Testing and Accountability, Data and Statistics and Learning Support.

California State PTA

2327 L Street
Sacramento, CA 95816-5014
www.capta.org
916-440-1985

California School Board Association

www.csba.org

You can find out who your board member is through this website. They also have meetings, trainings and events that support the school boards governance.

Contra Costa County Office of Education

77 Santa Barbara Road
Pleasant Hill, CA 94523
www.cccoe.k12.ca.us
925-942-3388

The County Office website provides information on educational related services for youths and their families throughout the county. Programs they provide include information about the State Superintendent of Schools, Educational Services, Business Services, and Student Programs and Services, such as special education and youth development.

National Association for the Education of Young Children

www.naeyc.org

Whether you're looking for a quality child care program, preschool, or school for your child, or you're interested in activities you can do at home to encourage your child's development, NAEYC has a great database of accredited schools and programs. Go to the parents and families link on their website to begin your search.

Charter Public Schools

Charter Schools are independent public schools designed and operated by educators, parents, community leaders, educational entrepreneurs and others. They are sponsored by designated local or state educational organizations that monitor their quality and effectiveness, but allow them to operate outside of the traditional system of public schools.

California Charter Schools—California Department of Education

www.cde.ca.gov/ds/si/cs/index.asp

The goal of charter schools is to provide additional educational options with quality outcomes for students and parents. Charter schools are public schools open to all students. They operate on public funds without tuition. We have not included all of the charter schools in each area, but just a few that are accredited, a candidate for accreditation or have different educational opportunities available.

Antioch

Antioch Charter Academy/Learner-Centered School

3325 Hacienda Way
Antioch, CA 94509
www.antiochcharteracademy.org

925-755-7311

They offer the basic educational necessities of K–8th grades. Their specialty is building upon the understanding of multiple intelligences and brain compatibility.

Berkeley

Walden Center & School

2446 McKinley Avenue
Berkeley, CA 94710
www.walden-school.net

510-841-7248

Walden is an Arts-based teacher-run elementary school. Our curriculum combines developmentally appropriate expectations with challenging units of study. The school's environment enhances each child's academic, emotional, social, creative and physical growth.

The Walden staff supports experiential learning, cooperative endeavor, creativity and appreciation of personal expression within a broader community. Children and adults at Walden value the racial, social, ethnic and economic diversity of the East Bay within the School's nonsectarian and multicultural learning environment.

Schools and Educational Resources

Walnut Creek

Eagle Peak Montessori School

800 Hutchinson Road
Walnut Creek, CA 94598
www.eaglepeakmontessori.org

925-946-0994

Eagle Peak Montessori is a tuition-free charter school and is opened to any student in the state of California. This school for grades 1-5 offers special programs outside of the normal classroom setting. These programs include environmental education, an art program and a music program

Richmond

Richmond College Prep K–5

214 South 11th Street
Richmond, CA 94804
510-235-2066

Grades: K–2

Manzanita Charter School

3200 Barrett Avenue
Richmond, CA 94804
www.manzy.org

510-232-3300

Grades: 6–8

At Manzanita Charter School, they believe in taking into consideration the individual learning styles of each student. Classes are small so the student-to-teacher ratios are smaller. Parents are encouraged to help in the day-to-day running of classes and the school.

Leadership Public Schools: Richmond

157 9th Street
Richmond, CA 94801
www.leadps.org/richmond.html

510-235-4522

Grades: 9–12

This school's main mission is to prepare students to be life long leaders in their communities. By showing students the skills for commitment, respect, responsibility, values and harnessing the power of the leadership network, LPS helps their students build a foundation for success in college and beyond.

West County Community High School

1615 Carlson Blvd.
Richmond, CA 94804
510-898-1495

Grades: 9–12

Private/Parochial Schools

Unlike public schools, private schools do not have rankings. Below is a list of most private schools in the Contra Costa County area. For a full listing of all private schools, visit the California Department of Education's website and search the county you are interested in: www.cde.ca.gov/re/sd/.

Antioch

Holy Rosary School

25 East 15th Street
Antioch, CA 94509
www.holyrosarycatholicschool.org

925-757-1270

Grades: PK–8

They see their primary mission as imparting of values and self-worth consistent with the Gospel message and the teachings of the Catholic Church.

Antioch Christian School

405 West 6th Street
Antioch, CA 94509
925-778-1639

Grades: K–6

Steppingstones Academy, Inc.

330 Worrell Road
Antioch, CA 94509
925-754-2209

Grades: K – 8

La Cheim Schools

1500 D Street, Portable 601
Antioch, CA 94509
www.lacheim.org

925-777-9550

Grades: 4–12

All students at La Cheim Schools receive core instruction in language arts, mathematics, social studies, the natural sciences, physical education/health, and the arts.

Brentwood

Dainty Center/Willow Wood School

1265 Dainty Avenue
Brentwood, CA 94513
www.daintycenter.com

925-634-4539

Grades: K–6

Diversity is an essential part of this school's program. Students represent a wide variety of income, ethnicity, cultural background and family composition.

Concord

The Concordia School
In the Montessori Tradition

2353 Fifth Avenue
Concord, CA 94518
www.concordiaschool.com

925-689-6910

Grades: Children's House: 2–6 yrs., Junior Elementary: 6–9 yrs., Advanced Elementary: 9–12 yrs.
The Concordia School is about developing physical, social and intellectual competency. Lessons here are carefully designed to teach specific skills and concepts when the child is ready to learn.

Queen of All Saints School

2391 Grant Street
Concord, CA 94520
www.qasconcord.org

925-685-8700

Grades: K–8

Queen of All Saints strives to develop the whole child in a spiritual, academic, social and emotional way. They believe in providing a child education with compassion and integrity.

Wood Rose Academy

4347 Cowell Road
Concord, CA 94518
www.woodroseacademy.org

925-825-4644

Grades: K–8

Their philosophy is to enable children to learn and live according to the Judeo-Christian principles as preserved and taught by the Roman Catholic Church.

Seneca Center—Oak Grove

1034 Oak Grove Road
Concord, CA 94518
www.senecacenter.org
925-603-1900 ext.112

Grades: 7–12
Seneca has developed an array of mental health and special education services designed to accelerate a child of need for academic progress and success. From preschool to high school, it offers specialized treatment and education services to help students with even the most intensive needs.

Carondelet High School

1133 Winton Drive
Concord, CA 94518
www.carondelet.pvt.k12.ca.us
925-686-5353

Grades: 9–12
Founded in 1965, Carondelet High School offers a Catholic education for young women. The mission of their school is "the education of women for leadership and Christian service in the twenty-first century." They also have available a College and Career Center where students can go for resources on colleges, financial aid, scholarships and careers to prepare them for their future.

De La Salle High School

1130 Winton Drive
Concord, CA 94518
www.dlshs.org
925-686-3310

Grades: 9–12
Founded in 1965, De La Salle High School is an all boys' Catholic school. The mission of their school is to "believe that diversity enriches the community and encourages the students to work together to build an environment of trust, acceptance, and brotherhood that will extend to their home communities." Student life here consists of academics, athletics and student government.

Danville

Fountainhead Montessori School

115 Estates Drive
Danville, CA 94526
www.fountainheadmontessori.org
925-820-1343

Grades: PK–K

The Montessori philosophy leads to the development of a child's strong sense of self esteem, dignity, independence, self direction and awareness of the community.

St. Isidore School

435 La Gonda Way
Danville, CA 94526
www.stisidore.org

925-837-2977

Grades: K–8

The St. Isidore curriculum and instruction are designed to provide students in Kindergarten through eighth grade the foundation of knowledge, characteristics, and skills needed for a quality and caring Catholic education.

The Athenian School

2100 Mt. Diablo Scenic Blvd.
Danville, CA 94506-2002
www.athenian.org

925-837-5375

Grades: 6–12

Athenian is a community that strives to uphold the ideals of democracy, responsibility and citizenship. Known as a distinctive San Francisco Bay Area College Preparatory School, its class size averages 15 students, and nearly 100 percent of the school's graduates gain admission to outstanding four-year colleges.

El Cerrito

Prospect Sierra School
Elementary Campus

2060 Tapscott Avenue
El Cerrito, CA 94530
www.prospectsierra.org

510-236-5800

Grades: K–4

Prospect Sierra School
Middle School Campus

960 Avis Drive
El Cerrito, CA 94530
www.prospectsierra.org

510-236-5800

Grades: 5–8

The Prospect School's curriculum is based on a framework of established themes of mathematics, literature, writing, art, music, science, social studies, computer technology and world languages such as French and Spanish. In addition to these courses, service learning and physical education are incorporated into a positive educational experience for each student.

Tehiyah Day School

2603 Tassajara Avenue
El Cerrito, CA 94530
www.tehiyah.org

510-233-3013

Grades: K–8

This Jewish Community Day School promotes excellence in general studies, math, science and humanities; depth of Judaic experience and knowledge of Hebrew; appreciation of the visual and performing arts and computer; and fostering the generous spirit of the child.

Windrush School

1800 Elm Street
El Cerrito, CA 94530
www.tehiyah.org

510-970-7580

Grades: K–8

This school offers child-centered classrooms which allow teachers to guide students in the development of personal initiative, critical thinking skills and the ability to think independently.

El Sobrante

East Bay Waldorf School

3800 Clark Road
El Sobrante, 94803
www.eastbaywaldorf.org

510-223-3570

The East Bay Waldorf School, WASC accredited for PK–12, is located on 11 beautiful acres. Waldorf education, a worldwide movement, inspires students to become creative thinkers and problem-solvers through its curriculum of rigorous academics, artistic discipline and practical challenge. The sciences, humanities and arts interweave to form an integrated whole, which includes visual and performing arts, foreign languages, music and movement. The faculty's personal approach offers the support students need to meet modern life with confidence, competence and initiative.

Lafayette

Diablo Valley Montessori School

3390 Deer Hill Road
Lafayette, CA 94549
www.dvms.org

925-283-6036

Grades: Infant–Toddler: 3 mo.–2yrs., Two Year Old and Transition: 2–3.5 yrs.
Preschool/Kindergarten: 3–6 yrs.

Known as one of the best educational facilities in the country, Diablo Valley Montessori School offers spacious classrooms, low student-to-teacher ratio, and the latest curriculum to support rapid academic and practical living development. They also pride themselves for their outstanding faculty—trained teachers with 5 to 25 years of experience at their facility.

Meher School

999 Leland Drive
Lafayette, CA 94549
www.meherschools.org

925-938-9958

Grades: PK–5

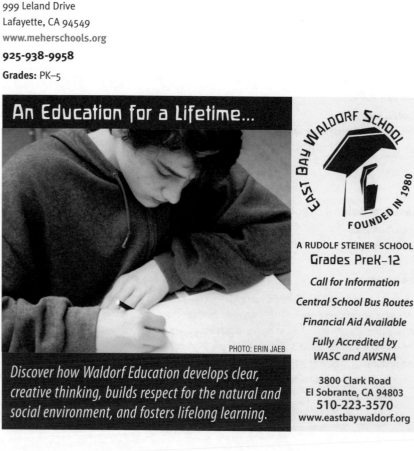

The Meher School is fully accredited by the Western Association of Schools and Colleges (WASC) since 1982. With 2 to 3 teachers per classroom, class sizes range from approximately 23 to 37 students. In the classrooms, they integrate the arts to complement and stimulate academic education.

Contra Costa Jewish Day School

3800 Mt. Diablo Blvd.
Lafayette, CA 94549
www.ccjds.org

925-284-8288

Grades: K–8
This Jewish Day School's curriculum includes accelerated academics in math, science and language arts. Students also have a chance to study art, music and drama, as well as Hebrew language and Jewish ethics. Advantages to this school include low student-to-teacher ratio, with full-time classroom assistants to insure that all students are taught to their individual levels.

St. Perpetua

3454 Hamlin Road
Lafayette, CA 94549
www.stperpetua.org

925-283-0272

Grades: K–8
At St. Perpetua, students are expected to exhibit the following characteristics: Catholic Faith; learning as a life-long endeavor; a healthy, well-rounded individual; and a respect of the world and all its cultures. In addition to the basic academic curriculum, religion is an essential part of each student's educational experience here. Their philosophy is to pass on the history of the Catholic Church to all their students.

Bentley School

Hiller Campus

Lower and Middle School
1 Hiller Drive
Oakland, California 94618

Lafayette Campus

Upper School
1000 Upper Happy Valley Road
Lafayette, California 94549
www.bentleyschool.net

510-843-2512

Bentley School is an independent coeducational college preparatory day school serving grades K through 12 on two campuses in Oakland, California (grades K through 8) and Lafayette, California (grades 9 to 12). The School was founded in 1920 and is accredited by both the California Association for Independent Schools and the National Association for Independent Schools. The school has a current enrollment of 683 students, serves families from the greater Bay Area and features an active Bentley Parents Association and committed Board of Trustees. Learn more about Bentley, we'd love to learn more about you.

Martinez

St. Catherine of Siena

604 Mellus Sreet
Martinez, CA 94553
www.stcath.net

925-228-4140

Grades: K–8

At St. Catherine of Siena, they want to teach their students to be committed Christians, enthusiastic learners, responsible communicators, creative problem solvers and involved citizens.

Moraga

Saklan Valley School

1678 School Street
Moraga, CA 94556
www.saklan.org

925-376-7900

Grades: PK–8

As an accredited school, their program features an excellent foreign language, technology, arts and music and physical education curriculum. Class size averages about 13 students per class. Test scores match or exceed those of the national independent school averages in all sections. In 2006, 70% of students scored at the 95th percentile or higher in one or more sections of the standardized national test of the Educational Records Bureau.

Orion Academy

350 Rheem Blvd.
Moraga, CA 94556
www.orionacademy.org

925-377-0789

Grades: 9–12

Orion Academy provides a college-preparatory program for students whose academic success is compromised by NLD (Non-verbal Learning Disorder), Aspergers syndrome or any other neurocognitive disability. The school program operates in six-week sessions and student to staff ratio is 1:8 to start in certain subjects and will increase as the students become more independent throughout the year. At Orion, they teach students how to achieve success even with their disorders.

Oakley

Faith Christian Learning Center

5400 Main Street
Oakley, CA 94561
www.faithchristianoakley.com

925-625-2161

Grades: K–12

Each student at this center sets his or her goals and with self-paced learning materials, students work until they achieve a mastery of the materials.

Orinda

Fountainhead Montessori School

30 Santa Maria Way
Orinda, CA 94563-2605
www.fountainheadmontessori.org

925-254-7110

Grades: PK–K

The Montessori philosophy is to develop a child's strong sense of self esteem, dignity, independence, self direction and awareness of the community.

Orinda Academy

19 Altarinda Road
Orinda, CA 94563
www.orindaacademy.org

925-254-7553

Orinda Academy is a non-profit, co-educational, college preparatory day school serving students in grades 7–12. Founded in 1982, Orinda Academy provides an academic setting that is highly structured, fosters communication and provides a nurturing, supportive environment. Small class sizes, innovative teaching strategies, and committed faculty, combined with a complete offering of music, arts, technology, athletic opportunities and summer classes, make Orinda Academy a viable choice for any student who has a desire to be challenged to their full potential. Contact admission@orindaacademy.org to schedule a personal tour.

Schools and Educational Resources

Christian Science Sunday School

24 Orinda Way (next to Library)
Orinda, CA 94563
www.christianscienceorinda.org

925-254-4212

Hours: 10 am–11 am every Sunday
Fees: Voluntary donation

Children up to age 20 are welcome to visit or enroll. Instruction is Bible-based, including the Psalms, Ten Commandments, Beatitudes, Sermon on the Mount, and the healings of Christ Jesus. Through informal discussion, students learn how to know God as Love, to feel and prove His power in their daily lives. Parents do not need to be church members for their children to benefit from Sunday School. Loving nursery care for toddlers.

Pittsburg

St. Peter Martyr Elementary

425 West Fourth Street
Pittsburg, CA 94565
www.stpetermartyrschool.org

925-439-1014

Grades: K–8

St. Peter Martyr School's mission statement is committed to share Christ's gospel through education.

Christian Center

1210 Stoneman Avenue
Pittsburg, CA 94565
www.ccenterschool.org

925-439-2552

Grades: K–12

Christian Center School is a fully accredited school with ACSI Accreditation for K-8 grades. Their curriculum exceeds California State Department of Education's standards. It has a Biblical basis and is traditional in approach.

Pleasant Hill

Fountainhead Montessori School

490 Golf Club Road
Pleasant Hill, CA 94523-1553
www.fountainheadmontessori.org

925-685-2949

Grades: PK–K

The Montessori philosophy leads to the development of a child's strong sense of self esteem, dignity, independence, self direction and awareness of the community.

Christ the King School

195-B Brandon Road
Pleasant Hill, CA 94526
www.ctkschool.org
925-685-1109

Grades: K–8

Christ the King School's philosophy is that parents are the prime educators of their children. They also believe that their school has the responsibility to communicate the Catholic message as well as to provide a sound academic education for their students. They are a fully accredited school and their courses meet and exceed the California State approved framework.

La Cheim Schools

1700 Oakpark Blvd.
Pleasant Hill, CA 94523
www.lacheim.org
925-930-7994

Grades: K–12

All students at La Cheim Schools receive core instruction in language arts, mathematics, social studies, the natural sciences, physical education/health and the arts.

San Ramon

Hidden Canyon Elementary School

18868 Bollinger Canyon Road
San Ramon, CA 94583
www.hiddencanyonschool.com
925-820-2515

The Hidden Canyon curriculum is organized to create deep, long-lasting learning in the core academic subjects of math, reading and language which are then integrated with science, history, social studies and the arts.

Montessori School of San Ramon

2400 Old Crow Canyon Road, Suite A2
San Ramon, CA 94583-1222
www.sanramont.com
925-855-7434

Grades: K–5

This Montessori school tries to incorporate major aspects of Piagetian educational philosophy such as maturation, experience, and social interaction to obtain equilibration. To simplify it, they utilize as many approaches as possible to encourage a child's love of learning and exploration.

Walnut Creek

The Dorris-Eaton School

1847 Newell Avenue
Walnut Creek, CA 94595
www.dorriseaton.com

925-933-5225

Grades: PK–8

The Dorris-Eaton School is recognized locally as well as nationally for its academic excellence. Each year nearly 70 percent of the 7th and 8th grade students qualify to take the SAT. A high percentage of them achieve Honors with Distinction or State Recognition in math, verbal or both.

The Seven Hills School

975 North San Carlos Drive
Walnut Creek, CA 94598
www.sevenhillsschool.org

925-933-0666

The Seven Hills School, founded in 1962, is an independent, not-for-profit, day school educating students enrolled in Preschool through 8th grade.

Nestled on nine acres behind Heather Farm Park, Seven Hills School is a student-centered environment that provides a myriad of experiences designed to develop the intellect, engage the spirit and foster respect for and responsibility to our world. With this mission, Seven Hills ensures the best for your child's educational journey by inspiring a love for learning that will last a lifetime.

Contra Costa Christian Schools

2721 Larkey Lane
Walnut Creek, CA 94597
www.cccss.org

925-934-4964

Grades: K–12

CCC Schools serve students and families from over 100 different churches. Their core value is to "prepare students through the creation of leadership and service opportunities, and extracurricular activities, how to grow in every aspect of their Christian faith and life."

Berean Christian High School

245 El Divisadero Avenue
Walnut Creek, CA 94598
www.berean-eagles.org

925-945-6464

Grades: 9–12

Berean Christian High School is an educational institution where young people receive a distinctive Christian education focused on college preparatory studies that are rooted in the Word of God.

Home Schooling

California Homeschooling

www.homeschooling.gomilpitas.com/regional/California.htm

Ann Zeise has assembled the most interesting and useful website links and articles about home education in California. On this one site you can find home schooling associations, events, field trips, legal information, online home school groups, home schooling publications and home schooling resources for your family. There are also home schooling support groups in Alameda and Contra Costa Counties.

California Homeschool Network

P.O. Box 55485
Hayward, CA 94545
www.californiahomeschool.net

800-327-5339

Founded in 1994, the California Homeschool Network informs families about the different styles and philosophies of home schooling.

California Teen Homeschoolers

www.groups.yahoo.com/group/CaliforniaTeenHomeschoolers

This is a support group for families of teen home schoolers. Teens who are home schooled typically have a difficult time interacting with other teens their age. This support groups provides teens with a way of communicating with other teens that are in a similar situation as far as education is concerned. This site allows them to set up activities with other teens in their area.

Christian Home Educators Association of California

www.cheaofca.org

The Christian Home Educators Association of California has put together some valuable information for your family and home schooling. They provide information about the most common questions and legal information. For those home schooling, and just starting, there is a section on getting started.

Homegrown Kids

www.homegrownkids.org

Serving the Richmond-El Cerrito-Berkeley-Oakland area, Homegrown kids is a group of home schooling families in the East Bay. These families meet weekly and organize trips and events to meet their interests. They ask that all families participate and contribute in some way to the group.

Homeschooling in California

www.homeschoolingincalifornia.com

Home schooling in California has put together some valuable information for your family and home schooling. For those home schooling and just starting, there is a section on getting started, how to home school, selecting curriculum and great support links for support groups and local and state events. This website is a great resource that provides teaching tips on a variety of different subjects including reading, writing, science, math, history and foreign languages.

LDS Homeschooling in California

www.ldshomeschoolinginca.org

This website was originally created so Latter-Day Saint home schoolers in California could communicate with each other; however it has expanded beyond California. They provide curriculum help, support groups and newsletters for families.

LDS Home School Resources—School of Abraham

www.schoolofabraham.com

This LDS (Latter-Day Saint) home school resource has home school resources like online LDS curriculum, commercial LDS curriculum providers, LDS home school authors, support groups and more.

Home School Association of California

www.hsc.org

On this site you can find home schooling associations, events, field trip, legal information, online home school groups, home schooling publications and home schooling resources for your family.

Tutors & Learning Centers

Boys & Girls Clubs

www.bgca.org/clubs

The Boys & Girls Club of America has national programs with arts and crafts, tutoring, leadership development, sports, friends and fun. There are many locations so visit online for locations and programs in your area.

Huntington Learning Center

www.huntingtonlearning.com

At Huntington Learning Center, they believe that "individual attention and an unwavering focus on the needs of the child are the keys to helping students do better in school." They pride themselves in creating individualized programs to fit the needs of each child.

Antioch
Orchard Square Shopping Center

2340 Buchanan Road
Antioch, CA 94509
925-776-4224

Moraga
Rheem Valley Shopping Center

490 Moraga Road
Moraga, CA 94556
925-377-0737

Walnut Creek

1399 Ygnacio Valley Road, Suite # 8
Walnut Creek, CA 94598
925-944-8774

Hurdles Dyslexia Clinic, Inc.

www.hurdlesdyslexia.com

925-337-3191

Does someone you know struggle with reading and spelling and getting his/er thoughts written down despite having average intelligence? It could be dyslexia (www.BrightSolultions.US) and/or a perceptual problem (www.irlen.com).Through evaluation we can informally diagnose and provide you with the tools to help him/er succeed through specialized tutoring and/or the use of colored overlays. Our in-depth reports will help you advocate for classroom accommodations while your student is being tutored and functioning below grade level in reading and spelling.

Kumon Math & Reading Center

www.kumon.com

This after-school math and reading program, founded in Japan in 1958, uses a systematic approach that helps children develop solid command of math and reading skills. Worldwide there are 3 million students enrolled in 43 countries. Visit the website for a location near you.

Alamo

21 Alamo Square
Alamo, CA 94507
925-552-8187

Antioch

3700 Delta Fair Blvd., Suite D
Antioch, CA 94509
925-672-8864

Clayton Valley

1460 Washington Blvd., #B-203
Concord, CA 94521
925-672-8864

Danville

4125 Blackhawk Plaza Circle, Suite 180
Danville, CA 94506
925-736-5544

Central Danville

117 Town And Country Drive, Suite B
Danville, CA 94526
925-838-2658

El Cerrito

11100 San Pablo Avenue, Suite 106
El Cerrito, CA 94530
510-235-8666

Lafayette

925 Village Center #3
Lafayette, CA 94549
925-284-9038

Moraga
2100 Donald Drive
Moraga, CA 94556
925-283-9228

Orinda
15 Altarinda Blvd., Suite 112
Orinda, CA 94563
925-283-9228

Pinole
610-M San Pablo Avenue
Pinole, CA 94564
510-724-3000

Pleasant Hill
2601 Pleasant Hill Road
Pleasant Hill, CA 94523
925-256-0420

San Ramon
9260 Alcosta Blvd., Bldg. B, Suite 14
San Ramon, CA 94583
925-803-9870

Walnut Creek North
3075 Citrus Circle, Ste. #250
Walnut Creek, CA 94598
925-256-0786

Walnut Creek
1904 Olympic Blvd. #10
Walnut Creek, CA 94596
925-256-0609

SCORE Educational Centers
35 Crescent Drive
Pleasant Hill, CA 94523
www.escore.com
925-676-8921

At SCORE, they help children develop a love for learning that keeps going long after their academic skills have expanded. They work with children from Grades: PK through the 10th grade on subjects like math, reading, writing and spelling.

Sylvan Learning Centers
El Cerrito
10612 San Pablo Avenue
El Cerrito, CA 94530
www.educate.com

510-559-1400

Programs include reading, math, writing, SAT preparation and study skills. Courses are also offered online.

Walnut Creek
2050 North Broadway
Walnut Creek, CA 94596
925-934-3000

Language Schools

A Plus Spanish Academy

801 San Ramon Valley Blvd.
Danville, CA 94526-4061
www.aplusspanish.com

925-820-2090

Prices: Week day preschool immersion—$240 per month; Saturdays $169 per 6 week session.
$35 annual registration fee per student/per year.
Ages: 3–5 for Preschool Immersion Program; K–8th grades for "FST" Friendly Spanish
Immersion Program.

Program: For the preschool immersion program, they offer a weekly 2 day program either Monday/Wednesday or Tuesday/Thursday. They also offer a 6 week Saturday program as well. A Spanish language school for children, teens and adults. Make sure to call the location of your choice before signing up.

Alamo Community Center

925-451-9176

Danville Community Center

925-314-3400

San Ramon Community Center

925-973-3200

Dougherty Station in San Ramon

925-973-3200

Dublin Community Center

925-556-4500

Livermore Community Center

925-373-5700

Berlitz

1646 North California Blvd.
Walnut Creek, CA 94596
www.berlitz.us

925-935-1386

Ages: Children and teens

With over 125 years of experience in language services Berlitz is well known for all of their languages they have to offer. Berlitz offers children's programs such as tutoring, group programs and after-school programs. Contact them directly for detailed information on their programs and prices.

CACC Chinese School
Amador Valley High School

1155 Santa Rita Road
Pleasanton, CA 94566
www.caccusa.org
cs@caccusa.org

Prices: $30 non-refundable registration fee for each family each school year. Upon request, a student can have a free class trial per class. Classes available for ages 4–12

Programs: Classes are held every Sunday morning. Registration is offered online only.

Entiendo Spanish Learning Center

www.entiendo.org
800-818-8394

Hours: Monday–Friday 8:30 am–8 pm, Saturday 9 am–5 pm, Sunday 10 am–4 pm
Fees: Visit our web site for details.

Serving all Contra Costa County. Come and learn Spanish. Entiendo offers a variety of programs for the student's convenience tailored to individual needs. Native instructors help foster rapid learning. We speak Spanish, dream in Spanish, and think in Spanish, and you will too! Also offering private tutoring, individual and group classes for adults and kids, opportunities to study abroad, and document translation services.

French for Fun
Corporate Terrace

3470 Mt. Diablo Blvd., Suite A115
Lafayette, CA 94549
www.frenchforfun.com/html/Philosophy.htm

925-283-9822

Ages: 2–5

Programs: Moms n' Tots, Total Immersion and Foreign Language at the Elementary School
French for Fun was established over 25 years ago and continues to introduce French as second language through physical experiences and not just through academics. Among the subjects they teach are: math, history, grammar, cooking, dance, music and geography.

Kids Into Speaking Spanish (KISS)

2780 Camino Diablo
Walnut Creek, CA 94597
www.kissprogram.com

925-952-9903

Ages: 2–6

Programs: Spanish is taught naturally, through active play and activities.
This is an immersion school program for preschoolers and kindergarteners.

Viva el Español

Lafayette, Alameda & Pleasanton
www.LamorindaSpanish.com

925-962-9177

Spanish Immersion Classes for Toddlers to Adults . Viva el Español, a non-profit Spanish Language Center, offers engaging, interactive Spanish programs for young amigos in pre-school through grade 8. Their programs offer full-immersion Spanish instruction by trained teachers, and have multiple proficiency levels. Classes include music, movement/dancing, storytelling, arts & crafts, puppets and more! Viva el Español has locations in Lafayette, Alameda, and Pleasanton and also teaches at numerous elementary schools throughout the East Bay. Viva el Español also offers Summer Camps, Teen "Fiesta" Nights, Adult Classes and private instruction. Come for storytelling, music, art, games and tons of fun!

Valley Community Church

4455 Del Valle Parkway
Pleasanton, CA 94566

Picking a School in Your Neighborhood

Lily Wescott/J.Rockliff Realtors

89 Davis Road, Suite 100
Orinda, CA 94563
www.LamorindaHome.com

925-330-6108

Hours: See website for details

Local realtor and resident serving Orinda, Moraga and Lafayette offers professional real estate services for single-family homes, income property and land opportunities. Lily Wescott of J. Rockliff Realtors ensures successful real estate outcomes supported by an in-depth knowledge of local neighborhoods, schools, businesses, zoning laws, and community resources. Now also serving the neighboring communities of Walnut Creek, Alamo, and Danville in Contra Costa County.

Parenting Resources

There are so many places to turn for parenting support in our community. If you're looking for more information on parenting classes and groups, contact your local school district or university sponsored Continuing Education to obtain a list of classes and workshops.

Love and Logic

www.loveandlogic.com

1-800-388-4065

For a list of facilitators in your area, call the Love and Logic Institute, Inc. If you are looking for easy to use techniques that will help you raise responsible kids who are fun to be around, you may want to attend Becoming a Love and Logic Parent classes. These classes are based on their Love and Logic philosophy, which is an easy to learn and unique approach that unlocks the secrets of successful parenting. You will learn specific instructions, not just theoretical concepts.

What is Love and Logic?

The Love and Logic Process

- Shared control: Gain control by giving away the control you don't need.

- Shared thinking and decision-making: Provide opportunities for the child to do the greatest amount of thinking and decision-making.

- Equal shares of empathy with consequences: An absence of anger causes a child to think and learn from his/her mistakes.

- Maintain the child's self-concept: Increased self-concept leads to improved behavior and improved achievement.

The Rules of Love and Logic

Rule #1: Adults take care of themselves by providing limits in a loving way.

- Adults avoid anger, threats, warnings or lectures.

- Adults use enforceable statements.

- Children are offered choices within limits.

- Limits are maintained with compassion, understanding or empathy.

Rule #2: Childhood misbehavior is treated as an opportunity for gaining wisdom.

- In a loving way, the adult holds the child accountable for solving his/her problems in a way that does not make a problem for others.

- Children are offered choices with limits.

- Adults use enforceable statements.

- Adults provide delayed/extended consequences.

- The adult's empathy is "locked in" before consequences are delivered.

California State PTA

2327 L Street
Sacramento, CA 95816-5014
www.capta.org

916-440-1985

The California State PTA's objectives are to promote the welfare of children and youth in home, school, community and place of worship; to raise the standards of home life; to secure adequate laws for the care and protection of children and youth; to bring into closer relation the home and the school, that parents and teachers may cooperate more intelligently in the education of children and youth; and to develop between educators and the general public such united efforts as will secure for all children and youth the highest advantages in physical, social and spiritual education. The National PTA developed a program called How to Help Your Child Succeed. Here are the key points of the program:

- Talk with your child. Talking early and often with your children helps them trust you as a source of information and guidance.

- Set high but realistic expectations. Paying attention to your children's strengths, whileacknowledging where they need assistance can help children develop realistic self-expectations.

- Build your child's self-esteem and confidence. Encourage your children to make choices even if it means making mistakes. This is how children learn and grow.

Parenting Resources

- Keep your child healthy. Promote your children's physical, emotional and social health.

- Support learning at home. Show that education is important to you and that you value learning.

- Communicate with your child's school. On a regular basis to stay informed and involved.

- Encourage exploration and discovery. By encouraging your children to develop their interests and seek opportunities to try new things you help them make the most of the world around them.

- Help your child develop good relationships. All children want to fit in and belong. Helping your children develop friendships that affirm them will go a long way to helping them build solid relationships as adults.

- Keep your child safe. Teach your children safety procedures and how to avoid dangerous situations.

- Participate in community service. Children's positive energy and talents can be acknowledged beyond the classroom when used to serve or help others.

From *How to Help Your Child Succeed*, a part of National PTA's Building Successful Partnerships program. *How to Help Your Child Succeed* is available as a two-part workshop in which participants learn more about the 10 ways and how to put them into practice. To find out how to bring a workshop to your community and for more information on this program, contact California PTA or visit the *How to Help Your Child Succeed* area on the National PTA website, www.pta.org.

Family Stress Center

2086 Commerce Avenue
Concord, CA 94520
www.familystresscenter.org

925-827-0212

315 G Street
Antioch, CA 94509
925-706-8477

Provides counseling and education to strengthen families.

John Muir Women's Health Center

1656 North California Blvd., Suite 100
Walnut Creek, CA 94596
www.johnmuirhealth.com/index.php/womens_services_whc.html

925-941-7900

The center offers great drop in support classes for new mothers and mothers with toddlers.

Parenting Resources

Kaiser Permanente

1425 South Main Street
Walnut Creek, CA 94596
www.Kaiserpermanente.com

925-295-4484

This hospital offers a new mother and baby support group. Make sure you call for dates, times, fees and specific location for group gatherings.

St. Paul's Episcopal Church

1924 Trinity Avenue
Walnut Creek, CA 94596
www.stpauls-wc.org

925-934-2324

Hours: Sunday 7:30 am and 9:30 am; Many weekday and evening events._Many free services, some donations and fees requested.

St. Paul's offers your child and you access to deep roots, growing community and living faith. Family fellowship, Ministry of Mothers Sharing (MOMS). Childcare for newborn to age 3 and for ages 3 to 11 Godly Play, an open classroom, respectful learning experience and a Summer Camp. Closed circuit TV room during service with armchairs for feeding baby, changing table and toys for restless ones. Ample free parking or walk from WC Bart.

Great Parenting Books

Caring for Your Baby and Young Child: Birth to Age 5
By American Academy of Pediatrics

Bring Up Boys: Practical Advice and Encouragement for Those Shaping the Next Generation of Men
By James C. Dobson

The Difficult Child
By Stanley Tureki, Leslie Tannery

The Emotional Problems of Normal Children—How Parents Can Understand and Help
By Stanley Tureck, Sarah Wernick

Finding the Path: A Novel for Parents of Teenagers
By Jeffrey P. Kaplan, Abby Lederman

Girls Will Be Girls: Raising Confident and Courageous Daughters
By JoAnn Deak, Teresa Barker

How to Talk So Kids Can Learn at Home and School: What Every Parent and Teacher Needs to Know
By Adele Faber, et al.

How to Talk So Kids Will Listen and Listen So Kids Will Talk
By Adele Faber, Elaine Mazlish

The Happiest Toddler on the Block: The New Way to Stop the Daily Battle of Wills and Raise a Secure and Well-Behaved One to Four-Year-Old
By Harvey Karp, Paula Spencer

Little Feelings
By Judy Spain Barton

Making the "Terrible" Twos Terrific
By John Rosemond

New Approach to Discipline: Logical Consequences
By Rudolph Dreikurs

1-2-3 Magic
By Thomas W. Phelan

Parenting With Love and Logic: Teaching Children Responsibility
By Foster W. Cline, Jim Fay

Parent/Teen Breakthrough: The Relationship Approach
By Mira Kirshenbaum, Charles Foster

Parenting Teens with Love & Logic: Preparing Adolescents for Responsible Adulthood
By Foster W. Cline, Jim Fay

Playful Parenting
By Lawrence J. Cohen

Perfect Parenting: The Dictionary of 1,000 Parenting Tips
By Elizabeth Pantley

Raising Boys: Why Boys are Different—And How to Help Them Become Happy and Well-Balanced Men
By Steve Biddulph

Raising Confident Boys: 100 Tips for Parents and Teachers
By Elizabeth Hartley-Brewer

Raising Preschoolers
By Sylvia Rimm

Raising Your Spirited Child: A Guide for Parents Whose Child is More Intense, Sensitive, Perceptive, Persistent, Energetic
By Mary Sheedy Kurcinka

Setting Limits with Your Strong-Willed Child: Eliminating Conflict by Establishing Clear, Firm, and Respectful Boundaries
By Robert J. MacKenzie Ed.D.

Siblings with Rivalry—How to Help Your Children Live Together So You Can Live Too
By Adele Faber, et al.

Toddlers and Pre-Schoolers: Love and Logic Parenting for Early Childhood
By Jim Fay, Foster Cline

Transforming the Difficult Child—The Nurtured Heart Approach

By Howard Glassner & Jennifer Easley

The Wish and Wonder Words of Wisdom for the Perfect Parent

By Gail Perry Johnston

The Way They Learn

By Cynthia Ulrich Tobias

Why Bright Kids Get Poor Grades—And What You Can Do About It

By Sylvia Rimm

Your 2 Year Old: Terrible or Tender

(A whole series including Your 1, 2, 3, 4, 5, 6, & 10-14 year old. They are all excellent.)

By Louise Bates Ames

Helpful Websites

The following Websites contain great information for parents and caregivers.

aap.org

American Academy of Pediatrics

They are dedicated to the health of all children.

babycenter.com

They offer pregnancy, baby, and toddler information, along with baby gifts, and a parenting community.

education.com

Learn and share your thoughts on parenting from the early years of 3–5 to the teen years of 13–18.

elainegibson.net/parenting

They have insights on parenting from a mother who wrote a parenting column for 13 years.

families.com

They offer ideas for family fun, blogs, homes, health, travel, parenting and marriage.

fatherhood.org

Everything a dad would want in a parenting website.

Parenting Resources

fathers.com

This website strengthens families by strengthening fathers.

extension.usu.edu/cooperative/publications

This is an online library of newsletters and other publications. Search and find anything from child development to parenting.

iamyourchild.org

They are the voice of America's parents.

parentcenter.com

They have help on parenting, children's health and education, family crafts and activities.

parenthood.com

Thy have information on parenting, pregnancy, conception and baby names.

parentingteenstoday.com

This is a website with great advice for parenting teenagers.

parentnetassociation.org

A great online resource to help parents and schools increase parent involvement and improve student academic achievement and success.

parenting.com

This is a great magazine with a great website. They offer advice, tips and resources for parents.

parenttime.com

They offer parenting topics on pregnancy, newborns and infants.

wholefamily.com

Strengthen your personal and family relations and solve the most challenging issues facing you and your family today with this website.

zerotothree.org

The nation's leading resource on the first years of life.

Family Finances

Teach Your Children the Value of Money

Before You Start

- Speak with your spouse or partner first so that you'll both be on the same page when it's time to talk to the kids about financial priorities.

- Put yourself in your children's shoes. Try to remember what your top financial concerns and priorities were at that age.

- Next, ask them about their thoughts on money. It'll show you're interested in their opinion and make financial conversations more productive.

1

Teach Your Children the Value of Money

"Reading, writing, arithmetic"—too bad that list doesn't include personal finance. Most kids learn the basics of money and making change in grammar school, but probably won't learn how to manage money unless they choose finance as a career path. That means it is up to all of us to see that our children reach adulthood prepared to face life's fiscal challenges.

2

Earlier Is Better

The benefits of teaching your children about money early on are both immediate and long term. In the short term, they may develop strong saving habits, learn how to make smart purchases, begin to understand the true meaning of "investment," and perhaps even learn why they can't immediately get everything they want. In the long term, you can help them avoid accumulating debt. And by teaching the value of saving for the future, you can help them plan for financial security.

As you think about how, what, and when to teach your children, consider letting them direct you by using their natural inquisitiveness. (But remember, it's never too late to start teaching—even adults can be taught the basics of personal finance.)

3

Where Does Money Come From?

An ideal time to begin teaching your children about the basics of money is when they first begin to notice it. In a child's world, money comes from Mom and Dad's pockets. And when Mom and Dad are tapped, a machine magically spouts dollars after merely pushing a few buttons. It's natural for them to assume that money is readily available whenever it's needed.

When they can't understand why you can't meet their every demand—and you're about to use a standby response such as, "Money doesn't grow on trees"—remember that a more constructive explanation may serve both of you better.

Even very young children can begin to understand the concept of earning money. Explain to your children that money is earned by working, and that you can only spend what you earn. To help them understand what it's like to get paid on a schedule, begin paying an allowance. Then help them set goals for how they spend and save their allowance. It's important, however, to make sure that you stick to the payment schedule; otherwise the lesson may be lost.

Your Child Could Become a Millionaire

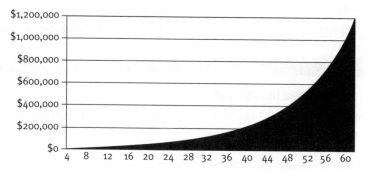

This chart shows the growth, compounded at 8% monthly, of an investment of $100 per month beginning at age 4 and ending at age 18, assuming that the investment remains untouched until age 62. This example is hypothetical and does not represent the performance of any actual investment.

4

Children and Allowances

Experts differ on whether or not allowances should be tied to household chores. Although many people say children will learn more about personal responsibility if they are NOT paid for pitching in around the home, others feel it teaches them valuable lessons about working and earning. You might consider paying your children for chores outside of daily duties, such as helping to garden or wash the family car.

5

Make Saving Interesting

You hear it every time you walk by a toy store: "I want...Buy me this... !" Again, pause and take a moment before responding. This situation presents a great opportunity to teach another important lesson about personal finance: savings and interest. Explain that people often save their money for items they want to buy.

A simple savings lesson involves using a piggy bank, shoe box, or empty peanut butter jar. Make the lesson fun by having your children decorate the "bank," while explaining to them how you also use a real bank to save your money. Encourage your children to save a portion of their allowance for a special goal. As they save money, you might reward them with a small additional amount, just like a bank pays interest. At the end of each month, calculate how much they have saved and then chip in a certain percentage as interest.

Last, to further encourage the learning process, you might consider plotting a visual chart of their savings (include the goal) so they can easily see their savings grow. Remember to keep it as simple as possible, geared toward each child's level of understanding.

6

Banking and Investing

Once your children have been saving enough to accumulate $10 or $20, take them to the bank to open their first savings account. Most community banks will allow children to open first accounts with low minimum deposits. Some even have accounts especially marketed to kids to make the learning process fun. Make sure that your children receive a passbook so they can see the progress of their savings efforts, as well as the interest that accrues.

Once your children have mastered banking with an institution, you can begin to teach them about investing. When your children want something that they can't quite afford, discuss the value of saving versus borrowing. If you do extend credit, use a written IOU, establish a repayment schedule, and charge interest. By doing this, you establish the framework for teaching your children that bonds and certificates of deposit are IOUs representing loans from investors to institutions.

7

Compounding

As your children get older and perhaps take on part-time jobs to earn more money, their savings will likely amass at a quicker rate. Now is the time to review the lesson of compounding, or the ability of earnings to build upon themselves. Explain how compounding can be more dramatic over time; the longer money is left alone, the greater the effect. This can lead into a discussion about investing and how certain investments can have a greater ability to compound over time.

Family Finances

Giving a gift of stocks of well-established or kid-oriented companies can be ideal ways to teach your children about investing. Most children would love to think of themselves as owners of Ben & Jerry's, Disney, or Toys "R" Us. Some companies even have shareholder meetings directed to children.

Mutual funds may be good vehicles as well. Like banks, some fund companies have specific programs to teach children about investing. Often such funds have low initial investments, as well as marketing materials designed to make the investing process fun.

8

A Little Learning Can Pay Off

Teaching your children about our complex financial system may seem daunting, but you can help put your child on the right track by encouraging smart habits now.

Is it worth your time and effort to help your children learn about money? As Benjamin Franklin once said, "An investment in knowledge always pays the best interest." Answering your children's questions honestly and in terms they'll understand can help them begin life on sound financial footing.

Summary

- The benefits of teaching your children about money can be both short and long term. Let your children help you determine how to teach them. Use their questions to develop lessons.

- Explain to children that money is earned. Consider paying them for helping with certain chores.

- Use a piggy bank to help teach about savings and interest. Set a savings goal to encourage your children to save some of their allowance. Calculate how much is saved each month and chip in a certain percentage as interest.

- Take your children to the bank to open a savings account requiring a lower minimum deposit.

- If you extend credit, issue an IOU, set a repayment schedule, and charge interest.

- Review compounding, or the ability of interest to build upon itself.

- Once your children begin earning their own money through part-time jobs, introduce them to investments such as stocks and mutual funds.

Checklist

- If they're old enough, help your children set up a plan to save for their own goals (such as a new video game) and other accounts for family goals (such as paying for college).

- Agree on an amount of their savings that you'll "match."

- Schedule time to talk about how investing works and how it may enable people to reach their financial goals faster.

- Talk to your children about good shopping habits. Perhaps you can ask them to clip coupons and let them keep some of the savings.

The Ten Worst Things To Say To Your Children About Money

As parents we want to communicate openly and honestly with our kids about money so that they won't experience problems—financial or emotional—later. But there are some words that should never leave our mouths. What and how you communicate to a child about money determines not just if he's fiscally responsible but socially responsible as well. Parents who learn to talk about money in appropriate ways usually raise well-adjusted, responsible, and value-conscious kids. Let's look at some words that shouldn't leave your mouth. We've found that focusing on these no-no's can make people more conscious about their money talk and help them edit out certain types of messages that can have a negative impact. Without further ado, here are the ten worst things parents can say when talking to children about money.

We can't afford it. This leads our list because it's such a common, dishonest response to a child's request (obviously, if you really can't afford it, then the response is appropriate). Your child has asked you to purchase something and you don't want to. Maybe it's a $79 plastic action figure that you don't want to buy because you consider it overpriced junk, or maybe it's a $275 pair of aviator sunglasses that you consider to be too expensive for a twelve-year-old who has lost his last two pairs of $8 sunglasses. Maybe it isn't overpriced or inappropriate but simply the third thing your kid has asked you to buy him today, and you feel that enough is enough. Saying you "can't afford it" when you just don't want to buy it is the easy way out. It's also dishonest; it involves lying to your child rather than explaining your values. It may instill a false impression of the family's actual financial situation, making your child needlessly anxious. And your child will probably see you buying other things, exposing the lie for what it is. As a parent, you need to be able to say no based on your values or your budget. State your values simply and in a manner that shows how those values relate to the topic at hand. "No, I've already bought you two things today that you wanted and that's enough." "No, I don't want to spend that much money to buy you sunglasses when you've lost the last two pairs. I'll pay half the cost of another pair of $8 sunglasses but you would have to use $4 from your savings to pay for the other half."

We'll talk about it later. Actually, this is fine to say if you follow through and talk about the money subject later. Many times, however, parents use this delaying tactic to avoid talking about money issues. This tactic, especially when it's repeated over time and forms a pattern, communicates to children that certain subjects can't or shouldn't be discussed. "Why were you and Mom fighting

Family Finances

about how much it costs to send me to that summer camp?" is the type of question that might earn the "We'll talk about it later" response. Rather than using the question as a springboard for discussion of important issues—what is the fair cost for a service, how do you measure the benefit versus the cost—parents end up demonstrating that these issues aren't worth talking about. Obviously, it takes more than one instance of this response to send this message, but when it becomes a patterned response, kids recognize what's happening. Plus, children see that you're being dishonest after this pattern is established; they know you have no intention of talking about it later. Thus, you send a doubly negative message.

We'll pay you $100 for every A on your report card. Variations on this gambit include "We'll increase your allowance if you clean your room" or "We'll get you that car you want if you can avoid getting a detention this semester." Bribery is not a particularly healthy child-raising policy. You are teaching your kids to associate being loved and getting paid with achieving goals, rather than achieving those goals to attain a sense of self-satisfaction. As your kid grows older, he is likely to associate using money to buy friends or love. And if your kid doesn't get an A or avoid detention, the failure to earn the money will be equated in his mind with failing to "earn" your love.

Money is the root of all evil. Woe be unto the parent who employs this adage. The Bible actually says that greed—the love of money—is the root of all evil. From our perspective, what's evil is hurting others in the quest to make money or being so obsessive about making money that it, rather than family and friends, becomes the top priority. If you communicate that money is evil, your children may well rebel and believe money is to be worshipped. Even if they develop a dislike of material things, they may also burden themselves with an inability to manage money. Kids who have been victimized by money-is-evil propaganda tend to disdain learning basic money-management techniques and can easily get themselves into chaotic financial situations.

Time is money. Time isn't money. Time is time. If you're always in a hurry and impressing your child with the importance of not wasting a minute, you're teaching her to place a monetary value on everything. We've seen parents try to impress their children with their hourly wages or go beyond the old adage when reprimanding their children for wasting time: "When you're an adult, you're not going to be allowed to dillydally around at work the way you do with your homework." Telling a child that you can't go to her dance recital because "someone in this family has to pay the bills" sends all sorts of negative messages about what's important in life.

They're disgustingly rich. This sentiment can come out many different ways in conversations with your child. You might make a disparaging comment about neighbors who buy a new car every year or you might make a negative remark about the thirty-something millionaire who got rich from stock options. The net effect is to associate money with negative images in your child's mind. If you want to express disagreement with how someone spends money, tie it to your values. For example, if you disagree with buying a new car every year, you might say "In our family, we like to save our money by not replacing our cars so frequently."

That's not an appropriate question. If you want to make your child feel guilty about talking about money, this response really does the trick. Younger children, especially, ask questions like "Are we rich?" "How much money do you make?" and "Do we have more money than Aunt Susie?" When kids ask these questions, we suggest that you respond with a question of your own: "Why do you want to know?" Often their underlying concern is "Am I secure?" and "Are you going to be able to take care of me?" For instance, five-year-old Grant came home from pre-school and asked, "Mommy, do we have $1 million dollars?" Instead of answering yes or no, she asked a question of her own: "Why are you asking?" It turned out that one of Grant's classmates had seen some homeless people at the local park and that a fellow five-year-old had asserted that one needed $1 million dollars to avoid becoming homeless. When it came to financial issues, Grant didn't know the difference between a million dollars and his elbow. He was really asking to be reassured that he was safe and wouldn't have to live on the street. Grant's mom explained to him the difference between their financial situation and that of a homeless person, rather than telling him that it wasn't nice to ask about the family's money.

Bruce and Diane recently bought a new home. One Sunday morning they were reading the newspaper and their fourteen-year-old son, Ethan, asked "How much did this house cost?" They looked up and saw that Ethan was holding the real estate section of the local newspaper. Bruce asked Ethan why he was interested and received the typical adolescent response: "Because I want to know." Instead of getting irked, Bruce and Diane treated the question as a teachable time. They told him the purchase price, adding that there were other houses in the neighborhood that cost more and others that cost less, and then engaged him in a discussion of what makes a house a home—how a house is a reflection of the attitudes and actions of the people who live in it, and that the biggest house in the world is worthless if people are rude to each other or don't respect each other. They ended the conversation by reminding him that certain subjects, such as family finances, should stay within the family and not be discussed with others.

Bruce and Diane are financially intelligent parents, and they handled this situation skillfully for two reasons. First, they used a question to engage Ethan in conversation. Responding to a difficult question with a question of your own—rather than a pronouncement—often increases your child's willingness to both talk and listen. Second, they expanded the discussion from money to values. Bruce and Diane used Ethan's curiosity about the value of their house to create a teachable moment where they were able to talk about the intangibles that make up a home: love, caring for one another, sharing in responsibilities and so on. By pointing out that there were other houses in the neighborhood that cost less and others that cost more, they were able to talk about the need to keep money in perspective and not to use it as a measure of self-worth. If you learn to treat money only as a scorecard, they told him, you will always be disappointed. Unless you are Bill Gates, there will always be someone with more money than you.

Finally, overcome your reluctance to discuss dollar-specific questions by reminding yourself that your kids probably know more about your finances than you think they do. We live in the information age. You would be amazed, or perhaps aghast, to discover that your kids can find general answers to many dollar-specific questions on the Internet. For example, a few minutes on

Family Finances

www.hotjobs.com discloses that the average income of an experienced advertising agency account executive in Fort Wayne, Indiana ranges between $73,000 and $89,000 a year, while an experienced tool and die maker in Detroit makes an average of $55,000 to $61,000 per year. In Ethan's case, the real estate section of the local newspaper gave him the asking price for houses in the neighborhood. Refusing to answer Ethan's question when he already had an idea of the range of values would simply tell him that Bruce and Diane were either excessively secretive about money or that they didn't trust him.

Don't ever tell anyone how much . . . . . . You can fill in the blank with everything from "our house cost" to "what Daddy makes." This response is closely related to "that's not an appropriate question." Privacy is important. On the other hand, excessive secrecy breeds paranoia and distrust. Although you probably don't want your children discussing the details of your finances with their friends, you also don't want them to view the family's finances as top secret. Money paranoia as a child can lead to unhealthy money relationships as an adult. Some of you may be horrified that Bruce and Diane told Ethan how much their home cost. Consider, though, the alternative of not saying anything: instilling anxiety through excessive money secrecy. Think about how this anxiety can affect your child's development. We have worked with financial advisors who tell us that they have clients who are so secretive about their money that they won't reveal their net worth to them; it's like refusing to tell a doctor about your overall physical condition. If your words and your behavior teach that money is a subject to be kept secret, your child may grow into an adult whose money anxiety may cause him to distrust his spouse, much less his financial advisor. A child who is taught to keep money details totally secret from everyone may find it difficult to have a trusting relationship with a spouse on any level, especially with finances. Keep a sense of balance. Stress the need for privacy without instilling distrust of others. Simply point out to your children that certain issues, including the family's finances, should stay within the family.

Why don't you have your friends come over here; we have a _____, after all. You can fill in the blank with swimming pool, pool table, or any number of expensive toys that might be attractive to kids. Even suggesting to a child that his friendships are based on the family's possessions is a terrible idea. You can foster cynicism in a child, who comes to believe that his friends only like him for what he has, rather than who he is. There are parents who are blatant about this issue, telling their children that they're going to buy a pool table or elaborate video-game setup because it will help them make friends. If you can afford to buy these toys, fine, but it's not a good idea to talk about them within the context of your child's friendships.

Be thankful you don't live there. The "there" might be everything from a poor urban neighborhood to a middle-class suburb. The implication is that life must be miserable for everyone who doesn't live in a community like your own. Although it may be appropriate to talk to your child about the problems in high-crime areas of the inner city or a homeless person living in a cardboard box under a freeway overpass, you need to be cautious about associating happiness with money. Kids should understand that money can't buy love or happiness. Fostering this false linkage between money and happiness can cause kids to pursue money as a means to a full, happy life. If they become financially successful at the cost of ignoring family and friends, they don't understand why they're not happy when they have all the things money can buy.

Variations on this statement can include everything from "If I had his money, I wouldn't have a care in the world" to "You don't know how easy your life is because of what we are able to buy for you." The former, envious statement communicates the power of money to solve all problems; the latter tells your kids that their problems are rendered trivial by what you've bought for them or how hard you work, and that they have no right to feel anxious, depressed, fearful, and so on. They need to understand that money is emotionally neutral and that you can be happy or miserable no matter how much money you have.

Talking to our kids about money is important. But sometimes, what we don't say is even more important.

Kids And Charity: Becoming A Charitable Family

As much as we want our children to be good money managers—to use their allowances wisely, to balance a checkbook and so on—it's equally important to provide our children with more than basic money skills. Our kids need to grow up to be "giving" human beings in the best sense of that word. Parents who simply recite the adage "It is better to give than receive" won't nurture their kids' generous impulses. It takes more than saying the right things to raise a kind, giving child. Involving kids in charity teaches them that they can do more with money than spend it on themselves. By participating as a family in volunteer and community activities, parents help their kids develop a sense of compassion and responsibility to others.

Despite all this, some of you may find it more difficult to embrace this money behavior than you might some of our other suggestions. Part of the problem is that becoming a charitable family requires a commitment of time, something that is in short supply in our society. Just as problematic, though, is that it's tough to know where to start. If you've never been involved in volunteer activities and don't have an easy entry point (such as membership in a church group with regularly scheduled volunteer opportunities), finding the right cause or venue can be challenging. Many parents say, "I'd really like to get my family involved in a good cause" but never do anything about it.

Charitable efforts should involve more than giving a dollar to a homeless person. "Living a life of purpose" and "making a difference" are more than just nice-sounding phrases. Happiness actually requires more than making a good living or having good relationships. In 2002, Jean Chatzky, the financial editor for NBC's Today show, and Money magazine engaged RoperASW, a major market research firm, to conduct extensive proprietary research on the influence that money has on an individual's overall happiness. One of the discoveries reported by Chatzky was that people who help others are happier with most aspects of their lives—friendships, marriage, children, lifestyle,

Family Finances

financial situation and self-esteem – than those who don't. Finally, kids gain a psychological benefit from giving; it teaches them they have the power to make life better for others. This empowering lesson will serve them well in many other areas of their lives.

Start introducing your children to the concept of charity about age four, when they begin to develop the capacity for empathy, which is the ability to understand other people's feelings. Empathy forms the basis for compassion and charity.

Money is a fairly abstract concept for small children; they have difficulty dealing with abstractions and need concrete experiences. Involvement in a volunteer activity, as opposed to writing a check to a charity, is key. Modeling charitable behaviors can jump start your child's empathy and desire to give. Sherry, for instance, began modeling charitable behavior when her daughter, Tracy, was four. She explained to Tracy that there were many children whose mommies and daddies didn't have the money to buy them toys, and that she might want to gather up the toys she was "too big for" and put them in a bag. Tracy was glad to do this task, and they drove over to a shelter run by a local church; Tracy carried the bag in. As Tracy became older, they would carry out this tradition a few times a year.

These simple activities not only showed Tracy that her mom was involved in helping the disadvantaged, but they also provided an accessible process for Tracy to become involved. Giving toys to kids who can't afford them is something most young children grasp. Sherry told us that on one or two occasions, Tracy had second thoughts about some toys she had donated and decided to keep a few of them for herself. This is fine. Expect these second thoughts and don't turn a learning experience into a fight. As long as children are willing to give up some of their toys, they are on the right track. When Tracy would decide to keep a toy she had originally designated for the church group, Sherry would suggest that next time they went, Tracy might want to contribute the withheld toy. This was a good approach, in that it gave her daughter a second chance to exhibit generous behavior.

Getting your children involved doesn't require a huge investment of time and effort. Grace and Hal, for instance, took advantage of an existing charitable endeavor in which their older children were involved, an experience that had an especially powerful impact on their four-year-old daughter. Their ten-year-old and twelve-year old kids attended a local public school that had adopted a homeless shelter. Once a week, both children brought two cans of food to school for the shelter. Grace and Hal decided that the experience would be more meaningful if every family member donated a few hours once a month to work at the shelter. Even their four-year-old daughter helped stack canned goods on the lower shelves. One day, she helped stack canned peaches. That evening, the family served dinner at the shelter, and the meal included canned peaches. Now that a number of years have passed, their younger daughter still recalls how good it made her feel when she was four years old and saw the homeless eating "her" peaches. Today, all three kids continue to be active volunteers.

While younger children will usually follow their parents' lead when it comes to volunteering, teenagers are another story, especially if they haven't been involved in these activities when they were younger. In fact, when we conduct our workshops, parents often ask us how to convince a reluctant 14 or 15-year-old to get involved in good causes.

Youth groups are often a good answer. Most teenagers are open to charitable opportunities, especially when they are working in concert with other teens. If you tell your 16-year-old out of the blue that you want him to drive down to a local soup kitchen and work there every Saturday, he'll probably resist your suggestion. You're asking him to do too much too fast. A much better approach is to take the following steps:

1. Do a little research on your own to determine what youth-oriented volunteering opportunities exist in your area. Churches and other religious institutions almost always have some ongoing programs. Schools often have eco-clubs and other charitable activities.

2. Discuss your research with your child and help him create a list of opportunities for involvement that appeal to him: some kids like the adventure of going overseas to build houses; others are more interested in doing something closer to home or in an area where they have a particular skill—your son might be a baseball player who teaches the game to developmentally disabled kids, for instance. Look for opportunities to involve the entire family.

3. Once your teenager is involved, ask her about the experience periodically. Give her the chance to explore her feelings about helping others, her fears or concerns related to poverty, death or disease and her pride in taking part in selfless acts.

In the vast majority of cases, compassionate, giving adults raise compassionate, giving children. But if your child rarely witnesses behaviors that reflect your belief in the importance of charity, your caring will have less impact. Therefore, don't overlook the importance of seizing opportunities to show your child your giving side. When you see a can on a restaurant counter seeking donations to cure a disease, drop some money in the slot. When you receive something in the mail soliciting funds for a cause you believe in, tell your child about it and ask how much he thinks you should give. When there's a walk or race designed to benefit a good cause, participate as a family. The net effect will help your child live a purposeful existence, not only throughout his childhood but also when he is adult.

Our friends Art and Penny modeled charitable behavior in many ways. Their story is especially unusual in that their son, Scott, died at 17 because of a congenital heart condition. Given Scott's four major heart operations and the knowledge that his life might be short, he could have understandably become focused on his own problems. It is to his parents' credit—not to mention Scott's own, considerable courage—that this was not case. He lived a full life in a short period of time, and helping others was a major part of that life. Scott saw early in his life that volunteering was important to his parents. When Scott was three, his parents donated some of their time to help at his preschool. Scott would get tired of playing in the sandbox and would come over to help

Family Finances

Mommy and Daddy paint a wall. He wasn't a particularly good painter, but he tried, and when he became bored painting, he'd go back to playing with his friends. A few weeks before he passed away, Scott was named Outstanding Youth Volunteer for the 2003 National Philanthropy Day Award of the Heart Association. When we asked Art and Penny why Scott was so involved in helping others when he was suffering from a life-threatening condition, they said simply, "We always did things as a family and children pick up on what they see."

All of us know that role models play an important part in our children's lives. It was only ten years ago, though, that scientists found out why as a result of an Italian researcher who wanted an ice cream cone and a chimpanzee who ended up eating it!

Marco Iacoboni is an Associate Professor at the UCLA Neuropsychiatric Institute. Ten years ago, he was in Italy, engaged in a research project that involved hooking up a chimp to an electroencephalogram (EEG), a device that records the electrical impulses in the brain. It was a hot day and Iacoboni took a break to buy one of those wonderful Italian gelato cones. When he came back to the lab and started to lick the gelato cone, the EEG showed a bunch of neurons firing in the chimp's brain. Iacoboni stopped licking the cone, and the neurons stopped firing in the chimp's brain. He took another lick, and the same neurons fired. He stopped; the neurons stopped firing in the chimp's brain. Iacoboni handed the cone to the chimp. The chimp started licking it and the same neurons fired!

Research on humans showed exactly the same result. Iacoboni had discovered mirror neurons. Chimps have them. So do we. Our brains are built out of about 100 billion or so long, narrow cells called neurons. Neurons have thousands of connections at each end and "talk" to one another through tiny electrical impulses that jump from connection to connection. When a neuron sends an electrical impulse to another neuron, it is said to be "firing." Thinking and memory actually consist of neurons talking to one another through these electrical impulses.

What Iacoboni discovered was that if we engage in an intentional activity, like licking an ice cream cone or giving money to a homeless person, an observer will have the same brain activity that would have occurred had she been licking the cone or giving the money! The existence of mirror neurons makes all types of parental modeling behaviors important, especially when it comes to charitable behavior. In this day and age, children are extremely vulnerable to a hedonistic, self-absorbed lifestyle. The cynicism and irony that dominates much of the music they listen to and the television shows they watch can steer them away from good causes. The media doesn't show people who are cool and hip spending their time working in soup kitchens or trying to help others less fortunate. Instead, they focus on satisfying their need to dress in the latest styles or to provide themselves with temporary escapes through drugs and alcohol.

When you model charitable giving, though, you provide your kids with a defense against these societal messages. You give them an alternative to the jaded, self-indulgent pose of some of their peers.

As important as it is to model giving behaviors, it's just as important to provide kids with a context for a given charitable act and help them see its real world impact. Context means giving your kids a reason why they should get involved. This doesn't just mean explaining why but choosing a particular activity where the why naturally emerges. For instance, if your child's grandparent has a particular disease, participating in a walk to fund research of that disease provides children with an obvious why.

Making it real is the second goal, and it simply means turning a donation or indirect charitable action into something that kids can experience directly. For instance, if your child contributes money to the local zoo to help provide a new habitat for the kangaroo, be involved yourself and, when it's completed, take your child to see the kangaroo's new home. Abstract concepts are not effective with younger children. Though you may be able to paint a good verbal picture, there is no substitute for seeing something with your own two eyes, no matter what age you are.

Giving your kids a context for giving and making the experience real are behaviors that will help you become a charitable family. Charitable families are highly conscious of opportunities to give and they make the most of them. Volunteering strengthens family relationships and teaches kids such values as kindness, empathy, respect for others, and, perhaps even more importantly, that happiness is not dependent on what we have.

A hallmark of charitable families is volunteerism. As a parent, you need to make a consistent effort to involve your entire family in activities that benefit others. This doesn't mean you have to devote every spare moment to good works or that you have to be dictatorial and declare to your family, "Get off your butts and start helping others!" The responsibility of a financially intelligent parent, though, is to provide options for and initiate interest in activities. To help you get started, here are some possibilities:

- Visit seniors in hospitals or nursing homes.
- Help clean up at the local park.
- Become a volunteer tutor in a literacy project—especially great if your child is bilingual.
- Join a local conservation organization and participate in their activities.
- Get involved in playtime and reading stories at a children's shelter.
- Become a storyteller in a children's reading program at the local library.
- Teach basic computer skills at a senior center.
- Help maintain a local bike path or hiking trail.

If you are looking for volunteer opportunities for your family, there are many resources available to you, especially when you have an Internet connection. Volunteer Match, (www.volunteermatch.org) provides a database of volunteer activities that can be searched by zip code and sorted by activities that are great for kids, teens, seniors or groups. When we input our zip code in Los Angeles and asked for volunteer opportunities within 20 miles of our house, VolunteerMatch came up with 64 hits for kids, 314 volunteer possibilities for teens and 346 hits for groups! Action Without Borders, located in New York, maintains the Idealist.org website (www.idealist.org) which offers the ability to match volunteers with as many as 36,000 non-profits world wide. The International Association for Volunteer Effort is an international non-governmental organization that promotes volunteerism worldwide. Their website (www.iave.org) contains links to volunteer organizations in over 80 countries.

Brthdays, holidays and special events can provide a charitable option for attendees. The Center for a New American Dream (www.newdream.org) offers "115 Tips For Raising Healthy Kids in a Commercial Culture." One tip is to opt out of giving "things" as birthday gifts; if your child agrees, give her a gift certificate redeemable as a donation in her name to a charity. You might also talk with your child and see if she is interested in asking guests to bring toys that can be donated to a children's shelter. An older child might be interested in earmarking a certain percentage of the money received for a bar mitzvah or other celebration as a donation to a charitable group.

You can also talk with your child about using part of her allowance for charity. For instance, let's say you give your kid $5 per week. Add an extra fifty cents to the allowance and explain to your child that this money is for her to give to a charity she wants to support. Saving fifty cents each week adds up to $26 she can give to charity each year. To a seven-year-old, $26 is a lot of money. Take your kid to visit the organization to see how his money was spent. Maybe it went to help build that new home for the kangaroo at the zoo. That's a powerful lesson for your child: her contribution is important.

Overcoming Inertia, Maintaining Momentum

If you're like most parents, you want to model these giving behaviors but you lack the time or energy to turn your wishes into action. It may also be that you've tried to get your family involved in a volunteer effort but after an initial burst of participation, the family's interest flagged. To overcome the inertia or maintain the momentum of this money behavior, we've created two approaches that you might want to try:

Here are the top seven excuses people often give to explain why they aren't more involved in charitable activities and our comments.

1. *I am too exhausted from work to get myself or my family to volunteer for anything.* Most people find volunteer work to be energizing. Because it is so different from what both adults and children usually are doing and because it has a clear, positive goal, people become revved up and engaged. It is nothing like a job or school work, and people leave volunteering activities more energized than when they started.

2. *The only time I have to volunteer are weekends, and weekends are for relaxing and fun activities.* Charitable participation is often fun. Weekends are often the time that walks, bike rides and races for good causes are held. In addition, kids often find it enjoyable to work in a soup kitchen or help clean up the environment. These aren't sedentary, clock-watching tasks, but ones where kids are in new environments meeting people they don't normally meet.

3. *My spouse and/or kids will never go along with my volunteering suggestions.* Your spouse and kids won't go along with your suggestions if you dictate them. Instead of telling them what volunteer effort you want them to participate in, ask for their ideas. Or you might use the ideas in this chapter to give them a host of options for participation.

4. *I can't find a cause or activity that will suit everyone in my family.* The previous response is one way to deal with this excuse. Another way is to try different activities until you find one that everyone enjoys. You can plan a rotation in which you spend the first quarter of the year volunteering at one place, then switch to a new group each quarter.

5. *We regularly give money to a number of good causes; that's enough.* As we've empha-sized, writing checks is great, but it's insufficient if you want to be a financially intelligent parent. Ask yourself if you want your kids to view you as someone who says the right things (about giving) but never sees you practice what you preach. Remember, when it comes to being a financially intelligent parent, later is now!.

6. *We just don't have the time; our schedules are filled.* This is probably the most common excuse, and the best way to eliminate it is designating one hour per week as "giving time". Everyone can spare one hour. Have everyone in your family make a commitment of one hour to volunteer or serve others in some way.

7. *I want to wait until my kids are teenagers and are better able to understand why it's important to help others in need.* Remind yourself that if you wait until your kids are teenagers, it's going to be much more difficult to get them involved in charitable activities than if you start them off when they are young.

Understandably, volunteer activities sometimes take a back seat to more pressing concerns: a child's involvement in sports, school work, and a hobby like music or art. You may also have events in your life that take you away from giving activities, such as a new, time-consuming job or more travel. Nonetheless, maintaining a consistent level of involvement may be easier if you put the following rewards and recognitions program into effect:

• When you do volunteer activities with your kids, discuss these activities and tell them how and why they're making valuable contributions. Don't assume that they'll understand that they're doing good. Pointing out that you're proud of them and the specific ways in which they've helped a given individual or group will validate their participation and increase the odds they'll stick with it.

Family Finances

- Start small and build involvement rather than making a huge commitment of your family's time. If you try to do too much too fast, you'll probably alienate your kids. They're going to feel resentful if you suddenly insist that they devote each Saturday to working on an environmental clean-up project while their friends are doing whatever they want. Ideally, you'll start with a small commitment of time and it will build naturally. The reward here is that they feel like they want to be more involved rather than that it's being forced upon them.

- Watch for signs that your kids are getting bored and try and make it a more positive experience. Is the initial enthusiasm your children exhibited when you began volunteering starting to fade? Are they asking, "Do we have to?" before you leave for a volunteer activity? Do they seem to be suffering in silence as you drive toward the shelter? If so, it may be time to switch volunteer activities. Find something more to their liking. Perhaps they would prefer joining an environmental group rather than working at a shelter because global warming is what has them concerned. Perhaps you can find a time for these activities that better suits their schedules.

- Add a fun element to volunteering. Realistically, some charitable activities may involve tedious or repetitive work. No one said that doing good for others is all fun and games. At the same time, you can help your children look forward to these activities by adding something that makes it more fun. For instance, you might schedule a family breakfast at a favorite pancake house before working in a shelter on Saturday morning. You might look for a museum, hiking trail or other family activity near where the volunteering is taking place, combining the two activities. At the same time, don't turn these rewards into bribes; don't say, "If you volunteer, I'll take you to the amusement park." Instead, take advantage of the proximity of fun places or create an enjoyable ritual out of volunteering.

Ultimately, the best reward for volunteering is internal. Sooner or later, your children will feel as if they're spending their time on something meaningful; that they are doing something that really matters to others. Sometimes it takes a while for this realization to dawn on them. When it does, though, you've achieved a significant breakthrough. You have helped your children learn that everything in life doesn't revolve around them and satisfying their own needs. You have given them the chance to feel good by focusing on other people. This is a great life lesson, and one that financially intelligent parents are able to teach effectively.

From Eileen and Jon Gallo, authors of the Financially Intelligent Parent, www.fiparent.com.

Local Advisors

Deanne Thompson
Mortgage Planner
Fountainhead Mortgage, Inc.
2 Theatre Square, Suite 310
Orinda, CA 94563
www.fountainheadmortgage.com

925-247-4162

Highly reputable mortgage planning firm creates intelligent custom plans for each individual based on his/her financial goals. This may include paying off your home in the most expeditious manner, revising financial goals to accommodate changing life needs, and/or leveraging current equity to build wealth while taking advantage of shifting market conditions. Specialized in local mortgage planning services for residents of Lamorinda and Northern California.

Rick & Nancy Booth, Coldwell Banker
5 Moraga Way
Orinda, CA 94563
www.BoothHomes.com

925-212-8867

Rick and Nancy Booth are top realtors and U.C. Berkeley MBAs who specialize in residential and investment properties in Contra Costa County. They are Contra Costa natives and are experts on neighborhoods and schools.

Chapter 17

Media in the Home

Today more than ever, parents need to be involved in their children's media choices. TV, video games and the Internet can and will expose your child to images, ideas and people you may not know or understand. Educating yourself and knowing your child's media choices will not only protect your child, but also maintain you as a participant in his or her life.

TV

What You Should Know About Television

• In a year, the average child spends 900 hours in school and nearly 1,023 hours in front of a TV (Kids Health).

• The average American child will witness 200,000 violent acts on television by age 18. Kids often imitate violent behavior seen on TV because violence is often demonstrated and promoted as a fun and effective way to get what you want.

• According to research, children ages 2 to 7 are particularly frightened by scary-looking images like ugly monsters. Simply telling children that monsters aren't real won't console them, because they can't yet distinguish between fantasy and reality.

• Kids ages 8 to 12 are frightened by the threat of violence, natural disasters, and the victimization of children, whether those images appear on fictional shows, the news, or reality-based shows. Reasoning with children this age helps, so it's important to provide reassuring and honest information to help ease your child's fears. The ultimate solution, however, is to avoid such content in the first place.

Media in the Home

• Studies have shown that teens who watch abundant sexual content on TV are more likely to initiate intercourse or participate in other sexual activities earlier than peers who don't watch sexually explicit shows.

• According to the AAP, children in the United States see 40,000 commercials each year. Kids are inundated with advertisements from junk food and toy ads during Saturday morning cartoons to the appealing promos on the backs of cereal boxes.

• In a study of fifth graders, 10-year-old girls and boys told researchers they were dissatisfied with their own bodies after watching a music video by Britney Spears or a clip from the TV show "Friends" (Mundell, 2002).

TV Parental Guidelines

Modeled after the movie rating system, this is an age-group rating system developed for TV programs. These ratings are listed in television guides, TV listings in your local newspaper, and on the screen in your cable program guide. They also appear in the upper left-hand corner of the screen during the first 15 seconds of TV programs—though not all channels offer the rating system. The ratings are as follows.

• TV-Y (All Children) found only in children's shows, means that the show is appropriate for all children.

• TV-7 (Directed to Older Children) found only in children's shows, means that the show is most appropriate for children age 7 and up.

• TV-G (General Audience) means that the show is suitable for all ages but is not necessarily a children's show.

• TV-PG (Parental Guidance Suggested) means that parental guidance is suggested and that the show may be unsuitable for younger children. This rating may also include a V for violence, S for sexual situations, L for language, or D for suggestive dialogue.

• TV-14 (Parents Strongly Cautioned) means that the show may be unsuitable for children under 14. V, S, L, or D may accompany a rating of TV-14.

• TV-MA (Mature Audience Only) means that the show is for mature audiences only and may be unsuitable for children under 17. V, S, L, or D may accompany a rating of TV-MA.

V-chip (V is for "violence"). This technology was designed to enable you to block television programs and movies you don't want your child to see. All new TV sets with screens of 13" or more have internal V-chips, but separate boxes are available for TV's made before 2000. The V-chip allows you to program your TV to display only appropriately-rated shows, and block out any other, more mature shows.

The Federal Communications Commission (FCC) requires that V-chips in new TV's recognize the TV Parental Guidelines and the age-group rating system and block those programs that don't adhere to these standards.

Good TV Habits

Here are some practical ways you can make TV-viewing more productive in your home:

- Limit the number of TV-watching hours.

- Keep books, kids' magazines, toys, puzzles, board games, etc. in your living room to encourage other types of entertainment.

- Keep TV's out of your child's bedroom.

- Turn the TV off during meals.

- No TV during homework.

- Treat TV as a privilege that your child needs to earn - not a right to which he or she is entitled. Tell your child that TV-viewing is allowed only after chores and homework are done.

- Try a weekday ban. Schoolwork, sports activities, and job responsibilities make it tough to find extra family time during the week. Record weekday shows or save TV time for weekends, and you'll have more family time to spend on meals, games, and reading during the week.

- Set a good example by limiting your own television viewing.

- Check the TV listings and program reviews ahead of time for programs your family can watch together (i.e., developmentally appropriate and nonviolent programs that reinforce your family's values). Choose shows, says the AAP, that foster interest and learning in hobbies and education.

- Preview programs before your child watches them.

- Create a family TV schedule that you all agree upon each week. Post the schedule in a visible area of the house so everyone knows which programs are OK to watch and when. Be sure to turn off the TV when the "scheduled" program is over, instead of channel surfing for another show.

- Watch TV with your child. If you can't sit through the whole program, at least watch the first few minutes to assess the tone and appropriateness, then check in throughout the show.

Media in the Home

• Talk to your child about what he or she sees on TV and share your own beliefs and values. If something you don't approve of appears on the screen, you can turn off the TV, then use the opportunity to ask your child thought-provoking questions such as, "Do you think it was OK when those men got in that fight? What else could they have done? What would you have done?" Or, "What do you think about how those teenagers were acting at that party? Do you think what they were doing was wrong?" If certain people or characters are mistreated or discriminated against, talk about why it's important to treat everyone equal, despite their differences. You can use TV to explain confusing situations and express your feelings about difficult topics (sex, love, drugs, alcohol, smoking, work, behavior, family life). Teach your child to question and learn from what he or she views on TV.

Helpful Websites About Television

Parents Television Council (PTC)

www.parentstv.org

The Parents Television Council was founded to ensure that children are not constantly assaulted by sex, violence and profanity on television and in other media. The website includes movie reviews and information for filing FCC complaints.

National Institute on Media and the Family: MediaWise

www.mediafamily.org

The National Institute on Media and the Family is a national resource for research, education and information about the likely impact of media on children and families. This is the home of the Kid Wise TV ratings.

Center for Screen-Time Awareness

www.tvturnoff.org

Discuss it, learn more about it and see how others have turned it off. Screen-Time helps children and adults watch less television in order to promote healthier lives and communities.

The Internet

The Internet is now a part of daily life at home, work and school. It is a valuable tool for school projects, homework, research, hobbies and games. For all its worthiness in these areas, it can also pose a very real danger to children and adults. Advertisements, faceless friends in chat rooms and an accidental click on a pop-up are just a few ways the Internet can turn from friend to foe in an instant.

The Internet: Pornography

- Nearly 90% of children aged 8-14 have been exposed to internet pornography. Simply misspelling a URL, receiving a pop-up ad or miss-clicking on a search engine list can lead to images and text inappropriate to this age group.

- Most boys have been exposed to internet pornography by the age of 8 1/2; girls by the age of 11.

- One in five online youth aged 10-17 received a sexual solicitation or approach over the Internet in the last year. One in thirty-three received an aggressive sexual solicitation—a solicitor asked to meet in person, called on the telephone, or sent postal mail, money or gifts. One in four had an unwanted exposure to pictures of naked people or people having sex (National Center for Missing and Exploited Children, Crimes Against Children Research Center and Office of Juvenile Justice and Delinquency Prevention).

- According to NetValue, children spent nearly 65% more time on pornography sites than on game sites in September 2000. Over _ of children aged 17 and under visited an adult website, which represents 3 million unique underage visitors. Of these minors, 21% were 14 or younger and 40% were female.

- Nearly 1/3 of kids aged 10–17 who live in households with computers say they've seen a pornographic website (NPR).

The Internet: Cyber-Bullying

- "Cyberbullying" is when a child is tormented, threatened, harassed, humiliated, embarrassed or otherwise targeted by another child using the Internet or mobile phones. It has to involve a minor on both sides, or at least have been instigated by a minor against another minor.

- The methods used are limited only by the child's imagination and access to technology. A cyberbully one moment may become the victim the next. The kids often change roles, going from victim to bully and back again.

- Children have killed each other and committed suicide after having been involved in a cyberbullying incident.

- Cyberbullying may arise to the level of a misdemeanor cyberharassment charge, or if the child is young enough may result in the charge of juvenile delinquency. It typically can result in a child losing their ISP or IM accounts as a term of service violation.

- When schools try to get involved by disciplining the student for cyberbullying actions that took place off-campus and outside of school hours, they are often sued for exceeding their authority and violating the student's free speech right.

- Cyber-bullying includes sending mean, vulgar, or threatening messages or images; posting sensitive, private information about another person; pretending to be someone else in order to make that person look bad; intentionally excluding someone from an online group (Willard, 2005).

Ways to Protect Your Children Online

- Check your Web History ("History" is a toolbar selection at the top of your screen)
- If the History is cleared, this may be a sign that someone in your family has visited an inappropriate website and then "cleaned the trail."
- It is possible to restrict the types of sites the web browser will allow (controlling language, nudity, sex and violence). Various browser packages will also place a safeguard to filter your Internet.

Interacting with Others on the Internet

Just as we tell our children to be wary of strangers on the street, we need to teach them to be cautious of strangers on the Internet. While many people are reasonable and decent, there are rude, mean and criminal people out there—and they're more dangerous because they're hiding miles away behind their own computer screen and keyboard.

- Never give personal information (including real name, home address, phone number, age, race, family income, school name or location or friends' names) or use a credit card online without parental permission.

- Never share passwords, even with friends. Shared passwords provide an opportunity for people (even friends) to steal your identity and say or do things online in your name.

- Never arrange a face-to-face meeting with someone met online, unless parents approve and accompany the child at the meeting.

- Never respond to messages that make you feel confused or uncomfortable. Ignore the sender, end the communication, block the sender and tell a parent or trusted adult immediately.

- Never use bad language or send mean messages online. This is cyberbullying, and is a dangerous social game to play.

- Never assume online "friends" are who they say they are (older men often pose as adolescents or even girls to gain trust), and never assume online information is private.

Limiting Children to Appropriate Content on the Internet

Without trying, your children can be exposed to Internet materials that are pornographic, obscene, violent, hate-filled, racist or otherwise offensive. Remember, child pornography is illegal. If you see child pornography, immediately report it to the Center for Missing and Exploited Children by calling 1-800-THE-LOST (843-5678) or go to www.missingkids.org.

> While other types of material aren't illegal, it is best to keep it away from your children and out of your home.

- Discuss with your children what you consider appropriate for them: What sites are good and what areas are off limits? How much time can they spend online, and when? Set clear rules.

- Keep the Internet in a trafficked area of your home. Put the computer in the kitchen or family room.

- Pay attention to the games your older children may download or copy.

- Check into software or online services that filter out offensive materials and sites. Options include stand-alone software that can be installed on your computer, online site blocking or restrictions and children's accounts that access specific services. Be aware that children are often more computer-savvy than you, and can often circumnavigate these controls. Stay vigilant and involved!

- Ask about the Internet use policy at your local library and school.

ClickAway Computers & Networking

4916 El Camino Real
Los Altos, CA 94022
650-964-9500
472 East El Camino Real
Sunnyvale, CA 94087
www.clickaway.com
408-732-4500

Family Contract for Online Safety

-From Safekids.com

Kids' Pledge

1. I will not give out personal information such as my address and telephone number, my parents' work address or telephone number, or the name and location of my school without my parents' permission.

2. I will tell my parents right away if I come across any information that makes me feel uncomfortable.

3. I will never agree to get together with someone I "meet" online without first checking with my parents. If my parents agree to the meeting, I will be sure it's in a public place and bring my mom or dad along.

4. I will never send a person my picture or anything else without first checking with my parents.

5. I will not respond to any messages that are mean or in any way make me feel uncomfortable. It's not my fault if I get a message like that. If I do, I will tell my parents right away so they can contact the service provider.

6. I will talk with my parents so we can set up rules for going online. We will decide what time of day I can be online, the length of time I can be online, and appropriate areas for me to visit. I will not access other areas or break these rules without their permission.

7. I will not give out my Internet passwords to anyone (even my best friends) other than my parents.

8. I will be a good online citizen and not do anything that hurts other people or is against the law.

I agree to the above.

_____

Child sign here

I will help my child follow this agreement and will allow reasonable use of the Internet as long as these rules and other family rules are followed.

_____

Parent(s) sign here

Chapter 18

Pregnancy and Infant Resources

Having a baby is one of the biggest events in life. Find out about community education and resources, books and support groups that can help you through the big event and beyond.

Community Education & Awareness Programs

American Red Cross—Bay Area Chapter
1-800-520-5433

Offers reasonably priced infant CPR and first aid classes. Call for class locations, time and registration in Contra Costa County.

Automotive Coalition for Safety, Inc.
www.actsinc.org

ACTS offers a wealth of information for keeping children and adults safe in motor vehicles. This website lists child safety seat manufacturer's toll free numbers, contacts and important links to help get consumers the most out of these life saving devices.

Bay Area Crisis Nursery
925-685-8052

24-hour hotline for families with children in danger of being abused or becoming homeless.

Bay Area Poison Control Hotline
1-800-523-2222

Pregnancy and Infant Resources

California Highway Patrol

Martinez, CA

925-646-4980

CHP offers service to the community with certified technicians to help you learn proper installation of safety seats and vehicle safety. Call to make an appointment or get a referral to alternative locations.

Contra Costa Child Care Council

3065 Richmond Parkway #112
Richmond, CA 94806
www.cocokids.org

510-758-5439

Free referrals to infant, preschool and after school programs as well as childcare.

DayOne Centers, Inc.

1403 North Main Street
Walnut Creek, CA 94596
www.dayonecenter.com

Hours: Monday–Friday 9:30 am–6 pm, Saturday 11 am–6 pm & Sunday 11 am–5 pm

DayOne provides a one stop solution for all of your pregnancy, baby and early parenthood needs in a welcoming environment. We offer prenatal classes, parenting and child development workshops, new parent groups and breastfeeding consultations. Our retail assortment offers the best and safest car seats, nursing bras, breastpumps, baby carriers, car seats, strollers, feeding products, layette and toys. Receive support from our expert staff of nurses, lactation consultants and retail associates, 7 days a week.

DayOne Center Locations:

San Francisco—Laurel Village

3490 California Street 2nd Floor, Suite 203
San Francisco, CA 94118
415-440-3291

Palo Alto—Town & Country Village

855 El Camino Real
Palo Alto, CA 94301
650-322-3291

International Cesarean Awareness Network, Inc.

1-800-686-ICAN

ICAN of Mt. Diablo—Holly Wiersma

www.ican-online.org

925-947-5874

ICAN is a non profit organization dedicated to improving maternal/child health through education, providing support for cesarean recovery, and promoting vaginal birth after cesarean (VBAC). Free monthly meetings.

March of Dimes

1050 Sansome Street, 4th Floor
San Francisco, CA 94111
www.marchofdimes.com/california

415-788-2202

The mission of the March of Dimes is to improve the health of babies by preventing birth defects and infant mortality. Find information on birth defects, newborn screening, premature babies, weight gain during pregnancy and most anything you'd like to know about babies. They have an amazing pregnancy and newborn health education center on their website. March of Dimes sponsors many local events to raise awareness and money for research and programs to prevent prematurity in babies.

National Center on Shaken Baby Syndrome

www.dontshake.com

1-888-273-0071

This is national referral and information center. They provide prevention information and community education classes. They have professionals available for parents in crisis due to the stress of a baby.

National Highway Traffic Safety Administration

Contra Costa County
925-941-7989

Learn how to properly install your child's car seat from a certified seat technician.

The Nurture Center

3399 Mt. Diablo Blvd.
Lafayette, CA 94549
www.nurturecenter.com

925-283-1346
1-888-998-BABY (2229)

This is a great resource center for new and expecting parents in the East Bay. Their store offers high quality and natural products, support, resources, classes, breast pump rentals, car seats and much more.

Postpartum Depression Resources

Bay Area Postpartum Depression Stress Hotline
1-888-773-7090

Postpartum Community Support Groups
925-552-5127

Pregnancy Risk Line
1-800-822-2229

Information and assistance provided anonymously concerning substance use and abuse during pregnancy.

Grief & Loss Support Groups

Beyond Choice
Oakland, CA
510-845-4656
510-752-6755

Beyond Choice is a free formal infant loss support group for parents. This is a safe place to share stories, feelings and concerns with others who have also suffered the loss of their baby. Located at Kaiser Oakland. An ongoing event every 1st and 3rd Tuesday of each month. Both Kaiser and non Kaiser member are welcome.

The Compassionate Friends, Inc.
P.O. Box 3696
Oak Brook, IL 60522-3696
www.compassionatefriends.org
1-877-969-0010 National
1-800-837-1818 Local chapter

The mission of The Compassionate Friends is to help families through the grief process following the death of a child. This is a nonprofit, self-help support organization with no religious affiliation and no membership dues or fees. They offer understanding, friendship and hope to bereaved parents and families. TCF holds regular monthly meetings the 4th Tuesday of every month except December located at Pleasant Hill City Hall Community Room, 100 Gregory Lane from 7:30 pm–9 pm. Check website for additional locations.

M.I.S.S. Foundation

www.missfoundation.org

1-888-455-MISS

A non-profit international organization available for the immediate and continuous support of bereaved families. Contact the organization for a local support group or to start your own.

Now I Lay Me Down To Sleep

www.nowilaymedowntosleep.org

1-877-834-5667

303-596-6935

This foundation is a photography service available to bereaved parents. They believe healing is helped through remembrance. There is a network of almost 3,000 professional photographers that will come to your hospital or hospice location for a free private portrait session including touch ups. You will be given a DVD or CD to print portraits of your cherished baby. Call or log on to locate a photographer in your area.

Share

P.O. Box 19538
Sacramento, CA 95819
www.sharingparents.org

916-424-5150

National Office

www.nationalshareoffice.com

1-800-821-6819

The loss of a pregnancy, newborn, or stillbirth is tragic and overwhelming. Share Pregnancy and Infant Loss Support, Inc. understands the grieving needs of those whose lives are touched by such loss. Share offers support and recovery help both physically, emotionally and spiritually. Support is free to bereaved parents.

SIDS Alliance of Northern California

1547 Palos Verdes Mall, #301
Walnut Creek, CA 94597
www.sidsnc.com

925-274-1109

1-877-938-7437

A non profit, volunteer group dedicated to support families, communities and professionals regarding sudden infant death syndrome. Grief support, community events and outreach are available to all.

Childbirth Education

Listed below are the various education and women's centers contact information. Call your local hospital or ask your healthcare provider about prenatal, childbirth and sibling classes and programs available. Most hospitals offer a variety of prenatal classes including various natural childbirth techniques.

John Muir Women's Health Center

1656 North California Blvd., Suite 100
Walnut Creek, CA 94596
www.johnmuirhealth.com
925-941-7900

Kaiser Permanente

Contact locations to find classes available to non members.

Antioch

3400 Delta Fair Blvd., Delta Square
Antioch, CA 94509
925-779-5147

Livermore

3000 Las Positas Road
Livermore, CA 94551
925-243-2920

Martinez

200 Muir Road
Martinez, CA 94553
925-372-1198

Park Shadelands

320 Lennon Lane
Walnut Creek, CA 94598
925-906-2190

Pleasanton

7601 Stoneridge Drive
Pleasanton, CA 94588
925-847-5172

Richmond

901 Nevin Avenue
Richmond, CA 94801
510-307-2210

Walnut Creek

1425 South Main Street
Walnut Creek, CA 94596
925-295-4410

San Ramon Regional Medical Center

6001 Norris Canyon Road
San Ramon, CA 94583
sanramonmedctr.com
1-800-284-2878

Sutter Delta Medical Center

3901 Lone Tree Way
Antioch, CA 94509
sutterdelta.org
925-779-7200

ValleyCare Health System

5555 West Positas Blvd.
Pleasanton, CA 94588
www.valleycare.com
925-847-3000

Instructors, Programs & Services

The Bradley Method

www.bradleybirth.com
1-800-4-A-BIRTH

The Bradley Method teaches natural childbirth and views birth as a natural process. It is their belief that most woman with proper education, preparation, and the help of a loving and supportive coach can be taught to give birth naturally. The Bradley Method is a system of natural labor techniques in which a woman and her coach play an active part. The Bradley Method encourages mothers to trust their bodies using natural breathing, relaxation, nutrition, exercise and education.

Pregnancy and Infant Resources

Doulas of North America

www.dona.org

1-888-788-DONA (3662)

A birth doula is a woman trained to give continuous support to the laboring mother. The service of a doula includes at least one prenatal visit that will allow the birthing family to communicate their needs and prepare for the birth. Throughout your labor, your doula will use a variety of comfort measures that include (but not limited to) massage, relaxation, breathing techniques, calm music, imagery, physical support and encouragement to enhance the experience of birth. You can find certified doulas in your area to call and interview.

Hypnobirthing—The Mongan Method

www.hypnobirthing.com

1-603-798-3286

Hypnobirthing offers natural childbirth education that uses self hypnosis, breathing techniques and guided imagery to have a joyful birth experience without the use of drugs. Go to the website and click "find a practitioner" to locate an instructor near you.

Lamaze International

www.lamaze.org

1-800-368-4404

Lamaze International is a nonprofit organization whose mission is to promote, support and protect normal birth through education and advocacy. The Lamaze vision is "a world of confident women choosing normal birth." The belief is that "normal" birth should unfold naturally and free from unnecessary intervention. Go to the Lamaze website and click "expectant parents" to find an instructor in your area.

Mount Diablo Doula Community

www.mtdiablodoulacommunity.org

This group of labor and postpartum doulas serving the greater San Francisco East Bay Area have a website listing local individual doulas and a direct link to their contact information and/or website. They have photos, valuable information and offer a free "meet the doula night" once a month.

Other Fabulous Pregnancy Ideas

Get a pregnancy massage. Indulge your body a little! Call any local spa or massage therapist and ask specifically for a pregnancy treatment. You'll be glad you did! Pregnancy massages are different from normal massages; there are certain pressure points that should be avoided in a regular massage for a pregnant woman. Check out the JUST FOR MOM'S chapter for listings of local spas!

Breastfeeding Resources

Barkasy, Denise IBCLC

1430 Tampico Place
Walnut Creek, CA 94598

925-945-7100

Board certified lactation consultant available for advice and consultation for breastfeeding issues. Fee applies.

Breastfeeding.com

This website provides a wealth of information to breastfeeding mothers including breastfeeding help, medication safety, pumps, books, articles and personal stories from breastfeeding mothers.

Goodyear, Kay RN, MN, IBCLC

925-313-8986

Breastfeeding guidance, home visits, pump rental, classes. Fee applies.

Hansen, Betsy IBCLC

925-284-5298

Spanish speaking, home visits, classes and guidance. Fee applies.

La Leche League International

Northern California Chapter

www.llli.org

925-274-3748

LLL provides valuable education, information, support and encouragement to all women who want to breastfeed. Monthly meetings are held at a number of locations by trained and accredited LLL leaders. Leaders are located throughout Contra Costa County.

Marine, Mary IBCLC

925-522-0494

Breastfeeding classes, guidance, home visits and pump rentals. Fee applies.

Nursing Mothers Council

www.nursingmothers.org

650-327-6455

NMC is a non profit organization available for help to nursing mothers. Most support is provided over the phone but they offer home visits as well, free of charge. The telephone number is a 24 hour referral hotline.

The Nurture Center

3399 Mt. Diablo Blvd.
Lafayette, CA 94549
www.nurturecenter.com

925-283-1346
1-888-998-BABY (2229)

Breast Pump rentals and sales. Lactation consultant on site.

Great Books

Gentle Birth Choices

By Barbara Harper, R.N.

What to Expect When You're Expecting

By Heidi E. Murkoff

Your Pregnancy Week by Week

By Glade B. Curtis, Judith Shuler

For Dads

The Birth Partner

By Penny Simkin

My Boys Can Swim! The Official Guys Guide to Pregnancy

By Ian Davis

The Expectant Father—Facts, Tips and Advice for Dads to Be

By Armin A. Brott

Websites

www.babycenter.com

Sign up for a weekly email about the stages and development of your pregnancy. There are a lot of great articles and comment boards found on this website.

www.drspock.com

Helpful information on all stages of raising a child can be found here.

Other Resources

ABC Diaper Delivery
925-935-4502
Serving all of Contra Costa County

Kids 'n Cribs
6061-B Lone Tree Way
Brentwood, California, 94513
www.kids-n-cribs.com
925-778-2229
Hours: Monday–Saturday 10 am–6pm, Sunday 11 am–5 pm
Cribs Starting at $249 & up, car seats starting at $149 & up, strollers starting at $149 and up.

Life's First Image
11700 Dublin Blvd.
Dublin, CA 94568
www.lifesfirstimage.com
925-833-9500
For all of the expectant parents out there, now you can see your unborn baby in live 4D motion. Lifes First Image uses cutting edge ultrasound technology to bring images of your unborn baby to life. You can actually see what your baby is going to look like before he or she is born! Use our Sonostream option to allow friends and family out of town to view your ultrasound LIVE! Specials going on NOW!

Safe and Sound Child Proofing
510-832-0222

Stork News of the East Bay
www.storknews.com
1-877-969-baby (2229)
925-683-7822
An original newborn announcement service offering 8' storks in pink or blue perched on your front lawn announcing your newest bundle(s). Call for rental packages.

They Grow So Fast—Child & Maternity Consignment Store
3413 Mt. Diablo Blvd.
Lafayette, CA 94549
www.theygrowsofast.com
925-283-8976

Children's Healthcare

Because finding all of the health care resources available can be a maze of confusion, we have done our best to track down some of the best resources in the community. Read on to find state health resources, immunization information, dental services, medical practitioners and more.

Health Organizations & Services

Access for Infants and Mothers (AIM)
1-800-433-2611

If you are pregnant and uninsured, the AIM program can provide health care to women whose income is too high to qualify for Medi-cal (free) health care. All applicants must be less than 30 weeks pregnant to apply. AIM benefits pregnant women with prenatal visits, hospital delivery, full health care during the pregnancy and for 60 days after the birth, and full health care services for the baby 0 – 2 years old. Call the toll-free number for more information and to receive an application.

California Department of Health Services
www.dhs.ca.gov

916-445-4171 Dept. of Health Care Services

916-558-1784 Dept. of Public Health

The mission of the California Department of Health Services is to promote and protect the health of all Californians. It is the state's point of contact for all public health issues in California. Public health relates to the matters of health of individuals and communities.

Facts of Life Line (a service of Planned Parenthood)

www.plannedparenthood.org

1-800-711-9848

If you need to talk to someone, call this toll-free information number for health related topics such as: Planned Parenthood, birth control and family planning, pregnancy options—prenatal care, sexuality, rape, sexual abuse, harassment, sexually transmitted infections, alcohol and drugs, mental health and well-being, parenting, nutrition, diet, weight control, safety and personal growth.

Healthy Families Program

www.healthyfamilies.ca.gov.

1-888-747-1222

Healthy Families is a low-cost private health care coverage program, including dental and vision, for children ages 0–19 years. Monthly premiums are from $4 per child up to a maximum of $27.00 per family with no-cost and low-cost ($5) co-payments depending on the type of service. This program is available to single and two-parent working families who meet the income eligibility requirements (family of four with incomes at or below $45,250) and does not count property (ie savings, cars) as income. Call for an application or to receive application assistance.

Medicaid of California

www.quickbrochures.net/medicare/california_medicaid_medicare.htm

Medicaid is a federally funded, state-run program that provides medical assistance for individuals and families with limited incomes and resources. It pays for your health care costs, including doctor's visits and eye care.

You can qualify if one of more of the following statements are true.

- You have children and a limited income.
- You receive or are eligible for Supplemental Security Income (SSI).
- You're a pregnant woman who meets income requirements. For example, a family of four making $23,225 a year or less qualifies.
- Your family's assets are less than $2,000.
- You receive adoption assistance or foster care assistance.

Scope of Services:

- Inpatient hospital services
- Outpatient hospital services
- Prenatal care
- Vaccines for children
- Physician services

- Nursing facility services for persons aged 21 or older
- Family planning services and supplies
- Rural health clinic services
- Home health care for persons eligible for skilled-nursing service
- Laboratory and x-ray services
- Pediatric and family nurse practitioner services
- Nurse-midwife services
- Early and periodic screening, diagnostic, and treatment services for children under age 21

Medi-Cal

Contra Costa County Employment and Human Service Dept.

30 Muir Road
Martinez, CA 94553
www.dhs.ca.gov

925-313-7987

Medi-Cal is California's Medicaid health care program. It is supported by federal and state taxes and provides health insurance and long term coverage to low-income adults, children, elderly, and disabled people in the state. Anyone can apply for coverage as long as they meet the state's eligibility requirements. Depending on your income, Medi-Cal will be either no-cost or low-cost. If your income is higher than the Medi-Cal limits, you will have to pay a Share of the Cost (SOC) but only for the month of that medical need. Once you meet your SOC, Medi-Cal will pay the rest of your medical bills for that month. Call for more information and to see how you can qualify for Medi-Cal.

National Women's Health Info Center

www.4woman.gov

1-800-994-WOMAN (9662)

The National Women's Health Information Center (NWHIC) is a reliable and current information resource on women's health today. Free women's health information is offered on more than 800 topics through their call center and web site including: pregnancy, breastfeeding, body image, HIV/AIDS, girls' health (www.girlshealth.gov), heart health, menopause and hormone therapy, mental health, quitting smoking and violence against women.

Planned Parenthood of California

www.plannedparenthood.org

1-800-230-PLAN (1-800-230-7526)

Planned Parenthood affiliate health centers provide culturally competent, high quality, affordable health care to millions of diverse women, men and teens every year. Planned Parenthood welcomes everyone—regardless of race, age, disability, sexual orientation, or income. Planned Parenthood health centers provide care to Medicaid recipients and participate in local managed health care programs.

Each Planned Parenthood affiliate is a unique, locally governed health service organization that reflects the diverse needs of its community. Planned Parenthood health centers offer a wide range of services that may include: family planning counseling and birth control, pregnancy testing and counseling, gynecological care, Pap tests, breast exams, midlife services, emergency contraception, HIV testing and counseling, infertility screening and counseling, prenatal care, adoption referrals, primary care, and referrals for specialized care.

Local Health Services

Your Local Public Health Department provides a variety of direct public health services and programs. The primary purpose of the Local Health Department is to protect and promote the health, safety and well-being of its citizens. The Local Health Department may service the following: car seat checks, influenza vaccine, cancer screening, children's special health care needs clinic, diabetes early intervention, environmental health, family planning, immunizations, infant development, infectious disease control, school health, well child physicals, WIC, family health, cholesterol screening and more.

Contra Costa County Health Services

50 Douglas Drive
Martinez, CA 94556
www.cchealth.org
925-957-5400

Check the website for an alphabetical directory of telephone numbers for Public Health Programs.

Contra Costa County Clinic Services

597 Center Avenue, Suite 375
Martinez, CA 94556
925-313-6250

Provides a wide variety of health and wellness services through out Contra Costa County through their mobile health vans. Many of the program services are free or low-cost.

Health Centers & Clinics

Antioch Health Center

3505 Lone Tree Way 1st Floor
Antioch, CA 94509
1-800-495-8885 Appointments only
1-877-905-4545

Bay Point Family Health Center

215 Pacifica Avenue
Baypoint, CA 94565
1-800-495-8885 Appointments only
1-877-905-4545
925-427-8302 Children's dental

Brentwood Health Center

171 Sand Creek Road Suite A
Brentwood, CA 94513
1-800-495-8885 Appointments only
1-877-905-4545

Concord Health Center

3052 Willow Pass Road
Concord, CA 94519
1-800-495-8885 Appointments only
1-877-905-4545

Concord Public Health Clinic

2355 Stanwell Circle
Concord, CA 94520
1-800-495-8885 Appointments only
1-877-905-4545 Immunization and WIC services

Martinez Family Practice Center

2500 Alhambra Avenue
Martinez, CA 94553
1-800-495-8885 Appointments only
1-877-905-4545

Pittsburg Health Center

2311 Loveridge Road
Pittsburg, CA 94565
1-800-495-8885 Appointments only
1-877-905-4545

Richmond Health Center

100 38th Street
Richmond, CA 94804
1-800-495-8885 Appointments only
1-877-905-4545
510-231-1240 Dental Clinic

N. Richmond Center for Health

1501 Third Street
Richmond, CA 94801
1-800-495-8885 Appointments only
1-877-905-4545

Dental Assistance

The following is a list of dental clinics and services in Contra Costa County that provide low-cost or free dental services. Eligibility must be met for each individual. Contact a location for more information.

County Clinics

Bay Point Family Health Center

215 Pacifica Avenue
Bay Point, CA 94565
925-427-8302

Martinez Dental Clinic

2500 Alhambra Avenue
Martinez, CA 94553
925-370-5300

Pittsburg Dental Clinic

2311 Loveridge Road
Pittsburg, CA 94565
925-431-2501

Richmond Dental Clinic

100 38th Street
Richmond, CA 94805
510-231-1240

Community Clinics

Brookside Community Health Center

2023 Vale Road, Suite 107
San Pablo, CA 94806
510-215-9092

La Clínica de la Raza—Monument

2100 Monument Boulevard,
Pleasant Hill, CA 94523
925-363-2000

La Clínica de la Raza—Pittsburg

335 East Leland Road,
Pittsburg, CA 94565
925-431-1250

Local Practices

Little Smile Makers Children's Dentistry

4536 Dublin Blvd.
Dublin, CA 94568
www.littlesmilemakers.com

925-828-9000

Little Smile Makers, we specialize in dental care for children. Growth monitoring, Air abrasion, Sealants, Digital X-rays=less radiation, Child-friendly environment, Nitrous oxide, oral sedation or general anesthesia

Pediatric Dentistry San Ramon

2301 Camino Ramon, Suite 284
San Ramon, CA 94583
www.pediatricdentistry-sanramon.com

925-806-0322

925-806-0310 Fax

Hours: Monday–Thursday 8 am–4:30 pm, Fridays and Saturdays 8 am–1 pm.

Prices: Vary by service

Pediatric Dentistry San Ramon is a new, fun, high tech, digital dental office devoted to dental care for all children. Our board-certified pediatric dentists provide various modalities for dental treatment such as nitrous, sedation, and general anesthesia. Our staff and doctors strive in making your child's visit as pleasant and positive as possible. The American Academy of Pediatrics and Pediatric Dentistry recommend that children see a dentist by their first birthday. Visit us at www.pediatricdentistry-sanramon.com.

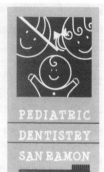

Robin Williams Orthodontics

901 Sunvalley Blvd., Suite. 201

Concord, CA 94520

www.DrRobinWilliams.com

925-680-4503

Offers a family-friendly environment and the most up-to-date technologies to provide beautiful smiles using clear or conventional braces, retainers and Invisalign®. Dr. Williams is a certified orthodontic specialist and is recognized as one of the top 5% Invisalign® providers in North America. Most insurance accepted; client financing available.

Eye & Vision Care

InfantSEE
American Optometric Association

www.infantsee.org

InfantSEE is a public health program designed to insure that eye and vision care becomes an integral part of infant wellness care to improve a child's quality of life. Under this program, member optometrists will provide a comprehensive infant eye assessment within the first year of life as a no-cost public health service.

An InfantSEE assessment between six and 12 months of age is recommended to determine if an infant is at risk for eye or vision disorders. Since many eye problems arise from conditions that can be identified by an eye doctor in the infant's first year of life, a parent can give an infant a great gift by seeking an InfantSEE assessment in addition to the wellness evaluation of the eyes that is done by a pediatrician or family practice doctor.

The web site can search by zip code for a participating optometrist near you under the Dr. Locator link. You can also subscribe to the InfantSEE Newsletter.

Lerner Eye Center

2333 San Ramon Valley Boulevard, Suite 145

San Ramon, CA 94583

www.lernereyecenter.com

925-820-9600

Immunizations

Immunizations play an important role in keeping your children healthy and preventing life threatening diseases. California has state recommended vaccines for children birth thru 12th grade. The following information was obtained from the California Department of Health Services and the National Center for Disease Control. For more information, contact your health care provider or local Public Health Department.

Children's Healthcare

What Shots Does My Child Need, and When?
(Information provided by CDHS)

Immunizations have been so successful at preventing disease that many parents have never seen most of the illnesses and complications that vaccines prevent. But these diseases still exist. Your child needs immunizations to be protected from them.

The CDHS recommends that children get the following immunizations before they begin kindergarten:

- Chickenpox vaccine (two doses)
- Tdap
- Hepatitis A
- Hepatitis B
- Hib
- MMR (two doses)
- Polio
- Pneumococcal conjugate vaccine
- An influenza vaccine every year in the fall

*HepB is taken in 3 doses. If given at birth, skip 4 month dose. If started at 2 months, give 3rd dose at least 4 months after 1st dose

They also recommend that children get the following immunizations at 11–12 years old:

- Tdap booster
- Human papillomavirus vaccine (for girls only)
- Varicella (chickenpox) booster (if they haven't had chickenpox)

Day Care, Head Start and K thru 12th Grade require:

DTP, HepB, Hib, MMR, Polio and Varicella.
Check with your practitioner or the local Public Health Department for age and vaccine schedules as boosters are needed at various age intervals.

For More Information:

A free copy of the "Parents Guide to Childhood Immunization" can be downloaded or requested online. This is a 94 page booklet introducing parents to 12 childhood diseases and the vaccines that can protect children from them. There are two ways for you to get a copy: Print your own copy at www.cdc.gov/nip/publications/parents-guide/ or order a free booklet from the National Immunization Program by filling out a section of the online order form at the link above.

American Academy of Pediatrics (AAP)

www.aap.org

The mission of the AAP is to attain optimal physical, mental, and social health well-being for all infants, children, adolescents and young adults.

American Medical Association (AMA)

www.ama-assn.org

The AMA disseminates up-to-date information on health and medical practice, medical ethics and education to physicians and to the public.

Bill and Melinda Gates Children's Vaccine Program (Gates CVP)

www.childrensvaccine.org

Gates CVP was established to promote equal access to lifesaving vaccines worldwide. This site provides information on advocacy issues, clinical issues, service delivery, immunization financing, safe injections, other related organizations, etc.

Every Child By Two (ECBT)

www.ecbt.org

The goals of ECBT are to raise awareness of the critical need for timely immunization and foster putting in place a systematic way to immunize all of America's children by the age of two.

Immunization Action Coalition (IAC)

www.immunize.org

They offer abundant useful information about immunization, including information about immunization resources and their newsletter "Needle Tips".

National Immunization Program (NIP)

www.cdc.org

This is a comprehensive web site that provides immunization information to the public and health professionals, including training, education materials, promotions, statistics, vaccine safety and disease surveillance.

National Network for Immunization Immunization (NNII)

www.immunizationinfo.org

This is information for the public, health professionals, policymakers, and the media about immunization. Site includes immunization news, a vaccine information database and a guide to evaluating vaccination information on the Web.

Health Education Resources

American Heart Association
East Bay Division
426 17th Street Suite 300
Oakland, CA 94612
510-904-4000
510-904-4004 Fax

American Red Cross of the Bay Area
85 Second Street
San Francisco, CA 94105
www.bayarea-redcross.org
415-427-8000

American Cancer Society
East Bay Metropolitan Unit
1700 Webster Street
Oakland, CA 94612
www.cancer.org
510-832-7012

California Department of Health Services
2151 Berkeley Way, Room 708
Berkeley, CA 94704
www.dhs.ca.gov
510-540-2067

California Department of Mental Health Headquarters
1600 9th Street, Room 151
Sacramento, CA 95814
1-800-896-4042

California Poison Control Center
San Francisco Division
San Francisco General Hospital
1001 Potrero Avenue Room 1E86
San Francisco, CA 94110
1-800-876-4766

Pediatric Urgent Care Clinics

Doctor's Medical Center

2000 Vale Road
San Pablo, CA 94806
www.doctorsmedicalcenter.org

510-970-5000

This is the only 24-hour emergency care serving West Contra Costa County. Across the street there is a pediatric clinic open 8 am–7:30 pm. It is advised to call first thing in the morning to get an appointment at 510-215-9092.

Night Owl Pediatrics

425 Gregory Lane, Suite 203
Pleasant Hill, CA 94523
www.nightowlpediatrics.com

925-288-3600

Hours: Monday–Saturday 1 pm–11 pm and Sunday 10 am–9 pm

Night Owl Pediatrics is an innovative after-hours pediatric urgent care dedicated to providing expert care to infants, children and adolescents. In this child friendly environment they offer care for illnesses and injuries when your primary physician's office may be closed. The physicians are nationally recognized leaders in Pediatrics and Pediatric Emergency Medicine, and the nursing team is specialized in the urgent needs of children.

Park Avenue Walk-In Clinic

2600 Park Avenue, Suite 105
Concord, CA 94520
www.parkaveclinic.com

925-825-8181

Park Avenue Walk-In Clinic provides affordable, reliable medical services in three languages (Spanish, English and Persian). They always welcome new patients and you do not need an appointment for urgent visits. The office is open Monday through Saturday. Discounted fees for non-insured patients.

San Ramon Regional Medical Center

6001 Norris Canyon Road
San Ramon, CA 94583

925-275-9200

San Ramon Regional Medical Center operates a 24-hour emergency service. The physicians are trained in emergency medicine, and additional specialist doctors are on-call.

Walnut Creek Urgent Care

112 La Casa Via
Walnut Creek, CA 94598
925-930-8200

Featuring General Practice medicine, doctors, clinics and urgent care. Operates 7 days a week. Call for office hours.

Miscellaneous

TruKid

www.Trukid.com
510-463-2682

TruKid's provides skincare, sunscreen, hair care and hero products for families who want only the best ingredients, attention and dedication to their well being. TruKid's products are free of all harmful chemicals in order to protect our children's growing bodies. Our products do not contain any controversial ingredients like Parabens, Sodium Lauryl Sulfate and Phthalates. TruKid creates Healthy Habits that'll last a lifetime (like brushing your teeth).

LoveBugs Salon

3746 Mt. Diablo Blvd., Suite 122
Lafayette, CA 94549
www.lovebugslice.com
925-283-7700

Hours: Open Monday–Saturday, Call for appointments

At LoveBugs private, garden-like salon nestled just above Mt. Diablo Blvd. in Downtown Lafayette, the trained staff will discretely take care of your lice problem with LoveBugs non-toxic, lice removal technique and special formula that were invented in Greece over 40 years ago. The LoveBugs Salon will service you as quickly, painlessly, and efficiently as possible. Recommended by San Francisco Bay Area Pediatricians. Convenient free Wi-Fi access while you wait.

St. Rose Hospital Women's Imaging Center

27200 Calaroga Avenue
Hayward, CA 94545
www.strosehospital.org
510-264-4000

The Women's Imaging Center at St. Rose Hospital has state-of-the-art equipment for digital breast imaging, bone mineral density testing and diagnostic ultrasound all found in a facility that offers comfort, privacy in a caring environment to meet the needs of today's women. The center is accredited by the American College of Radiology and all examinations are performed to meet specific guidelines of the ACR and the FDA. We also use "mammopad" to cushion the breast for more comfort.

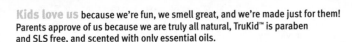

State and Community Resources

I t's often said "It takes a village to raise a child." This statement couldn't be more true. In this chapter you'll find the
programs and resources available in the "village." Browse
through this chapter even if you don't think that you'd utilize
any of the programs and services. Chances are, you might know
someone who can.

211 Information & Referral

Dial 211 Or 800-273-6222

211 San Francisco—United Way of the Bay Area Help link

www.211.org

This is one of the best resources in the state. Their operators are friendly, helpful and they have a
vast database full of information that you need. Contact them to find local, nonprofit, state, government, health and human services information.

These typical calls tell the story of how critical The Information and Referral Center is to the community:

Typical Calls

• My husband just left me. I have very little money and very little food. The rent and utilities
are coming due. I have four children. What do I do?

• My mom was recently diagnosed with Alzheimer's. I know we are going to need help as her
symptoms get worse. Are there support groups? What about day care when my husband
and I are at work?

State and Community Resources

- My daughter is being abused by her live in boyfriend, but she denies it's a serious problem. Can he stop abusing her without counseling? How can I express my concerns for her without alienating her?

- I think I'm pregnant. I haven't been feeling well for about a month. I came to the East Bay with my boyfriend because his family lives here, but he left. They don't like me and won't tell me where he is. I need a place to stay and a free pregnancy test. I don't have any money.

- I have a very bad sore on my leg that is infected, but I cannot afford a doctor. Who will examine my leg?

- Sometimes I get really out of control with my anger and yell at my wife. Last night I beat her up and I don't ever want to do it again. Where can I go to get some counseling?

Food Assistance Programs

Did you know ...

- In 2004 California ranked as the 15th worst state for food insecurity.
  -California Food Advocates 2004

- 25,104 children live in poverty in Contra Costa County. *-2004 California Food Advocates*

- More than 325,251 individuals (both adults and children) are vulnerable to the indignity of hunger, frequently skipping meals or eating too little.
  -U.S. Census Bureau 2003 American Community Survey

- Preschool and school-aged children who experience sever hunger have higher levels of chronic illness, anxiety and depression, and behavior problems than children without hunger. As a result these children miss more days of school and are less ready to learn when they are able to attend school. *-Center on Hunger and Poverty*

Food Bank of Contra Costa County

www.foodbankccs.org

1-800-870-FOOD

The mission of the Food Bank of Contra Costa is to alleviate hunger and provide an efficient, coordinated system for collecting and distributing food that reduces food waste and increases public awareness regarding hunger and food security issues in Contra Costa and Solano counties. Through the activities of the Food Bank and its member agencies, all people in Contra Costa and Solano counties will receive at least one nutritious meal a day. Call their toll free number or look them up on the web to find a local food distribution location.

Catholic Charities of the East Bay

Catholic Charities services people in need who reside in the East Bay. These include the elderly, the hungry and the homeless, families and children, immigrants and refugees, the unemployed and underemployed, people with HIV/AIDS, victims of violence, at-risk youth, and others. Below are Contra Costa locations:

Concord Family Service Center

3540 Chestnut Street
Concord, CA 94519
925-825-3099

Brentwood Family Service Center

654 Third Street
Brentwood, CA 94513
925-308-7775

Richmond Family Service Center

2369 Barrett Avenue
Richmond, CA 94804
510-234-5110

Food Stamps

There are over 240 food stamp offices in California operated by local county welfare departments. Low-income people may apply for food stamps at any office located in the county where they live. To find information on a food stamp office near you, call the Contra Costa County Social Services Department nearest you.

Richmond

510-412-3280
510-231-8114

Hercules

510-262-7709

Antioch

925-706-4990

Martinez

925-313-7987

State and Community Resources

St. Vincent de Paul Charity Services

Contra Costa County Diocese

2210 Gladstone Drive

Pittsburg, CA 94565

925-439-5063

The Society of St. Vincent de Paul offers tangible assistance to those in need on a person-to-person basis. It is this personalized involvement that makes the work of the Society unique. This aid may take the form of intervention, consultation, or often through direct dollar or in-kind service. An essential precept of the Society's work is to provide help while conscientiously maintaining the confidentiality and dignity of those who are served. The Society recognizes that it must also assume a role of advocacy for those who are defenseless or voiceless. Some 12 million persons are helped annually by Vincentians in the United States.

To secure assistance, contact the nearest Catholic Church in your community and ask if they have a Society of St. Vincent de Paul Conference in their parish or know of one in the vicinity. Or, look for "Society of St. Vincent de Paul" in your local White Pages to find the District or Diocesan Council closest to you.

Woman, Infants and Children (WIC)

www.wicworks.ca.gov

1-888-942-9675 Info line

1-800-852-5770 State office

WIC is a supplemental nutrition program for Women, Infants and Children. WIC provides nutritious foods, nutrition education, breastfeeding support and counseling to pregnant, postpartum and breastfeeding women. Eligibility is determined by income level, medical and nutritional need. Information can be obtained by calling the toll-free number. You will be directed to the WIC office closest to you.

To qualify for WIC, you must:

- Have a family income less than WIC guidelines. A person receiving Medicaid or food stamps already meets the eligibility requirements.

- Have a special nutritional need.

- Be one of the following groups: pregnant, breastfeeding, a woman who has just had a baby, an infant, a child less than 5 years of age.

State and Community Resources

WIC Income Guidelines
185% Federal Poverty Level
Effective May 1, 2007 to June 30,2008

Gross Income				
# of persons in Family Unit	Annual	Monthly	Weekly	Hourly
1	$18, 889	$1, 575	$364	$9.09
2	$25,327	$2,111	$488	$12.18
3	$31,765	$2,648	$611	$15.28
4	$38,203	$3,184	$735	$18.37
5	$44,641	$3,721	$859	$21.47
6	$51,079	$4,257	$983	$24.56
7	$55,517	$4,794	$1,107	$27.66
8	$63,955	$5,330	$1,230	$30.75
8+	$6,438 per added family member	$537 per added family member	$124 per added family member	$3.10 per added family member

Child Abuse

What is the definition of child abuse?

- Neglect is the failure to provide for a child's basic needs including physical, medical, educational and emotional needs.

- Physical abuse is physical injury (ranging from minor bruises to severe fractures or death) as a result of punching, beating, kicking, biting, shaking, throwing, stabbing, choking, hitting, or otherwise physically harming a child.

- Sexual abuse includes activities such as fondling a child's genitals, penetration, incest, rape, sodomy, indecent exposure, and commercial exploitation through prostitution or the production of pornographic materials.

- Emotional abuse is a pattern of behavior that impairs a child's emotional development or sense of self-worth. This may include constant criticism, threats, or rejection, as well as withholding love, support, or guidance.

State and Community Resources

Child Abuse Prevention Council of Contra Costa County

1410 Danzig Plaza, Suite 110
Concord, CA 94520
925-798-0546

They promote the safety of children, raise community awareness, provide resources and support families.

Children's Hospital—Oakland

510-428-3000 24-hours a day

510-428-3742 business hours

Provides counseling and services for children and families affected by violence or abuse and conduct forensic medical exams of children.

Contra Costa County 24-hour Child Abuse Hotline

925-646-1680 Local

1-877-881-1116 National

Your report will be kept confidential. You may also remain anonymous.

Contra Costa County Child Protection Services

510-374-3324 West County

925-427-8811 East County

925-646-1680 Central County

Contra Costa County Crisis Hotline

1-800-833-2900

Resource and referral service

Mental Health Countywide Access

1-888-678-7277

925-646-2800 Adult Services

925-646-5488 Children's Crisis

Provides referrals for counseling and mental health services, housing, medical services, parenting, and other issues for children and adults.

National Child Abuse Hotline

1-800-422-4453

YWCA Contra Costa County

1320 Arnold Drive
Martinez, CA 94553
www.ywca.org

925-372-4213

The mission of the YWCA is to empower women and girls and to eliminate racism. They provide shelter for battered women, children's advocacy and intervention services, childcare, after school recreation, etc. Call for locations near you or visit their website.

Domestic Violence

Did you know...

- In the United States, every nine seconds a woman is physically abused by her husband.

- Battering is the single largest cause of injury to women in the United States. It exceeds all rapes, muggings, and auto accidents combined.

- Child abuse is 15 times more likely to occur in families where domestic violence is present. Men, who have witnessed domestic violence as children, are three times more likely to abuse their own wives/partners than children of non-violent parents.

- Children living in poverty are 18-22 times more likely to be abused, 44 times more likely to be neglected, and 60 times more likely to die from maltreatment, compared to children living above the poverty line. *-Public Health Department*

Contra Costa County District Attorney's Office

925-646-2200 County Main
925-646-2625 Central/East
925-646-4770 Domestic Violence/Sexual Assault

National Domestic Violence Hotline

1-800-799-7233

They offer 24-hour crisis counseling and referrals to local agencies. They have interpreters available for most languages.

Bay Area Legal Aid

1025 MacDonald Avenue
Richmond, CA 94801
510-250-5270 Contra Costa West
925-219-3325 Contra Costa East

Bay Area Legal Aid provides free legal services in the priority areas of housing, domestic violence, public benefits and health access to eligible clients.

Building Futures with Women and Children
1-866-A-WAY-OUT
1-866-292-9688

This is a certified volunteer and staff 24-hour, 365 days a year telephone service providing intake for shelters, offering outside referrals, resources and telephone counseling.

Northern California Family Center
www.ncfc.us
925 370-1990

Northern California Family Center is a non-profit agency that has been serving the needs of Contra Costa County since 1978. They offer counseling and mediation for individuals and families, and are the headquarters for the Safe Place Program for both Contra Costa and Solano counties. N.C.F.C. serves children and adolescents, individuals, parents, couples and families. They help with a wide variety of problems ranging from depression and anxiety, domestic violence and abuse, to personal growth and development. Fees are based on a sliding scale.

Martinez
2244 Pacheco Blvd.
Martinez, CA 94553

Walnut Creek
1621 North Broadway
Walnut Creek, CA 94598

Shelter Hotline
1-800-799-6599

The Shelter hotline is a toll free number dedicated to assisting homeless persons to access the adult interim-housing program (shelter).

Shepherd's Gate
Livermore, CA
925-443-4283

They provide a safe haven for women and their children who are homeless because of abusive relationships, addictions, loss of financial support and other factors. Shelter and transitional housing.

STAND Against Domestic Violence
1410 Danzig Plaza, 2nd Floor
Concord, CA 94520
925-676-2845
1-888-215-5555 Crisis line

STAND! is the sole provider of comprehensive domestic violence services in Contra Costa County. During the past three years STAND! has answered more than 18,000 calls on their crisis line. They have housed nearly 300 women and 350 children in their emergency shelter and in their transitional housing facility. Nearly 800 clients received legal advocacy services. All STAND! services are provided by a highly trained, culturally competent group of 58 staff and more than 100 volunteers.

Ethnic & Minority Groups

Asian Women's Resource Center

940 Washington Street
San Francisco, CA 94108
415-421-8827
415-788-1008

AWRC is a project of the Methodist Church established to address the unmet needs of women and children in geographic and social transition. In providing a safe sanctuary to live in and programs that develop life skills, they empower these individuals, fostering stability, self-reliance, self-determination, and full access to opportunity.

The Friendship House

Association of American Indians Inc.

Lodge Program

1815 39th Avenue
Oakland, CA 94601
510-535-7100

Residential program for women with their children.

NAACP

Berkeley Youth Council Branch

www.naacp.org
510-435-3101
1-877-NAACP-98

They provide protection and enhancement of civil rights for African Americans.

ANewAmerica Community Corporation

1918 University Avenue
Berkeley, CA 94704
510-540-7785

ANewAmerica's mission is to promote the long-term economic empowerment of new Americans—new citizens, immigrants, and refugees—and to encourage their full participation in the political, social and cultural growth of America.

Housing

SHELTER, Inc.

1815 Arnold Drive
Martinez, CA 94553
925-335-0698
1-800-808-6444 Crisis Line

SHELTER Inc. is working to realize a vision: A Home For Everyone. Everyday, one family at a time, SHELTER, Inc. staff and volunteers help individuals find and keep a home. As an innovative leader, they have helped 3,707 Contra Costans, half of them children, overcome homelessness last year. If you or someone you know is homeless, call the Crisis Line.

East Bay Housing Organization.

538 9th Street, Suite 200
Oakland, CA 94607
510-663-3830

East Bay Housing Organization is a 23-year-old affordable housing advocacy coalition dedicated to working with communities in Alameda and Contra Costa counties to preserve, protect and expand affordable housing opportunities through education and advocacy.

Eden Council for Hope and Opportunity (ECHO)
Contra Costa Office
925-679-8023

ECHO's goal is to promote equal access in housing and provide support services. They offer rental assistance, housing assistance, and counseling. They provide education and charitable assistance to the general public in matters relating to obtaining and maintaining housing.

YWCA Contra Costa County

1320 Arnold Drive
Martinez, CA 94553
www.ywca.org

925-372-4213

The mission of the YWCA is to empower women and girls and to eliminate racism. They provide shelter for battered women, children's advocacy and intervention services, childcare, after school recreation, etc.
Call for locations near you or visit their website.

Job Training & Education

One-Stop Career Centers

The Career Centers are a self-directed career resource center. The Center provides resources and services that are focused on assisting any member of the community with job search, training information and career assistance.

Brentwood

281 Pine Street
Brentwood, CA 94513
925-634-2195

Concord

4071 Port Chicago Highway, Suite 250
Concord, CA 94520
925-671-450

Pittsburg

415 Railroad Avenue
Pittsburg, CA 94565
925-439-4875

Richmond Main

330 25th Street
Richmond, CA 94804
510-307-8014

Richmond Downtown

334 11th Street
Richmond, CA 94801
510-970-7379

San Pablo

2300 El Portal Drive
San Pablo, CA 4806
510-374-7440

State and Community Resources

School Districts

Contra Costa County Office of Education

77 Santa Barbara Road
Pleasant Hill, CA 94523
www.cccoe.k12.ca.us

925-942-3388

Call the school district in your area for more information about receiving your high school diploma and/or adult education through their alternative education program. The Contra Costa County Office of Education's website lists all the schools and their phone numbers by District, Adult Education, Community Colleges and Occupational Programs.

Legal Assistance

Contra Costa County Bar Association

704 Main Street
Martinez, CA 94553
925-686-6900

925-825-5700 Lawyer Referral and Information Service

The CCCBA provides many services for the public, including referrals, pro bono legal assistance for those who qualify, attorney-client fee disputes and more. Contact the office for assistance.

Bay Area Legal Aid

Contra Costa County

1025 MacDonald Avenue
Richmond, CA 94801
510-250-5270
510-233-9954

Eastern Contra Costa County

1901 Railroad Avenue
Danville, CA 94565
www.baylegal.org

925-219-3325

Provides free legal services to low income residents of 7 Bay Area Counties.

State and Community Resources

The Law Center
Contra Costa County
1-866-543-8017

Helps low income residents of CCC to obtain free or low cost legal services. Will also assist in getting pro bono representation or other assistance for callers who do not qualify for, or cannot be helped by, existing legal services.

Public Defender
925-335-8000

Represents low-income defendants in criminal court.

TAX AID
www.tax-aid.org
415-963-8911

Non-profit service that prepares taxes for low income Bay Area families or individuals for free.

Rape

Rape is a serious crime. If you have experienced sexual abuse, there are several outreach programs available to you. You deserve legal support, confidential help, and a safe place to go. Contact your local police department or any of the listed outreach centers for help.

Bay Area Woman Against Rape
510-845-7273 Hotline

CALCASA
www.calcasa.org
916-446-2520

The California Coalition Against Sexual Assault provides information on how to seek help, file a police report and provide information for emotional healing.

A Safe Place
510-536-SAFE (7233)

A Safe Place offers shelter and professional supportive services to victims of domestic violence.

Tri-Valley Haven for Woman
925-449-5842 Hotline

Home Hazards

Sometimes there are dangers lurking inside our home and we don't even know it. The California Department of Health and several other Federal Agencies are there to help. Safeguard your home and family from these hidden dangers:

Carbon Monoxide

www.carbonmonoxidekills.com

Carbon Monoxide is produced whenever a fuel such as gas, oil, kerosene, wood, or charcoal is burned. Hundreds of people die accidentally every year from CO poisoning caused by malfunctioning or improperly used fuel-burning appliances and even more die from CO produced by idling cars. Symptoms include severe headaches, dizziness, mental confusion, nausea or faintness. If you think you are suffering from CO poisoning get fresh air immediately, and go to an emergency room. For more information on ways to prevent Carbon Monoxide Poisoning please visit the link listed above.

Lead

www.epa.gov/lead/

Visit the link above to find out important information about lead and how it can affect your health. Most problems come from old paint and water pipes. If you suspect that you have lead-based paint in your house you should have your children tested for blood-lead levels.

Radon

www.epa.gov/radon/

Radon is an odorless, tasteless gas that causes no immediate symptoms or health effect. It occurs from natural radioactive decay of uranium and radium in the soil. It enters the home through cracks and openings in the concrete that are in contact with the ground. Lung cancer is a long-term affect of continual exposure to Radon. To test your home for Radon levels look for Radon test kits that say "meets EPA requirements".

Mold

www.epa.gov/mold/moldguide.html

Molds are usually not a problem indoors, unless mold spores land on a wet or damp spot and begin growing. Molds have the potential to cause health problems. Molds produce allergens (substances that can cause allergic reactions), irritants, and in some cases, potentially toxic substances (mycotoxins). Inhaling or touching mold or mold spores may cause allergic reactions in sensitive individuals. Allergic responses include hay fever-type symptoms, such as sneezing, runny nose, red eyes, and skin rash (dermatitis). Allergic reactions to mold are common. They can be immediate or delayed. Molds can also cause asthma attacks in people with asthma who are allergic to mold. In addition, mold exposure can irritate the eyes, skin, nose, throat, and lungs of both mold-allergic and non-allergic people. Symptoms other than the allergic and irritant types are not commonly reported as a result of inhaling mold.

Special Needs and Disabilities

H aving a child with special needs or disabilities requires parents to have additional resources at hand. Read on to find out about helpful programs and services in our community to ensure that your child utilizes the opportunities that are available.

The American Academy of Pediatrics' studies on early child development have proven that a child's environment and what a child experiences during their first few years of life significantly influences the development of their brain structure. By accessing specialized services for your child you will enhance and improve their abilities for the rest of their life.

Did you know . . .

- Almost 20% of all people with disabilities live in poverty households, which is twice the rate of people without disabilties. *-Center for Technical Assistance and Training*

- The likelihood of abuse and neglect is between 1.6 and 3.9 times greater for children with disabilities. *-U.S. Department of Health and Human Services*

- 45 million Americans suffer from psychiatric disorders *-Surgeon General of the United States*

- 1 in 5 will suffer from mental illness sometime in life. *- National Institute of Mental Health*

- Only 49% of people in mental health services are currently receiving treatment. *-Valley Mental Health*

- One of every 33 babies is born with a birth defect. A birth defect can affect almost any part of the body. The well being of the child depends mostly on which organ or body part is involved and how much it is affected. *-Center for Disease Control and Prevention*

Special Needs and Disabilities

- In 1996 and 2000 respectively, 29% and 35% of children with intellectual disabilities also had one or more other developmental disabilities. *-MADDSP.*

If you suspect that your child is not developing appropriately contact your pediatrician to discuss your concerns. For children with developmental delays early intervention and treatment can make a significant difference. California offers free services for all children 0–3 through the early start program. Your pediatrician can refer your child to a regional center for an evaluation by a developmental pediatrician to determine if there are any significant concerns that need to be addressed.

711 California Relay Service
Dial 711

711 is a new statewide and nationwide telephone relay number that connects standard voice telephone users with the deaf, hard of hearing and/or speech disabled people who use text telephones (TTYs).

ADA Technical Assistance Center

www.ada-infonet.org

1-800-514-0301 Voice

1-800-514-0383 TTY

They provide individuals and organizations with information relating to the Americans with Disabilities Act.

Alexander Graham Bell Association of California
Local Chapter—SF Bay Area

www.agbell.org

www.calif-agbell.org

The California Chapter of the Alexander Graham Bell Association for the deaf and hard of hearing is an organization that supports and empowers people who are hearing impaired and function independently. They "Advocate Independence through Listening and Talking." Check the website to find a list of Parent and Educator volunteers who offer advice and/or direction.

Autism Society of America

www.autism-society.org

1-800-328-8476

This is a volunteer-run, non-profit organization that offers networking, support, information and referral for parents and professionals who are involved with autism, PPD and Asperger's Syndrome.

Blind Babies Foundation

1841 Franklin Street, 11th Floor
Oakland, CA 94612
www.blindbabies.org

510 446-2229

Free: Low Income

Families of infants and preschoolers (ages birth to sixth birthday) who are visually impaired/blind receive early intervention services in their homes, consultation with ophthalmologists and schools, family support and referrals. Serves the following counties: Alameda, San Francisco, Contra Costa, Santa Clara, Sonoma, Napa, Marin, San Mateo, Kings, Tulare, Solano. Please call main Oakland office for services in all locations.

California Chapter of the National Association Autism Spectrum Parent Support

110 East Richmond
Point Richmond, CA 94801

510-237-9454

This is a parent-to-parent support group for families in and around West Contra Costa and Alameda Counties. They share strategies, resources and more.

California Department of Education

1430 N Street
Sacramento, CA 95814
www.cde.ca.gov

916-319-0800

Contact the State Office of Education or your school district to find any special schools, programs and services available for your child.

CARE Parent Network

1340 Arnold Drive, Suite 115
Martinez, CA 94553
www.careparentnetwork.org

1-800-281-3023

CARE Parent Network is a one-stop family resource center serving families of children with disabilities. They provide support, information and resources specially designed to help families meet the unique challenges of parenting a child with special needs.

Contra Costa County Office of Education

77 Santa Barbara Road
Pleasant Hill, CA 94523
www.cccoe.k12.ca.us

925-942-3388

Contact the CCCOE to find special education schools and resources.

CHADD of Northern California

369 Santa Paula
San Leandro, CA 94579
www.chaddnorcal.org

1-888-759-9751

Children and Adults with Attention Deficit Disorder can call the number given above to receive information about support group meetings. They provide support through education, advocacy and great resources. They also offer information on summer camps as well as parenting classes.

Contra Costa County Community Services Department

2425 Bisso Lane, Suite 120
Concord, CA 94520
www.co.contra-costa.ca.us/depart/service/faq
www.ehsd.org

925-646-5540

CCC Community Services' mission is to support individuals and families to thrive as contributing members of the community by providing high quality services and learning opportunities. They have a very large Child Development program to provide early childhood education services. They also have many other valuable comprehensive services.

Disability Rights Education and Defense Fund Inc.

2212 Sixth Street
Berkeley, CA 94710
www.dredf.org

510-644-2555

Founded in 1979 by people with disabilities and parents of children with disabilities, the Disability Rights Education and Defense Fund, Inc. (DREDF) is a national law and policy center dedicated to protecting and advancing the civil rights of people with disabilities through legislation, litigation, advocacy, technical assistance, and education and training of attorneys, advocates, persons with disabilities, and parents of children with disabilities.

Down Syndrome Clinic
Children's Hospital Medical Center of Northern California

747 52nd Street
Oakland, CA 94609
510-428-3550

Patients are seen with general public.

Down Syndrome Connection of the Bay Area

117 A Town & Country Drive
Danville, CA 94526
www.dsconnection.org
925-362-8660

The Down Syndrome Connection, consisting of parents, educators, therapists and concerned persons, seeks to optimize the quality of life for individuals with Down syndrome by offering direct services to them and their caregivers, and by educating the general public about the special concerns and unique contributions of the Down syndrome community.

Easter Seals Bay Area
Early Intervention

180 Grand Avenue, Suite 300
Oakland, CA 94612
www.bayarea.easterseals.com
510-835-2131

Easter Seals has been helping individuals with disabilities and special needs, and their families, live better lives for more than 85 years. From child development centers to physical rehabilitation and job training for people with disabilities, Easter Seals offers a variety of services to help people with disabilities address life's challenges and achieve personal goal

After School Programs

7425 Larkdale Avenue
Dublin, CA 94568
925-828-8857

Timpany Center of Santa Clara County

730 Empey Way
San Jose, CA 95128
408-295-0228

Child Development Center

75 Hawthorne Street
San Francisco, CA 94105
415-744-875

Enhanced Learning and Growth Center (ELGC)

Sindy Wilkinson, Director

2940 Camino Diablo, Suite 105
Walnut Creek, CA 94597
www.learningandgrowth.com

925-934-3500

ELGC provides HANDLE® and counseling services to assist people efficiently overcome life's challenges in a gentle, safe, caring environment.

HANDLE: Holistic Approach to NeuroDevelopment and Learning Efficiency is an effective, non-drug, non-invasive approach that addresses the underlying causes for conditions commonly diagnosed as learning disabilities, ADD/ADHD, Autistic Spectrum Disorders, and other perplexing behaviors.

Through an observational assessment and a home based program of individualized activities we address irregularities in how a person accesses and processes information, gently reorganizing and strengthening the body/brain connection. This results in easier and more productive functioning. Free informational evenings are given regularly.

Epilepsy Foundation of Northern California

5700 Stoneridge Mall Road, Suite 295
Pleasanton, CA 94588

925-224-7760

1-800-632-3532

The Epilepsy Foundation of Northern California is your local center providing services to families affected by epilepsy since 1953. They are dedicated to serving the nearly 133,000 people with epilepsy in our region and seek to ensure that people with seizures are able to participate in all life experiences and prevent, control and cure epilepsy.

NAMI—National Alliance for the Mentally Ill

www.nami.org

1-800-950-6264

NAMI is the nation's largest grassroots mental health organization dedicated to improving the lives of persons living with serious mental illness and their families. They provide educational programs for families and friends of those who suffer from a mental illness. Education programs, Family to Family, Hope for Tomorrow, Bridges, Crisis Intervention, Advocacy, Research, and Support Groups are located throughout the state.

If you have a family member that struggles with any form of mental illness, NAMI's education programs and support groups would be beneficial for you and your family. Often people don't see mental illness for what it is: an illness. Mental illness becomes an issue that most families would rather just sweep under the rug and not talk about. People often rationalize someone else's mental illness with comments like, "If they would just decide to change their lives everything would be fine!" or "They're just feeling sorry for themselves and being lazy" NAMI can help your family and friends better understand mental illness, how to deal with it and how to support others who struggle with it.

Local NAMI's:

Concord

www.namicontracosta.org

925-465-3864

Livermore

www.namitrivalley.org

925-980-5331

Oakland

www.nami-alamedacounty.org

510-835-5010

Pittsburg

925-431-2622

National Fragile X Foundation

Walnut Creek, CA
925-938-0300
1-800-688-8765

The National Fragile X Foundation unites the Fragile X community to enrich lives through educational and emotional support, promote public and professional awareness, and advance research toward improved treatments and a cure for Fragile X.

Northern California Fragile X Association

www.fragilex.org/html/nocfxa.htm
510-864-4268

The Northern California Fragile X Association of California (NOCFXA) was formed by parents to promote public awareness of Fragile X Syndrome with special emphasis on educators and health professionals. They also provide a forum for families of children with Fragile X to meet and share their ideas, concerns, and problems; and to support scientific research on Fragile X Syndrome.

Regional Center of the East Bay

Oakland Main Office: Airport Corporate Center

7677 Oakport Street, Suite 300
Oakland, CA 94621
510-383-1200

The Regional Center of the East Bay supports persons with developmental disabilities and their families with the tools needed to achieve lives of quality and satisfaction, and builds partnerships that result in inclusive communities.

RCEB provides or coordinates quality services and supports that may include:

- Adaptive Equipment and Supplies
- Behavioral Intervention Programs
- Camps
- Child Care
- Diapers
- Early intervention
- Independent Living Services
- Infant Programs
- Parent Services
- Respite Services and many other services

The Regional Center is a fantastic resource. A child can remain a member for life if they qualify by diagnosis. After you apply, you will have a case manager assigned to your child who will help get your child the services he/she needs. Contact the office closest to you to receive more information on how the RCEB can be a part of your life.

Salvio Pacheco Square (Concord Office)

2151 Salvio Street, Suite 365
Concord, CA 94520
www.rceb.org
925-798-3001

Ronald McDonald House

1640 Scott Street
San Francisco, CA 94115
www.rmhc.org
415-673-0891

The mission of Ronald McDonald House Charities, Inc. (RMHC®) is to create, find and support programs that directly improve the health and well being of children. RMHC has three core programs that help families in need: Ronald McDonald House®, Ronald McDonald Family Room® and Ronald McDonald Care Mobile®. As the most well-known program, Ronald McDonald House provides a home away from home for families of seriously ill children receiving treatment at nearby hospitals. Visit their website to find a local chapter.

Shriners Hospitals for Children—Northern California

2425 Stockton Blvd.
Sacramento, CA 95817
916-453-2000
1-800-237-5055

Shriners Hospitals for Children Northern California is the newest addition to the Shriners 22-hospital pediatric healthcare system. It is the only hospital in the Shriners system that houses facilities for treatment of all three Shriner specialties—spinal cord injuries, orthopaedics, and burns. The hospital features 80 patient beds, nine parent apartments, five state-of-the-art operating rooms, a high-tech Motion Analysis Lab, and an entire floor devoted to research. The Shriners Hospital in Sacramento provides many ways in which professionals work in partnership to make a difference in the lives of children.

To best ensure comprehensive recovery for the patient and the patient's family, the Northern California Hospital medical staff includes a broad range of sub-specialists, including pediatricians, general and plastic surgeons, urologists, psychiatrists, geneticists, neurologists, and many others. Children up to age 18 are eligible for admission to Shriners Hospitals for Children if, in the opinion of the physicians, there is a reasonable possibility they can benefit from the specialized services available. Admission is based solely on a child's medical needs, regardless of financial need. There is no charge for any care or services provided within Shriners Hospitals for Children facilities.

Special Needs Alliance, Attorneys

www.specialneedsalliance.com

1-877-572-8472

The Special Needs Alliance is a national, non-profit organization committed to helping individuals with disabilities, their families and the professionals who represent them. The attorneys are some of the most credentialed public benefits and disability law attorneys in the country, many of whom are themselves parents and siblings of children with disabilities.

Services include:
- Drafting Special Needs Trusts
- Drafting Special Needs Wills
- Estate Planning
- Financial Planning & Legal Assistance for disabled persons
- Living Trusts
- Conservatorship
- Guardianship
- Personal Injury and Medical Malpractice Settlements
- Preparation of Trust Accountings
- Structured Settlement Negotiations
- Trust Distributions

Spina Bifida Association of Greater Bay Area
Traci Whittemore—President

100 West South Street

Tracy, CA 95376

www.sbaa.org

925-215-1503

The mission of the Spina Bifida Association is to promote prevention and enhance the lives of all those affected by it.

United Advocates for Children of California

1401 El Camino Avenue, Suite 340

Sacramento, CA 95815

information@uacc4families.org

916-643-1530 UACC

1-866-643-1530

916-643-1532 TA Center

1-866-807-7687

The United Advocates for Children of California is a non-profit advocacy organization that works on behalf of children and youth with serious emotional disturbances and their families. UACC is a family organization with the majority of the board and staff being parents of youth who have received services for mental health. They have a very informative website as well as local assistance in Alameda County.

United Cerebral Palsy of the Golden Gate

1970 Broadway, Suite 115
Oakland, CA 94612
www.ucpgg.org

510-832-7430

Your local UCP affiliates provide support groups for consumers and their family members and friends, share important information and services across the developmental disability community and advocate for improved services. Activities and Camps for Special Needs*

*CARE Parent Network has a listing of most camps available in Northern California listed on their website at www.careparentnetwork.org

Residential Camps

Berkeley Toulumne Family Camp

(Berkeley Office of Recreation)

510-981-5140

Located near Yosemite National Park. Youth must be accompanied by a parent or guardian. Some tents are ramped and there is a wheelchair accessible shower. Some terrain may be difficult without assistance.

Boy Scouts of America

www.sfbac.org

510-577-9000 ext. 118

Offers summer camping experiences for all Scouts ages 7–18.

Building Bridges Camp

650-696-7295 ext.105

This is a camp for children ages 6–18 who use augmentative and alternative communication systems and assistive technology for learning.

Camp Costanoan

www.viaservices.org

408-243-7861

Sponsored by Via Services, Inc., this camp serves children ages 5+ and adults with developmental and physical disabilities. Located in the Santa Cruz Mountains, it offers fully-equipped playground, nature trails, petting zoo, horseback riding ring, arts and crafts, music, sports and 2 heated pools. Sessions are 6, 8 or 9 days.

Camp Krem

www.campingunlimited.com

510-222-6662

Offers 7, 8, 10 and 12 day sessions for all ages and disabilities, June through August near Santa Cruz.

Camp Lotsafun

www.camplotsafun.com

1-888-825-2267

Offers one week, two week and weekend mini sessions of structured indoor and outdoor activities for individuals 6+.

Camp New Hope

www.campnewhope.net

Designed for children and adolescents diagnosed with bipolar/mood disorder. Located in the Livermore Valley, this camp includes a variety of activities, in a supportive environment.

Camp Ohlone

www.ebparks.org

510-562-2267

This is an accessible campsite in the Sunol area, which is available for group use. The camp is part of the East Bay Regional Parks.

Camp Okizu

www.okizu.org

415-382-9083

A free resident camp for children with cancer and their family members.

Disabled Sports USA and Tahoe Adaptive Ski School

www.dsusafw.org

530-581-4161

They operate year-round programs for people age 4+. All disabilities are welcome, but some activities may require specific abilities. Summer programs include lake kayaking, cycling, rafting, water skiing, golf, 4-wheel drive outings and family camp. Cost and dates vary.

Easter Seals Camp
831-684-2380
www.centralcal.easterseals.com

They feature various activities at two different locations.

Enchanted Hills Camp
www.lighthouse-sf.org
415-431-1481

For children ages 5–19, who are legally blind, ambulatory and do not require 1:1 supervision. Located at Mt. Veeder above Napa Valley.

Muscular Distrophy Association
415-673-7500

Free program at Camp Harmon in the Santa Cruz mountains. For people ages 6–21 who have a neuromuscular disease. Swimming, arts and crafts and recreational activities. Contact them for dates.

Sequoia Lake
1-800-989-1165

Near Kings Canyon National Park, boasts swimming, backpacking, boating, sports and much more for teens 13-17 with diabetes. For 8–12 year olds, Larry L. Hillblom Camp is available.

YMCA Camp Jones Gulch
www.campjonesgulch.org
650-747-1200

Located in La Honda, it offers a wide variety of camping experiences for children ages 8–18. Children with disabilities are integrated on a case-by-case basis.

Day Camps & Programs

Albany Contra Costa Youth Soccer League
510-301-1747
TOPSoccer program for youths with disabilities. West County youth are encouraged to apply.

Special Needs and Disabilities

Albany Sports Camp
510-559-8208

Baseball, basketball, t-ball, soccer, tennis, capture the flag, bocce ball, board games, art and more.

Adventures and Outings and B.A.T.I (Blind Accessible Trails Initiative)
www.borp.org

510-849-4663

Offers a wide range of recreation opportunities to children and youth with disabilities.

Aquatics Program
510-238-2196

A swimming program through City of Oakland Office of Parks and Recreation. Learn-to-swim programs for special needs.

Axis Dance Company
510-625-0110

Offers creative dance for youth with and without disabilities. Wheelchair accessible.

Bay Area Disabled Sailors
www.baads.org

415-281-0212

Offers a free Bay sailing opportunity for disabled individuals on Sundays at noon in San Francisco.

Berkeley High School Pool
510-644-6843

Very warm indoor pool open to people with disabilities. Check for pool dates and times.

Berkeley Recreation Program
510-981-6651

After-school and all day summer program for kids and teens with and without disabilities.

Cal Adventures
www.oski.org

510-642-4000

Accepts children with mild disabilities. Offers outdoor activities like rock-climbing, sailing and windsurfing for youth ages 8–17.

Camp Tzofim

www.opjcs.org

510-530-9222

Summer day camp opportunity for kids K thru 9th grade. Daily schedule from 9 am to 4 pm sponsored by the Jewish Community Center. The camp has experience with the inclusion of children with disabilities on a case-by-case basis.

City of Danville

925-314-3477

Recreation Activities for the Developmentally Disabled (RADD) offers dances and excursions for ages 15 and up.

City of Pleasant Hill

www.pleasanthillrec.com

925-676-5200

Offers a dance once a month for individuals with developmental disabilities.

City of Richmond

510-620-6814

Disabled people's recreation center after school program for youth ages 11–22.

City of Walnut Creek Specialized Recreation

925-256-3531

Offers weekly activities, including yoga and karate, and special trips.

Halleck Creek 4-H Riding Club

www.halleckcreekranch.org

415-662-2488

Located in Marin County, they operate three sessions year-round every Saturday, including therapeutic exercises on horseback. FREE.

Music and Movement for the Special Needs Child

510-524-9283

Meets at the Albany Community Center for children 6 and under.

Oakland Ice Center Special Skater Program

www.oaklandice.com

510-268-9000

Special date and time slots for families of children with mental or physical challenges. Wheelchair/walkers allowed on ice with volunteer help.

Pinole-Hercules Little League Challenger Division

510-433-9943

Baseball program for children with disabilities.

Quest Therapeutic Camp

925-743-1370

For ages 6–14, camp provides intensive therapeutic intervention for kids with behavioral, emotional and social problems and/or LD, ADD. Not for children with major physical handicaps. 6:1 ratio.

Special Olympics of Northern California

www.sonc.org

925-944-8801

The Special Olympics mission is to provide year-round sports training and athletic competition for persons 6 years and older with mental retardation. A wide variety of activities are available.

Great Sports Websites

www.adaptiveadventures.org Adaptive Adventures

www.disabledonline.com Disabled Online

www.ushf.org Hand Cycling Federation

www.nscd.org National Sports Center for the Disabled

www.narha.org North American Riding for the Handicapped Association

General Disability Websites

www.capc-coco.org Child Abuse Prevention Council

www.cckids.org Contra Costa Children and Family Council

www.chadd.org Children and Adults with ADHD

www.chasa.org Children's Hemiplegia and Stroke Association

www.childrensdefense.org Children's Defense Fund

www.cocokids.org Contra Costa Childcare Council

www.contracostaarc.com CARE Parent Network - see Contra Costa ARC

www.crisis-center.org Crisis Center

www.dds.cahwnet.gov/index.cfm California Dept of Developmental Services

www.dmh.cahwnet.gov California Dept of Mental Health

www.downsyndrome.com Down Syndrome

www.dralegal.org Disability Rights Advocates

www.dredf.org Disability Rights Education Defense Fund

www.easter-seals.org Easter Seals

www.ehsnrc.org Early Head Start National Resource

www.enablingdevices.com Battery operated switch toys and devices

www.familyvoices.org Information on how to contact senators

www.fathersnetwork.org Supports fathers raising children with special needs

www.handspeak.com Animated sign language dictionary

www.healthyfamilies.ca.gov Healthy Families

www.irissoft.com/cccc Contra Costa County online resource database

www.naeyc.org National Association for Young Children

www.nationalautismassociation.org National Autism Association

www.ncd.gov National Council on Disability

www.pai-ca.org Protection and Advocates

www.php.com Parents Helping Parents
   -offers support and information group meetings.

www.preemies.org Information on preemie development

www.rarediseases.org Information on rare disorders

www.rceb.org Regional Center of the East Bay

www.specialchild.com Disability awareness, includes success stories and horror stories

www.ssa.gov/kids/parents1htm Social Security information for parents

www.supportforfamilies.org Support for Families

www.ucpa.org United Cerebral Palsy Association

www.wecarebmcc.org We Care

www.zerotothree.org Zero to Three

Special Needs and Disabilities

Helpful Mental Illness Websites

www.dbsalliance.org Depression and Bipolar Support Alliance

www.surgeongeneral.gov Surgeon General's Conference on Children's Mental Health

www.pfizer.com/brain Pfizer Brain: The World Inside Your Head

www.depressedteens.com A resource for recognizing depression in teens

www.nationaleatingdisorders.org National Eating Disorders Association

www.aacap.org Academy of Child and Adolescent Psychiatry

www.mentalhealth.org Mental Health Organization and Information Center

www.drugdigest.org Drug Digest

www.hopeandrecovery.org Hope and Recovery

www.anred.com Anorexia Nervosa and Related Eating Disorders

Chapter 22

Volunteer Opportunities

About 61.2 million people volunteered through, or for, an organization at least once between September 2005 and September 2006. Was your family one of them?

-Bureau of Labor Statistics of the U.S. Department of Labor 2006.

Did you know...?

- Youth who volunteer are more likely to do well in school, graduate, vote and be philanthropic. *-UCLA 1991*

- Young people who volunteer just one hour or more a week are 50% less likely to abuse drugs and engage in at-risk behavior. *-America's Promise 2001*

- 89% of households give to charities each year

- 44% of American adults volunteer

- 83.9 million American adults volunteer each year. That's equivalent to over 9 million full-time employees at a value of $239 billon!

A new study shows that people who begin volunteering as students are

- Twice as likely to volunteer as adults.

- More likely to give generously to charitable causes.

- More likely to teach their own children to volunteer.

Information courtesy of www.independentsector.org

What to Expect When Volunteering

Volunteering is different for every person. No two people will have the same volunteer experience. But there are few things that will be similar in volunteering, especially when you are first starting. Here's a short list of what you should know and what you might expect.

- Be prepared to work.
- Be prepared to wait.
- Be prepared to fill out forms.
- Wear reasonable clothes.
- Remember you only get out what you put in.

The Rights of a Volunteer.

- Volunteerism itself is a basic right.
- Volunteers have a right to know what is expected of them.
- Volunteers have the right to good training.
- Volunteers have the right to be treated with respect.
- Volunteers have the right to set goals for themselves.
- Volunteers have the right to feel good about their service.

Ways Kids Can Help

Donate food to a food pantry. Have your child pick out one item each time you go to the store. When you get a bagful, take it to a local food pantry.

Walk to fight disease. Many organizations use walks to increase awareness and raise funds. Kids 5 and up can walk a few miles, and you can push little ones in a stroller.

Put together activity boxes. If your child is a preschooler, decorate shoe boxes and fill them with a deck of cards, small games and puzzle books for kids at the local hospital.

Visit a nursing home. Your family can be matched with one person to call on regularly.

Clean up. Pick up litter at a local park or while you take a walk in the neighborhood.

Deliver Meals. You and your child can bring both hot food and companionship to homebound people through local charity food service.

Ideas taken from Parents Magazine—January 2005

Random Acts of Kindness

Your family can start a chain of kindness beginning with one generous act. Then make it a daily practice. Promote kindness in your home, school, community and workplace. Below are some simple acts of kindness to help you get started.

- Offer your mail carrier a refreshing drink, a kind word or a thank you note.

- Phone or email someone who has been going through a tough time, just to let them know you care.

- Pick up any litter you see as you go through the day.

- Leave a bouquet of flowers on someone's front door step.

- Make a balloon bouquet and ask the nurses at a children's hospital to deliver it to a child.

- Leave an extra large tip for the waitress the next time your family goes out for dinner. Talk to your children about generosity.

- Send a "thinking of you" card to someone you know who is struggling.

- Call a friend or family member and tell them why you love them

Information provided by www.doinggoodtogether.org

Volunteer Centers & Locations

Here are a few of the many organizations in need of volunteers throughout Contra Costa County and Northern California.

ARF—Animal Rescue Foundation

2890 Mitchell Drive
Walnut Creek, CA 94598
www.arf.net
925-256-1ARF
800-567-1ARF

Their mission is to rescue and adopt animals in Contra Costa. ARF asks for a six month commitment of at least eight hours a month if you are interested in volunteering your time.

Contra Costa County Library

www.ccclib.org/donations/volunteer.html

Be prepared to be able to volunteer at least 2 hours a week.

East Bay Trail Dogs

www.eastbaytraildogs.org

925-443-3925

East Bay Trail Dogs is a volunteer organization maintaining trails throughout Contra Costa and Alameda Counties.

East Bay Volunteer Opportunities

www.volunteerinfo.org/eastbay.htm

There are many organizations in need of volunteers. This is a great site you can go to for organizations needing volunteers in Contra Costa and Alameda Counties.

Families First Inc.

www.familiesfirstinc.org

800-698-4968

This organization provides a safe environment and shelter for families and children in California.

Greater Bay Area Make-A-Wish Foundation

235 Pine Street, 6th Floor
San Francisco, CA 94104
www.makewish.org

800-464-9474

Guide Dogs for the Blind
California Campus

350 Los Ranchitos Road
San Rafael, CA 94903
www.guidedogs.com

415-499-4000

Provide loving homes for puppies in training for the visually impaired. Be prepared for the commitment to last anywhere from 13 to 14 months.

Habitat for Humanity East Bay

2619 Broadway
Oakland, CA 94612
www.eastbayhabitat.org/volunteer

510-251-6304

Loaves and Fishes of Contra Costa

www.loavesandfishesofcontracosta.org

925-837-8758

This non-profit organization was developed to provide hot meals for very low income people. They do so by providing them with food and a place to go where they can enjoy their meal in a friendly atmosphere, without charge, conditions or questions.

Make-A-Wish Foundation of Sacramento and Northeastern California

3841 North Freeway Blvd., Suite 185
Sacramento, CA 95834
www.makeawish-sacto.org

888-828-9474

Volunteers help grant wishes to children who are suffering from a life-threatening medical condition.

Meals on Wheels of Contra Costa, Inc.

1330 Arnold Drive, #252
Martinez, CA 94553
www.mealsonwheelsofcontracosta.org/volunteer.php

866-669-6697

The Meals on Wheels volunteer program enlists the support of volunteers who are able to deliver hot meals once a week during a lunch hour to senior citizens who are unable to provide a meal for themselves. There are many different chapters throughout Contra Costa County. Visit the website and contact the local chapters in your area for more volunteer opportunities.

Ronald McDonald House of San Francisco

1640 Scott Street
San Francisco, CA 94115
www.ronaldhouse-sf.org/volunteer.asp

415-673-0891

Volunteering is vital to this organization. There are many ways to help such as providing a-home-away-from-home for ill children and home cooked meals for the families after they come home from their hospital visits. To achieve this, duties may include welcoming families, stocking supplies, and any special projects that need to be done. Please plan to work two three-hour shifts per month; six month minimum. For meals, once a month is preferred, but one-time meals are accepted as well.

Special Olympics East Bay

3480 Buskirk Avenue #340
Pleasant Hill, CA 94523
www.sonc.org

925-944-8801
510-553-9833

Volunteer Opportunities

Stitches from the Heart

3316 Pico Blvd.
Santa Monica, CA 90405
www.stitchesfromtheheart.org

866-472-6903

If you can knit or crochet, this might be up your alley. This organization provides hats, booties, sweaters and blankets for premature babies and babies in need. All of the items are hand knit or crocheted by volunteers and then donated to hospitals across the country.

The Holiday Project

www.holiday-project.org

The mission of The Holiday Project is to enrich the experience of the holidays by arranging visits to people confined to nursing homes, hospitals and other institutions.

The Volunteer Center of Contra Costa

2401 Shadelands Drive, Suite 112
Walnut Creek, CA 94598
www.helpnow.org

925-472-5760

The following are service and program opportunities provided through the Volunteer Center:

Community Agency Services
Help non-profit organizations list their volunteer opportunities and build capacity for volunteers.

Corporate Volunteer Council (CVC)
Convene monthly meetings for local business representatives to discuss corporate volunteer programs.

Disaster Response Network
Work with agencies to help them plan for effective use of emergentcy volunteers in the event of a disaster.

Holiday Volunteer Services
Teach individuals and groups about holiday activities and volunteer opportunities by publishing a comprehensive holiday list.

Volunteer Services
Individuals or groups can find more that 600 opportunities available for community volunteers.

Youth Action Council (YAC)
Students join the Youth Action Council to serve as leaders by planning volunteer events.

<u>Annual Special Event:</u>

Human Race

A community fundraiser that helps 100 community non-profits by encouraging walkers to raise funds through pledged sponsorships.

Information provided by www.volunteercentersca.org/vc_walnutcreek.htm

Volunteer Match

www.volunteermatch.org

Find volunteer opportunities throughout the country on this site.

The Volunteer Services Program for Contra Costa County

www.co.contra-costa.ca.us/vol.html

This site provides a directory of organizations that are in need of volunteer services.

Volunteer Solutions

www.volunteersolutions.org

They connect those who desire to volunteer with opportunities in their community. Enter your zip code to see the organizations near you in need of service.

Youth Service America

www.ysa.org

This national center provides the largest database of volunteer opportunities for people ages 5–25.

Have We Missed Anything?

Do you know of a great family activity, resource or family oriented business? Have any great "Mama" secrets you'd like to share? Send us your information and we may include it in next year's edition!

Bay Area Mama
2527 Camino Ramon, Suite 300
San Ramon, CA 94583
www.bayareamama.com

To purchase additional copies of The Bay Area Mama Handbook
please visit our website: www.bayareamama.com

Emergency Preparedness

Nearly half of Americans say they believe a major natural disaster or terrorist attack is likely to occur in their area in the next five years. A new survey shows more than three quarters admit they are ill prepared should it occur. According to a recent Red Cross poll 60% of Americans have not put together a basic disaster kit nor have they created a family emergency plan. Are you one of them? Read on to find helpful information to safeguard your family in the event of a natural disaster.

-Consumer Affairs www.consumeraffairs.com/news04/2006/01/disaster_planning.html

Ready America

www.ready.gov

Some of the things you can do to prepare for the unexpected, such as assembling a supply kit and developing a family communications plan, are the same for both a natural or man-made emergency. However, as you will see throughout the pages of **Ready.gov**, there are important differences among potential terrorist threats that will impact the decisions you make and the actions you take. With a little planning and common sense, you can be better prepared for the unexpected.

Ready Kids

www.ready.gov/kids

Ready Kids is a tool to help parents and teachers educate children in grades 4–5 about emergencies and how they can help get their family prepared. Ready Kids is part of the U.S. Department of Homeland Security's Ready campaign, a national public service advertising campaign designed to educate and empower Americans to prepare for and respond to natural disasters, potential terrorist attacks and other emergencies. The Ready Kids web site features age-appropriate, step-by-step instructions on what families can do to be better prepared and the role kids can play in this effort.

Water & Food

Water

- One gallon of water per person per day, for drinking and sanitation.
- Children, nursing mothers, and sick people may need more water.
- If you live in a warm weather climate more water may be necessary.
- Store water tightly in clean plastic containers such as soft drink bottles.
- Keep at least a three-day supply of water per person.
- Use rainwater, streams, rivers and other moving bodies of water, ponds, lakes, and natural springs for emergency water sources. Be sure to purify.

Food

- Store at least a three-day supply of non-perishable food.
- Select foods that require no refrigeration, preparation or cooking and little or no water.
- Include vitamin, mineral and protein supplements in your stockpile to assure adequate nutrition.
- Pack a manual can opener and eating utensils.
- Choose foods your family will eat.
- Ready-to-eat canned meats, fruits and vegetables
- Protein or fruit bars
- Dry cereal or granola
- Peanut butter
- Dried fruit
- Nuts
- Crackers
- Canned juices
- Non-perishable pasteurized milk
- High energy foods
- Vitamins
- Food for infants
- Comfort/stress foods

Clean Air

Many potential terrorist attacks could send tiny microscopic "junk" into the air. For example, an explosion may release very fine debris that can cause lung damage. A biological attack may release germs that can make you sick if inhaled or absorbed through open cuts. Many of these agents can only hurt you if they get into your body, so think about creating a barrier between yourself and any contamination.

Nose and Mouth Protection

You should have face masks or dense-weave cotton material, that snugly covers your nose and mouth and is specifically fit for each member of the family. Do whatever you can to make the best fit possible for children.

Be prepared to improvise with what you have on hand to protect your nose, mouth, eyes and cuts in your skin. Anything that fits snugly over your nose and mouth, including any dense-weave cotton material, can help filter contaminants in an emergency. It is very important that most of the air you breathe comes through the mask or cloth, not around it. There are also a variety of face masks readily available in hardware stores that are rated based on how small a particle they can filter in an industrial setting.

Given the different types of attacks that could occur, there is not one solution for masking. For instance, simple cloth face masks can filter some of the airborne "junk" or germs you might breathe into your body, but will probably not protect you from chemical gases. Still, something over your nose and mouth in an emergency is better than nothing. Limiting how much "junk" gets into your body may impact whether or not you get sick or develop disease.

First Aid Kit

In any emergency a family member or you yourself may be cut, burned or suffer other injuries. If you have these basic supplies you are better prepared to help your loved ones when they are hurt. Remember, many injuries are not life threatening and do not require immediate medical attention. Knowing how to treat minor injuries can make a difference in an emergency. Consider taking a first aid class, but simply having the following items on hand can help you stop bleeding, prevent infection and assist in decontamination.

Things you should have:

- Two pairs of Latex, or other sterile gloves (if you are allergic to Latex).
- Sterile dressings to stop bleeding.
- Cleansing agent/soap and antibiotic towelettes to disinfect.
- Antibiotic ointment to prevent infection.
- Burn ointment to prevent infection.
- Adhesive bandages in a variety of sizes.
- Eye wash solution to flush the eyes or as general decontaminant.
- Thermometer

- Prescription medications you take every day such as insulin, heart medicine and asthma inhalers. You should periodically rotate medicines to account for expiration dates.
- Prescribed medical supplies such as glucose and blood pressure monitoring equipment and supplies.

Things it may be good to have:

- Cell Phone
- Scissors
- Tweezers
- Tube of petroleum jelly or other lubricant

Non-prescription drugs:

- Aspirin or non-aspirin pain reliever
- Anti-diarrhea medication
- Antacid for upset stomach
- Laxative

Portable Kits

Emergency Supplies

Water, food, and clean air are the essential items for survival. Each family or individual's kit should be customized to meet specific needs, such as medications and infant formula. It should also be customized to include important family documents.

Recommended Supplies to Include in a Portable Kit:

- Water, amounts for portable kits will vary. Individuals should determine what amount they are able to both store comfortably outside the home and be able to transport to other locations.
- Food, at least a three-day supply of non-perishable food.
- Battery-powered radio and a NOAA Weather Radio with tone alert and extra batteries for both.
- Flashlight and extra batteries.
- First Aid kit.
- Whistle to signal for help.
- Dust mask or cotton t-shirt, to help filter the air.
- Moist towelettes for sanitation.
- Wrench or pliers to turn off utilities.
- Can opener for food if kit contains canned food.
- Plastic sheeting and duct tape to shelter-in-place.
- Unique family needs, such as daily prescription medications, infant formula or diapers, and important family documents.
- Garbage bags and plastic ties for personal sanitation.

Special Needs Items

Remember the special needs of your family members. In the event of a terrorist attack, infants, the elderly and persons with disabilities need the same planning as everyone else, and sometimes a little more.

For Baby:

- Formula
- Diapers
- Bottles
- Powdered milk
- Medications
- Moist towelettes
- Diaper rash ointment

For Adults:

- Ask your doctor about storing prescription medications such as heart and high blood pressure medication, insulin and other prescription drugs.
- Denture needs
- Contact lenses and supplies
- Extra eye glasses

For Seniors:

- Plan how you will evacuate or signal for help.
- Plan emergency procedures with home health care agencies or workers.
- Tell others where you keep your emergency supplies.
- Teach others how to operate necessary equipment.
- Label equipment like wheelchairs, canes or walkers.
- *Additional supplies for seniors:*
  - List of prescription medications including dosage in your supply kits. Include any allergies.
  - Extra eyeglasses and hearing-aid batteries.
  - Extra wheelchair batteries or other special equipment in your supply kit.
  - A list of the style and serial numbers of medical devices such as pacemakers in your emergency supply kits.
  - Copies of medical insurance and Medicare cards.
  - List of doctors and emergency contacts.

For People with Disabilities:

- Create a support network to help in an emergency.
- Tell these people where you keep your emergency supplies.
- Give one member of your support network a key to your house or apartment.
- Contact your city or county government's emergency information management office. Many local offices keep lists of people with disabilities so they can be located quickly in a sudden emergency.
- Wear medical alert tags or bracelets to help identify your disability.
- If you are dependent on dialysis or other life sustaining treatment, know the location and availability of more than one facility.
- Show others how to operate your wheelchair.
- Know the size and weight of your wheelchair, in addition to whether or not it is collapsible, in case it has to be transported.
- *Additional Supplies for People with Disabilities:*
  - Prescription medicines, list of medications including dosage, list of any allergies.
  - Extra eyeglasses and hearing-aid batteries.
  - Extra wheelchair batteries, oxygen.
  - Keep a list of the style and serial number of medical devices.
  - Medical insurance and Medicare cards.
  - List of doctors, relatives or friends who should be notified if you are hurt.

Creating a Family Plan

Your family may not be together when disaster strikes, so plan how you will contact one another and review what you will do in different situations.

- It may be easier to make a long-distance phone call than to call across town, so an out-of-town contact may be in a better position to communicate among separated family members.
- Be sure every member of your family knows the phone number and has coins or a prepaid phone card to call the emergency contact.
- You may have trouble getting through or the telephone system may be down altogether, but be patient.

Emergency Information

Find out what kinds of disasters, both natural and man-made, are most likely to occur in your area and how you will be notified. Methods of getting your attention vary from community to community. One common method is to broadcast via emergency radio and TV broadcasts. You might hear a special siren, or get a telephone call, or emergency workers may go door-to-door. Call the closest chapter of the American Red Cross for emergency information that applies to your community.

Emergency Plans

You may also want to inquire about emergency plans at places where your family spends time: work, daycare and school. If no plans exist, consider volunteering to help create one. Talk to your neighbors about how you can work together in the event of an emergency. You will be better prepared to safely reunite your family and loved ones during an emergency if you think ahead and communicate with others in advance.

Go to this website to download a copy of a Family Communication Plan to fill out with your family. www.ready.gov/america/_downloads/family_communications_plan.pdf

Food Storage

Helpful Food Storage Tips

Be Practical: Store the food you eat, eat the food you store: It doesn't make sense to buy food storage that your family isn't accustomed to eating.

Store foods properly: Quality is best maintained by minimum exposure to light, heat, moisture and air. Items stored in a basement will last much longer than in your pantry or garage. Store them on shelves or on raised platforms rather than directly in contact with concrete floors or walls. Avoid storing items next to items that may impart an odor such as soaps or fuel.

Temperature: Where possible, always store your food indoors. Temperature affects shelf life the very most. Canned goods will store 2 to 3 times longer at 70°f than they do at 90°f. Most dry goods store indefinitely below 70°f but for less time at higher temperatures. Temperature affects nutrition, texture, and taste.

Moisture: Dry goods should be below 10% moisture and kept dry. The more a container is opened, the more moisture is introduced. The humidity in the air the day food is dry packed or "home canned" can also affect the storage life. Weevil cannot grow in grain with less than 10% moisture. Beans with less than 10% moisture won't go hard as quickly. Non-fat dry milk should have no more than 2.8% moisture for the longest life.

Light: Store in opaque containers or in dark cupboards. Light fades colors, destroys vitamins, and speeds the rancidity of fats.

Air: Containers should have airtight seams and lids. If in doubt, seal with duct tape. Plastic buckets with rubber gaskets are airtight if the gasket has not been damaged. Insects cannot grow and multiply without air.

Use Variety: Add items for variety and nutrition in meal preparation. This will provide a more balanced nutrition and greater flexibility in cooking such as pasta, flour, canned goods, dehydrated or freeze dried foods, yeast, baking soda, baking powder and spices.

Use Labels: Label your containers with the date you purchased it.

Rotate Your Storage: Rotate as many items as you can by using something in your food storage at least twice a week. This will allow complete rotation of a years supply every three years and will help your family become accustomed to the items you have stored.

Store Water: Be sure to store water (at least 14 gallons per person for a 2-week supply). Soda/juice bottles will work for water storage or larger food grade plastic containers may also be used. For larger quantities you can purchase food grade water barrels in sizes of: 5, 15, 30, or 55 gallons. Water will need to be treated before storage. The Federal Emergency Management Agency recommends 4 drops of bleach per-quart of water. Replace your water supply yearly.

Store Non Food Items: Food storage is only part of Emergency Preparedness. Don't forget to store non-food items such as medicines, toiletries soap, cleaning supplies, paper products, laundry detergent, and a limited amount of clothes.

Grow a Garden: Grow a garden so you can have fresh produce. Store and rotate seeds. If you don't have garden space, try growing vegetables in pots etc.

Information provided by Shelf Reliance.

Disaster Preparedness Checklists for Specific Natural Disasters

Earthquakes

If a major earthquake struck in your area today, you might be without direct assistance for up to 72 hours. Are you prepared to be self-sufficient? Is your family? Your neighborhood?

Individual and Family Preparedness

- Know the safe spots in each room—under sturdy tables, desks, against inside walls or in hallways that are not crowded with objects.
- Know the danger spots—windows, mirrors, hanging objects, fireplaces, tall or heavy furniture, appliances or shelves holding heavy objects. Kitchens and garages tend to be the most dangerous.
- Practice drop, cover, and hold-on in each safe place. Drop under a sturdy desk or table and hold on to one leg of the table or desk. Protect your eyes by keeping your head down.
- Know the exit routes of different locations in your house.
- Learn first aid and CPR (cardiopulmonary resuscitation) from your local Red Cross Chapter or other community organization.
- Decide where your family will reunite if separated.
- Keep a list of emergency phone numbers.

- Choose an out-of-state friend or relative whom family members can call after the quake to report whereabouts and conditions.

Home Preparedness

- Learn how to shut off gas, water and electricity in case the lines are damaged.
- Check chimneys, roofs and wall foundations for stability. Make sure your home is bolted to its foundation. Call a licensed contractor if there are any questions.
- Bolt bookcases, china cabinets, and other tall furniture to a wall stud. Brace or anchor high or top-heavy objects.
- Secure water heater and appliances that could move enough to rupture utility lines.
- Keep breakable and heavy objects on lower shelves.
- Secure hanging plants and heavy picture frames or mirrors (especially those hanging over beds).
- Put latches on cabinet doors to keep them closed during shaking.
- Keep flammable or hazardous liquids such as paints, pest sprays or cleaning products in cabinets or secured on lower shelves.
- Maintain emergency food, water and other supplies, including medicine, first aid kit and clothing.

Community Preparedness

- Suggest that local organizations of which you are a member undertake a specific preparedness program or acquire special training to be of assistance in the event of a damaging earthquake.
- Organize a neighborhood earthquake preparedness program.
- Conduct training for neighborhood residents in preparedness, first aid, fire suppression, damage assessment and search and rescue.
- Develop self-help networks between families and neighborhood through a skills and resource bank which includes a listing of tools, equipment, materials and neighborhood members who have special skills and resources to share.
- Identify neighbors who have special needs or will require special assistance.
- Have neighbors agree to hang a white flag out after the quake if everyone and everything is OK.

Source: www.oes.ca.gov

Floods

How to prepare for a flood:

- Find out if you are in a flood prone area.
  - FEMA Flood Hazard Maps Information on locating Flood Insurance Rate Maps (FIRM), instructions on how to read them, and requesting a map change.

  - FEMA Flood Map Store, Online Map Viewer Order or view current Flood Insurance Rate Maps online (registration required, no charge to view maps)

Emergency Preparedness

- Update flood procedures for your family. Make sure everyone knows emergency phone numbers, meeting places if family is separated, how to turn off gas, electricity and water lines.
- Learn the safest route from your home or business to high ground.
- Talk to neighbors and share information on preparedness and previous experiences.
- Buy sand and sandbags ahead of time.
- Keep emergency supplies on hand (Disaster Supply Kit).

Minimize flood damage:

- Store valuables at higher elevations (second story, if possible).
- Store household chemicals above flood levels.
- Ensure that underground storage tanks are fully sealed and secure.
- Close storm shutters and sandbag doorways.
- Move vehicles and RVs to higher ground.
- Keep street drains, storm grates and flap gates free of leaves and other debris.

Consider buying flood insurance to protect your property.

- Homeowners' insurance does not cover flood loss, but most homeowners' insurance agents also sell flood insurance. Anyone can get flood insurance, even if you are located in an area not mapped as a floodplain, or even if you have never been flooded before. Learn More: FloodSmart.gov

Source: dnr.metrokc.gov/wlr/flood/Before.htm

Fires

How to make your home fire safe- Outside
Maintenance

- Enclose the underside of eaves, balconies and above ground decks with fire resistant materials.
- Install only dual-paned or triple-paned windows.
- Make sure that electric service lines, fuse boxes and circuit breaker panels are maintained as prescribed by code.

Access

- Make sure your house address is easily visible from the street, especially at night.
- Identify at least two exit routes from your neighborhood.
- Clear flammable vegetation at least 10 feet from roads and five feet from driveways.
- Cut back overhanging tree branches above access roads.

Roof

- Install a fire resistant roof. Contact your local fire department for current roofing requirements.
- Remove dead leaves and needles from your roof and gutters.
- Remove dead branches overhanging your roof and keep branches 10 feet from your chimney.
- Cover your chimney outlet and stovepipe with a nonflammable screen of 1/2 inch or smaller mesh.

Landscape

- Create a Defensible Space of 100 feet around your home. It is required by law.
- Create a "LEAN, CLEAN and GREEN ZONE" by removing all flammable vegetation within 30 feet immediately surrounding your home.
- Remove lower tree branches at least six feet from the ground.
- Landscape with fire resistant plants.
- Maintain all plants with regular water, and keep dead braches, leaves and needles removed.

Yard

- Stack woodpiles at least 30 feet from all structures and remove vegetation within 10 feet of woodpiles.
- Contact your local fire department to see if debris burning is allowed in your area; if so, obtain a burning permit and follow all local air quality restrictions.

Emergency Water Supply

- Maintain an emergency water supply that meets fire department standards through one of the following:
- a community water/hydrant system
- a cooperative emergency storage tank with neighbors
- a minimum storage supply of 2,500 gallons on your property (like a pond or pool)
- Clearly mark all emergency water sources.
- If your water comes from a well, consider an emergency generator to operate the pump during a power failure.

How to make your home fire safe—Inside

Kitchen

- Keep a working fire extinguisher in the kitchen.
- Maintain electric and gas stoves in good operating condition.
- Keep baking soda on hand to extinguish stovetop grease fires.
- Turn the handles of pots and pans away from the front of the stove.
- Install curtains and towel holders away from stove burners.

Emergency Preparedness

- Store matches and lighters out of reach of children.
- Make sure that electrical outlets are designed to handle appliance loads.

Living Room

- Install a screen in front of fireplace or wood stove.
- Store the ashes from your fireplace (and barbecue) in a metal container and dispose of only when cold.
- Clean fireplace chimneys and flues at least once a year.

Hallway

- Install smoke detectors between living and sleeping areas.
- Test smoke detectors monthly and replace batteries twice a year, when clocks are changed in the spring and fall.
- Replace electrical cords that do not work properly, have loose connections, or are frayed.

Bedroom

- If you sleep with the door closed, install a smoke detector in the bedroom.
- Turn off electric blankets and other electrical appliances when not in use.
- Do not smoke in bed.
- If you have security bars on your windows or doors, be sure they have an approved quick release mechanism so you and your family can get out in the event of a fire.

Bathroom

- Disconnect appliances such as curling irons and hair dryers when done; store in a safe location until cool.
- Keep items such as towels away from wall and floor heaters.

Garage

- Mount a working fire extinguisher in the garage.
- Have tools such as a shovel, hoe, rake and bucket available for use in a wildfire emergency.
- Install a solid door with self-closing hinges between living areas and the garage.
- Dispose of oily rags in Underwriters Laboratories approved metal containers.
- Store all combustibles away from ignition sources such as water heaters.
- Disconnect electrical tools and appliances when not in use.
- Allow hot tools such as glue guns and soldering irons to cool before storing.
- Properly store flammable liquids in approved containers and away from ignition sources such as pilot lights.

Source: www.fire.ca.gov.php

Emergency Information & Products

Here are some great resources to get you prepared. Contact them to get all the essentials mentioned above. If you don't have time to make your own; they have 72-hr and first aid kits as well as food storage to purchase.

Emergency Essentials

Kits 4 Disaster Survival

4435 First Street, Suite 365
Livermore, CA 94551
www.kits4disastersurvival.com

888-510-0678

Kits 4 Disaster Survival is an on-line company that believes that everyone should be equipped with an emergency survival kit. They have emergency disaster survival kits and supplies for just about every situation. They think you should "Be prepared with peace of mind".

REI

www.rei.com

1-800-426-4840

REI has everything you can imagine for your emergency or disaster preparedness kit. Order a custom kit on-line or call to find the location of a store near you

Provident Living
Food Storage and Emergency Preparedness

www.providentliving.org/channel/1,11677,1706-1,00.html

Storing food is an important part of becoming self-reliant. Help your family by beginning or improving your own storage. This website gives information on:

- Why Food Storage?
- What to Store
- How to Store
- Using Food Storage
- Gardening
- Emergency Preparedness

Helpful Websites

Check out these websites for other information about Emergency Preparedness and Food Storage.

Pet Emergency Preparedness
Contra Costa County Animal Services

4800 Imhoff Place
Martinez, CA 94553
www.cccpep.org

925-335-8340

Our cats and dogs are our family too. Learn how to keep them safe during any emergency.

FEMA- Are You Ready?

www.fema.org/areyouready

Homeland Security—Emergencies and Disasters

www.dhs.gov/dhspublic/theme_home2.jsp

Center for Disease Control and Prevention

www.bt.cdc.gov

Home Canning—Pure and Simple

www.homecanning.com

Learn More

If you are interested in learning more about how to prepare for emergencies, contact your local State Office of Emergency Management or local American Red Cross chapter or write:

FEMA
P.O. Box 2012
Jessup MD 20794

Request the following publications:

- Emergency Preparedness Checklist L-154-Item #8–0872 ARC 4471
- Your Family Disaster Supplies Kit L-189-Item # 9–0941 ARC 4463
- Your Family Disaster Plan L-191-Item #8–0954 ARC 4466
- Are You Ready? Your Guide to Disaster Preparedness H-34-Item #8–0980
- Emergency Preparedness Publications L-164- Item #8–0822

Car Clinic

2655 Monument Blvd. #1
Concord, CA 94520
www.concordcarclinic.com

925-676-5590

Ready for auto repair with a woman's touch? Ann is the owner of Car Clinic and a mother of two. The Car Clinic will never sell you an unnecessary repair. Ann truly understands the importance of driving a safe car while transporting children. Car Clinic has been serving Contra Costa for 26 years. Visit their website to learn more. Car Clinic is located less than 1 mile north of COSTCO in Concord.

Emergency Preparedness Numbers & Info

911 For Fire, Medical Emergency, or Child Abuse

Poison Control
800-222-1222
www.calpoison.org

FEMA- Federal Emergency
Management Team
800-525-0321

American Red Cross,
Disaster Relief
866-438-4636

After Hours / Emergency / Hospitals

Kaiser Permanente
3400 Delta Fair Blvd.
Antioch, CA 94509
925-779-5105

Sutter Delta Medical Center
3901 Lone Tree Way
Antioch, CA 94509
925-779-7200

Brentwood Urgent Care Center
2400 Balfour Road
Brentwood, CA 94513
925-308-8111

Contra Costa Regional
Medical Center
118 Oak Street
Brentwood, CA 94513
925-634-1102

John Muir Urgent Care
2700 Grant Street # 200
Concord, CA 94520
925-677-0500

John Muir Medical Center—Concord
2540 East Street
Concord, CA 94520
925-682-8200

Contra Costa Regional
Medical Center
2500 Alhambra Avenue
Martinez, CA 94553
925-370-5000

Doctor's Medical Center
2151 Appian Way
Pinole, CA 94564
510-741-2400

Night Owl Pediatrics
425 Gregory Lane
Pleasant Hill, CA 94523
925-288-3600

Doctor's Medical Center

2000 Vale Road #4
San Pablo, CA 94806
510-970-5000

John Muir Medical Center

1601 Ygnacio Valley Road
Walnut Creek, CA 94598
925-939-3000

John Muir Urgent Care

1455 Montego #205
Walnut Creek, CA 94598
925-939-4444

Kaiser Foundation Hospital

1425 South Main Street
Walnut Creek, CA 94596
925-295-4000

Bishop Ranch Urgent Care

2305 Camino Ramon #100
San Ramon, CA 94583
925-866-8050

San Ramon Regional Medical Center

6001 Norris Canyon Road
San Ramon, CA 94583
925-275-9200

Police Departments

Alamo County Sheriff Office

150 Alamo Plaza #C
Alamo, CA 94507
925-837-2902

Antioch Police Dept

300 L Street
Antioch, CA 94509
925-778-3911

Brentwood Police Dept

100 Chestnut Street
Brentwood, CA 94513
925-634-6911

Clayton Police Dept

6000 Heritage Trail
Clayton, CA 94517
925-673-7350

Concord Police Dept

4467 Clayton Road
Concord, CA 94521
925-671-3377

Concord Police Dept

1500 Monument Blvd #F17
Concord, CA 94520
925-671-3483

Danville Police Dept

510 La Gonda Way
Danville, CA 94526
925-314-3410

El Cerrito Police Dept

10900 San Pablo Avenue
El Cerrito, CA 94530
510-215-4400

Hercules Police Dept

111 Civic Drive
Hercules, CA 94547
510-799-8260

Lafayette Police Dept

3675 Mt. Diablo Blvd. #130
Lafayette, CA 94549
925-284-5010

Martinez Police Dept
525 Henrietta Street
Martinez, CA 94553
925-372-3400

Moraga Town Police Dept
329 Rheem Blvd.
Moraga, CA 94556
925-376-2515

Oakley Police Dept
210 Ohara Avenue
Oakley, CA 94561
925-625-6700

Orinda Police Dept
14 Altarinda Road
Orinda, CA 94563
925-254-6820

Pinole Police Dept
880 Tennent Avenue
Pinole, CA 94564
510-724-8950

Pittsburg Police Dept
65 Civic Avenue
Pittsburg, CA 94565
925-252-4980

Pleasant Hill Police Dept
330 Civic Drive
Pleasant Hill, CA 94523
925-288-4600

Richmond Police Dept
401 27th Street
Richmond, CA 94804
510-620-6655

San Pablo Police Dept
13880 San Pablo Avenue
San Pablo, CA 94806
510-215-3130

San Ramon Police Dept
2222 Camino Ramon
San Ramon, CA 94583
925-973-2700

Walnut Creek Police Dept
1666 North Main Street
Walnut Creek, CA 94596
925-943-5844

Glossy Advertiser Index

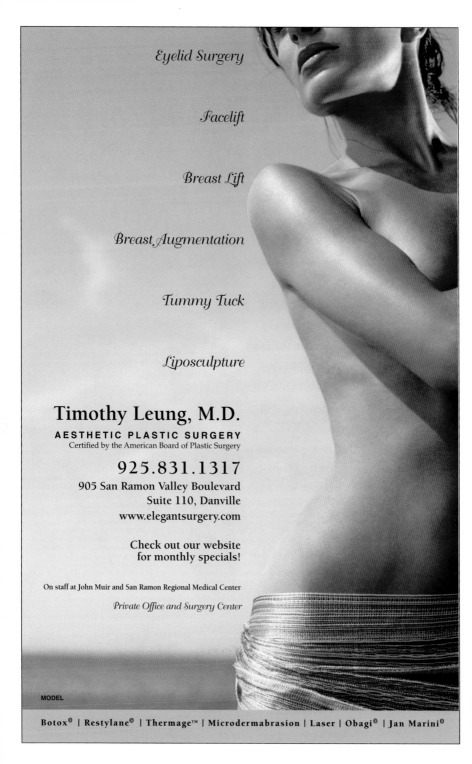

535

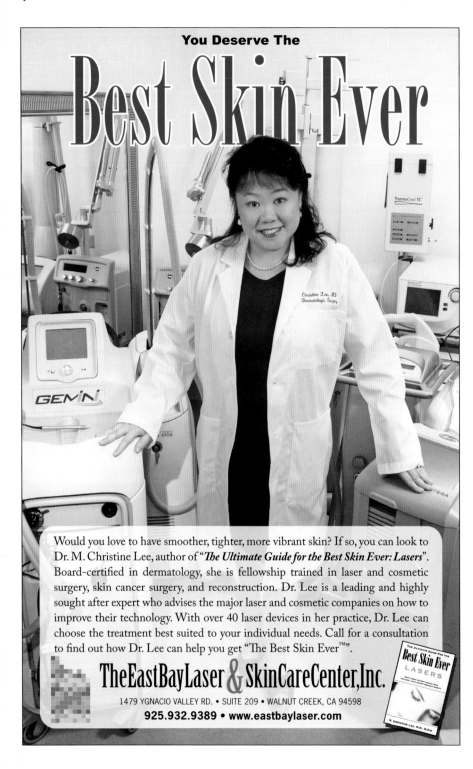

ROBIN WILLIAMS ORTHODONTICS

Get your happy, healthy smile at **ROBIN WILLIAMS ORTHODONTICS.** Featuring the latest technology, including digital radiography and computer-aided diagnosis, we offer personalized care and a family-friendly orthodontic experience with beautiful outcomes for all ages!

ORTHODONTIC SERVICES

- **Conventional Metal Braces**
- **Clear Ceramic Braces**
- **Traditional & Invisible Retainers**
- **Invisalign® (no metal wires)**

901 Sunvalley Blvd., Suite 201, Concord, CA 94520
Located near Sunvalley Mall at the corner of Contra Costa Blvd. and Sunvalley Blvd. above Baja Fresh!

925.680.4500

www.DrRobinWilliams.com

A simply beautiful smile

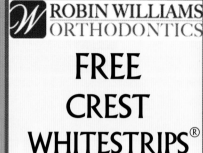

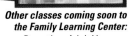
543

EVERYDAY
IS A *New Way*
TO PLAY

Today, over one in five children are overweight or obese and more likely to persist into adult life with increased health risks. Help your children maintain a healthy lifestyle with Club One's youth programs.

> Youth dance, yoga and martial arts classes
> Year-round swim lessons
> Spring & summer camps
> Family changing & dedicated infant rooms
> Birthday parties
> Arts & crafts
> Sports conditioning
> Movie nights for the entire family

925/755-9111
www.ClubOneBrentwood.com

3690ADV18COBR

CLUB ONE AT BRENTWOOD
120 Guthrie Lane
Brentwood

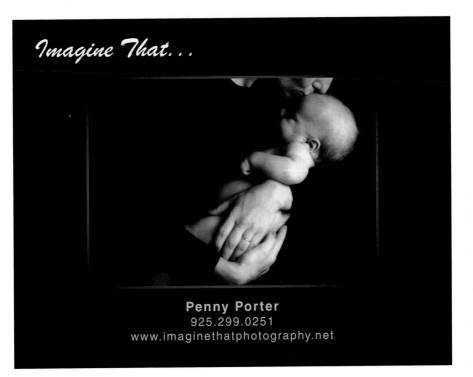

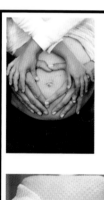

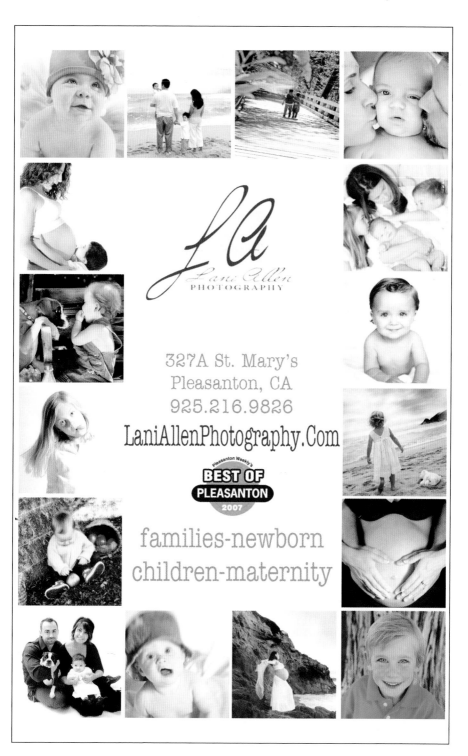

Dedicated to the young child as a total and individual person - accepted for himself alone and given materials and guidance to grow at his pace emotionally, physically, mentally, and spiritually.

Walnut Avenue
COMMUNITY CHRISTIAN PRESCHOOL

OUR PHILOSOPHY

Our program is highly individualized, offering a wide range of materials and utilization of ideas and experiences from several schools of educational thought.

The child is free to work independently according to his/her developmental level as well as in groups through teacher led activities. There are learning stations for a broad range of science, music, art, creative drama, pre-math and pre-reading on sequential levels.

Each child is a valued individual. Our teaching staff is well educated and experienced. We strive to build a community amongst our preschool families. We welcome all cultural and religious backgrounds.

KINDERGARTEN READINESS PROGRAMS
(For 2 to 5 years of age)

MON thru THURS - 11:45 to 2:15

MON + WED + FRI - 9 to 11:30am

TUE + THUR - 9 to 11:30am

TUE +/OR WED +/OR THUR
9 to 11:30am

**LUNCH BUNCH
&
EXTENDED CARE**
may be available upon request.

_Mention this ad
and we will waive the
registration fee
(a $40 value!)_

WALNUT AVENUE COMMUNITY CHRISTIAN PRESCHOOL
260 Walnut Ave., Walnut Creek CA 94598
925.937.7063

559

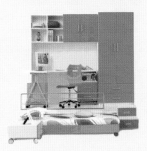

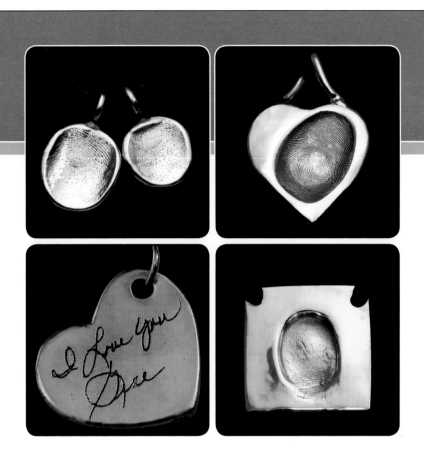

Learn to swim!

- Indoor pools heated to 92°
- Instruction for all ages and abilities: infant through adult
- Small class size: four students per instructor

- Open year-round, 7 days a week with morning, afternoon & evening classes
- Safety is our priority: instructors are fully-trained & CPR certified

FREMONT SWIM SCHOOL

**LIVERMORE
FREMONT
NEWARK**

AMERICAN SWIM ACADEMY

DUBLIN

The Bay Area's trusted swim school since 1973

1.800.810.SWIM

www.FremontSwimSchool.com   www.AmericanSwimAcademy.com

Other Important Numbers

_____

_____

_____

_____

_____

_____

_____

_____

Emergency Numbers for Kids

Emergency Dial

9 1 1

Emergency # to call: _____

Mom's Work #: _____

Mom's Cell Phone #: _____

Dad's Work #: _____

Dad's Cell Phone #: _____

Friend's #: _____

Neighbor's #: _____

My Address: _____

My Home Phone #: _____

Bay Area Poison Control Center
1-800-222-1222